Prospect Heights Public Library
3 1530 00215 7823

D0072308

Enduring the Great War

An innovative comparative history of how German and British soldiers endured the horror of the First World War. Unlike existing literature, which emphasises the strength of societies or military institutions, this study argues that at the heart of armies' robustness lay natural human resilience. Drawing widely on contemporary letters and diaries of British and German soldiers, psychiatric reports and official documentation, and interpreting these sources with modern psychological research, this unique account provides new insights into the soldiers' fears, motivations and coping mechanisms. It explains why the British outlasted their opponents by examining and comparing the motives for fighting, the effectiveness with which armies and societies supported men and the combatants' morale throughout the conflict on both sides. Finally it challenges the current consensus on the war's end, arguing that not a 'covert strike' but rather an 'ordered surrender' led by junior officers brought about Germany's defeat in 1918.

ALEXANDER WATSON is a Research Fellow at Clare Hall, Cambridge. In manuscript form *Enduring the Great War* was joint-winner of the Institute of Contemporary History and Wiener Library's Fraenkel Prize for 2006.

Enduring the Great War

Combat, Morale and Collapse in the German and British Armies, 1914–1918

Alexander Watson

CAMBRIDGE UNIVERSITY PRESS
Cambridge, New York, Melbourne, Madrid, Cape Town, Singapore,
São Paulo, Delhi

Cambridge University Press
The Edinburgh Building, Cambridge CB2 8RU, UK
Published in the United States of America by Cambridge University Press,
New York

www.cambridge.org
Information on this title: www.cambridge.org/9780521881012

First published 2008

Printed in the United Kingdom at the University Press, Cambridge

A catalogue record for this publication is available from the British Library

ISBN 978-0-521-88101-2 hardback

Contents

Plates

Figures

Tables

Acknowledgements

This book began life as a doctoral thesis in October 2001, and it is to my former supervisor, Professor Niall Ferguson, that I owe the greatest thanks. It was he who persuaded me to conduct research in Germany, and at every stage of my work I have benefited enormously from his wisdom and support.

I have also been fortunate to receive help from a number of other academics. Special gratitude is due to Professor Hew Strachan, who as editor of the Cambridge Military Histories series has been very supportive of this project. The comments made by him and my external examiner, Professor Richard Bessel, at my doctoral viva proved extremely useful when I came to prepare my thesis for publication. I am also grateful to Dr Patrick Porter, who besides acting as a sounding board for some of the ideas in this book, kindly allowed me access to his notes from the Nuremberg church archive. During my research, I benefited greatly from attendance at a number of conferences. In particular, I would like to thank the participants of the 'German–British–French Summer Course on Violence in Politics, War and Everyday Life in the Twentieth Century' at the Max-Planck-Institut für Geschichte, Göttingen in September 2001, the 'Culture and Combat Motivation' workshop held at King's College, Cambridge in February 2005 and the International Society for First World War Studies' third conference, 'Uncovering the First World War', which took place in Dublin in September 2005. The papers which I presented at the latter two meetings were earlier or modified versions of chapters 3 and 4 and have since appeared in the *Journal of Contemporary History* and *War in History*, and I am grateful to both publications for allowing me to reuse material from these articles in this book. Finally, I would like to thank the two anonymous readers commissioned by Cambridge University Press to review the first draft of the work. Their advice was highly constructive and saved me from several errors.

No research is possible without funding and institutional support, and in these respects I have been particularly fortunate. I am extremely grateful to the Arts and Humanities Research Board and also to the Alfred Toepfer Stiftung F.V.S., which provided me with the opportunity to research in Germany. In England, Jesus and Balliol Colleges, Oxford, and Clare Hall, Cambridge offered unrivalled environments in which to think and write, while in Germany I was privileged to be a member of Freiburg's Alban Stolz Haus, whose community made my stay enormously enjoyable and rewarding, on a personal level as well as academically. The research itself was materially aided by staff at the following libraries and archives: in Germany, the Bundesarchiv-Militärarchiv in Freiburg, the Hauptstaatsarchive in Dresden, Munich (Abteilung IV) and Stuttgart, the Generallandesarchiv in Karlsruhe, the Handschriftabteilungen in the Staatsbibliothek zu Berlin and the Staats- und Universitätsbibliothek in Hamburg, the Bibliothek für Zeitgeschichte in Stuttgart and, most particularly, the Deutsches Tagebucharchiv in Emmendingen. In Britain, I would like to thank staff at the National Archives, the Imperial War Museum, the Wellcome Library for the History and Understanding of Medicine and especially the Archive of Modern Conflict, all in London.

This study has drawn on the personal papers of over one hundred soldiers. The descendants of those Germans cited are no longer contactable, and, except in the case of letters from my own collection and those of Dr Hans Carossa, I have therefore used pseudonyms in order to protect authors' identities. In the case of British combatants, however, contact can sometimes be made with families and where possible I have sought permission to quote from their writings. My gratitude goes to the following copyright holders: Mr P. Arnold, Ms S. Ashton, Mr N. Calverley, Mr G. Copson, Mrs A.E. Deal, the Rt Revd Lord Habgood, Earl Haig of Bemersyde, Ms H. Hamilton, Mrs M. Freeman, Mr G.H. Loyd, Mr T. Myatt, Mrs H.J.S. Pietrzak, Ms S. Rixon, Ms P. Stone, Mr H. Wilkinson and the trustees of the Imperial War Museum. Photographs and line drawings are reproduced courtesy of the Department of Photographs, Imperial War Museum, the Archive of Modern Conflict and the Costelloe family. Every effort has been made to contact copyright holders and the author would be grateful for any information which might help to trace those whose identities or addresses are not currently known.

The process of producing a book is a complicated one, and I have been lucky to have had the support of an excellent editorial team. The help, advice and patience which I have received from Michael Watson, Helen Waterhouse, Elizabeth Davey and Monica Kendall at Cambridge University Press were crucial throughout the publishing process. Additionally, I am grateful to Martin Lubikowski of ML Design for drawing and granting permission to use the book's map.

Thanks of a more personal nature are also due. First must come the Kuhbier family in Hamburg, whose generosity and hospitality considerably cushioned the first shock of learning the German language. Ailsa Wallace's company was instrumental in my survival during the first nine months abroad, and I am also hugely grateful to Philipp Stiasny, who always offered a sympathetic and interested ear and a roof over my head on research forays to Berlin. I am indebted to two very long-standing friends, Chris Costelloe and Peter James, who not only endured years of extended monologues on the First World War, but also respectively allowed me to examine family documents pertaining to that conflict and provided invaluable technical help. Judy Wright and David Winter kindly checked through parts of an earlier version of the work, and special mention is due to John Crouch, who tirelessly proofread the original thesis and offered a constant stream of thought and criticism throughout the research, for which I cannot express enough gratitude.

Finally, and most importantly, my thanks go to my loved ones: to Ania, without whose love, support and patience I would probably still be writing this book, and to my family, Susan, Henry and Tim, for their love, help and encouragement. This book is dedicated to them.

NOTE

For clarity, German terms have been placed in italics throughout the text.

Abbreviations

ARCHIVES

BA-MA Freiburg	Bundesarchiv-Militärarchiv Freiburg
BZ	Bibliothek für Zeitgeschichte, Stuttgart
DTA	Deutsches Tagebucharchiv, Emmendingen
GLA Karlsruhe	Generallandesarchiv Karlsruhe
HStA Dresden	Sächsisches Hauptstaatsarchiv Dresden
HStA Munich/IV	Bayerisches Hauptstaatsarchiv München, Abteilung IV: Kriegsarchiv
HStA Stuttgart	Hauptstaatsarchiv Stuttgart
IWM	Imperial War Museum, London
LA Nuremberg	Landeskirchliches Archiv Nürnberg
Staatsbib. Berlin	Staatsbibliothek zu Berlin, Preussischer Kulturbesitz, Handschriftabteilung, Berlin
Staatsbib. Hamburg	Staats- und Universitätsbibliothek, Handschriftabteilung, Hamburg
TNA	The National Archives, Kew (formerly Public Record Office)
WLHM	Wellcome Library for the History and Understanding of Medicine, London

BOOKS

J&R	Johnson, W. and Rows, R.G., 'Neurasthenia and War Neuroses', in W.G. MacPherson, W.P. Herringham, T.R. Elliott and A. Balfour (eds.), *History of the Great War based on Official Documents*. Vol. II: *Medical Services. Diseases of the War* (London: HMSO, 1923), pp. 1–67
Medical Services	Mitchell, T.J. and Smith, G.M. (eds.), *History of the Great War based on Official Documents. Medical Services. Casualties and Medical*

	Statistics of the Great War (London: Imperial War Museum, 1931, 1997)
Military Effort	War Office (ed.), *Statistics of the Military Effort of the British Empire during the Great War. 1914–1920* (London: HMSO, 1922)
RWOCIS	War Office (ed.), *Report of the War Committee of Enquiry into 'Shell-Shock'* (London: HMSO, 1922)
Sanitätsbericht II	Heeres-Sanitätsinspektion des Reichskriegsministeriums (ed.), *Sanitätsbericht über das Deutsche Heer (Deutsches Feld- und Besatzungsheer) im Weltkriege 1914/1918 (Deutscher Kriegssanitätsbericht 1914/18)*. Vol. II: *Der Sanitätsdienst im Gefechts- und Schlachtenverlauf im Weltkriege 1914/1918* (Berlin: E.S. Mittler & Sohn, 1938)
Sanitätsbericht III	Heeres-Sanitätsinspektion des Reichskriegsministeriums (ed.), *Sanitätsbericht über das Deutsche Heer (Deutsches Feld- und Besatzungsheer) im Weltkriege 1914/1918 (Deutscher Kriegssanitätsbericht 1914/18)*. Vol. III: *Die Krankenbewegung bei dem deutschen Feld- und Besatzungsheer im Weltkriege 1914/1918* (Berlin: E.S. Mittler & Sohn, 1934)

GENERAL

ADMS	Assistant Director of Medical Services
AEF	American Expeditionary Force
AK	*Armeekorps*
ANZAC	Australian and New Zealand Army Corps; a man from this formation
AOK	*Armee-Oberkommando*
AWOL	Absence without leave; a man guilty of absconding
BEF	British Expeditionary Force
CO	Commanding Officer
GHQ	General Headquarters, British Expeditionary Force
MO	Medical Officer

NCO	Non-commissioned Officer
NO	*Nachrichtenoffizier*
OHL	*Oberheeresleitung*, German Field Army
I/bayerisches Reserve-Infanterie-Regiment Nr. 23	*I Bataillon des bayerischen Reserve-Infanterie-Regiments Nr. 23* (same form used for other German regiments)
1/5 Durham Light Infantry	5th Battalion of First Line Territorials, Durham Light Infantry (same form used for other British regiments)

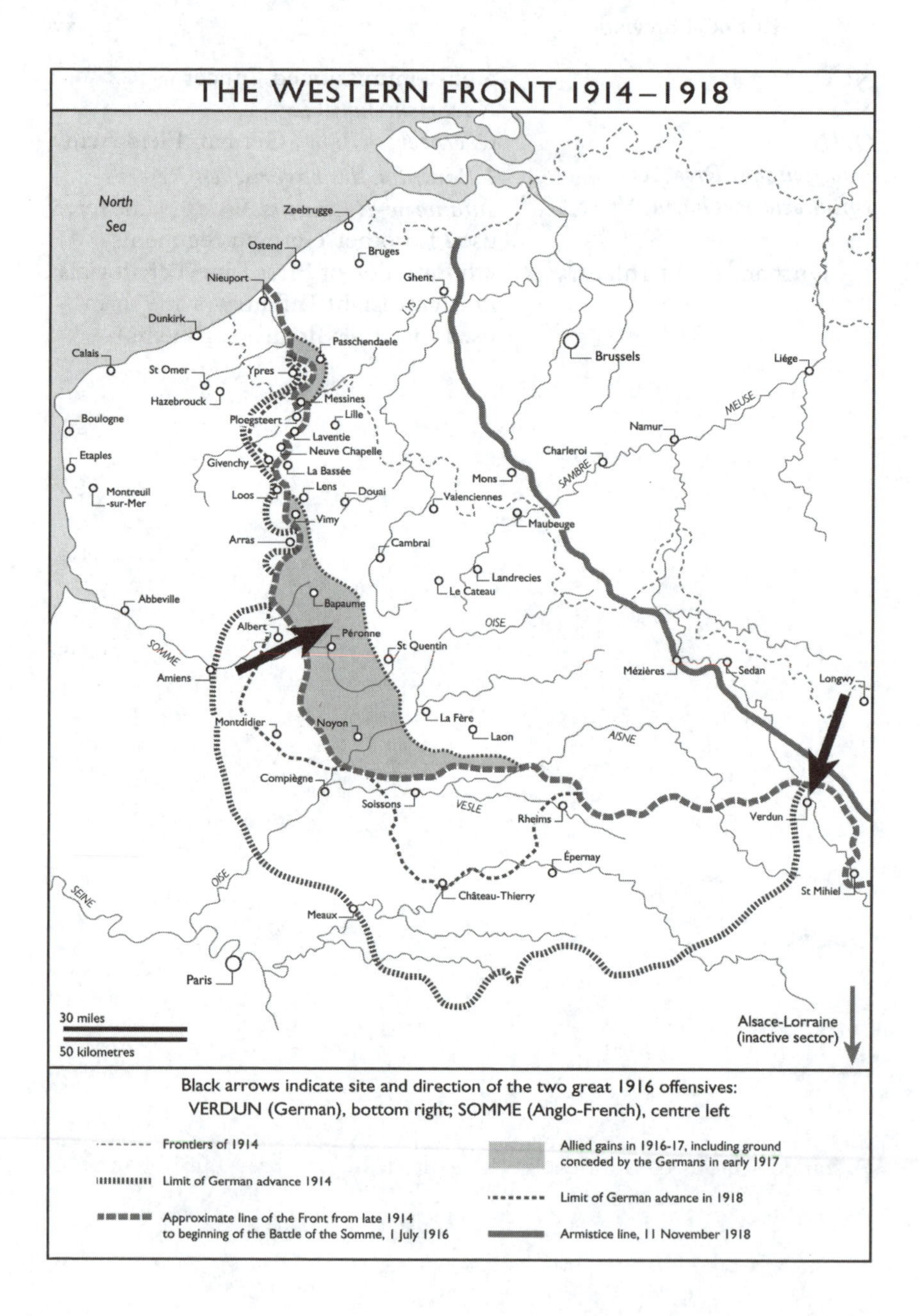
THE WESTERN FRONT 1914–1918
North Sea
Zeebrugge
Ostend
Bruges
Nieuport
Ghent
Dunkirk
Passchendaele
Brussels
Calais
St Omer
Ypres
Liége
Hazebrouck
Messines
Boulogne
Ploegsteert
Lille
Laventie
Namur
Neuve Chapelle
Etaples
Givenchy
La Bassée
Charleroi
Montreuil -sur-Mer
Loos
Lens
Douai
Mons
Valenciennes
Vimy
Maubeuge
Arras
Cambrai
Landrecies
Le Cateau
Abbeville
Bapaume
Albert
Péronne
St Quentin
Amiens
Mézières
Sedan
Longwy
La Fère
Montdidier
Noyon
Laon
Compiègne
Soissons
Rheims
Verdun
Épernay
St Mihiel
Château-Thierry
Meaux
Paris
LYS
MEUSE
SAMBRE
OISE
SOMME
AISNE
VESLE
SEINE
30 miles
50 kilometres
Alsace-Lorraine (inactive sector)
Black arrows indicate site and direction of the two great 1916 offensives: VERDUN (German), bottom right; SOMME (Anglo-French), centre left
Frontiers of 1914
Limit of German advance 1914
Approximate line of the Front from late 1914 to beginning of the Battle of the Somme, 1 July 1916
Allied gains in 1916-17, including ground conceded by the Germans in early 1917
Limit of German advance in 1918
Armistice line, 11 November 1918

Introduction

> Victory will go to him who has the best nerves.
>
> *Generalfeldmarschall* Paul von Hindenburg, 1916[1]

Although usually remembered as a conflict of attrition or material, the First World War was, above all, a contest of endurance. Nowhere was this truer than on the Western Front where, for the four years following August 1914, the French, Belgian and British armies, later joined by the Americans, fought the German army in some of the most costly battles in history. The conflict's long duration, unprecedented bloodiness and particularly horrendous and indecisive 'trench warfare' placed extreme strain on individuals, armies and nations. Yet it was only in the second half of 1918, after enduring months of inconclusive static combat followed by a dramatic offensive which almost broke through Entente lines, that the overstrained German war effort finally collapsed. The rapid decline in combat motivation at the front and the outbreak of revolution at home indicated clearly that Hindenburg's soldiers, army and nation had reached the end of their mental resources.

Historians have adopted a number of approaches to account for the longevity and outcome of the war. Some, such as Gerald Feldman and Avner Offer, have focused on the Central Powers' material shortages and inefficiencies in order to explain the eventual collapse of their armies and economies.[2] Other scholars, most notably Paddy Griffith, Tim Travers, Robin Prior and Trevor Wilson, have examined the Allied success in breaking the German line at the end of the war, producing detailed studies of the development of strategy, tactics and technology

1 Hindenburg, quoted in M. Hirschfeld, *Deutsche Kriegsschriften*. Part 20: *Kriegspsychologisches* (Bonn: A. Marcus & E. Webers Verlag, 1916), p. 24.

2 G.D. Feldman, *Army, Industry, and Labor in Germany 1914–1918* (Princeton University Press, 1966) and A. Offer, *The First World War. An Agrarian Interpretation* (Oxford: Clarendon Press, 1989).

on the Western Front.[3] Both of these approaches will be addressed only in so far as they relate to a third line of investigation: the examination of soldiers' and armies' morale. This is the main focus of this monograph.

Considerable effort has been invested by historians into understanding whence the formidable resilience of First World War armies originated and why the Allies apparently possessed 'better nerves' than their opponents. Particular attention has been focused on the British and German armies, two of the most resilient forces which fought through the conflict. Many explanations emphasise the role of military institutional factors. John Baynes has argued in his pioneering study of the 2/ Scottish Rifles at Neuve Chapelle in March 1915 that the unique British regimental system was 'the quintessence of the morale of the pre-1914 Army'.[4] James Brent Wilson has evaluated the success with which the high command tracked and maintained morale in the BEF during the war, while Timothy Bowman has focused on how Irish regiments supported their men.[5] Anglo-American historians studying the German army have emphasised the role played by superior combat preparation in enabling the force to endure the prolonged hostilities. Trevor Dupuy argues that the personnel, doctrine and methods of the General Staff 'institutionalized military excellence' in the army, while Hew Strachan has emphasised the superiority of the force's training over that of its opponents.[6] Perhaps for cultural reasons, explanations by German historians tend to be much darker, focusing on the ability of the Kaiser's army to coerce and manipulate men into remaining obedient. Benjamin Ziemann argues that successful military socialisation ensured cooperation: temporary reliefs, such as leave or rest behind the lines, made active service bearable, while 'the disciplinary corset, in which the men moved,

[3] P. Griffith, *Battle Tactics on the Western Front. The British Army's Art of Attack, 1916–18* (New Haven: Yale University Press, 1994), T. Travers, *How the War Was Won. Command and Technology in the British Army on the Western Front, 1917–1918* (London: Routledge, 1992) and R. Prior and T. Wilson, *Command on the Western Front. The Military Career of Sir Henry Rawlinson, 1914–18* (Oxford: Blackwell, 1992).

[4] J. Baynes, *Morale. A Study of Men and Courage. The Second Scottish Rifles at the Battle of Neuve Chapelle 1915* (London: Leo Cooper, 1967, 1987), p. 163.

[5] J.B. Wilson, 'Morale and Discipline in the British Expeditionary Force, 1914–1918' unpublished MA thesis, University of New Brunswick (1978) and T. Bowman, *The Irish Regiments in the Great War. Discipline and Morale* (Manchester University Press, 2003).

[6] T.N. Dupuy, *A Genius for War. The German Army and General Staff, 1807–1945* (London: MacDonald and Jane's, 1977), p. 302 and H. Strachan, 'Ausbildung, Kampfgeist und die zwei Weltkriege', in B. Thoß and H.-E. Volkmann (eds.), *Erster Weltkrieg Zweiter Weltkrieg. Ein Vergleich* (Paderborn: Ferdinand Schöningh, 2002), pp. 265–78. For a comparative but highly contested study of training and doctrine in the British and German armies, see M. Samuels, *Command or Control? Command, Training and Tactics in the British and German Armies, 1888–1918* (London: Frank Cass, 1995).

offered them in practice no freedom and, in cooperation with the in actuality ineffective right of complaint, effectually suppressed for a long time the first manifestations of serious insubordination'.[7] For Anne Lipp, it was skilful propaganda, combined with ordinary soldiers' position as 'subordinates of no prestige at the bottom end of the hierarchy' which ensured continued compliance.[8] The most influential theory on the German army's collapse, put forward by Wilhelm Deist, also presents coercion as the principal force holding troops together by 1918. Only when soldiers discovered how to circumvent military discipline by means of a mass 'covert strike' in the second half of that year did units disintegrate and further fighting cease to be possible.[9]

Military factors alone have not been considered fully sufficient to explain armies' resilience, however. The improvised nature of the wartime BEF, the self-consciously civilian identity of its soldiers and the antagonism generated by official morale-raisers such as strict Regular Army discipline, 'bull' and raiding have resulted in societal explanations of this force's resilience remaining dominant. As Peter Simkins has observed, most historians 'are in broad agreement that the nature of British society in 1914–18 provided a bedrock of social cohesion which prevented the BEF from total collapse'.[10] J.G. Fuller, one of the earliest and most influential exponents of this view, has argued that civilian, working-class leisure activities, particularly football and music hall, helped British citizen-soldiers relax when out of the line and encouraged an attitude of 'humour and sceptical stoicism' to danger and hardship.[11] John Bourne similarly suggests that the working-class culture of

[7] B. Ziemann, *Front und Heimat. Ländliche Kriegserfahrung im südlichen Bayern 1914–1923* (Essen: Klartext, 1997), pp. 120 and 462–72.

[8] A. Lipp, *Meinungslenkung im Krieg. Kriegserfahrungen deutscher Soldaten und ihre Deutung 1914–1918* (Göttingen: Vandenhoeck & Ruprecht, 2003), pp. 113 and 307–20.

[9] W. Deist, 'The Military Collapse of the German Empire. The Reality Behind the Stab-in-the-Back Myth', *War in History* 3, 2 (April 1996), 204–7. See also the original German version of this article, 'Der militärische Zusammenbruch des Kaiserreichs. Zur Realität der "Dolchstoßlegende"', in U. Büttner (ed.), *Das Unrechtsregime. Internationale Forschung über den Nationalsozialismus*. Vol. I: *Ideologie-Herrschaftssystem-Wirkung in Europa* (Hamburg: Christians, 1986), pp. 101–29 and Deist's similar piece, entitled, 'Verdeckter Militärstreik im Kriegsjahr 1918?', in W. Wette (ed.), *Der Krieg des kleinen Mannes. Eine Militärgeschichte von unten* (Munich: Piper, 1992, 1995), pp. 146–67.

[10] P. Simkins, 'Everyman at War. Recent Interpretations of the Front Line Experience', in B. Bond (ed.), *The First World War and British Military History* (Oxford: Clarendon Press, 1991), p. 301.

[11] J.G. Fuller, *Troop Morale and Popular Culture in the British and Dominion Armies 1914–1918* (Oxford: Clarendon Press, 1990), particularly pp. 175–80.

impassivity and mutual solidarity developed in response to the boredom, discomfort and subordination of peacetime industrial life paid dividends in the trenches.[12] For Jay Winter, the fact that Britain possessed 'probably the most highly disciplined industrial labor force in the world' accounts for the BEF's obedience and robustness.[13] Gary Sheffield also considers peacetime industrial relations to hold the key to British military resilience in the First World War. He demonstrates convincingly that the paternalism–deference exchange which regulated pre-war class interaction was transferred to the officer–man relationship in the army, creating good inter-rank relations and strong cohesion.[14]

In contrast to the resilience which their pre-war upbringing and culture provided to British troops, peacetime societal influences have generally been seen to have disadvantaged German soldiers. Bernd Hüppauf and Bernd Ulrich have condemned the exaggerated militarism of the *Kaiserreich*, arguing that 'war-enthused' volunteers inculcated with naive, glorified images of war quickly became disillusioned or suffered mental collapse when they experienced real combat.[15] Christoph Jahr, noting that desertion rates remained far more stable in the British army than in its German opponent, has suggested that the BEF's strength derived from the fact that it was 'a "citizen army" constituted by amateurs'. Drawing on Fuller's work, he contends that 'the adoption of civilian thought and behaviour in the army bestowed it with a flexible steadfastness, so that it came through the war without fundamental shock'.[16] Moreover, unlike in the British army, where peacetime class relations provided the basis of an excellent officer–man relationship, the reproduction of peacetime social divisions within the German military hierarchy is thought to have been highly damaging. Wolfgang Kruse argues that the resentment caused by the privileges and insensitivity of

12 J. Bourne, 'The British Working Man in Arms', in H. Cecil and P.H. Liddle (eds.), *Facing Armageddon. The First World War Experienced* (London: Leo Cooper, 1996), pp. 342–50.

13 J. Winter, *The Experience of World War I* (London: Greenwich Editions, 1988, 2000), p. 159.

14 G. Sheffield, *Leadership in the Trenches. Officer–Man Relations, Morale and Discipline in the British Army in the Era of the First World War* (Basingstoke: Macmillan, 2000), particularly pp. 72–3.

15 B. Hüppauf, '"Der Tod ist verschlungen in den Sieg". Todesbilder aus dem Ersten Weltkrieg und Nachkriegszeit', in B. Hüppauf (ed.), *Ansichten vom Krieg. Vergleichende Studien zum Ersten Weltkrieg in Literatur und Gesellschaft* (Königsten: Forum Academicum, 1984), pp. 68–71 and B. Ulrich, 'Kriegsfreiwillige. Motivationen – Erfahrungen – Wirkungen', in Berliner Geschichtswerkstatt (ed.), *August 1914. Ein Volk zieht in den Krieg* (Berlin: Dirk Nishen, 1989), pp. 235–41.

16 C. Jahr, *Gewöhnliche Soldaten. Desertion und Deserteure im deutschen und britischen Heer 1914–1918* (Göttingen: Vandenhoeck & Ruprecht, 1998), p. 176.

upper-class officers led inevitably to bitterness and ultimately the radicalisation of the common soldiery. Revolution and collapse thus derived ultimately from the undemocratic nature of Germany's society and military.[17]

Other historians have studied the dynamics of the battlefield to explain why soldiers were prepared to fight. John Keegan was the first to develop this approach, when he analysed the factors which propelled British Kitchener soldiers towards German lines on 1 July 1916.[18] Tony Ashworth's sociological view of trench warfare has shed light on the 'live and let live' truces which prevailed in some front sectors and eased the lives of the soldiers. He contends that the primary conflict in the trenches lay not between the combatants themselves but rather between the infantry at the front, which sought to avoid danger, and staff officers in the rear, who by a variety of methods broke up informal truces and successfully compelled troops to fight.[19] More recently, Leonard V. Smith's study of the French Fifth Infantry Division has addressed similar questions to those posed by Ashworth but utilises a more complex theoretical framework of Foucaultian proportionality to explain men's behaviour at the front. Correcting Ashworth's misapprehension that belligerent soldiers were 'warlike deviants', he demonstrates that not only the will of the high command but also often the dynamics of the battlefield and combatants' own value systems made fighting the most attractive or only possible course of action.[20]

Curiously, although questions of human resilience are at root psychological rather than sociological or military institutional, there has been little interest in examining individual coping strategies in the trenches. Those historians who have addressed the experience of the First World War from a psychological standpoint have tended to stress the difficulty faced by individuals in coping with battle. Eric Leed has portrayed soldiers as incapable of processing the monstrous machine warfare raging about them, while Modris Eksteins has argued that 'men stopped

[17] W. Kruse, 'Krieg und Klassenheer. Zur Revolutionierung der deutschen Armee im Ersten Weltkrieg', *Geschichte und Gesellschaft. Zeitschrift für Historische Sozialwissenschaft* 22, 4 (1996), 533–4 and 539–49.

[18] J. Keegan, *The Face of Battle. A Study of Agincourt, Waterloo and the Somme* (Harmondsworth: Penguin, 1976, 1983), pp. 207–89.

[19] T. Ashworth, *Trench Warfare 1914–1918. The Live and Let Live System* (Basingstoke: Macmillan, 1980, 2000).

[20] L.V. Smith, *Between Mutiny and Obedience. The Case of the French Fifth Infantry Division during World War I* (Princeton University Press, 1994), particularly pp. 11–17.

asking questions, deliberately. They ceased to interpret'. Peter Knoch similarly asserts that combatants typically experienced 'paralysis before the all-powerfulness of war' in the trenches.[21] Rather than focusing on the majority of men who successfully coped with conditions at the front, disproportionate attention has been paid by historians to the minority who developed psychiatric disorders. The confusing impression given is that while societies and armies proved to be very resilient during the war, the individuals who comprised them were victims of their situation and susceptible to mental collapse.[22]

Recently, historians have begun to question whether soldiers were quite so helpless and vulnerable as hitherto portrayed. Niall Ferguson has argued that fighting went on for so long and armies were so obedient because many men 'simply took pleasure in killing'. Joanna Bourke has arrived at a similar conclusion from her study of combatants in the First and Second World Wars and the Vietnam conflict. Declaring that 'the characteristic act of men at war is not dying, it is killing', she contends that soldiers actually 'insisted upon emotional relationships and responsibility' with and for their victims.[23] As will be demonstrated, the emphasis on 'face-to-face killing' found in the work of these authors in fact represents a misunderstanding of the overwhelmingly anonymous and impersonal warfare conducted on the Western Front in the First World War. Nonetheless, their suggestion that soldiers were by no means as fragile as usually argued is convincing. Modern psychological research has consistently demonstrated that humans in fact possess a considerable level of innate resilience. The National Vietnam Veterans Readjustment Study, examining the modern psychiatric disease Post-traumatic

[21] E.J. Leed, *No Man's Land. Combat and Identity in World War I* (Cambridge University Press, 1979, 1981), pp. 130–3, M. Eksteins, *Rites of Spring. The Great War and the Birth of the Modern Age* (London: Bantam Press, 1989), p. 174 and P. Knoch, 'Erleben und Nacherleben. Das Kriegserlebnis im Augenzeugenbericht und im Geschichtsunterricht', in G. Hirschfeld, G. Krumeich and I. Renz (eds.), *Keiner fühlt sich hier mehr als Mensch ... Erlebnis und Wirkung des Ersten Weltkriegs* (Essen: Klartext, 1993), pp. 211–12.

[22] See, particularly, P. Leese, *Shell Shock. Traumatic Neurosis and the British Soldiers of the First World War* (Basingstoke: Palgrave Macmillan, 2002) and B. Shephard, *A War of Nerves. Soldiers and Psychiatrists 1914–1994* (London: Pimlico, 2002), pp. 1–168. For Germany, see P. Lerner, *Hysterical Men. War, Psychiatry, and the Politics of Trauma in Germany, 1890–1930* (Ithaca: Cornell University Press, 2003).

[23] N. Ferguson, *The Pity of War* (London: Allen Lane. The Penguin Press, 1998), p. 363 and J. Bourke, *An Intimate History of Killing. Face-to-Face Killing in Twentieth-Century Warfare* (London: Granta Books, 1999), pp. 1 and 6. The idea has also been adopted in S. Audoin-Rouzeau and A. Becker, *1914–1918. Understanding the Great War* (London: Profile Books, 2002), p. 37.

Stress Disorder, found, for example, that 'the majority of Vietnam theater veterans have made a successful reentry into civilian life'.[24] After reviewing literature studying the reactions of mid- and late twentieth-century civilians and soldiers under fire, the psychologist S.J. Rachman concluded that 'the large majority coped extraordinarily well'.[25] There seems no reason why this should not have also been true of men fighting in the First World War. Indeed, the testimonies of contemporary psychiatrists indicate that this was the case. As T.W. Salmon, one of the founding fathers of American military psychiatry, observed of British combatants, 'neurosis provides a means of escape so convenient that the real source of wonder is not that it should play such an important part in military life but that so many men should find a satisfactory adjustment without its intervention'.[26]

The purpose of this book is, therefore, to provide a new understanding of the impressive resilience demonstrated by the British and German armies during the First World War by focusing on individual soldiers' psychology. Knowledge of combatants' fears, motivations, mental defence mechanisms and coping strategies will not only explain why they were able and willing to fight so hard for so long but should also shed light on why certain military institutions were effective in providing support while others failed. A comparative approach has been chosen in order to avoid the cultural biases which may have crept into some of the existing almost exclusively national historiography. Allegedly society-specific qualities identified by historians as beneficial to resilience were often, it will be argued, common human responses to stress. By focusing on individuals' strategies for coping with risk and death, it will thus become possible to explain the resilience of soldiers and armies, analyse whether the British did indeed have 'better nerves' than their opponents and clarify how and why German soldiers eventually stopped fighting.

Attitudes to risk and death in the trenches involved transitory calculations and emotions liable to be distorted by the passage of time. In order to construct an accurate picture of contemporary perspectives on trench warfare and battle, the letters and diaries of more than one

[24] R.A. Kulka, W.E. Schlenger, J.A. Fairbank, R.L. Hough, B.K. Jordan, L.R. Marmar and D.S. Weiss, *Trauma and the Vietnam War Generation. Report of Findings from the National Vietnam Veterans Readjustment Study* (New York: Brunner / Mazel, 1990), p. xxvii.

[25] S.J. Rachman, *Fear and Courage* (New York: W.H. Freeman and Company, 1978, 1990), pp. 35–6.

[26] T.W. Salmon, 'The Care and Treatment of Mental Diseases and War Neuroses ("Shell Shock") in the British Army', *Mental Hygiene* 1, 4 (October 1917), 516.

hundred British and German combatants have been studied. Written directly after or sometimes even during the events they describe, these sources offer the best possibility for the historian to see trench warfare as soldiers did at the time. They are, however, not without their problems. Letters were often tailored for their audiences; predictably, soldiers were most likely to be frank about their feelings and experiences when the recipient was male and least likely when writing to a child. Female addressees stood in between, although the amount of information depended on their relationship with the soldier. Mothers, sisters or girlfriends might become confidantes and receive unvarnished accounts of the front. More often, disturbing events might be excluded or a cheerful tone adopted in order to spare loved ones from worry. Censorship, either through company officers or, later in the war, an official censor, also may have influenced letters' style and content.[27] Diaries were less vulnerable to these problems; usually soldiers seem to have written them for personal consumption and comfort, as a way of releasing tension, although sometimes they were consciously kept for posterity. In the case of both sources, often little is known about the background of the author, other than what can be inferred from the text. In some ways, however, this is not so important. As will be seen, although class origin, education and religion might influence style or vocabulary, the similarities in soldiers' correspondence generally outweigh the differences, suggesting that psychological coping strategies were only coloured, not shaped, by social influences. Finally, the individual nature of such sources is necessary but problematic. Each letter collection or diary sheds light on the attitudes and perspectives of only one soldier. As 20 million men passed through the German and British armies between 1914 and 1918, generalisations can hardly be made solely from a sample of 100 combatants' writings.

In order to overcome these difficulties, other contemporary sources have also been consulted. A number of excellent German wartime psychological studies of troops in the field exist. By far the most sophisticated is that undertaken by the psychologist and front officer Walter Ludwig, who set 200 officer cadets and wounded soldiers an essay entitled, 'Observations from the field regarding what the soldier thinks in the moment of greatest danger in order to overcome the fear of death'. He analysed their writings and later published his results in what

[27] For the pitfalls of using letters as historical sources, see P. Fussell, *The Great War and Modern Memory* (Oxford University Press, 1975), p. 183 and B. Ulrich, *Die Augenzeugen. Deutsche Feldpostbriefe in Kriegs- und Nachkriegszeit 1914–1933* (Essen: Klartext, 1997), pp. 16–18.

remains one of the earliest and most valuable articles on combat motivation in the twentieth century.[28] Other, more subjective but nonetheless useful research also survives. Paul Plaut published two studies on war psychology based partly on his own experience of service at the front and partly on soldiers' answers to questionnaires disseminated at the outbreak of war by the Institüt für angewandte Psychologie in Klein Glienicke, near Potsdam.[29] During the war, the neurologist Ludwig Scholz drew on his own service on the Eastern Front to write his observations of soldiers' behaviour, as did the psychologist Erich Everth.[30] A study of British troops, based on published sources, was produced by the American psychologist Charles Bird in 1917.[31] Wartime research conducted by military psychiatrists on both sides of the lines provides valuable information on the factors exposing men to nervous disorders and the process of adaptation at the front, much of which can be cross-referenced with the results of modern studies.[32] The post-war Southborough Committee's enquiry into 'shellshock' also yields useful material, despite its undoubted political agenda.[33] Finally, in order to provide the results of the research with breadth as well as depth, documentation pertaining to the armies' morale has been consulted. The studies of German and British soldiers' songs produced by

[28] The original German title was 'Beobachtung aus dem Feld, an was der Soldat im Augenblick der höchsten Gefahr denkt, um die Furcht vor dem Tod zu überwinden'. W. Ludwig, 'Beiträge zur Psychologie der Furcht im Kriege', in W. Stern and O. Lipmann (eds.), *Beihefte zur Zeitschrift für angewandte Psychologie. 21. Beiträge zur Psychologie des Krieges* (Leipzig: Johann Ambrosius Barth, 1920), p. 130. See Appendix 1 for more details.

[29] P. Plaut, 'Psychographie des Kriegers', in W. Stern and O. Lipmann (eds.), *Beihefte zur Zeitschrift für angewandte Psychologie. 21. Beiträge zur Psychologie des Krieges* (Leipzig: Johann Ambrosius Barth, 1920), pp. 1–123 and P. Plaut, 'Prinzipien und Methoden der Kriegspsychologie', in E. Abderhalden (ed.), *Handbuch der biologischen Arbeitsmethoden*. Part VI: *Methoden der experimentellen Psychologie*. Part C/I (Berlin: Urban & Schwarzenberg, 1928), pp. 621–87.

[30] L. Scholz, *Seelenleben des Soldaten an der Front. Hinterlassene Aufzeichnungen des im Kriege gefallenen Nervenarztes* (Tübingen: J.C.B. Mohr, 1920) and E. Everth, *Tat-Flugschriften 10. Von der Seele des Soldaten im Felde. Bemerkungen eines Kriegsteilnehmers* (Jena: Eugen Diederich, 1915).

[31] C. Bird, 'From Home to the Charge. A Psychological Study of the Soldier', *American Journal of Psychology* 28, 3 (July 1917), 315–48.

[32] See, for example, C. Stanford Read, *Military Psychiatry in Peace and War* (London: H.K. Lewis, 1920) and K. Bonhoeffer (ed.), *Geistes- und Nervenkrankheiten*. Part I (Leipzig: Johann Ambrosius Barth, 1922).

[33] War Office (ed.), *Report of the War Committee of Enquiry into 'Shell-Shock'* (London: HMSO, 1922). As Peter Barham argues, a primary concern of this report was to counter more progressive views towards psychiatric disorder and reinstate a pre-war moral vision distinguishing between neuroses and insanity and condemning nervous breakdown. See Barham, *Forgotten Lunatics of the Great War* (New Haven: Yale University Press, 2004), pp. 233–7.

veterans after the war provide a useful window into contemporary motives for fighting and, most especially, sources of grievance.[34] Among surviving official military sources, the most valuable are the letter-censorship reports produced in the British army from the end of 1916 and in the Kaiser's force from mid-1917, which were compiled from the correspondence of tens of thousands of combatants. Prisoner-interrogation reports and, in the German army, the reports of the *Eisenbahnreisende* (railway police) also provide information on the morale and coping strategies of large numbers of soldiers.

Armed with this material, the book will examine human resilience in the First World War trenches. In doing so, it will address three broad questions: why did soldiers and armies fight for such a long time? How were they able to cope psychologically with conditions at the front? And, finally, why did they eventually stop fighting?

[34] Studies of particular note are W. Schuhmacher, *Leben und Seele unseres Soldatenlieds im Weltkrieg* (Frankfurt am Main: Moritz Diesterweg, 1928) and J. Brophy and E. Partridge, *The Long Trail. Soldiers' Songs and Slang 1914–18*, revised edn (London: Sphere Books, 1965, 1969).

1 War of endurance

Deadlock

The trench fighting that predominated on the Western Front during the First World War was distinguished not only by its bloodiness and longevity but also by its indecisiveness. For three and a half years between November 1914 and March 1918 the lines moved significantly only once, in the spring of 1917, when a German strategic decision, not an Allied breakthrough, prompted the Kaiser's Field Army to retreat to new positions 20 miles to the rear. The stasis persisted until the German *Kaiserschlacht* in March 1918, despite great efforts on the part of all belligerents. Major offensives were launched: by the British at Neuve Chapelle, Aubers Ridge and Loos in 1915, on the Somme in 1916 and at Arras and Ypres in 1917, by the French in the Champagne in 1915 and 1917 and by the Germans at Ypres in 1915 and Verdun in 1916. Despite their lack of success these attacks caused enormous suffering and loss of life: casualties on the Somme during the second half of 1916 numbered 419,654 Britons, 204,353 Frenchmen and perhaps 465,000 Germans. During the ten months of fighting at Verdun, the French and Germans suffered a further 315,000 and 281,000 casualties respectively, while losses at the Third Battle of Ypres totalled 200,000 German and 275,000 British troops. By the end of the war, British fatalities had reached 723,000 men, the French had lost 1,398,000 and German fallen numbered 2,037,000.[1]

[1] See, respectively, G. Hirschfeld, 'Die Somme-Schlacht von 1916', in G. Hirschfeld, G. Krumeich and I. Renz (eds.), *Die Deutschen an der Somme 1914–1918* (Essen: Klartext, 2006), p. 87, R.T. Foley, *German Strategy and the Path to Verdun. Erich von Falkenhayn and the Development of Attrition, 1870–1916* (Cambridge University Press, 2005), p. 259, R. Prior and T. Wilson, *Passchendaele. The Untold Story* (New Haven: Yale University Press, 1996), p. 195 and Ferguson, *Pity*, p. 295. Exact German casualties on the Somme remain contested but most modern authorities reject the claims of the official British historian, J.E. Edmonds, that they numbered 680,000 and argue that, in fact, Entente losses were far heavier. See especially M.J. Williams, 'Thirty per cent. A Study in Casualty

The difficulties which would hinder a decisive breakthrough for most of the conflict already manifested themselves during the initial war of movement in 1914, when the German army surged through Belgium into France. Martin van Creveld has explained the severe logistical problems experienced by the army during this time. Damaged Belgian railways forced reliance on slow supply columns shuttling between railheads and the front, which were quickly outrun by the headlong advance of combat troops.[2] The success of this advance was primarily the result of the vast local superiority which the German army in the north possessed, helped greatly by the poor strategic decision of the French to sacrifice many of their best troops in vain attacks on prepared defensive positions in Alsace-Lorraine. Once the army came into contact with large Anglo-French forces on the Marne, the difficulties of battlefield communication, coordination and assault could not be overcome and the defeat inflicted there sent it reeling back along a front of 250 miles to the Aisne. The misnamed 'race to the sea' followed, in which each army rushed northwards in an attempt to outflank its enemy, and ended with the failure of the German assault on Ypres, where that army again experienced the perils of attacking even hurriedly prepared earth fortifications.[3]

By November 1914, heavy casualties and the need to release men for further offensives had prompted both sides to construct trenches along a line stretching 475 miles from the Swiss border to the Belgian coast. At first these were little more than rifle pits linked together but they quickly became habitable earth fortresses consisting of front, reserve and support positions. One typical German trench in early 1915 possessed duckboards, walls reinforced with brushwood revetments, sandbagged parapets, a steel sniper plate and dugouts which the officer in charge compared to 'ship cabins'.[4] The exact construction varied according to the stage of the war, the terrain and the nationality of the builders. Dry chalk soil allowed trenches to be dug deeply and equipped with expansive dugouts; those built by the Germans around Serre in the Somme sector during 1916, for example, typically consisted of two levels with

Statistics', *Journal of the Royal United Services Institution* 109, 633 (February 1964), 51–5 and M.J. Williams, 'The Treatment of the German Losses on the Somme in the British Official History. "Military Operations France and Belgium, 1916" Volume II', *Journal of the Royal United Services Institution* 111, 641 (February 1966), 69–74.

[2] M. van Creveld, *Supplying War. Logistics from Wallenstein to Patton*, 2nd edn (Cambridge University Press, 1977, 2004), pp. 113–41.

[3] The most thorough account of this period can be found in H. Strachan, *The First World War. To Arms* (3 vols., Oxford University Press, 2001), I, pp. 208–80.

[4] BA-MA Freiburg, MSg 2/ 5254: E.W. Küpper, letter to wife, 20 Mar. 1915.

Plate 1. The battlefield: British trenches from the air, September 1915. The traverses and winding communication lines effectively minimised the physical effect of shellfire. Detail from a photograph in the album of *II/Feldartillerie-Regiment Nr. 84*.

beds and a kitchen for their garrison. Another larger dugout taken by the British in the same area possessed four entrances with twenty-five steps leading below ground and contained dry boots, socks, shirts, blankets and also rations 'for a considerable number of men'.[5] Where the water table was high, as in Flanders, such extensive excavation was not possible and troops were forced to build breastworks or, later in the war, rely on concrete pillboxes for protection. By contrast, in the rocky ground of the Vosges, stone *sangars* were the favoured means of defence. German trench construction was generally considered the most thorough; British troops, burdened by a high command obsessed with the 'offensive spirit', were not usually given the materials to build shelters similar to the deep *Stollen* of their opponents. The French seem to have been the most lackadaisical builders, their trenches consisting generally of zigzags rather than the more defensible but also more labour-intensive traverses employed by the British and Germans. Although trenches never went out of use in practice, later in the war the promulgation of doctrines such as 'elastic' and 'blob' defence encouraged the dispersion of troops into shell-holes or pre-prepared strongpoints.[6]

The problem for generals attempting to break through enemy lines was that contemporary weaponry favoured the defence; even in 1918, after all the war's tactical and technical innovations, attackers still suffered the most killed and wounded.[7] Bolt-action rifles, machineguns and, above all, artillery fire were extremely effective against men in the open, providing attackers with little chance of closing for hand-to-hand combat: a fact reflected in the war's casualty statistics (see Table 1).

The strip of land separating belligerents was often narrow (the 1915 trench described above was only 25 metres – 27 yards – away from

[5] TNA, WO 157/ 15: Annexe to GHQ Summary, 26 Nov. 1916.

[6] For trench construction, see R. Holmes, *Tommy. The British Soldier on the Western Front 1914–1918* (London: HarperCollins, 2004), pp. 245–72. For 'elastic' and 'blob' defence, see Samuels, *Command or Control?*, pp. 192–7 and 214–21. For German scorn at British trenches, see TNA, WO 157/ 10: Summary of Information (GHQ), 13 June 1916 and Ferguson, *Pity*, p. 350.

[7] Ferguson, *Pity*, pp. 300–2. Only at Verdun in 1916 did the defenders' casualties outnumber those of the attacking force. Partly, this exception may have resulted from the unique operational plan of the battle; the Germans advanced principally in order to provoke French counterattacks, against which they could then exploit the natural advantages of the defence. Additionally, however, it may also have been due to the French failure to garrison the virtually impregnable fortress of Douaumont, enabling the Germans to effect its nearly bloodless capture early in the battle (the Brandenburg *Infanterie-Regiment Nr. 24* suffered only thirty-two dead on the day it took the fortress). The attacks launched to retrieve it contributed greatly to overall French losses, costing, in the opinion of one divisional commander, 100,000 men. See Foley, *German Strategy*, pp. 192–3 and A. Horne, *The Price of Glory. Verdun 1916* (London: Macmillan, 1962), p. 116.

Table 1. *Weaponry responsible for wounds and fatalities in the British and German armies (percentage)*

Casualties/weapon	Artillery	Small arms	Grenades	Edged weapons	Other
British wounded (no date)	58.5	39.0	2.2	0.3	N/A
German wounded (2.8.14–31.1.17)	43.0	50.9	2.6	0.6	3.0
German killed (2.8.14–31.1.17)	54.7	39.1	1.3	0.3	4.6
German wounded (15.4.–15.5.17)	76.1	17.8	0.8	0.1	5.2

Sources: *Medical Services*, p. 40 and *Sanitätsbericht III*, pp. 71 and 73. British figures were drawn from an undated sample of 212,659 soldiers treated in casualty clearing stations.

French lines) but was nonetheless extremely difficult for troops to negotiate when churned up by the heavy preparatory bombardments particularly characteristic of the war's middle years. Attackers were often burdened by the extra arms and ammunition, sometimes weighing as much as 70 pounds, which were needed to hold any ground they captured. In the estimation of one veteran, only a quarter of heavily laden troops who successfully crossed no-man's-land in an assault were capable of engaging in hand-to-hand combat; the rest were usually too exhausted.[8] The inadequacy of contemporary communications meant that once soldiers passed across no-man's-land, staff officers were largely powerless to direct them. Telephone cables were cut by artillery, carrier pigeons lost their way in the smoke of the battlefield or refused to fly in fog and runners were killed, leaving generals in the rear ignorant of success or failure until well after the event. It was not unknown for men who had taken a trench to be forced out again by their own artillery, which was bombarding the position in the belief that it was still occupied by the enemy.

Technological and doctrinal innovation during the war did provide some solutions to these difficulties. By early 1917, enhanced assault tactics based around more flexible platoons armed with not only rifles

[8] W.D. Croft, 'The Application of Recent Developments in Mechanics and other Scientific Knowledge to Preparation and Training for Future War on Land', *Journal of the Royal United Services Institution* 65, 459 (August 1920), 447.

and bayonets but also light machineguns, hand and rifle grenades were being widely disseminated in both the German and British armies.[9] Facilitated by improvements in communications, inter-arms cooperation grew better, and, by the end of the year, artillery on both sides had recognised the costs to their own infantry caused by efforts to obliterate defensive obstacles; instead, they developed short, intense bombardments and creeping barrages designed to neutralise the enemy.[10] Nonetheless, while these advances greatly helped attackers to break into opponents' positions, the logistical difficulties of bringing up the vast amounts of supplies, guns and munitions required quickly in order to exploit an opportunity or continue an advance remained. All too often, the pause enabled the enemy, having fallen back on his railheads, to reinforce his troops and win back the position. Not until the second half of 1918, once Allied armies finally possessed a large pool of motorised transport, were these problems also partially overcome.[11]

The difficulty of decisively breaking through enemy lines led generals and politicians to turn to strategies of attrition. For Lord Kitchener at the end of 1914, this approach simply meant holding Britain's New Armies at home until their German opponent had been sufficiently weakened by French and Russian action. During the following year, however, attrition began to be considered more constructively: from the summer, the British undertook serious analyses of German manpower and casualties, and, in the late autumn, small-scale assaults were launched with the intention of wearing down the enemy's reserves. By December, Entente generals agreed at the Chantilly conference that victory would be achieved in 1916 through preparatory attacks costing the Germans 200,000 men a month followed up with a coordinated offensive on all fronts designed to smash through the fatally weakened enemy.[12]

9 See B.I. Gudmundsson, *Stormtroop Tactics. Innovation in the German Army, 1914–1918* (London: Praeger, 1989, 1995), pp. 83–5, 97 and 101–2 and J. Lee, 'Some Lessons of the Somme. The British Infantry in 1917', in British Commission for Military History (ed.), '*Look to Your Front*'. *Studies in the First World War* (Staplehurst: Spellmount, 1999), pp. 79–88.

10 J. Bailey, 'British Artillery in the Great War', in P. Griffith (ed.), *British Fighting Methods in the Great War* (London: Frank Cass, 1996), pp. 31–43 and H. Linnenkohl, *Vom Einzelschuß zur Feuerwalze. Der Wettlauf zwischen Technik und Taktik im Ersten Weltkrieg* (Koblenz: Bernard & Graefe, 1990). For improved communications, see Griffith, *Battle Tactics*, pp. 169–75.

11 G. Sheffield, *Forgotten Victory. The First World War. Myths and Realities* (London: Headline, 2001), pp. 98–103.

12 See D. French, 'The Meaning of Attrition, 1914–1916', *English Historical Review* 103, 407 (April 1988), 389 and 397–8 and J.M. Beach, 'British Intelligence and the German Army, 1914–1918' unpublished Ph.D. thesis, University College London (2005), pp. 141–4.

Similar calculations were being made at the same time on the German side of the lines. Recognising the extreme difficulty of achieving a decisive breakthrough, the Chief of the General Staff, *General* von Falkenhayn, concluded at the end of 1915 that a new approach designed to wear out the opponents' strength was necessary. The Verdun offensive begun in February 1916 was therefore consciously conceived as an attritional battle, the first stage of a plan intended to apply such pressure on the French that it would not only destroy their reserves but also force the British to launch an inadequately prepared relief operation which would, in turn, sap their strength. This, it was hoped, would then enable the Germans to launch one final attack, sweeping their enemies from the field and enabling the negotiation of a favourable peace.[13]

Neither strategy succeeded. At Verdun, the German tactic of advancing a short way and then using the defensive power of heavy artillery to destroy counterattacks did indeed cause heavy French casualties, but the lack of understanding of Falkenhayn's concept at lower command levels combined with the failure to capture key positions early meant that the battle soon degenerated into a gruelling fight for territory costing the Germans similarly devastating losses.[14] In the Entente's Somme offensive, operational confusion at the highest levels marred execution. Despite his later attempt to present the action as a 'wearing-out battle', the first stage in a carefully planned attritional campaign which brought Germany to its knees, General Douglas Haig at first aimed for a decisive breakthrough. By altering the limited objectives initially set for the attack to much more ambitious goals without a corresponding increase in firepower, he reduced the intensity and effectiveness of the preparatory artillery barrage with catastrophic consequences for both the advance and his men's lives. The Battle of the Somme became an attritional contest by default, not design, and while not without success, particularly in psychological terms, it did not wipe out German manpower reserves. Indeed, Entente casualties vastly outnumbered those of their enemy, and, far from declining, the German Field Army continued to expand until the second half of 1917.[15]

13 Foley, *German Strategy*, pp. 266–7. Cf. also the review of Foley's book by T.M. Holmes in *English Historical Review* 121, 492 (June 2006), 872–4.

14 Foley, *German Strategy*, particularly pp. 209–36.

15 See the excellent account in R. Prior and T. Wilson, *The Somme* (New Haven: Yale University Press, 2005), pp. 41–51 and 306. For Haig's subsequent justification of the battle, see J.H. Boraston (ed.), *Sir Douglas Haig's Despatches (December 1915–April 1919)* (London: J.M. Dent & Sons, 1919, 1979), pp. 19 and 51–3. For the German Field Army's strength, see *Sanitätsbericht III*, pp. 6*–7*.

Plate 2. The cost: German corpses after the French Artois Offensive, September 1915. Defence, although generally less expensive in human lives than the attack, could still be bloody. German photograph (anonymous).

In the absence of strategies enabling decisive breakthrough or the annihilation of the enemy, the conflict on the Western Front became a war of endurance. Conditions at the front sorely tested soldiers' morale and armies' discipline. As the censor of the British Third Army observed in mid-1917:

> It is perfectly plain that the minds of men are adversely affected far more by their continued absence from home and by the dread of winter conditions than by the prospect of actual conflict with the enemy. References to winter privations and to lack of leave outnumber references to the horror of fighting in the ratio of 5 to 1.[16]

Dirty and unpleasant trenches sapped soldiers' will to endure; Ernst Huthmacher, a middle-aged infantryman serving with *bayerisches Landwehr-Infanterie-Regiment Nr. 1*, described the men's accommodation in his front line as being like 'pigsties', commenting, 'I can only be amazed that I have not been suffocated in filth'.[17] The basic trenches in the winter of 1914 were worst for combatants, offering such inadequate protection against the harsh elements that men on both sides died of exposure.[18] Even after this early period, it was not unknown for men to be stationed in positions flooded by heavy rainfall or melting snow. One particularly bad position visited by *Hauptmann* Helmuth Fuchs in April 1915 was almost waist-deep in water and had two sodden corpses stuck in its breastworks.[19] Battlefield hygiene was often poor, attracting flies and vermin. Lice also caused troops considerable discomfort: not just due to the skin irritation they caused but also, as one soldier, Franz Brussig, complained in his diary, because their noise kept men awake.[20] Food and water had to be brought up from the rear, a very time-consuming process if the narrow communication trenches leading to the front line were filled with mud. The machine-gunner Richard Williams recorded that a relief battalion had taken almost an entire day to negotiate the mile-long communication trench which led to his position in

16 IWM, 84/46/1: M. Hardie, Report on Moral, &c., 25 Aug. 1917.
17 DTA, 930: E. Huthmacher, letter to wife, 12 Mar. 1915.
18 *Medical Services*, p. 135 and *Sanitätsbericht III*, p. 19. For letter accounts, see IWM, Con Shelf: R.P. Harker, letter to Ethel, 16 Dec. 1914, and DTA, 865: H. Weber, letter to friends, 7 Jan. 1915.
19 BA-MA Freiburg, MSg 1/ 2965: H. Fuchs, diary, 7 Apr. 1915.
20 For rats, see IWM, P 317 Con Shelf: H.W. Yoxall, letter to family, 1 June 1916 and IWM, 92/3/1: E.F. Chapman, letter to mother, 15 Sept. 1916. For flies, see BA-MA Freiburg, MSg 1/ 2966: H. Fuchs, diary, 1 Sept. 1916. For lice, see IWM, 84/46/1: M. Hardie, Report on Complaints, Moral, etc., 23 Nov. 1916, pp. 4 and 11; Staatsbib. Berlin, Ms. Boruss. fol. 1084: F. Brussig, diary, 2 Feb. 1916 and BA-MA Freiburg, MSg 1/ 161: K. Reiter, diary, 20 June 1916.

December 1915.[21] In the heat of summer, thirst could become a major problem for troops, as, although each carried a flask, the difficulty of bringing water up to the trenches limited the possibility of refilling. It was not unknown for men to be given only a quarter of a litre to share between two, with the result that some would drink from dubious sources and contract dysentery.[22] Hunger was a less serious problem in the front line itself, as combatants were better fed than rear troops and were allocated extra rations when a major action was expected. Nonetheless, the fact that food often reached the front cold and was bland in character, particularly in the German army during the second half of the war, did prove to be a major source of demoralisation.[23] Equally debilitating was the exhaustion of active service. Williams remarked that 'there is little or no sleep during the 48 hours we are in' and Lieutenant Yoxall described his men as being 'never warm enough to go to sleep' during the six- or seven-day periods they spent in the trenches.[24] In the opinion of the former medical officer William Tyrrell, exhaustion was the 'most potent single cause of "shell-shock" and nervous breakdown' at the front.[25]

The risk of death and dismemberment also placed considerable strain on soldiers. One doctor serving in a pioneer company in 1914 recorded seeing some of the men, convinced that they would be killed, repeatedly writing a 'last' goodbye card to relatives at every opportunity.[26] Such behaviour was by no means unrealistic, for soldiers faced terrible danger: in the British army, 11.8% of men mobilised were killed and overall, including wounded, missing and captured, 43% became casualties during the conflict. The chances of unscathed survival were still less for German

[21] IWM, 82/26/1: A.R. Williams, letter to brother, 3 Dec. 1915.

[22] See Plaut, 'Psychographie des Kriegers', p. 49. In the British army, each battalion possessed two water carts which brought water up as far as battalion headquarters. In 1918, 100-gallon tanks were issued and positioned just behind the line, so that the carts could shuttle back and forth, keeping them supplied, rather than remaining in the danger zone. See O.W. White, 'Battle Supply', *Journal of the Royal United Services Institution* 67, 465 (February 1922), 96–7.

[23] For rations, see *Military Effort*, pp. 584 and 586 and also TNA, WO 157/ 13: Reductions in the Scale of Rations in the German Army, Sept. 1916 and Plaut, 'Psychographie des Kriegers', p. 48.

[24] IWM, 82/26/1: A.R. Williams, letter to family, 16 Dec. 1915 and IWM, P 317 Con Shelf: H.W. Yoxall, letter to mother, 30 Jan. 1917.

[25] W. Tyrrell in *RWOCIS*, p. 31. Cf. IWM, P 317 Con Shelf: H.W. Yoxall, letter to family, 1 June 1916; IWM, 80/43/1: P.D. Mundy, letter to Ruby, 16 July 1916 and IWM, 69/25/1: G. Donaldson, letter to mother, 18 July 1916. Also, cf. Plaut, 'Psychographie des Kriegers', pp. 50–1.

[26] K.E. Neumann, 'Psychologische Beobachtungen im Felde', *Neurologisches Centralblatt* 33, 23 (1 December 1914), 1244.

soldiers, of whom around 15% were killed and 51% became battle casualties.[27] These were figures for entire armies. For combatant troops and above all for their officers, the risks were far greater. Second Lieutenant Robert Hamilton, serving with the 1/20 London Regiment, estimated in June 1915 that 'before this war is over 90% of Captains & subalterns of infantry will be washed out, as will 50% of the men'. Lieutenant St Leger, a twenty-one-year-old serving with the 2/Coldstream Guards, remarked with equal pessimism in February 1917 that among his officer friends, 'those of us who are not hit by this time nine months will be very, very lucky'.[28]

Perhaps worst of all, however, was the lack of progress or a foreseeable end to hostilities. The long exposure to risk proved debilitating: in the opinion of the former commander of the tank corps J.F.C. Fuller, the psychiatric disease 'shellshock' was less the result of sudden trauma than the 'prolonged danger in a static position, where the man cannot get away from it'.[29] Middle-aged men found the long absence from their wives and children extremely depressing. Huthmacher, for example, suffered intense homesickness, writing to his spouse: 'how gladly I would give up everything, just [to go] home again, home to you, to my loved ones'.[30] For *Offizierstellvertreter* Ludwig Moeller, the strain of being apart from his beloved 'Mariele' was also very great: 'long, long and often have I looked at your picture; sadly, sadly it was only the picture; for how gladly I would have embraced you once again and looked into your beloved eyes'.[31] Simply the lack of progress itself was also highly disheartening. Lord Moran, medical officer of 1/Royal Fusiliers during the war, remarked that 'for most men there is no rest, no peace of mind, without an end in view'. He described the winter of 1916–17 as 'interminable' and 'prayed that something, that anything might

[27] Ferguson, *Pity*, p. 295, *Sanitätsbericht III*, p. 12, J. Winter, 'Britain's "Lost Generation" of the First World War', *Population Studies. A Journal of Demography* 31 (November 1977), 451 and I. Beckett, 'The Nation in Arms', in I.F.W. Beckett and K. Simpson (eds.), *A Nation in Arms. A Social Study of the British Army in the First World War* (Manchester University Press, 1985), p. 8.

[28] IWM, 87/8/1: R.P. Hamilton, letter to cousin, 3 June 1915 and IWM, P 239: W.B. St Leger, diary, 14 Feb. 1917. Cf. M. Middlebrook, *The Kaiser's Battle, 21 March 1918. The First Day of the German Spring Offensive* (London: Allen Lane. The Penguin Press, 1978), pp. 405–6. Middlebrook calculates the average subaltern's front-line service in the 10/West Yorks as 6.17 months, although just under half of those who left the battalion did so by being transferred rather than as casualties.

[29] J.F.C. Fuller in *RWOCIS*, p. 29.

[30] DTA, 930: E. Huthmacher, letter to wife, 23 June 1915.

[31] BA-MA Freiburg, MSg 2/ 428: L. Moeller, postcard to wife, 26 Apr. 1916.

happen; but nothing did happen, until at last I had given up anticipating anything'.[32] Moran was not alone in despairingly submitting to the long duration of his ordeal. As the Bavarian infantryman Josef Kohler remarked in the spring of 1916, 'we absolutely no longer believe that [the war] will ever come to an end; it appears that we are all condemned for life'.[33] In other cases, the lack of progress prompted soldiers to question the value of their sacrifices and the point of the bloodshed. 'What impressed me most about the whole thing was the hopelessness of it all,' wrote Captain Geoffrey Donaldson, after his first time in the line. 'I feel that fighting will never end the war'.[34]

The effects of hunger, homesickness, exhaustion and continual danger were exacerbated by the apparent purposelessness of combat. The difficulty of keeping men motivated in such conditions was a primary concern of all armies fighting on the Western Front. Unable to advance except at extremely heavy cost and incapable of annihilating their enemies, generals had little option other than to hope that morale and discipline would endure. Under such circumstances, resilience became the key quality necessary for men and armies to survive and was the determining factor in the long and bloody conflict.

Loss of control

The war on the Western Front was not only a conflict of endurance because of its longevity and indecisiveness but also because of the peculiar way in which the fighting was conducted. Trench warfare was an especially stressful form of combat, as most soldiers testified. The sentiment expressed by one British officer when the Germans withdrew to the Hindenburg Line, 'I hope to God trench warfare is dead, though I'm afraid it isn't. It's a rotten business, and one's nerves get worse and worse. Open fighting would do us all a lot of good,' was by no means uncommon.[35] One year later on the eve of the *Kaiserschlacht*, the postal censor of the German *5. Armee* similarly noted 'to a portion of the letter writers, the mobile war which, in their view, will now soon begin, appears to be considerably more pleasant than the previous

32 Lord Moran [C. Wilson], *The Anatomy of Courage* (London: Constable, 1945, 1966), p. 145.
33 BA-MA Freiburg, MSg 2/ 5458: J. Kohler, 2 Mar. 1916. Cf. Plaut, 'Psychographie des Kriegers', p. 42.
34 IWM, 69/25/1: G. Donaldson, letter to mother, 1 June 1916.
35 IWM, 92/3/1: E.F. Chapman, letter to mother, 23 Mar. 1917.

position warfare'.[36] From very early in the conflict, service on the Western Front gained a reputation among German soldiers as far more stressful than the more mobile fighting in eastern theatres. *Gefreiter* Heinrich Genscher, for example, remarked in the spring of 1915 that while 'reserves of physical strength' was the main characteristic needed by troops in the mobile war of the east, those fighting in France and Flanders required 'moral strength' in order to survive. His opinion was echoed after the war by the army doctor Hermann Hofmann, who pithily asserted that 'mobile warfare is more muscle war, position warfare more nerve war'.[37] Narrative evidence supports these observations. German divisions used to the eastern war of movement arrived completely unprepared for the conditions of the Western Front. The *11. bayerische Division*, for example, which had served in Russia and Serbia before being positioned opposite the French in March 1916, went to battle confident of success but was quickly disillusioned. 'From the first day's fighting on our front', an Entente intelligence report observed, 'the moral[e] [of the division] sank and the men became discouraged. Under the avalanche of shells, they bent and crumpled. One officer went mad'.[38]

Discomfort alone hardly accounts for the particular strain engendered by trench warfare. It is true that often the front line was unpleasant, particularly if troops were positioned in waterlogged ground or in an 'active' sector with heavy fighting (the area around Ypres, which fulfilled both of these conditions, was particularly feared by soldiers).[39] On the many quiet sectors of the front, however, the static nature of the warfare actually allowed troops to organise quite comfortable living quarters. Private Arthur Wrench was surprised on taking over French trenches in 1916 at the relative luxury they afforded: 'these French soldiers certainly spared nothing to make these quarters habitable for they seem to have ransacked the entire neighbourhood for all sorts of furniture and kitchen equipment', he observed. 'We have here beds, stoves, tables, chairs, mirrors, pots and pans, and dishes. Even some clocks and other ornaments'.[40] If British tastes in dugout furnishing tended to be more spartan than those of their allies, they nonetheless excelled

36 BA-MA Freiburg, W-10/ 50794: Postüberwachung der *5. Armee*, 24 Feb. 1918, p. 45.

37 BA-MA Freiburg, MSg 2/ 2735: H. Genscher, letter to father, 10 Apr. 1915 and H. Hofmann, 'Die deutsche Nervenkraft im Stellungskrieg', in F. Seeßelberg (ed.), *Der Stellungskrieg 1914–18* (Berlin: E.S. Mittler & Sohn, 1926), p. 445.

38 TNA, WO 157/ 6: Annexe to [GHQ] Summary, 11 Apr. 1916. Cf. F. Schauwecker, *Im Todesrachen. Die deutsche Seele im Weltkriege* (Halle: Heinrich Diekmann, 1921), pp. 49–50.

39 For Ypres, see particularly J.S.Y. Rogers in *RWOCIS*, p. 63.

40 IWM, 85/51/1: A.E. Wrench, diary, 11 Mar. 1916.

stereotypically at front-line gardening. One trench in 1915 possessed a 'square garden with diagonal lattice wood paths with quite a profusion of old-fashioned flowers, marsh marigold, mignonette, snapdragon, convolvulus, nasturtium, all flourishing right under the parapet', on which friendly nocturnal visitors were warned not to tread. The startling assertion of normality given by such a garden in the battle environment appears to have reassured soldiers, who found it 'a pleasant surprise to hear there were flowers even in the mud and darkness'.[41] The Germans also took advantage of the stasis to dabble in battle-zone horticulture, their artillerymen cultivating neat lawns around their dugouts.[42] Considerable effort was also invested in the shelters themselves: the mortar man who wrote from the Vosges that he was the proud owner of 'a pretty shelter' with a sofa, four chairs, a table, a cupboard, a coat rack and a telephone was by no means exceptional.[43] A British interrogator reported with astonishment that prisoners of *Infanterie-Regiment Nr. 181* had 'spent several months in [the] front line without being relieved, and did not seem to object to the system, as they said their trenches and dug-outs were very comfortable, heated with stoves and lit by electricity'.[44] German officers' shelters could even be luxurious: those captured by British soldiers at Beaumont Hamel in 1916 were not only papered and hung with tapestries but also allegedly contained women's clothing, suggesting, if true, that on occasion officers brought female companions to the line.[45] In contrast, German troops in the east, engaged in combat on a constantly fluctuating front, were unable to establish themselves comfortably. Harsher weather conditions, a poorer rail network than that in the west and a war of movement placed far greater physical strain on the men of the eastern German armies than those in France and Flanders.

Equally important, and contrary to popular perceptions, trench warfare did not increase casualty rates but actually limited fatalities: as Hew Strachan has observed, 'the war would have been far more horrific if there had been no trenches'.[46] Open combat was usually far bloodier than static fighting. The German western Field Army sustained its heaviest battle casualties during the three-month war of movement in

41 IWM, 91/3/1: P.A. Brown, letter to mother, 8 Oct. 1915.
42 Plaut, 'Psychographie des Kriegers', p. 107.
43 DTA, 91: Letter of Fr. W. Steinbach, 26 Aug. 1915, reproduced in A. Schulz's compilation.
44 TNA, WO 157/ 4: Summary of Information (GHQ), 22 Jan. 1916.
45 IWM, 85/51/1: A.E. Wrench, diary, 15 Nov. 1916.
46 H. Strachan, *The First World War. A New Illustrated History* (London: Simon and Schuster, 2003), p. 159.

Plate 3. The power of artillery: shell exploding in no-man's-land, December 1916. Sitting under a disempowering artillery bombardment was the archetypal combat experience on the Western Front. Official British photograph.

1914 and suffered grievously again during the mobile fighting in March 1918.[47] In the east during the early stages of the conflict, battle losses far exceeded those in the west. The highest casualty rate experienced by the German army during the First World War on any front was that of the 1914–15 campaign in East Prussia and Poland, where losses amounted to 476 wounded per 1,000 men. Against this figure, the casualties from the more famous western trench warfare and attritional battles of 1916 and 1917, at 182–3 wounded per 1,000 men, appear positively modest.[48]

Crucially, however, regardless of battle casualties, losses from psychiatric causes were always higher in the static warfare of the west than in the more mobile eastern fighting: as German medical authorities observed, 'mobile warfare ... eroded the psychological strength of the army less than did static warfare'.[49] Contemporary psychiatrists blamed

47 See *Sanitätsbericht II*, p. 2 and table 9 and *Sanitätsbericht III*, p. 19.
48 *Sanitätsbericht III*, pp. 82*–5*.
49 Ibid., pp. 146 and 42*–3*.

'the excessive incidence of nervous disorders' in the west on 'the sustained shell fire with high explosives which has characterized most of the fighting'.[50] The connection between artillery fire and psychiatric casualties seemed logical for two reasons. Firstly, as the historian John Terraine observed, 'the war of 1914–18 was an artillery war'.[51] According to British statistics, shellfire was responsible for nearly 60 per cent of wounds during the conflict. The numbers of guns and weight of the projectiles fired increased during the war, with the result that the weapon gained in importance: German medical authorities estimated that in its later stages, these projectiles caused as many as 76 per cent of all wounds.[52] Artillery was three and a half times more densely positioned in the west than it was in the east and the industrial capacity of the western Allies was larger than that of Russia, enabling the former to produce more shells.[53] The officer of the *11. bayerische Division* who collapsed in the front line had almost certainly never before experienced anything like the rapid, sustained fire of the amply supplied French 75mm artillery batteries, which could sweep an area of 4 hectares with over 10,000 shrapnel balls in less than a minute.[54]

Secondly, the connection between psychiatric disorders and shellfire made sense because it was clear that few other weapons had such a great morale effect on troops. As one German memorandum on artillery fire commented in July 1918, 'more difficult to bear than the physical losses is often the psychological impact of a heavy bombardment'.[55] Men described shelling as 'beastly' and wrote that 'nobody cares a rap about anything else'.[56] Heavy bombardments were particularly frightening: 'I was flat on my stomach in the trenches at that time for two hours and didn't dare to move,' wrote Huthmacher, attempting to explain the terror of being in the midst of such an event.[57] Lethargy was another very common response to artillery fire. The battalion doctor Ernst

50 Salmon, 'Care and Treatment', 512. Cf. W. Aldren Turner, 'Remarks on Cases of Nervous and Mental Shock Observed in the Base Hospitals in France', *British Medical Journal* (15 May 1915), 833 and M. Rohde, 'Neurologische Betrachtungen eines Truppenarztes im Felde', *Zeitschrift für die gesamte Neurologie und Psychiatrie* 29, 5 (19 October 1915), 380.

51 J. Terraine, *White Heat. The New Warfare 1914–18* (London: Sidgwick and Jackson, 1982), p. 95.

52 See Table 1.

53 See N. Stone, *The Eastern Front 1914–1917* (Abingdon: Purnell Book Services, 1975, 1976), p. 93.

54 Strachan, *First World War*, I, p. 229.

55 BA-MA Freiburg, PH 3/ 455: Memorandum on shellfire from *Chef des Generalstabes*, 9 July 1918.

56 Respectively, IWM, 96/29/1: S.A. Knight, letter to girlfriend, 19 June 1915 and IWM, P 317 Con Shelf: H.W. Yoxall, letter to father, 22 Sept. 1916, and IWM, 82/26/1: A.R. Williams, letter to brother, 12 Aug. 1916.

57 DTA, 930: E. Huthmacher, letter to wife, 31 Mar. 1915.

Wittermann recorded that men reacted 'for the most part with a feeling of enormous sleepiness'.[58] Both emotions were apparent in the physical alterations visible among soldiers under bombardment:

> The eyes pop out of their sockets, the expression becomes fixed and glassy, the facial skin loses all of its red colour, the skin becomes yellow, the cheekbones protrude. The lips are shut tight and sticky spittle tacks up the tongue to the roof of the mouth. The heart works in short, convulsive beats, breathing becomes slower ... From time to time a cold shudder runs through the body and the teeth chatter ... Every spoken word is felt as agony.[59]

The tremendous strain of such experiences proved too much for many men to bear. The former medical officer William Tyrrell remembered that 'acute breakdown ... occurred especially during bombardments when the men, sometimes in large numbers, lost their heads and lost their control'.[60] It was unsurprising that the term 'shellshock', coined to describe wartime psychiatric disorders but soon discredited among doctors, was quickly adopted by the troops.[61]

Shellfire owed its psychological effect to several factors. The noise of projectiles played a major role in generating terror and exhaustion. Private E.A. Luther of the 3/Rifle Brigade described the sound of approaching 'Jack Johnsons' as 'like being on the platform when an express train is coming through at full speed' and rated the detonation as 'worse than any thunder owing to its proximity'.[62] Wittermann attributed shells' morale effect both to the time delay between their firing and arrival, during which their scream intensified, forcing soldiers to brace themselves, and also to the nerve-jarring effects of the subsequent explosion.[63] Guns with a flat trajectory and a supersonic projectile were more feared than howitzers, whose shell approached more slowly. The size of the explosion, which was influenced by the shell's size and filling, its fuse and the type of land on which it fell, was also an important determinant of psychological impact. So frightening was the noise of shellfire that

58 E. Wittermann, 'Kriegspsychiatrische Erfahrungen aus der Front', *Münchener Medizinische Wochenschrift* 62, 34, *Feldärztliche Beilage* 34 (24 August 1915), 1165.
59 Ludwig, 'Psychologie der Furcht', p. 132. Second World War research similarly found that air-raid victims often displayed excessive docility. See Rachman, *Fear and Courage*, p. 27.
60 *RWOCIS*, p. 34.
61 Shephard, *War of Nerves*, p. 1.
62 IWM, P 262: E.A. Luther, diary / memoir, 23 Sept. 1914.
63 Wittermann, 'Kriegspsychiatrische Erfahrungen', 1165. Cf. C.S. Myers, *Shell Shock in France 1914–18. Based on a War Diary* (Cambridge University Press, 1940), p. 39 and, for a similar observation from a combatant, IWM, 79/51/1: C.J. Paterson, diary, 18 Sept. 1914.

even when completely safe, men could still react to it with anxiety. One British captain, watching his own side bombard enemy trenches, remarked that 'although there was no danger, the sharp reports & the roar and scream of the shells over our heads seemed to give some of the men more "wind" than the front line'.[64]

Although the noise of shellfire alone was emotive, it would not have been so frightening had the potential threat it heralded not been so great. Not only did artillery cause more casualties than any other weapon on the Western Front but those injuries that it did inflict were often grievous. Contemporary psychiatrists agreed that men's primary fear was not death but mutilation; wounds to the stomach, jaw and eyes were particularly dreaded. It is thus significant that artillery fire was more likely than other weapons to cause head wounds.[65] Moreover, shells were terrifying because, as Lieutenant St Leger somewhat coyly observed, they could 'make such a mess of one'. The weapon eviscerated, maimed and disfigured. Body parts could be scattered over wide distances and legs and arms blown into trees by the force of explosions.[66] Such sights were obviously extremely disturbing, especially when the victims were friends or comrades. As Lieutenant Yoxall remarked, 'when you have seen a shell fall into the midst of six men and packed three of them away in a sandbag ... one wonders whether anything matters'.[67]

Above all, however, it was the disempowering nature of artillery fire which made it so stressful and frightening. Infantrymen felt 'caught like rats in a trap by such terrific shelling ... without a chance in the world to help ourselves'.[68] One British Regular officer, who had been hoping for a war of movement, wrote that 'under continuous shellfire ... one

[64] BA-MA Freiburg, PH 3/ 455: Memorandum on shellfire from *Chef des Generalstabes*, 9 July 1918 and IWM, 69/25/1: G. Donaldson, letter to mother, 5 June 1916.

[65] Schauwecker, *Im Todesrachen*, pp. 365–6. Cf. Scholz, *Seelenleben*, p. 155, Plaut, 'Psychographie des Kriegers', pp. 26–7, 65, Ludwig, 'Psychologie der Furcht', p. 166 and IWM, 82/25/1: H.M. Dillon, letter to 'K.D.', 29 Oct. 1914. For head wounds, see *Sanitätsbericht III*, pp. 68–9 and *Medical Services*, p. 41. Cf. Table 1.

[66] IWM, P 239: W.B. St Leger, diary, 28 Nov. 1917 and Dr Krüger-Franke, 'Ueber truppenärztliche Erfahrungen in der Schlacht', *Berliner Klinische Wochenschrift* 1 (4 January 1915), 8. Perhaps due to the great fear, horror and disgust they caused, vivid descriptions of mutilation or evisceration are rare in combatants' letters and diaries. Already by early 1915, however, the number of crippled German troops was estimated at 30,000 men. After the war, 237,433 men were awarded pensions for wounds and amputations in Britain. See, respectively, B. Ulrich, '"...als wenn nichts geschehen wäre". Anmerkungen zur Behandlung der Kriegsopfer während des Weltkriegs', in G. Hirschfeld, G. Krumeich and I. Renz (eds.), *Keiner fühlt sich hier mehr als Mensch ... Erlebnis und Wirkung des Ersten Weltkriegs* (Essen: Klartext, 1993), p. 118 and *Medical Services*, p. 326.

[67] IWM, P 317 Con Shelf: H.W. Yoxall, letter to mother, 5 Feb. 1917.

[68] IWM, 85/51/1: A.E. Wrench, diary, 16 Apr. 1917.

feels so helpless'.[69] Helmuth Fuchs, a German professional officer, summed up the problem succinctly when he observed that, 'holding out under a psychologically wearing, even if in practice ineffectual, shellfire is very difficult for the infantry because they stand defenceless and must let it go over them'.[70] Doctors and psychologists with front experience emphasised that men's behaviour was determined less by objective assessments of danger than by subjective perceptions of helplessness. The psychologist Erich Everth argued that heavy shellfire was only frightening when troops had to face it passively: 'in such circumstances', he noted, 'the urge to do something is often so strong that one would gladly change places, even if in doing so one was certain to come into even greater danger'.[71] His colleague, Walter Ludwig, who fought on the Western Front during the war, similarly contended that soldiers who were distracted by activity or who felt they could defend themselves experienced less fear than men who felt powerless in the face of a danger.[72] This was also noted by Wittermann, who suggested that small-arms fire had little psychological impact on infantrymen because they could actively defend and distract themselves by discharging their own rifles.[73] Many artillerymen, in contrast, were undisturbed by shellfire, against which they could retaliate, but were terrified of infantry fire.[74] Modern psychological research supports these observations: S.J. Rachman, for example, has argued that 'there is a connection between our ability to control potentially threatening situations and the experience of fear. In the face of threats, if a person feels unable to control the probable outcome, he or she is likely to experience fear'.[75]

Static warfare was less bloody than its more mobile counterpart precisely because trenches were extremely effective at limiting the material damage inflicted by shellfire. When troops lay protected in trenches, it took 329 shells to hit one German soldier and approximately four times that number to kill him.[76] The heavy bombardments fired by

69 IWM, 02/16/1: W.H.J.St L. Atkinson, letter to mother, 1 Nov. 1914.
70 BA-MA Freiburg, MSg 1/ 2965: H. Fuchs, letter to wife, 9 Sept. 1914.
71 Everth, *Seele des Soldaten*, p. 41.
72 Ludwig, 'Psychologie der Furcht', p. 152.
73 Wittermann, 'Kriegspsychiatrische Erfahrungen', 1165.
74 See Ludwig, 'Psychologie der Furcht', p. 148. Cf. Plaut, 'Psychographie des Kriegers', pp. 21–2 and IWM, 88/7/1: R. Downing, letter to father, 25 Aug. 1915.
75 Rachman, *Fear and Courage*, p. 13.
76 See *Sanitätsbericht III*, p. 71 and Bourke, *Intimate History of Killing*, p. 6. The British manufactured 210,300,676 high explosive and shrapnel shells between 1914 and 1918, fifteen shells for every man who served in the German army. See *Military Effort*, pp. 474–7.

Plate 4. A constrictive environment: the trenches from the ground. The restrictive confines of the front line (in this case a sector opposite Messines being held by the Lancashire Fusiliers in January 1917) protected men physically against shellfire but magnified its psychological impact. Official British photograph.

belligerents on the Western Front were necessary precisely because most shells did no physical damage to the enemy. The 1.5 million shells fired during the seven-day bombardment preceding the opening of the Somme Offensive on 1 July 1916, for example, inflicted less than 7,000 casualties.[77] Crucially, however, although they protected men from the fatal effects of shellfire, trenches amplified the weapon's psychological impact. The restrictions on movement and vision imposed by such defences, when combined with their helplessness against artillery fire, thwarted soldiers' 'flight or fight instinct', correspondingly increasing the mental tension experienced in danger. The veteran and psychologist Paul Plaut recognised this when he observed that static warfare was 'psychologically more concentrated' than mobile combat because 'the spatial restriction of the vital living conditions channels this tension

[77] Figure for killed, wounded and missing of *2. Armee* from 21 to 30 June 1916. *Sanitätsbericht III*, p. 51.

inwards, so that one's head threatens to burst'.[78] It was also confirmed by a British officer who had collapsed while sheltering from shellfire in a trench:

> Owing to the small area to which we were confined, there was no opportunity of being able to give vent to the pent-up feelings that were in me, and in consequence my nerves were strung up to such a pitch that I felt that something in me would snap.[79]

Although illogical in terms of their chances of survival, many soldiers preferred not to restrict their freedom of movement in a bombardment. Ludwig noted this behaviour in his investigation of fear and Moran also remembered a man 'who could not keep still in a bombardment but who would walk up and down the trench, though he must have known that he was much safer in a dug-out'.[80] Huthmacher similarly recorded that he had hesitated to slide into a funk hole during a heavy bombardment due to fear of being buried. Only on the urgent entreaty of a comrade did he do so, narrowly avoiding death or serious injury from a shell which fell immediately afterwards.[81] Such behaviour could become extreme, even pathological. One psychiatrist treated a medical officer, 'P.', who, after one near miss by a shell, developed severe claustrophobia. He became unable to use a shellproof tunnel leading to the front lines, instead preferring to walk above ground in much greater danger.[82]

Not only the constrictive nature of the trenches but also the peculiar style of fighting in static warfare increased the level of disempowerment experienced by soldiers. Opposing trenches in France and Flanders were normally only between 200 and 300 yards apart. Sometimes they were even closer, especially after attacks, when nothing more than an improvised blockage in a trench might separate enemies. The ease of attack added to soldiers' fear and uncertainty, particularly at night, the time when raids and patrols were usually undertaken and when a primitive fear of the dark might take hold. As the American psychologist Charles Bird observed, 'tremendous psychic tension' resulted from 'watching and seeing nothing'.[83] Mistakes by nervous sentries with overactive imaginations could arouse considerable agitation. *Leutnant* Hans

78 Plaut, 'Psychographie des Kriegers', p. 42.
79 W. Brown, *Psychology and Psychotherapy* (London: Edward Arnold, 1921), p. 121.
80 Ludwig, 'Psychologie der Furcht', p. 138 and Moran, *Anatomy*, p. 178.
81 DTA, 930: E. Huthmacher, letter to wife, 31 Mar. 1915.
82 Steiner, 'Neurologie und Psychiatrie im Kriegslazarett', *Zeitschrift für die gesamte Neurologie und Psychiatrie* 30, 2/3 (27 November 1915), 316.
83 Bird, 'From Home to the Charge', 333.

Muhsal, serving in the Vosges, recorded how an NCO caused panic by claiming to have seen three Frenchmen in no-man's-land. The company stood to alarm in the forward line and convinced themselves that the position was surrounded, only for it to transpire half an hour later that the 'Frenchmen' were in fact bushes.[84]

The very invisibility of the enemy, despite his proximity, further increased the sense of uncertainty and uncontrollability in the trenches. It was, as one British officer remarked in early 1917, 'a bit of a shock ... to the ordinary men to see a German'.[85] Unable to look behind the enemy parapet, infantrymen had little idea when the next raid might be launched, artillery bombardment begin or mine explode. Moreover, the difficulty of retaliating or actively defending themselves in trench warfare added to soldiers' sense of disempowerment and stress. The historians Stéphane Audoin-Rouzeau and Annette Becker have noted that 'the brutality described [by soldiers] is always anonymous and blind' and have suggested that this was the result of social taboos or an attempt to escape the guilt of having taken a human life.[86] Yet, casualty figures and contemporary testimonies both clearly indicate that such portrayals were common precisely because this was exactly how violence was usually experienced. As Lieutenant Roland Hely Owen bitterly explained to his brother in the navy, 'One goes thro' a fortnight of alternately sitting down under (s)hellfire & hobbling away, without necessarily seeing a single enemy, and then one's parents write and say "it was glorious"!'[87] Hans Carossa, a battalion doctor serving at Passchendaele, agreed, observing ruefully that, 'No one knows whom he kills, that is the terrible thing.'[88] 'Face-to-face' killing with bayonets and sharpened entrenching tools accounted for only about half a per cent of wounds in the German and British armies, while grenades, another weapon used at close quarters, caused less than 3 per cent of wounds.[89] Even small-arms fire, which was responsible for

[84] BA-MA Freiburg, MSg 1/ 3109: H. Muhsal, diary, 3 Oct. 1914. Similar stories abounded on the Western Front. See, for example, Scholz, *Seelenleben*, p. 224 and G. vom Holtz, *Das Württembergische Reserve-Inf.-Regiment Nr. 121 im Weltkrieg 1914–1918* (Stuttgart: Chr. Belsersche Verlagsbuchhandlung, 1922), p. 32.

[85] IWM, P 317 Con Shelf: H.W. Yoxall, letter to mother, 30 Jan. 1917.

[86] S. Audoin-Rouzeau and A. Becker, *1914–1918. Understanding the Great War* (London: Profile Books, 2002), p. 39. Cf. K. Latzel, 'Die mißlungene Flucht vor dem Tod. Töten und Sterben vor und nach 1918', in J. Duppler and G.P. Groß (eds.), *Kriegsende 1918. Ereignis, Wirkung, Nachwirkung. Beiträge zur Militärgeschichte. Herausgegeben vom Militärgeschichtlichen Forschungsamt*. Vol. LIII (Munich: R. Oldenbourg, 1999), p. 189.

[87] IWM, 90/37/1: R.H. Owen, letter to brother, 22 Sept. 1914.

[88] Staatsbib. Hamburg, 6179: H. Carossa, letter to R. Dehmel, 27 Nov. 1917.

[89] See Table 1.

rather more casualties and could be used at close quarters, was usually long range and often came from well-hidden professional snipers, indirect machinegun 'strafes' on reserve lines or fixed rifles fired randomly at sentry posts.[90]

New inventions in technology and tactics did little to lessen the psychological strain on soldiers: 'how harmless was the war of 1914–15 compared with the chasing about of 1916', exclaimed *Leutnant* Friedrich Nawrath as he considered the patrols, raids and gas attacks which were a feature of the middle of the war. In fact, as has been noted, even on the Western Front, the open fighting of 1914 had been objectively more than twice as dangerous as the trench warfare and *Materialschlachten* of 1916. Nawrath himself should have recognised this fact, for, as a volunteer, he had watched British rifle and artillery fire wipe out his unit at the First Battle of Ypres in October and November 1914.[91] It was because the growth in importance of artillery fire and the introduction of new weapons and tactics had added to the unpredictability and uncontrollability of the fighting that the war appeared subjectively more dangerous in 1916. The advent of raids and patrols forced soldiers to maintain a high level of concentration during trench duty, imposing more strain on them. Although rarely fatal, gas was relatively effective at injuring men, one casualty being caused by every twenty-five shells.[92] The intense fear which it elicited, especially among British troops, was, however, primarily because of the uncertainty it produced. Its novelty, difficulty of detection and, in the case of mustard gas, its delayed effects left men wondering uneasily after gas attacks whether they had been affected. Moreover, unlike other weapons which attacked externally, gas raised the level of uncontrollability by killing men from inside; as Colonel A.B. Soltau, the British army's Consultant Physician in France for Gas Cases, observed, it was 'the dread of being slowly strangled' which made the weapon so terrifying.[93] It was hardly surprising that, in Lord Moran's words, 'the majority of men who left the front line in 1917 "gassed" were frankly frightened'.[94]

90 *Sanitätsbericht III*, p. 70.

91 BA-MA Freiburg, MSg 1/ 1383: F.O. Nawrath, letter to Anne, 18 July 1916. For his experience at Ypres in 1914, see, particularly, letter to parents, 3 Dec. 1914.

92 H.L. Gilchrist, *A Comparative Study of World War Casualties from Gas and other Weapons* (Washington, DC: United States Government Printing Office, 1928), p. 13.

93 *RWOCIS*, pp. 73–4.

94 Lord Moran, 'Wear and Tear', *The Lancet* (17 June 1950), 1100. Cf. Rogers, in *RWOCIS*, p. 63.

The notion that uncontrollability, rather than discomfort or the objective danger of the trenches, was the primary cause of stress in static warfare is indicated by the fact that the dreams of men in or just behind the line frequently took disempowerment as their leitmotif. A study undertaken in 1915 is worth quoting at length:

> Horror of isolation constitutes the commonest nightmare of men in the first fighting line. They dream that they are wandering through endless trenches as complicated as an artificial maze, or are picking their way through lonesome forests whence all but they have fled ... Another common night terror is the dream of a sudden call to arms and the inability to find some indispensable article of attire or combat, a conception productive of intense mental agony. Live shells naturally occupy a large share of subconscious attention, and an exasperating nightmare is the discovery in one's bed of a shell ready and willing to burst, associated with the usual nightmare incapacity to execute the necessary movements to get rid of it. Several men have had dreams centring round the inability to withdraw the bayonet from the enemy's body when urgently required for self-defence.[95]

'Isolation', 'inability' and 'incapacity' in the dream world all reflected soldiers' impotence to determine their own chances of survival in everyday life.[96] Not simply death and discomfort but above all disempowerment made service in the trenches of the Western Front a uniquely frightening, depressing and stressful experience.

Resilience

The strain which men experienced at the front was highly destructive to both individual combat motivation and unit cohesion. Danger and uncontrollability were unsurprisingly closely linked to the incidence of psychiatric casualties; according to the official British medical history, periods of 'prolonged fighting and heavy bombardments' were most likely to produce large numbers of breakdowns.[97] Men who were left 'too long in any lonely position or in a lonely nature of employment', such as battalion runners, were remembered by veterans as particularly prone to suffering mental collapse, probably because, unlike their peers, they lacked the certainty and sense of control which the company of

95 [Editorial], 'Soldiers' Dreams', *The Lancet* (23 January 1915), 210.

96 See J.T. MacCurdy, *War Neuroses* (Cambridge University Press, 1918), pp. 22 and 26 and for a diary account of such a dream, see IWM, P 239: W.B. St Leger, diary, 28 Oct. 1917.

97 *J&R*, p. 16.

trusted comrades could provide.[98] The fact that soldiers who suffered psychological disorders either often had been, or believed themselves to have been, buried alive, again strongly suggests a connection with loss of control. Incarceration in a tomb-like hole, unable to move or escape, was an intensely disempowering and frightening experience; soldiers who saw men buried thought it a 'beastly business' or 'dreadful affair' and described those rescued as 'half crazy' when they were dug out.[99]

Much depended on a soldier's luck. Sometimes men collapsed after a single, particularly horrendous experience. One officer treated by the psychiatrist John MacCurdy suffered a mental breakdown after receiving a 'terrible "turn"' when he had touched what he thought was a living man, only for the back of the corpse's head to roll off.[100] Lord Moran described how a stretcher-bearer temporarily lost his senses after a shell killed three of his comrades, throwing their remains over him.[101] Such intensely traumatic events were, however, by no means necessary to push a man over the threshold of his endurance; the accumulated strain of prolonged active service was alone sufficient. As the official British medical history noted, among psychiatric patients were many 'once sturdy soldiers ... broken by wounds, sickness and the length of their service in the battle line'. Even among those who managed to cope without reporting sick or collapsing, there were few, in the estimation of the German psychiatrist Robert Gaupp, who returned home with 'entirely unscathed nerves'.[102]

Historians have tended to criticise contemporary psychiatrists for their propensity to see men who collapsed as weaklings, constitutionally inferior or psychopaths.[103] Yet although, as by 1916 most doctors in

98 Sir John Goodwin, Director General of the Army Medical Service, and J.S.Y. Rogers, former MO of 4/Black Watch, in *RWOCIS*, pp. 15 and 65–6 respectively.

99 IWM, P 317 Con Shelf: H.W. Yoxall, letter to mother, 13 July 1916 and Staatsbib. Berlin, Ms. Germ. fol. 1651: C.F. Müller, diary, 7 Dec. 1917. See also J.S.Y. Rogers in *RWOCIS*, p. 67 and, for descriptions of being buried alive, the anonymous testimony in ibid., pp. 90–1 and DTA, 506,1: K. Kramer, diary, 10–22 Oct. 1918.

100 MacCurdy, *War Neuroses*, p. 111.

101 Moran, *Anatomy*, p. 22.

102 *J&R*, p. 18 and R. Gaupp, 'Schreckneurosen und Neurasthenie', in K. Bonhoeffer (ed.), *Geistes- und Nervenkrankheiten*. Part I (Leipzig: Johann Ambrosius Barth, 1922), p. 88.

103 G. Komo, '*Für Volk und Vaterland*'. *Die Militärpsychiatrie in den Weltkriegen* (Münster: Lit, 1992), p. 86 and K.H. Roth, 'Die Modernisierung der Folter in den beiden Weltkriegen. Der Konflikt der Psychotherapeuten und Schulpsychiater um die deutschen "Kriegsneurotiker" 1915–1945', *1999. Zeitschrift für Sozialgeschichte des 20. und 21. Jahrhunderts* 2, 3 (1987), 11–17.

Britain and Germany recognised, even 'the strongest man ... may become subject to mental derangement', the fact that psychiatric disorders affected only a small minority of soldiers indicates that their judgements, while harshly expressed, were essentially not unreasonable.[104] Certainly, recent psychological research emphasises the role played by personal vulnerability factors in the genesis of the modern mental complaint, Post-traumatic Stress Disorder.[105] Contemporary statistics also support this, for they record that in many cases the extreme stresses of combat were by no means necessary to engender psychiatric disorders; 15 per cent of hysterics from the Bavarian army actually became ill before reaching the front.[106] In the German army as a whole, psychiatric casualties were more prevalent in the Home Army than at the front, probably partly because less capable men either broke down or were deliberately removed at this stage.[107] In the British army, units serving at home and abroad suffered an annual psychiatric casualty rate of 3 and 10 per 1,000 respectively in 1917, suggesting that while battlefield experiences played a major role in causing such disorders, some men were too frail even to cope with the lesser stresses of basic training. In the absence of any psychological screening at the recruitment stage, these men came to pose a serious burden on the army's medical services; according to Lieutenant-Colonel Burton-Fanning, a psychiatrist working in the 1st Eastern General Hospital, patients suffering from neurasthenia accounted for almost one-third of admissions into medical wards from the Home Forces during 1917.[108]

Although some contemporary beliefs regarding psychiatric disease were certainly chauvinistic, there were serious attempts to carry out scientific studies in order to establish predisposing factors. One study published by Captain J.M. Wolfsohn in 1918 tried to isolate these by

104 G. Elliot Smith, 'Shock and the Soldier', *The Lancet* (22 April 1916), 855. For the wartime debate over whether physically healthy men could suffer psychiatric disorders, see Shephard, *War of Nerves*, pp. 30–1 and Lerner, *Hysterical Men*, pp. 75–7.

105 R.J. McNally, R.A. Bryant and A. Ehlers, 'Does Early Psychological Intervention Promote Recovery from Posttraumatic Stress?', *Psychological Science in the Public Interest* 4, 2 (November 2003), 49.

106 K. Weiler, *Arbeit und Gesundheit. Sozialmedizinische Schriftenreihe aus dem Gebiete des Reichsministeriums.* Part 22: *Nervöse und seelische Störungen bei Teilnehmern am Weltkriege, ihre ärztliche und rechtliche Beurteilung.* Part I: *Nervöse und seelische Störungen psychogener und funktioneller Art* (Leipzig: Georg Thieme, 1933), pp. 130 and 190.

107 *Sanitätsbericht III*, p. 145.

108 See Salmon, 'Care and Treatment', 518 and F.W. Burton-Fanning, 'Neurasthenia in Soldiers of the Home Forces', *The Lancet* (16 June 1917), 907. For neurasthenia, see *J&R*, pp. 20–4.

comparing the family histories and wartime service of psychiatric casualties and physically wounded. It found that 34% of the psychiatric patients and none of the wounded had a family history of insanity; 66% had a personal background of nervousness, in contrast to only 12% of the wounded. Psychiatric patients were more likely to have experienced 'frights in childhood', and suffer from or have a family history of epilepsy. Curiously, they also had a greater propensity to tend towards 'excessive religion' and be teetotal.[109] In line with pre-war theories, there was a wide consensus that a history of mental instability prejudiced a man's chances of coping successfully with the stress of active service. Estimates of its influence varied, but one psychiatrist who testified to the 1922 War Committee of Enquiry into 'Shell-Shock' put the incidence of 'marked nervous hereditary' characteristics among psychiatric casualties at over 77 per cent. Others argued that previous 'mental conflict and maladjustments' and '"fits" in childhood' were also indicative of greater vulnerability to psychiatric disorder.[110] Intelligence, which today is recognised as one of the most important determinants of human resilience, was regarded with mixed views. Some psychiatrists asserted that it had no influence, while others, in line with contemporary military prejudices, argued that the 'natural fool' could make a good soldier.[111] Edward Mapother, Medical Superintendent of the Maudsley Neurological Hospital, and Charles Myers, the former Consulting Psychologist to the Army, pre-empted modern findings, however, when they concluded from extensive experience of 'shellshock' patients that 'the intellectually defective' were at a disadvantage on active service.[112] The evidence that intelligence was relevant in the onset of psychiatric disease was good enough to convince the US army to set 1.75

[109] J.M. Wolfsohn, 'The Predisposing Factors of War Psycho-Neuroses', *The Lancet* (2 February 1918), 178–9. Most psychiatrists, however, believed that excessive alcohol consumption was indicative of predisposition to mental disease. See K. Bonhoeffer, 'Über die Bedeutung der Kriegserfahrungen für die allgemeine Psychopathologie und Ätiologie der Geisteskrankheiten', in K. Bonhoeffer (ed.), *Geistes- und Nervenkrankheiten*. Part I (Leipzig: Johann Ambrosius Barth, 1922), pp. 21–3, Scholz, *Seelenleben*, p. 220 and O.P. Napier Pearn, 'Psychoses in the Expeditionary Forces', *Journal of Mental Science* 65, 269 (April 1919), 102.

[110] Statement of L.C. Bruce (Medical Superintendent, Perth District Asylum) in *RWOCIS*, p. 82 and Myers, *Shell Shock*, p. 38.

[111] Statement of A.F. Hurst (Physician, Nervous Diseases, Guy's Hospital) in *RWOCIS*, p. 23 and Colonel J. Heatly-Spencer in United Services Section with Section of Psychiatry, 'Discussion on Functional Nervous Disease in the Fighting Services', *Proceedings of the Royal Society of Medicine* 29 (1935–6), 857. Cf. statement of Lieutenant-Colonel E. Hewlett (late Inspector of Infantry Training), in *RWOCIS*, p. 18.

[112] *RWOCIS*, pp. 27–8. Testimony of E. Mapother, Medical Superintendent, Maudsley Neurological Hospital. Cf. Myers, *Shell Shock*, pp. 38 and 86.

million recruits a pioneering, albeit highly flawed, intelligence test from 1917.[113]

The extreme stress experienced by men at the front did not necessarily manifest itself as a diagnosable psychiatric disorder. Intense psychological or physical fatigue could cause men to become timid or apathetic, decreasing their combat motivation and prompting them, in contemporary parlance, to 'shirk'. Lieutenant R.H. Owen, for example, who arrived in mid-August 1914, was gradually worn down emotionally by the danger and hardships of the front. Already by the end of September, his letters were displaying signs of nervousness and, in October, he began to complain, 'I wish these shells wouldn't come so close over head [*sic*]. They have a way of getting on one's nerves'. After being shot in the knee in November 1914, he spent some time in hospital and returned to the front with great reluctance in February 1915, where he did not exhibit a particularly high level of devotion to duty. Ordered into no-man's-land on a raid to capture a German, he 'went out a very short way, and then prayed for someone to shoot at us as an excuse for coming back ... presently someone made three very good shots at us – by the 3rd one we were nearly home'.[114] Exhausted units lost what GHQ referred to as 'the offensive spirit' and were more likely to conduct 'live and let live' truces with the enemy. They also manifested high rates of illness, not only because their personnel were more likely to seek escape through the sick parade but also because apathetic and depressed men were genuinely more vulnerable to disease than happy and well-rested comrades. Thus, for example, when Ernst Huthmacher arrived at the front, he found his regiment, after three months in the line, 'completely depressed', with many of its officers and nearly one-third of its surviving

113 J.D. Keene, 'Intelligence and Morale in the Army of a Democracy. The Genesis of Military Psychology during the First World War', *Military Psychology* 6, 4 (1994), 235–7 and 240–3. The test was flawed because many of its questions contained cultural bias. For modern research into predisposing causes of psychiatric diseases, see especially Kulka *et al.*, *Trauma and the Vietnam War Generation*, p. 83, which found that 'problem behaviors in childhood, meeting the criteria for a diagnosis of antisocial personality disorder before age 18, having been a member of a family that had trouble making (economic) ends meet, and having one or more first-degree relatives with a mental disorder' all predisposed Vietnam veterans to PTSD. For intelligence, see R.K. Pitman, S.P. Orr, M.J. Lowenhagen, M.L. Macklin and B. Altman, 'Pre-Vietnam Contents of Posttraumatic Stress Disorder Veterans' Service Medical and Personal Records', *Comparative Psychology* 32 (1991), 420 and R.J. McNally and L.M. Shin, 'Association of Intelligence with Severity of Posttraumatic Stress Disorder Symptoms in Vietnam Combat Veterans', *American Journal of Psychology* 152 (1995), 936–7.

114 IWM, 90/37/1: R.H. Owen, letter to parents, 27 Mar. 1915. See also letters of 24 Sept., 11 Oct 1914 and 21 Feb. 1915.

men ill. The mood in Hans Muhsal's unit was probably worse when, after six months in the line, its doctor reported that the men were physically and psychologically run-down and deemed them unsuitable for military operations.[115] Trench foot, a disease similar to frostbite, was actually used by the British army as a guide to discipline and morale. If the weekly incidence in any unit rose, a report was demanded from its officers.[116]

More extreme forms of shirking also existed. The passivity and apathy caused by extreme physical and mental fatigue could shade into more active attempts to gain respite from the trenches. Some soldiers sought deliberately to infect themselves with venereal disease. This appears to have been a problem in the German western Field Army during the final year of hostilities, when, despite the fact that much of the force was stationed in areas devoid of civilians and involved in extremely heavy fighting, the average annual rate rose from being consistently under 15 men per 1,000 to 17.7 men per 1,000. In the British army, rates of venereal disease were higher still, fluctuating between 17.32 and 29.65 per 1,000. Less efficient preventative measures, rather than lower morale, probably accounts for this difference, however.[117] Venereal disease gave relief from the trenches for about seven weeks only. The really desperate instead sought permanent release through a self-inflicted wound; 3,478 British soldiers were tried abroad for self-inflicted wounds before October 1918, but the arbitrariness with which the crime was classified suggests that many other cases remain hidden within the statistics.[118] Suicide, an even more extreme form of escape, was also underreported. The 3,828 wartime suicides recorded by the German army exclude those deeply depressed men who had killed themselves through wanton exposure to fire and overlooks other,

[115] DTA, 930: E. Huthmacher, letter to wife, 19 Mar. 1915 and BA-MA Freiburg, MSg 1/ 3109: H. Muhsal, diary, 2 Mar. 1918.

[116] *Medical Services*, pp. 87–90.

[117] *Sanitätsbericht III*, pp. 66*–7* and *Medical Services*, pp. 73 and 77–9. Cf. also M. Hirschfeld, *Sittengeschichte des Ersten Weltkrieges*, revised edn (Hanau am Main: Karl Schustek, 1929, *c.* 1965), pp. 171–94.

[118] Many self-inflicted wounds were disguised by being tried under Section 40 of the Army Act: 'conduct to the prejudice of good order and military discipline'. See H.B. McCartney, *Citizen Soldiers. The Liverpool Territorials in the First World War* (Cambridge University Press, 2005), pp. 171–6. For British statistics, see *Military Effort*, pp. 660–6. For German self-inflicted wounds, see *Sanitätsbericht III*, p. 147 and B. Ziemann, 'Verweigerungsformen von Frontsoldaten in der deutschen Armee 1914–1918', in A. Gestrich (ed.), *Gewalt im Krieg. Ausübung, Erfahrung und Verweigerung von Gewalt in Kriegen des 20. Jahrhunderts* (Münster: Lit, 1996), pp. 108–9.

unambiguous cases which had been reported as combat deaths in order to spare families pain.[119]

Rather than turning to self-harm to escape the trenches, some individuals absconded temporarily from their units; 25,844 men were sentenced for 'Absence Without Leave' in the BEF between the beginning of the war and October 1918.[120] The roughly equivalent sentence in the German army, *unerlaubte Entfernung*, was between ten and fifteen times more common than convictions for permanent desertion, *Fahnenflucht*. Together, in the estimation of the German historian Christoph Jahr, they totalled 50,000 cases during the war.[121] Often, the men who committed these offences were less resilient than average: an examination of Second World War American AWOLs and deserters found that they were 'more neurotic' than troops who remained in combat.[122] In the First World War, opinion remained divided on the cause of military crime. Gaupp contended that most wayward soldiers were by nature 'psychopaths and mild imbeciles', while the British official medical history argued that it was often an alternative manifestation of psychological collapse. Most deserters, it argued, were 'cases of chronic and acute nerve exhaustion with a history of war sickness and wounds, who had suffered complete breakdown at the time of their action'.[123] Certainly, narrative testimony supports the notion that some of these men had been under severe and sustained stress before committing their offences. Gunner Peter Fraser, for example, recorded allowing a sergeant who had absconded from the Royal Field Artillery to sleep in his billet for two nights. The man, Fraser commented, had 'had a bad time and is very near a complete breakdown'.[124] Another deserter, a member of *Infanterie-Regiment Nr. 121*, had also suffered a long-drawn-out emotional struggle. The soldier, who was sentenced to ten months' imprisonment for two counts of *unerlaubte Entfernung* eight weeks before the war's end, had served since 1 September 1914 and had been wounded twice. When he deserted his unit in April 1918 he felt unable to face

119 *Sanitätsbericht III*, p. 27. For false reporting of suicides, see R. Graves, *Goodbye to All That*, revised edn (London: Penguin, 1929, 1960), pp. 105–6. For soldiers exposing themselves intentionally to enemy fire in the hope of being shot, see *J&R*, p. 51 and MacCurdy, *War Neuroses*, p. 23.

120 *Military Effort*, pp. 660–6.

121 Jahr, *Gewöhnliche Soldaten*, pp. 128 and 155. For the differences in how the two armies classified and tried absconders, see ibid., pp. 147–8.

122 A.M. Rose, 'The Social Psychology of Desertion from Combat', in P. Karsten (ed.), *Motivating Soldiers. Morale or Mutiny* (New York: Garland Publishing, 1998), p. 263.

123 Gaupp, 'Schreckneurosen', p. 100 and *J&R*, p. 41. The division of opinion appears to have been along national lines: cf. Scholz, *Seelenleben*, p. 220.

124 IWM, 85/32/1: P. Fraser, diary, 14 Sept. 1917.

shellfire and a doctor's report of the previous month had described him as 'nervous and anxious' but had refused him respite on the grounds that 'extreme nervousness is not outside the scale of normal war nervousness'.[125]

It was most dangerous for armies' combat performance when not just individuals but also groups began to shirk or commit acts of indiscipline. The most spontaneous, yet also one of the most serious, was the phenomenon of group panic on the battlefield. Intense fear, often brought about by a sudden, unexpected and dangerous or horrific event, could spread quickly through a group causing officers to lose control and a unit to disintegrate. Plaut recalled how discipline had collapsed in his company when a sudden bombardment began, maiming some of its members, who began to scream. The remainder broke into 'a complete, senseless dissolution and flight which resulted in many wounded'.[126] Surprise attacks relied on the shock and panic caused by the unexpected in order to disorganise opponents and hasten their defeat. Often, they were highly successful: a patrol of ten German soldiers, for example, defeated a numerically superior British machinegun post on the night of 20–21 August 1917 by launching a sudden assault with hand grenades. Two or three of the defenders were immediately killed, while others, shocked by the attack, attempted to flee.[127] Poorly trained, inexperienced and exhausted troops were particularly prone to such disorganisation. The severe British defeat at Cambrai on 30 November 1917 appears to have stemmed partially from the inability of raw drafts sent into the line to cope with the heavy bombardment and fierce attack of veteran German stormtroops.[128]

Panic was a spontaneous reaction to an unexpected and frightening event. Exhaustion and grievances against officers or the pursuit of the war could lead to more conscious breaches of discipline. An instructive example of collective disobedience took place on 10 July 1916, when 11/Border Regiment, depressed and exhausted after having lost all its officers and half of its complement of men on the first day of the Somme, was ordered to raid enemy lines. Those soldiers chosen for the raid immediately reported sick with 'shellshock' and, when

[125] HStA Stuttgart, M 30/ 2 Bü 702: Court records of Johann Karl Klinkhamer, 14 Sept. 1918.

[126] Plaut, 'Psychographie des Kriegers', p. 39.

[127] BA-MA Freiburg, PH 3/ 585: Vernehmungsprotokolle, AOK 4: Vernehmung [of one man from 6/Border Regiment], 27 Aug. 1917.

[128] See TNA, CAB 24/ 37: War Cabinet. Cambrai Inquiry. Memorandum by General Smuts. G.T.-3198, 3 Jan. 1918. Also, IWM, P 239: W.B. St Leger, diary, 30 Nov. 1917. For exhausted troops' propensity to panic, see Bonhoeffer, 'Über die Bedeutung der Kriegserfahrungen', p. 10.

refused evacuation and ordered to execute the operation, failed to pick up bombs, lagged behind on the way up to the trenches and took wrong turnings. Consequently, the operation had to be cancelled.[129] It was, however, usually behind the lines, where men were better rested, safer and possessed the time to organise themselves, that group indiscipline took place. Probably the most famous example is the rioting which took place at the British base camp of Étaples after a confrontation between ANZACs and Military Police led to a corporal being shot. The police were stoned and 1,000 men broke out of the camp and went to the neighbouring town. Demonstrations continued during the following three evenings, men forcing their way through pickets into Étaples. The disorder was only quelled once the camp's police had been replaced and the Honourable Artillery Company had been called in to keep the men in the camp. The riots seem primarily to have had general local causes, most notably the harsh disciplinary regime of the camp, and were directed against the camp authorities, particularly the police.[130] Mutiny, which had broader goals such as challenging the authority of commanders or questioning the management of the war, was far more threatening for armies' ability to continue fighting. The French mutinies of 1917, which did exactly that and encompassed 40,000 men, had no equivalent in either the German or British armies.[131]

Remarkably, however, not only was large-scale mutiny not a feature of either the British or the German military experience, but indiscipline in general remained at an extremely low level. Jahr's estimate of 50,000 deserters represents well under 0.5 per cent of the men who passed through the German army during the war, fully justifying his claim that desertion was 'from a purely military standpoint . . . insignificant'.[132] Similarly, only 31,405 British soldiers, representing just over 0.5 per cent of the army's manpower, were tried for absence without leave or desertion abroad between the beginning of the war and the end of September 1918, and some of these were acquitted. Other military crimes were even less significant: for example, no more than forty-two men were charged with mutiny by the British army on the Western Front between 1914 and the

129 WLHM, RAMC 446/18 Box 66: Extracts from Proceedings of a Court of Enquiry into failure of a party of 11th Border Regiment 97th Inf. Bde 32nd Division to carry out an attack, as ordered, on 10 July 1916.

130 D. Gill and G. Dallas, 'Mutiny at Etaples Base in 1917', *Past and Present* 69 (November 1975), 91–7.

131 See C. Corns and J. Hughes-Wilson, *Blindfold and Alone. British Military Executions in the Great War* (London: Cassell, 2001, 2002), p. 380. The classic account of the French mutinies is G. Pedroncini, *Les mutineries de 1917* (Paris: Presses Universitaires de France, 1967).

132 Jahr, *Gewöhnliche Soldaten*, pp. 155 and 335.

beginning of 1918.[133] More subtle transgressions, such as individuals going sick unnecessarily or units conducting 'live and let live' truces in inactive sectors were, if the impression given by narrative accounts is correct, more common, yet there is no evidence that such phenomena ever seriously undermined either army's fighting potential. The good disciplinary records of both forces have generally been viewed as evidence of the efficacy of their coercive mechanisms. More importantly, however, they also reflected the sheer resilience of the men who composed these armies; a fact supported by surviving statistics for psychiatric disorders. In total, 613,047 German psychiatric casualties were treated: only 4.58 per cent of the men who passed through the army during the war. British army figures are more fragmentary, but extrapolation suggests that it treated approximately 325,000 psychiatric casualties (among them 144,000 cases of neurasthenia and 'shellshock'), comprising 5.70 per cent of its military manpower.[134] Of course, even these figures are probably incomplete; somatic cases were often misdiagnosed as organic ailments and modern authorities rightly argue that the collection of data on psychiatric disorders was 'haphazard and inconsistent'.[135] Nonetheless, the impressive resilience demonstrated by men at the front may also be inferred from contemporary studies of those men who did suffer mental collapse. A sample of 200 British troops suffering from nervous disorders calculated their average length of active service at ten months. Karl Weiler's post-war examination of Bavarian psychiatric casualties found that their average length of field service was, at just over fifteen months, even more impressive.[136] As these were the frailest, least fortunate or hardest pressed men, it seems reasonable to assume that many of those who did not suffer psychological collapse served a lot longer. Men in the First World War thus proved themselves astonishingly resilient on the battlefield. The next chapters explain why and how they fought so hard for so long.

133 For mutiny, see Corns and Hughes-Wilson, *Blindfold*, p. 380. Desertion figure calculated from *Military Effort*, pp. 660–6.

134 See Appendix 2.

135 E. Jones and S. Wessely, 'Psychiatric Battle Casualties. An Intra- and Interwar Comparison', *British Journal of Psychiatry* 178 (2001), 242. Cf. Shephard, *War of Nerves*, p. 41.

136 Napier Pearn, 'Psychoses in the Expeditionary Forces', 105 and Weiler, *Nervöse und seelische Störungen*, p. 107. The former study excluded from its calculations Regular soldiers, who had the longest service records of any soldiers in the British army, and thus perhaps underestimated the time British soldiers with nervous disorders had spent in the field.

2 Why men fought: combat motivation in the trenches

Enlistment

Given the strain of fighting, why did most soldiers agree to do so? Traditional historiography held that the First World War had been welcomed by the belligerent populations. Contemporary publications in Germany claimed that huge, 'war-enthused' crowds had roared approval at the outbreak of hostilities and that more than 1 million volunteers had flooded into barracks.[1] Echoing this propaganda, historians have until recently also reported that 'enormous jubilation greeted the announcement [of mobilisation]'.[2] The research undertaken by Jeffrey Verhey, Wolfgang Kruse and Benjamin Ziemann in the 1990s effectively exposed these myths. Verhey found from an extensive analysis of newspaper accounts that 'the majority of Germans in July and August did not feel "war enthusiasm"'. Kruse uncovered the forgotten fact that 750,000 people took part in peace demonstrations directly before the war and argued that, when the conflict began, the industrial working classes reacted 'with a serious, frequently also despairing mood'. Ziemann has shown convincingly that people in the Bavarian countryside similarly responded to news of mobilisation with depression and pessimism.[3] On the other side, the British seem to have been little more enthused by the onset of hostilities: Adrian Gregory contends that belligerence and

[1] See, for example, *Berliner Tageblatt und Handels-Zeitung*, *Morgen Ausgabe* 43, 405 (12 August 1914) and M. Erzberger, *Die Mobilmachung* (Stuttgart: Deutsche Verlags-Anstalt, 1914), p. 14.

[2] R. Rürup, 'Der "Geist von 1914" in Deutschland. Kriegsbegeisterung und Ideologisierung des Krieges im Ersten Weltkrieg', in B. Hüppauf (ed.), *Ansichten vom Krieg. Vergleichende Studien zum Ersten Weltkrieg in Literatur und Gesellschaft* (Königsten: Forum Academicum, 1984), p. 2.

[3] J. Verhey, *The Spirit of 1914. Militarism, Myth and Mobilization in Germany* (Cambridge University Press, 2000), p. 113, W. Kruse, *Krieg und nationale Integration. Eine Neuinterpretation des sozialdemokratischen Burgfriedensschlusses 1914/15* (Essen: Klartext, 1993), p. 58 and Ziemann, *Front*, particularly pp. 39–49. For a good review of other studies, see C. Nonn, 'Oh What a Lovely War? German Common People and the First World War', *German History* 18, 1 (January 2000), 104–8.

jingoism were not dominant and the public were 'quite clear-headed about the perils of war'.[4]

The new consensus leaves a vacuum in our understanding of why men went to war and fought so hard for so long, for despite the lack of general 'war enthusiasm', the public response seen in both countries to the outbreak of the conflict was impressive. In Germany, the peacetime conscript army of 808,280 soldiers quadrupled in twelve days to a force 3,502,700 strong.[5] Additionally, 250,000 men volunteered during August 1914; not as many as the propaganda claimed but nonetheless an extremely impressive figure for a country which had already conscripted 36.5 per cent of its military-aged manpower.[6] In Britain, which lacked conscription, 298,923 men enlisted in August followed by a further 462,901 in September 1914.[7] Older historiography ascribed popular readiness to fight to peacetime socialisation. Thomas Rohkrämer, for example, has emphasised the role of schools, universities, patriotic societies and veterans' organisations in inculcating Germans with militarism and nationalism.[8] Other historians have seen the 1890 school conference, at which Wilhelm II had declared, 'I am looking for soldiers; we want to have a strong generation,' as the first stage on the route to the Hitler Youth four decades later.[9] In Britain too, education was not without military influences: working-class children were taught drill in schools while upper-class pupils at public schools were inculcated with notions of classical heroism and manly athleticism.[10] Yet the widespread depression and anxiety at the outbreak of war undermine these theories. Why then, did Germans and Britons prove so willing to fight?

The absence of evidence for extensive 'war enthusiasm' in Germany does not negate the possibility that societal influences did affect the population's response to war. German pedagogic aims were, after all,

[4] A. Gregory, 'British "War Enthusiasm" in 1914. A Reassessment', in G. Braybon (ed.), *Evidence, History and the Great War. Historians and the Impact of 1914–18* (New York: Berghahn Books, 2003), p. 75.

[5] *Sanitätsbericht III*, p. 12. The fully mobilised force was divided roughly equally between the *Feldheer* (Field Army) and *Besatzungsheer* (Home or Garrison Army) in August 1914 (see ibid., pp. 5* and 8*).

[6] A. Watson, '"For Kaiser and Reich". The Identity and Fate of the German Volunteers, 1914–1918', *War in History* 12, 1 (January 2005), 48.

[7] *Military Effort*, p. 364.

[8] T. Rohkrämer, 'August 1914 – Kriegsmentalität und ihre Voraussetzungen', in W. Michalka (ed.), *Der Erste Weltkrieg. Wirkung, Wahrnehmung, Analyse* (Munich: Piper, 1992), pp. 760–1.

[9] C. Schubert-Weller, *'Kein schönrer Tod'. Die Militarisierung der männlichen Jugend und ihr Einsatz im Ersten Weltkrieg 1890–1918* (Weinheim: Juventa, 1998), p. 25. Cf. U. Bendele, *Krieg Kopf und Körper. Lernen für das Leben – Erziehung zum Tod* (Frankfurt am Main: Ullstein, 1984), pp. 213–15.

[10] Sheffield, *Leadership*, pp. 68–9 and 43–53 respectively. Cf. P. Parker, *The Old Lie. The Great War and the Public-School Ethos* (London: Constable, 1987), pp. 69–105.

intended primarily to inculcate men with devotion to the monarch and Fatherland, not make them war-crazed, belligerent 'militarists'. Inoculating working-class children against the attractions of the Social Democratic Party was more important to the Kaiser in 1890 than any thoughts of world domination.[11] The army, which annually called up 50 per cent of twenty-year-olds for two years of military service, continued the work begun in schools by instilling men with loyalty and obedience.[12] Afterwards, *Kriegervereine* (veterans' associations), which together claimed 2,837,944 mainly lower middle- and working-class members in October 1913, ensured that the men remained socially conservative.[13] Given this background, it is hardly surprising that many contemporaries saw culturally ingrained discipline as a primary cause of the general obedience to mobilisation orders witnessed in Germany at the outbreak of war. The American psychologist George Crile suggested that encirclement by powerful neighbours had forced Germans to accept that 'if the people as a whole were to survive, they must renounce their individuality, must surrender themselves to the state, to be used by the state, for the advantage of the people themselves'.[14] His interpretation fits neatly with the historian Erich Marcks' view of his countrymen as disciplined, strict and strongly politically and militarily cohesive.[15] The roots of this discipline lay with the socialisation of the German populace through peacetime conscription, according to Dr Ernst Schultze-Großborstel. For him, it was 'the education of all conscripts into voluntary obedience in the service of the Fatherland' which made Germany strong.[16] British psychologists also adopted this theme, although they framed it in a less favourable light. Germans had no great cause to which to rally or ideological motivation inspiring them to fight; rather, they responded to mobilisation orders because they were, in the words of Edmond Holmes, 'the most obedient people on the face of the earth'.[17] 'The triumph of

[11] Schubert-Weller, *Kein schönrer Tod*, pp. 23–4.

[12] M. Ingenlath, *Mentale Aufrüstung. Militarisierungstendenzen in Frankreich und Deutschland vor dem Ersten Weltkrieg* (Frankfurt: Campus, 1998), pp. 154–5 and 391.

[13] See G.A. Ritter and K. Tenfelde, *Arbeiter im Deutschen Kaiserreich 1871 bis 1914* (Bonn: J.H.W. Dietz Nachf., 1992), pp. 738–40.

[14] G.W. Crile, *A Mechanistic View of War and Peace* (London: T. Werner Laurie, 1915), p. 70.

[15] H. Delbrück, *Über den kriegerischen Charakter des deutschen Volkes. Rede am 11. September 1914* (Berlin: Carl Heymann, 1914), p. 26 and E. Marcks, *Politische Flugschriften. Der Deutsche Krieg.* Part 19: *Wo Stehen Wir? Die politischen, sittlichen und kulturellen Zusammenhänge unseres Krieges* (Stuttgart: Deutsche Verlagsanstalt, 1914), p. 19.

[16] E. Schultze-Großborstel, *Deutsche Kriegsschriften.* Part 16: *Die Mobilmachung der Seelen* (Bonn: A. Marcus & E. Webers Verlag, 1915), pp. 60–8.

[17] E. Holmes, *The Nemesis of Docility. A Study of German Character* (London: Constable and Company, 1916), p. 1.

Prussianism', wrote the psychologist G.R. Stirling Taylor, was that 'it has made a whole nation fit for nothing else than to obey its rulers'.[18]

Unlike Germany, Britain maintained no system of peacetime conscription and did not introduce one on the outbreak of war. Youth organisations, many of which were quasi-military, were popular in Edwardian society; figures provided by Paul Wilkinson suggest that perhaps 40 per cent of all male adolescents had passed through such groups by 1914.[19] The Regular Army, however, was emphatically not favoured as a career choice. The low standing, poor pay and limited opportunities open to men after military service left the majority of the population deeply suspicious or even hostile to it. Such was the stigma attached to soldiering that wartime volunteers captured by the Germans insisted on informing bemused interrogators that they considered themselves 'amateur soldiers'.[20] This attitude makes the huge influx of volunteers in August and September 1914 even more astonishing. Contemporaries explained the popular willingness to serve, however, as a moral crusade. As one academic, T.H. Procter, asserted after the war, the German invasion of Belgium had been crucial in mobilising public opinion:

> We might have entered the war as a matter of policy even if Germany had never invaded Belgium but we should have been a nation split from top to bottom ... Moral people would not fight willingly for English interests, but they responded readily to the appeal of Belgium.[21]

Certainly, the German invasion of Belgium on 3 August was the official reason given for Britain's declaration of war, and Procter's assertion is supported by some post-war memoirs, which recorded 'a great feeling of indignation and patriotic fervour, and hate for the Germans for what they had done, or had been reported to have done to "Little Belgium"'.[22] Yet it also fitted neatly with British intellectuals' favoured view of their

18 G.R. Stirling Taylor, *The Psychology of the Great War* (London: Martin Secker, 1915), p. 180.

19 P. Wilkinson, 'English Youth Movements, 1908–30', *Journal of Contemporary History* 14, 2 (April 1969), 3.

20 BA-MA Freiburg, PH 3/ 573: Nachrichtenoffizier, AOK 4, p. 157: Vernehmung der am 30.7. früh bei Hooge gefangenen 15 Engländer, 30 July 1915. For the poor conditions and pre-war disapproval of soldiering, see E.M. Spiers, 'The Regular Army in 1914', in I.F.W. Beckett and K. Simpson (eds.), *A Nation in Arms. A Social Study of the British Army in the First World War* (Manchester University Press, 1985), pp. 45–6.

21 T.H. Procter, 'The Motives of the Soldier', *International Journal of Ethics* 31, 1 (October 1920), 34–5.

22 IWM, 02/30/1: G. Calverley, memoir, p. 2. For German atrocities and their public representation in Entente and neutral countries, see J. Horne and A. Kramer, *German Atrocities, 1914. A History of Denial* (New Haven: Yale University Press, 2001).

countrymen as principled and independent, in contrast to the unthinking obedience attributed to the Germans. So entrenched were these national stereotypes that they even featured in military calculations: a secret intelligence assessment of the German army in 1914 argued that Britons' alleged 'elastic, open-minded, give-and-take character' would prove advantageous when set against the Germans' 'circumscribed, police-regulated view of matters'.[23]

Certainly, if the stereotypes have any truth in them at all, there could have been serious consequences for each army's robustness during the war. Modern sociologists argue that only organisations relying on 'normative power', through which soldiers possess a moral involvement with their aims and goals, can survive conditions on the twentieth-century battlefield.[24] Such arguments lead to the satisfying conclusion that the British ultimately won the war because their idealism outlasted the mindless discipline-based combat motivation attributed by British contemporaries and some modern German historians to the Kaiser's army. The fact that, as will be seen, discontent with the state and war-weariness began sooner and reached greater intensity in the German military, seems on face value to support this notion. Yet such a simplistic explanation for the eventual outcome of the war remains highly dubious, not least because it vastly exaggerates the differences between the belligerents and their motives for fighting. Despite the lack of peacetime military service in their country, conservatism, obedience and discipline were probably no less strongly inculcated in the industrial working classes comprising the majority of Britons than in conscripted continentals.[25] British other ranks were not known for their fervent idealism during the war; indeed, contemporaries on both sides more often remarked on their apathy and indifference.[26] Moreover, although popular sympathy for France and Belgium existed in August 1914, it is likely that had men not felt that Britain too was under threat, there would have been fewer volunteers. Suggestions that Germany might invade were

[23] TNA, WO 33/ 613: Intelligence Series. Belgium. 1914, p. 61. Unlike in Germany, in Britain, the myth of 'war enthusiasm' was cultivated by the left after the war, perhaps because it was thought to show the people's liberal credentials. See Gregory, 'British "War Enthusiasm" in 1914', p. 84 note 6.

[24] S.D. Wesbrook, 'The Potential for Military Disintegration', in S.C. Sarkesian (ed.), *Combat Effectiveness. Cohesion, Stress and the Volunteer Military* (London: Sage Publications, 1980), p. 274.

[25] See Introduction, pp. 3–4.

[26] See Fuller, *Troop Morale*, pp. 167–8. English troops' unquestioning acceptance of authority was also commented upon: see ibid., pp. 162–3. For apathy, cf. BA-MA Freiburg, PH 3/ 589: Gefangenen-Aussagen, AOK 4, p. 157: Vernehmung von 8 Gefangenen des I/R.Irish.Fus. 108. Brigade 36. Division, 19 July 1918.

well established in popular fiction and had been given more credence by the 1909 invasion scare.[27] Working-class men were warned by contemporary propaganda that, 'in the event of British territory passing under German rule, the man who refused to fight for his country of his own free-will one day would the next day be compelled to fight for his new masters, whether he wished or not'.[28] Although the moral abhorrence of German brutality in Belgium provoked expressions of outrage from middle-class volunteers, for most men the significance of these atrocities lay in their import for the fate of British homes and families if Germany attacked. As the Regular soldier B.C. Myatt reasoned in his diary:

> We know we are suffering these awful hardships to protect our beloved one's [*sic*] at home from the torture and rape of these German pigs [who] have done some awful deeds in France and Belgium cutting off childrens [*sic*] hands and cutting off womans [*sic*] breasts awful deeds.[29]

Underlining the importance of self-interested national defence, as opposed to altruistic idealism, is the timing of British recruiting, which peaked in the first week of September, just after the *Times*' emotive dispatch reporting disaster at Mons (see Figure 1). As Gregory has observed, 'the largest single component of volunteers enlisted at *exactly* the moment when the war turned serious. Men did not join the British army expecting a picnic stroll to Berlin but in the expectation of a desperate fight for national defence'.[30]

Despite the claims of British propagandists, German obedience to mobilisation orders, far from being the product of socially ingrained, mindless discipline, was also highly conditional on the belief that the conflict was defensive. German wartime propaganda has been criticised on many different grounds, but its success in blaming the war on Russia was a masterstroke, mobilising widespread Russophobia in the working classes, the people most opposed to armed conflict, and playing on the threat of invasion. As the *Berliner Tageblatt* told its readers on 2 August 1914, 'the German people may honestly say once more in this hour that it did not want this war ... But it will not allow the soil of the Fatherland to

27 Ferguson, *Pity*, pp. 1–4.

28 W. Harbutt Dawson, *The German Danger and the Working Man* (London: The Central Committee for National Patriotic Organisations, n.d.), p. 7.

29 IWM, 97/4/1: B.C. Myatt, diary, 15 Feb. 1915. Cf. Ferguson, *Pity*, pp. 199–201.

30 Gregory, 'British "War Enthusiasm" in 1914', p. 80. For an example of a volunteer motivated by events in France, see R.S. Ashley, *War-Diary of Private R.S. (Jack) Ashley 2472 7th London Regiment 1914–1918* (London: Philippa Stone, 1982), p. 1. Ashley remarked on 1 Sept. 1914, 'bad news from France, and another appeal for men which set me thinking it was time to get along'.

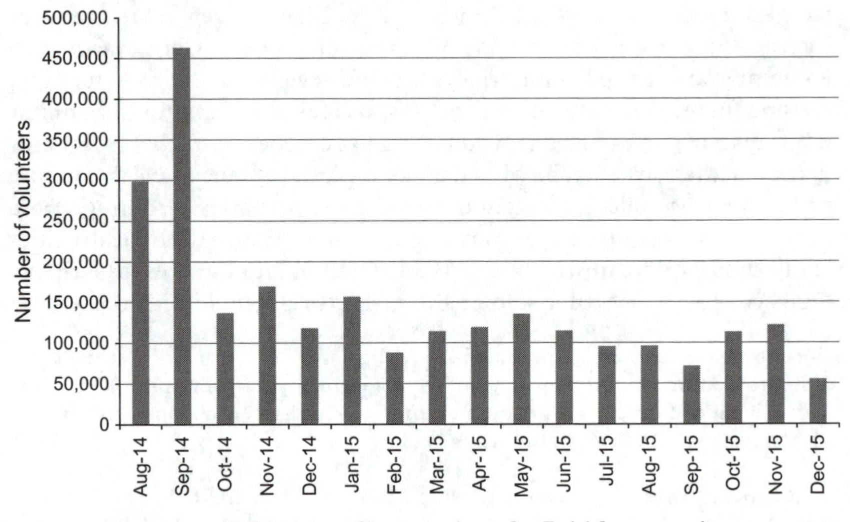

Figure 1. *Voluntary enlistments into the British army, August 1914 – December 1915*
Source: *Military Effort*, p. 364

be overrun and devastated by Russian regiments'.[31] The brief occupation of East Prussian territory by Russian units at the end of August fanned fears of the so-called 'blood Tsar' and his 'Cossack hordes' further. Exaggerated atrocity stories appeared in the press and were given credibility by the letters of men serving in the theatre: 'the war is very hard for our poor East Prussians; you will certainly have already read in the newspapers about the atrocities which these Russian dogs have perpetrated on defenceless women and children', wrote one soldier to his parents after a week spent patrolling the battle zone.[32]

Under such circumstances, it was hardly surprising that men of all classes decided that it was their patriotic duty to fight. Whereas in Britain, protected by sea and by the Royal Navy, volunteering only gathered pace when Kitchener issued his call to arms on 8 August and only reached its

[31] *Berliner Tageblatt und Handels-Zeitung. Morgen-Ausgabe* 43, 387 (2 August 1914). For a critique of German propaganda, see A.G. Marquis, 'Words as Weapons. Propaganda in Britain and Germany during the First World War', *Journal of Contemporary History* 13, 3 (July 1978), 467–98 and for pre-war Russophobia, see Kruse, *Krieg und nationale Integration*, p. 72.

[32] BA-MA Freiburg, MSg 2/ 3788: G. Klein, letter to parents, 31 Aug. 1914. The behaviour of Russian troops in East Prussia is still a matter of controversy. See V.G. Liulevicius, 'Ostpreußen', in G. Hirschfeld, G. Krumeich and I. Renz (eds.), *Enzyklopädie Erster Weltkrieg* (Paderborn: Ferdinand Schöningh, 2004), pp. 764–6.

peak almost a month later, in Germany, surrounded on all sides by enemies, the rush to volunteer was immediate and spontaneous. With no official encouragement, 260,672 enlistment requests were received in Prussia alone during the first *week* of mobilisation, of which 143,922 were accepted.[33] Unlike in Britain, August 1914 represented the high-point of German volunteering; the only surviving figures, compiled by the Württemberg army, indicate that in this month enlistments were almost four times those of September and more than ten times those of October 1914 (see Figure 2). Moreover, contrary to the usual historiographical claim that volunteers were 'war-enthused' students or schoolchildren, examination of muster rolls and letters demonstrates that a broad cross-section of urban society enlisted, mainly for reasons of patriotic self-defence.[34] As a survey of volunteer motivations concluded, 'patriotic feeling . . . was there to a great degree – as an impulsive, categorical imperative: we have a duty to protect the Fatherland. War has been declared, weapons are our only remaining resort'.[35] For the majority of men who were conscripts, motives for fighting were little different and many arrived at their depots early. *Feldunterarzt* Kurt Neumann, for example, observed that the reservists in his company 'all, with only a few exceptions, who professed illness, went willingly into the war forced upon us, firmly resolved to protect the Fatherland'.[36] As in Britain, many soldiers were particularly concerned to guard their homes and families from the horrors of foreign occupation: *Gefreiter* Georg Kirchner, a twenty-one-year-old trainee teacher mobilised as a reservist, wept on leaving his family yet simultaneously believed that his participation in the war was necessary: 'I . . . would look on it as fortunate to die for the loved ones at home in this sad time,' he wrote.[37]

The similarity of German and British motivations for fighting was reflected in the fact that on both sides it was the language of duty or *Pflicht*

[33] BA-MA Freiburg, W-10/ 50902: Denkenschrift über die Ersatzstellung für das Deutsche Heer von Mitte September bis Ende 1914, p. 53.

[34] Watson 'For Kaiser and Reich', 50–62. For the traditional historiographical view of volunteers, see Nonn, 'Oh What a Lovely War?', 107 and A. Gestrich, '"Leicht trennt sich nur die Jugend vom Leben"– Jugendliche im Ersten Weltkrieg', in R. Spilker and B. Ulrich (eds.), *Der Tod als Maschinist. Der industrialisierte Krieg 1914–1918. Eine Ausstellung des Museums Industriekultur Osnabrück im Rahmen des Jubiläums, 350 Jahre Westfälischer Friede, 17. Mai–23. August 1998. Katalog* (Bramsche: Rasch, 1998), p. 36.

[35] Plaut, 'Psychographie des Kriegers', p. 13.

[36] Neumann, 'Psychologische Beobachtungen', 1243. Cf. H. Rahne, *Militärische Mobilmachungsplanung und -technik in Preußen und im Deutschen Reich von Mitte des 19. Jahrhunderts bis zum Zweiten Weltkrieg* (Berlin: Militärverlag der deutschen Demokratischen Republik, 1983), p. 143.

[37] DTA, 9/II: G. Kirchner, letter to family, 10 Aug. 1914.

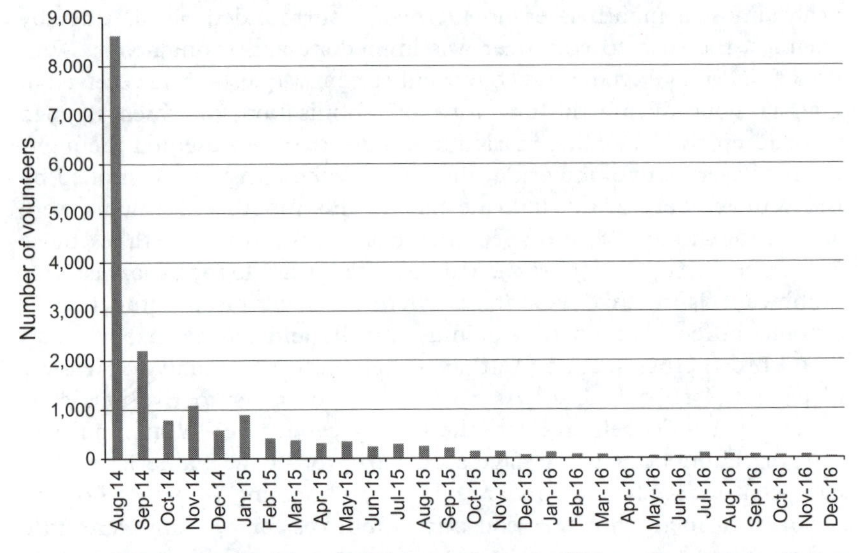

Figure 2. *Voluntary enlistments into the Württemberg army, August 1914 – December 1916*
Source: HStA Stuttgart, M 77/ 2/ 4: Stellv. Generalkommando XIII A K Nr. 4. Abteilung II b. (Kriegsarbeits-u.Ersatzwesen-Abteilung) Denkschriften über die Erfahrungen bei der Mobilmachung im Jahre 1914 und während des Krieges betr. Vorbereitung der Mobilmachung, Organisation usw. Juni 1918

which was most often utilised to explain the decision to enlist. When asked why he had volunteered, the sixty-eight-year-old Professor of Theology E.R. Gregorn responded, 'I did not become a soldier in order to make psychological studies, in order to be able to travel, in order to have "fun", in order to be allowed to wear a uniform or in order to satisfy my ambition. I became a soldier, because I considered it my duty'. Younger German volunteers similarly wrote of their 'solemn duty' to defend Germany.[38] The concept was no less emotive for conscripts, who sang as they were marching to war, 'Es hat mich der König gerufen / Zu schützen treu das Land' ('The King called me / Loyally to protect the land').[39] On the other

[38] Respectively, J.E. Hottenroth (ed.), *Sachsen in großer Zeit in Wort und Bild. Gemeinverständliche sächsische Kriegsgeschichte und vaterländisches Gedenkswerk des Weltkrieges* (3 vols., Leipzig: Verlag der Literaturwerke 'Minerva' R. Max Lippold, 1923), III, p. 181 and BA-MA Freiburg, MSg 2/ 2735: H. Genscher, letter to father, 6 Nov. 1914.

[39] C. Sieber, 'Das Soldatenlied im 1. WK – Analyse und didaktische Verwertbarkeit' unpublished Wissenschaftliche Hausarbeit, Pädagogische Hochschule Freiburg (1995), p. 98.

hand, as Kirchner's case demonstrates, 'duty' or *Pflicht* could express less a sense of patriotic feeling than more personal allegiances. It is not without significance that a favourite wartime British army song went, 'Good-bye, Nellie, / I'm going across the main. / Farewell, Nellie, / This parting gives me pain. / I shall always love you / As true as the stars above. / I'm going to do my duty / For the girl I love'. The composition, according to the authors of the definitive dictionary of British soldiers' songs and slang, was 'sung with great sentiment, and no notion that it was ridiculous'. As it went to the heart of why its singers were risking their lives in France and Flanders, this was hardly surprising.[40]

In both countries, men's sense of duty and fear of invasion were backed up by coercive mechanisms. Already in Germany in 1914 and in Britain from the beginning of 1916, governments possessed legislative powers compelling men to enlist. Equally potent in forcing reluctant combatants to go to the front was the social pressure placed on military-aged males. The nearly universal acceptance of the war by both societies meant that many men experienced what one psychologist referred to as a feeling of *dabei-sein-dürfen* (the need to be 'allowed to take part').[41] Those not in uniform felt suddenly excluded from their communities: the London factory worker Robert Cude expressed both patriotism and a sense of social exclusion when, after being rejected from the Navy, he contrasted the 'Personal Pride in being a part, (if a very minor part), of the War Machine' with the feeling that he was now 'plain Mr Nobody'.[42] Older men also evinced similar emotions. The sixty-five-year-old Franco-Prussian war veteran A.O. Stein wrote to *Fußartillerie-Regiment Nr. 12* to demand a posting: 'I can no longer find peace,' he declared. 'Five sons and one son-in-law perform their duty and I'm supposed to sit back and twiddle my thumbs?'[43] British recruiters cleverly exploited community ties both to make service more desirable and peer pressure more intense by setting up so-called 'Pals Battalions', which promised men from the same localities, clubs or families the opportunity to serve together. More explicit pressure was applied through poster campaigns, many of which played on men's fear of ostracism, and most particularly through the October 1915 'Derby Scheme', under which every male Briton between the ages of eighteen and forty-one was personally asked to pledge that he would enlist when called for on the basis that young,

40 Brophy and Partridge, *The Long Trail*, p. 53.
41 Plaut, 'Psychographie des Kriegers', p. 10.
42 IWM, Con Shelf: R. Cude, memoir section of diary, p. 2.
43 HStA Dresden: 11363 Ersatz-Bataillon Fussartillerie 12, 34288: A.O. Stein, letter to *das königliche Kommando des königl. sächsischen Ersatz-Bataillons Fußartill. Regt. 12*, 25 August 1914.

single men would be taken first. Additional to such official measures was informal pressure exerted by female patriots, who took it upon themselves to help swell the ranks of the volunteers; Gunner J.P. MacKay neatly satirised their role in a cartoon depicting a warlike Amazon punching her inoffensive husband while shouting, 'Get out you lout you should be at the front protecting poor women like me' (see Plate 5). More often, coercion by women relied on embarrassment: according to Procter, the practice of presenting white feathers to male civilians 'reached extraordinary intensity' in the second year of the war.[44]

Although compulsion became more important in recruitment the longer the conflict lasted, the acceptance of army service as a necessary duty remained extraordinarily high throughout the war. In Britain, 2,675,149 men volunteered (more than half of the 4,970,902 who enlisted during the war), 208,430 of whom did so in the two years after the introduction of conscription in January 1916.[45] Although the conscripts who comprised the majority of drafts after 1916 were denigrated in some quarters, there is little evidence to suggest that they were any less or differently motivated than their volunteer predecessors. Percy Copson was probably not untypical in repressing anxiety for the future on his departure for the front in March 1918 with the thought that, 'I was at least doing my duty, and with the band playing our "march past" and the cheers from the crowd on the platform outside the train, it made one feel proud to go'.[46] In Germany, where the level of mobilisation was far higher than in Britain and where a system of conscription operated throughout the war, volunteering reached the lesser but still impressive figure of half a million men.[47] Moreover, among the majority of troops who were conscripts, a sense of patriotic duty remained present throughout the war. Even in the autumn of 1916, at a time of intense stress for the Kaiser's army, German other ranks could still be heard to declare, 'we won't fail, however, for we are still Germans and want to remain so'.

44 Private Collection (Costelloe): J.P. MacKay, cartoon, no date and Procter, 'Motives', 31. For British posters, see M.L. Sanders and P.M. Taylor, *British Propaganda during the First World War* (London: Macmillan, 1982), pp. 138–9 and, for recruiting techniques and organisation, R. Douglas, 'Voluntary Enlistment in the First World War and the Work of the Parliamentary Recruiting Committee', *Journal of Modern History* 42, 4 (December 1970), 564–85.

45 For volunteers, see *Military Effort*, p. 364 and Winter, 'Britain's "Lost Generation"', 451. Volunteering figures refer to the period up to 31 October 1917. More men may have volunteered during the following year.

46 IWM, 86/30/1: P.G. Copson: diary / memoir, 19 Mar. 1918. Cf. Sheffield, *Leadership*, pp. 182–3. With regard to combat motivation, Sheffield argues that 'the method by which a man joined the army was relatively unimportant'.

47 Watson, 'For Kaiser and Reich', 50.

Plate 5. Volunteering: female coercion. The pressure applied by women on their menfolk to enlist was usually more subtle, but no less potent. From the sketches of John Patrick MacKay.

In mid-1918, when the military situation on the Western Front was deteriorating, *Vertrauensleute* – men appointed to report on morale within their units – serving in home units were often still able to report that young conscripts were in good spirits and prepared for the front.[48]

Motivations for volunteering or enlisting were naturally complex. In individual cases, unemployment, excitement, official compulsion or social coercion might all have been factors in determining men's actions. Middle-class men in both countries were more likely to volunteer, partly because they were more prone to 'war enthusiasm' than their lower-class peers, but mainly because their education and place in society meant that morally and socially there was no other course of action open to them.[49] Most men did not wish for war and hoped that it would soon end: as one Saxon conscript was already telling his wife on 15 August 1914, 'each hopes that he can go home soon'.[50] Nonetheless, the high level of social integration in Britain and Germany and the serious threat of invasion perceived by men of both nationalities resulted in almost universal resolution, however reluctant, to accept that participation in the war was necessary. Societal differences and ideological variations in national war aims were relatively unimportant for most men of whatever nationality; rather, as the psychologist and veteran Paul Plaut accurately observed, 'the uniform wearer is carrier of the unifying thought: protect the home'.[51] Fear of the consequences of an enemy invasion for their countries, and still more for their homes, families and loved ones, meant that for four long and bloody years most Britons and Germans, however scared or reluctant, were nonetheless willing recruits for their national armies.

Military and combat dynamics

When a man joined his nation's army, he entered an organisation designed to survive extreme levels of stress. Effective operation under intensely hostile battlefield conditions required militaries to demand that their personnel act in ways totally at odds with most civilian inclinations or experience: soldiers were expected to endure severe discomfort, place themselves in mortal danger and even break the ultimate taboo of taking

48 For the quotation, see BA-MA Freiburg, MSg 2/ 5799: A. Meier, letter to *Oberpostsekretär* Dölker, 6 Sept. 1916. For conscripts in 1918, see chapter 6, p. 213 and for *Vertrauensleute*, see Lipp, *Meinungslenkung*, pp. 77–8.

49 See J. Winter, *The Great War and the British People* (London: Macmillan, 1986), pp. 26–9, J.S.K. Watson, *Fighting Different Wars. Experience, Memory, and the First World War in Britain* (Cambridge University Press, 2004), pp. 298–9 and Watson, 'For Kaiser and Reich', 52–3.

50 Private Collection (Author): K. Beier, letter to wife, 15 Aug. 1914.

51 Plaut, 'Psychographie des Kriegers', p. 96.

human life. All individual priorities, even the survival instinct, were to come second to the goals of the organisation. In order to ensure that such behaviour became the norm, armies attempted to socialise men into a specifically martial culture of obedience and group loyalty. An environment was constructed in which dissension was not only unattractive but quite often unthinkable: troops were inculcated with new military allegiances and habituated to obey. Those who chose not to conform were punished, while conduct which exceeded the bare minimum of compliance was rewarded symbolically or materially. On active service, the stress of battle could cause this organisation and value system to collapse, prompting soldiers to place self-preservation before military priorities. More often, however, the experience of facing a dangerous enemy actually confirmed troops' predominantly defensive reasons for fighting and encouraged them to sink their identities further into their fighting organisations.

The process of military socialisation commenced immediately a man enlisted. In both Britain and Germany, recruits were inducted into the army with a mandatory oath of allegiance, in which they swore to 'serve faithfully' their king and (in the German case) Kaiser, promised 'all superiors the due respect and obedience' and pledged to prove themselves 'at every opportunity a brave and loyal soldier'.[52] The meaning of these words was elaborated during basic training, an exercise designed partially to confer the physical robustness and technical skill necessary for functioning in combat but also intended, as David French has observed, 'to instil into young soldiers ... the belief that the military authorities possessed the legitimate authority to govern their every action'.[53] Visible evidence of individuality was eliminated, as men were clothed uniformly, quartered communally and subordinated together at the bottom of an inflexible and dominating hierarchy, personified by the stereotypical bawling NCO.[54] Close-order drill, the first task which both

52 DTA, 1040, II: L. Wernicke, handwritten copy of oath to Ludwig III of Bavaria and the German Kaiser in diary as taken in May 1916. For the similar British attestation oath, see TNA, WO 363/ FO 22 (p. 340): Short Service Attestation Form for Private Henry Fairhurst, 14/York and Lancs.

53 D. French, *Military Identities. The Regimental System, the British Army, and the British People, c. 1870–2000* (Oxford University Press, 2005), p. 62.

54 See P. Simkins, *Kitchener's Army. The Raising of the New Armies, 1914–16* (Manchester University Press, 1988), pp. 296 and 313 and French, *Military Identities*, pp. 61–75 for British training. Details of the similar form of German instruction can be found in TNA, WO 157/ 13: 'German Recruit Training'. Annexe to GHQ Summary of 20 Sept. 1916 and TNA, WO 157/ 24: 'Report on the Training of Two Men of the 1918 Class Belonging to the 450th Inf. Regt., 233rd Division'. Annexe to Advanced GHQ Summary of 29 June 1917. For a more personal account, see also V. Klemperer, *Curriculum Vitae. Erinnerungen 1881–1918*, ed. W. Nowojski (2 vols., Berlin: Aufbau Taschenbuch Verlag, 1996), II, pp. 306–10.

British and German soldiers were required to master, illustrated the value of teamwork and graphically expressed the military's claim to absolute power over the recruit by obliging him to hold his body in a prescribed fashion.[55] The same message was underlined by the strict regimentation of troops' lives during the entire period of instruction: one German finishing his training at a field recruit depot in the autumn of 1918 described a typically exhausting day as beginning at 5.30 a.m. and ending only after almost continual, organised activity at 7 p.m., 'around the time that it's already beginning to get dark'.[56] Through establishing its right to regulate and control their every action, the army, in the words of the social psychologists Herbert C. Kelman and V. Lee Hamilton, came 'to define reality for its members'. Once an obligation to obey an authority has been accepted, 'people's reactions ... are governed not so much by motivational processes – what they want – as by perceptual ones – what they see required of them'.[57] For most First World War soldiers, this meant that during basic training obedience ceased largely to be a conscious choice and instead became a default option.

Punishment performed an essential role in men's military socialisation by both clearly marking certain behaviour as unacceptable to the organisation and frightening the less committed into compliance. The sanctions at armies' disposal were wide-ranging. Minor misdemeanours might be punished by binding offenders to a wheel or tree, a practice which soldiers on both sides found deeply humiliating and which was abolished in the German army in May 1917.[58] Greater disobedience was met with imprisonment or hard labour, and the most serious crimes before the enemy could occasionally provoke the death penalty: 48 German soldiers were executed during the war, while the British implemented 346 death sentences, including 266 for desertion, 18 for cowardice and 3 for mutiny.[59] Draconian punishment was by no means always necessary to guarantee compliance. Early in the war, discipline in British Territorial units was often laxer than in Regular battalions partly because fear of disgrace was

55 French, *Military Identities*, p. 64. Cf. S.D. Jackman, 'Shoulder to Shoulder. Close Control and "Old Prussian Drill" in German Offensive Infantry Tactics, 1871–1914', *Journal of Military History* 68, 1 (January 2004), 90–104.

56 Private Collection (Author): G. Schneider, letter to parents, 20 Sept. 1918. For the similar form (if not content) of British training earlier in the war, see IWM, Con Shelf: R. Cude, memoir section of diary, pp. 2–3.

57 H.C. Kelman and V.L. Hamilton, *Crimes of Obedience. Toward a Social Psychology of Authority and Responsibility* (New Haven: Yale University Press, 1989), pp. 90–1.

58 See Holmes, *Tommy*, p. 558 and Ziemann, *Front*, pp. 110–12. For soldiers' reactions, see IWM, 78/4/1: T.H. Cubbon, diary, 17 Aug. 1914 and B. Ulrich and B. Ziemann (eds.), *Frontalltag im Ersten Weltkrieg. Wahn und Wirklichkeit* (Frankfurt am Main: Fischer Taschenbuch, 1994), pp. 121–2.

59 Corns and Hughes-Wilson, *Blindfold*, pp. 103–4.

itself sufficient to deter dissent among their socially superior manpower.[60] When shame or guilt was less emotive, however, harsh penalties could be useful in casting obedience as the least unattractive course of action. Concerned about its troops' commitment and suspecting that imprisonment simply offered a desirable escape from active service, the German army established seventy-eight penal companies in October 1917 in order to ensure that malcontents remained at the front and suffered more than their obedient compatriots.[61] The BEF was even more eager to exploit the deterrent effect of tough penalties. According to Christoph Jahr, the army's discipline was both stricter and more arbitrary than that of its opponent, particularly at the beginning of the war and during offensives, when harsh sentences were meted out not only with justice in mind but also with an exemplary object. Executions were publicised in General Routine Orders with this purpose and there is some evidence that knowledge of this penalty figured in at least some soldiers' risk calculations. Private Arthur Wrench, in an emotional state after hearing of the death of his brother and considering whether to debunk while on leave, thought of the severe punishment for desertion and concluded 'that I am more afraid NOT to return for that would be a greater ignominy to die that way. And that way would be more certain too'.[62]

Armies not only sanctioned heavy punishments for dissent but, through the creation of an environment of close supervision, also ensured that deviant behaviour was unlikely to go undiscovered. In both forces, formations specifically tasked with maintaining discipline grew during the conflict. In the British army, the Corps of Military Police expanded from 405 to 13,414 men. Whereas in 1914 there had been only 1 military policeman for every 3,306 soldiers, by 1918 the ratio was 1 to 292. The Corps was supported by Regimental Police and Garrison Police, both of whom were soldiers ordered to perform police duties on a temporary basis.[63] In the German army, the Field Police, of whom

60 See Sheffield, *Leadership*, pp. 1–28. Cf. also I. Beckett, 'The Territorial Force', in I.F.W. Beckett and K. Simpson (eds.), *A Nation in Arms. A Social Study of the British Army in the First World War* (Manchester University Press, 1985), pp. 144–5.

61 See H. Cron, *Imperial German Army 1914–18. Organisation, Structure, Orders of Battle* (Solihull: Helion and Company, 1937, 2002), p. 234 and Jahr, *Gewöhnliche Soldaten*, p. 178.

62 IWM, 85/51/1: A. Wrench, diary, 6 Dec. 1917. Cf. statement of Polish deserter in TNA, WO 157/ 12: Summary of Information (GHQ), 28 Aug. 1916. For British arbitrariness and deterrence measures, see Jahr, *Gewöhnliche Soldaten*, pp. 244–51 and D. Gill and G. Dallas, *The Unknown Army* (London: Verso, 1985), pp. 40–3.

63 See *Military Effort*, p. 642, D. Englander and J. Osborne, 'Jack, Tommy and Henry Dubb. The Armed Forces and the Working Class', *Historical Journal* 21, 3 (1978), 595 and G. Sheffield, 'British Military Police and their Battlefield Role, 1914–18', *Sandhurst Journal of Military Studies* 1 (1990), 33–46.

one-third were NCOs, one-third senior personnel from the provincial police and one-third lance-corporals of the cavalry, underwent a significant albeit less dramatic expansion from 33 to 115 sections.[64] Partly, this growth resulted from the need for more men to direct the traffic on armies' increasingly congested supply lines, not disciplinary concerns. Nonetheless, helped by the static nature of trench warfare and the fact that both armies were fighting abroad, the ever larger body of police found it relatively easy to close off potential escape routes. Railway lines and (in the case of the British army) French ports were closely watched, in order to deter and capture deserters.[65]

On an everyday basis, however, it was not military police but rather officers, NCOs and the men themselves who maintained discipline. Behind the lines, company officers could offer alternative punishments to those inflicted by official military justice. Often these were lighter, although occasionally they could be severe or even dangerous: one German artillery volunteer, for example, recorded how an argument with an officer in October 1914 had led to one of his comrades being ordered to carry shell panniers across the battery front.[66] In battle, officers were crucial, maintaining discipline by their own example but also, if necessary, by coercion. Although such incidents were rare, fleeing soldiers might (contrary to military law) be shot down by their officer, while reliable troops were sometimes posted behind wavering comrades in order to ensure their compliance: one order from the CO of *II/Infanterie-Regiment Nr.* 65 in November 1916 intercepted by British intelligence instructed a company officer to station 'a NCO and several energetic men' to his rear with the purpose of 'preventing ... your men from running away'.[67] Deserters or men attempting to surrender to the enemy could be dealt with summarily. Two unfortunate soldiers who wished to escape to enemy trenches made it only so far as the barbed wire before their own side spotted them and began shooting with machineguns, artillery and mortars, eventually dispatching a patrol to bring them back.[68]

64 Cron, *Imperial German Army*, p. 229.
65 Jahr, *Gewöhnliche Soldaten*, pp. 180 and 202–3.
66 BA-MA Freiburg, MSg 1/ 121: R. Güldenberg, 28 Oct. 1914. For lenient punishments, see Sheffield, *Leadership*, pp. 87–8.
67 TNA, WO 157/ 15: Summary of Information (GHQ), 15 Nov. 1916. Cf. also the incident described in IWM, 78/4/1: T.H. Cubbon, diary, 11 Nov. 1914. For officers shooting their men, see BA-MA Freiburg, MSg 1/ 2970: H. Fuchs, diary, 25 Dec. 1914; IWM, P 239: W.B. St Leger, diary, 30 Nov. 1917 and BA-MA Freiburg, PH 3/ 585: Vernehmungsprotokolle, AOK 4: Vernehmung [of eight men from 10/Royal West Kents, six men from 11/Royal West Surreys, one man from 23/Middlesex and twenty-three men from 20/Durham Light Infantry]. 3 Aug. 1917.
68 Staatsbib. Berlin, Ms. Germ. fol. 1651: C.F. Müller, diary, 25 Apr. 1917.

NCOs and even ordinary soldiers were also willing to use violence in order to secure the obedience of their comrades. Walter Enders, a cavalryman serving on the Eastern Front, was horrified during an inspection to see his *Wachtmeister* beat, kick and swear at a man with an imperfectly cleaned weapon.[69] On the other side, Sergeant A. Reeve gave his section what he termed 'a quiet hint' when he found three of them drunk. The offenders, he wrote, 'looked lovely objects as they crawled out of the green pond'.[70] Fear of penalties from higher up the chain of command prompted other ranks to police themselves. One letter picked up by the Third Army censor in August 1917 observed that 'Albert – will probably get 28 days first field punishment for staying over his leave, and if these is [*sic*] any soldiers serving in his unit he will probably be thrown in the horse pond, besides getting a rough handling, as it [is] such men as he who get the leaves stopped'.[71] According to prisoner interrogations, some soldiers decided to 'make it their business' to stop desertion attempts and it was not unknown for sentries to fire on comrades trying to abscond.[72]

While coercion could induce a minimum level of compliance, it provided troops with no incentive to fulfil orders actively or enthusiastically. Accompanying the negative incentive of punishment in both forces were therefore promotions, medals and material prizes such as cash bonuses or extra leave intended to encourage men to act beyond the call of duty. The British army exploited these more successfully than its enemy. Promotion within non-commissioned ranks was, for example, purely meritocratic in the BEF, whereas the German army's system of favouring middle-class reserve officer aspirants (*Einjährig-Freiwillige*) with NCO positions before they were commissioned caused resentment among some soldiers of inferior education and social background, whose own prospects were correspondingly reduced.[73] Worse still, perhaps in a misguided attempt to compensate, the German army devalued its own awards system by conferring far too many medals: almost every other German soldier,

69 Private Collection (Author): W. Enders, letter to father, 17 Feb. 1915.

70 IWM, 90/20/1: A. Reeve, diary, 13 Jan. 1915.

71 IWM, 84/46/1: M. Hardie, handwritten note from censored letter, 8 Aug. 1917.

72 TNA, WO 157/ 15: Summary of Information (GHQ), 26 Nov. 1916.

73 For German complaints about this system, see G. Gothein, *Warum verloren wir den Krieg?* (Stuttgart: Deutsche Verlags-Anstalt, 1919), p. 86. After its initial enormous expansion in 1914, when almost universal lack of military experience meant that class and education were sometimes used as criteria to appoint NCOs, promotion within the non-commissioned ranks was purely meritocratic in the British army. Many units were scrupulous in their fairness: German interrogators found that some Australian units demoted replacement NCOs arriving at the front for the first time, in order to ensure that veterans' promotion prospects would not be disadvantaged. See, respectively, Simkins, *Kitchener's Army*, p. 227 and BA-MA Freiburg, PH 3/ 556: Note from AOK 2. Nachr. Offz. at Gefangenlager Cambrai, 29 Aug. 1916.

5,209,000 in total, was awarded an Iron Cross Class II during the war, with 218,000 also receiving Class I.[74] In contrast, although the British became more generous as the war dragged on, the total number of medals awarded to BEF personnel still only reached 239,853.[75] While complaints about undeserving recipients in the rear were heard in both armies, winning a distinction remained a source of pride for British troops, whereas in the German army, the value of decorations was already being questioned in some quarters by the autumn of 1914.[76]

At the root of military forces' formidable discipline and cohesion, however, lay the close identification felt by the majority of soldiers for their army and its aims. Social psychologists observe that 'the internalization of organizational goals is ... the most effective of motive patterns'.[77] In the First World War, acceptance of armies' authority as legitimate derived primarily from citizen-soldiers' attachment to civilian roles and loyalties, which prompted them to recognise a duty to defend their home communities in time of national emergency. Additionally, however, voluntary compliance was bolstered by emotional integration into the army through the adoption of new military allegiances. It is notable that although middle-ranking staff officers were often viewed with disdain, expressions of loyalty and respect for higher commanders were very common. This was above all the case in the German army, where even in 1918, Hindenburg remained a figure of hope for many soldiers.[78] With the possible exception of Lord Kitchener, no figure of comparable stature emerged on the British side, but soldiers nonetheless

74 H. Ostertag, *Bildung, Ausbildung und Erziehung des Offizierkorps im deutschen Kaiserreich 1871–1918. Eliteideal, Anspruch und Wirklichkeit* (Frankfurt am Main: Peter Lang, 1990), p. 292.

75 *Military Effort*, foldout facing p. 560; 205,685 of these awards went to troops on the Western Front.

76 See BA-MA Freiburg, MSg 1/ 2965: H. Fuchs, letter to wife, 23 Oct. 1914 and BA-MA Freiburg, MSg 2/ 2735: H. Genscher, letter to father, 13 Nov. 1914. For German complaints in general, see H. Kantorowicz, *Der Offiziershaß im deutschen Heer* (Freiburg im Breisgau: J. Bielefelds Verlag, 1919), pp. 19–21. For pride in British decorations, see BA-MA Freiburg, PH 3/ 556: Interrogations undertaken in the Cambrai POW Camp: Vernehmung eines Mannes des X. West York Ba[taill]ons, 50. Brig. XVII Division. 17 Sept. 1916, p. 2 and the letter of 17 Sept. 1918 written by the 6/Connaught Rangers' CO and reproduced in J. Laffin (ed.), *Letters from the Front 1914–1918* (London: J.M. Dent & Sons, 1973), p. 100.

77 D. Katz and R.L. Kahn, *The Social Psychology of Organizations*, 2nd edn (Chichester: John Wiley & Sons, 1978), p. 425. Cf. pp. 361–3 and 374–7 and also Kelman and Hamilton, *Crimes of Obedience*, pp. 89–95. The other 'motive patterns' identified by Katz and Kahn are 'legal compliance', which comprises obedience imposed through punitive threats, and 'instrumental satisfaction', which relies on motivation through reward.

78 See, for example, BA-MA Freiburg, MSg 1/ 161: K. Reiter, diary, 2 Mar. 1918. Cf. BA-MA Freiburg, W-10/ 50794: Postüberwachung der *5. Armee*. 10 Jan. 1918, p. 36.

reported in glowing terms if they met their leaders. Howard Panton, returning from the Loos battlefield in 1915, recorded that being thanked personally by Sir John French 'was like a tonic' after his unit's ordeal.[79] Two years later, a British prisoner told his German interrogators that a speech by General Plumer had motivated his tired battalion to man the line only days after it had been involved in a heavy attack.[80]

It was not the army or its leaders, however, but rather subsidiary units which were the primary objects of soldiers' military loyalties. As Procter observed, 'one did not love the army. But it was possible to love a battalion or a regiment, to identify oneself with its purposes, to feel proud of its achievement, – and, still more strongly, to feel the shame that clung to the name of a division that had broken'.[81] Battalions, which at the beginning of the war contained 1,000 men, were the visible communities and tactical units in which soldiers on both sides lived, fought and died. Regiments, in contrast, were larger, 'culturally defined organizations' which, as David French has explained, 'were bound together by shared historical memories, customs, and a myth of descent'.[82] Through dress distinctions, ceremonial parades and the cultivation of a mythologised, glorious past, regiments in both armies aimed to imbue recruits with the sense of belonging to a unique, arcane community with glorious traditions to uphold.[83] Long-serving British Regulars were most thoroughly inculcated with this ideology, and, according to the former medical officer Lord Moran, regimental loyalty became a 'religion' among them.[84] Such intense devotion was rarer among wartime citizen-soldiers, although by no means unknown. As Captain Yoxall, serving with the prestigious 18/King's Royal Rifle Corps, observed:

> When you're a member of a great regiment like the Sixtieth you feel yourself in a sense immortal. If the battalion lives the loss of the individual doesn't matter. To go up the scale, if the battalion is wiped out & the regiment lives still it doesn't matter. You can go further & take it up to the country (as Kipling -
>
> 'Who lives if England dies?

79 IWM, P 262: H. Panton, letter to brother, 29 Sept. 1915.

80 BA-MA Freiburg, PH 3/ 585: Vernehmungsprotokolle, AOK 4: Vernehmung [of man of 1/Hertfordshires], 22 Aug. 1917. For generals' efforts to motivate their men, see also D. Englander, 'Discipline and Morale in the British Army, 1917–1918', in J. Horne (ed.), *State, Society and Mobilization in Europe during the First World War* (Cambridge University Press, 1997), p. 129.

81 Procter, 'Motives', 40–1.

82 French, *Military Identities*, p. 98.

83 For the British, see ibid., pp. 78–94. For the Germans, see U. Frevert, *A Nation in Barracks. Modern Germany, Military Conscription and Civil Society* (Oxford: Berg, 2004), pp. 183–4.

84 Moran, *Anatomy*, pp. 184–5. Cf. Baynes, *Morale*, p. 163.

'Who dies if England lives?')

& so on to the cause.[85]

The flexible and purely administrative and historical (rather than tactical) nature of British regiments helped the army to imbue wartime soldiers with such loyalties. Whereas the German army maintained three-battalion regiments throughout the conflict (comprising a tactical unit equivalent to a British brigade) and expanded by creating totally new regiments lacking traditions, the British equipped new battalions with an instant pedigree by founding them within the existing regimental framework. By the end of the conflict, some British regiments possessed over forty battalions serving all over the world, the vast majority of which were totally new wartime creations, yet which linked themselves to and derived their *esprit de corps* from a glorious martial past.[86]

While regimental tradition was thus more important in the BEF than its opponent, wartime troops' allegiances on both sides were probably most influenced by their regiments' local connections. These not only raised units' legitimacy through direct association with the communities for which citizen-soldiers were fighting but also strengthened cohesion by enabling men of similar origin to serve together. British infantry regiments were generally linked to one or two counties (thus, for example, 'the Middlesex Regiment' or the 'Oxfordshire and Buckinghamshire Light Infantry'), although in the pre-war Regular Army only a minority of personnel were commonly native to their unit's locality. Conversely, pre-war Territorials and the Kitchener 'Pals Battalions' were often raised from men of the same professions, sports associations and districts and evinced very strong local ties.[87] The disadvantage of such overly narrow recruiting was revealed on the Somme in 1916, when the annihilation of

[85] IWM, P 317 Con Shelf: H.W. Yoxall, letter to mother, 2 Sept. 1916. For other evidence of wartime soldiers' regimental loyalties, see IWM, 86/32/1: S.T. Fuller, diary / memoir, 19 May 1918 and IWM, 97/37/1: A.H. Roberts, diary, 7 and 12–13 Aug. 1918.

[86] Thus, for example, the Royal Welch Fusiliers expanded from seven to forty-two and the Middlesex Regiment from ten to forty-six battalions during the war. See, respectively, E.O. Skaife, *R.W.F. A Short History of the Royal Welch Fusiliers* (London: Gale & Polden, n.d.), pp. 56–7 and E. Wyrall, *The Die-Hards in the Great War. A History of the Duke of Cambridge's own (Middlesex Regiment), 1914–1919, Compiled from the Records of the Line, Special Reserve, Service, and Territorial Battalions* (2 vols., London: Harrison & Sons, n.d.), I, pp. 1–2. For the continued cultivation of regimental loyalties during wartime, see S.P. MacKenzie, 'Morale and the Cause. The Campaign to Shape the Outlook of Soldiers in the British Expeditionary Force, 1914–1918', *Canadian Journal of History* 25, 2 (August 1990), 218.

[87] For the composition of pre-war Regular battalions, see French, *Military Identities*, pp. 57–60. For 'Pals Battalions', see Strachan, *First World War*, I, p. 161 and Simkins, *Kitchener's Army*, pp. 79–100 and for pre-war Territorials, see McCartney, *Citizen Soldiers*, pp. 17–22.

these units devastated their home communities. Under the pressure of heavy casualties, British battalions became more heterogeneous during the second half of the war, even absorbing reinforcements from outside their own shires and regiments. Nonetheless, local loyalties did not become irrelevant. Some units, particularly Territorial battalions from major conurbations, did successfully maintain a high proportion of county men. Moreover, even where battalions lacked adequate reinforcement from their own recruiting districts, the existence of regional Commands in Britain ensured that further drafts would usually be drawn from nearby shires, thereby preserving broader regional identities.[88] Such identities were also favoured by the German army, which allocated reinforcements through regional corps Commands throughout the war. Although heavy losses caused some disruption to the system in the middle years of hostilities, the army placed such importance on these loyalties that, in 1917, it exchanged men between regiments and even reorganised its divisions in order to ensure that most were geographically homogeneous.[89] Such efforts to cultivate *esprit de corps* had a highly beneficial effect on morale. As a Saxon *Vertrauensmann* in a home depot noted in June 1918, 'a particularly favourable influence on the mood of the drafts is observed when these same know that they are designated as replacements for their own regiment or battalion and won't be transferred to unfamiliar units'.[90]

[88] A small sample taken by French suggests that 67 per cent of soldiers in Territorial regiments during the war came from their units' home counties, in contrast to 49 and 46 per cent of those in Regular and service battalions respectively. French, *Military Identities*, pp. 280–1. For recruitment, drafting and amalgamation policies favouring the maintenance of local loyalties, see McCartney, *Citizen Soldiers*, pp. 57–74. Her research indicates that, at least among Territorial units, county homogeneity was retained to an even greater extent than implied by French's figures and convincingly refutes the argument that recruitment was nationalised after the Somme, as suggested in K.W. Mitchinson, *Gentlemen and Officers. The Impact and Experience of War on a Territorial Regiment 1914–1918* (London: Imperial War Museum, 1995), pp. 130–6 and Samuels, *Command or Control?*, pp. 224–5.

[89] Thus, for example, *Grenadier-Regiment Nr. 89* exchanged its Schleswig-Holsteiners for *Infanterie-Regiment Nr. 31*'s Mecklenburgers in mid-1917 and the *52. Division* replaced its *Infanterie-Regiment Nr. 66* (from Magdeburg) with *Infanterie-Regiment Nr. 111* to become a homogeneous Baden formation. See, respectively, TNA, WO 157/ 21: Summary of Information (GHQ), 28 June 1917 and P. Camena d'Almeida, *L'armée allemande avant et pendant la guerre de 1914–1918* (Nancy: Berger-Levrault, 1919), pp. 269–73. See also Ziemann, *Front*, p. 68.

[90] HStA Dresden, 11348 Stellv. Gen.-Kdo XIX AK KA(P) 12888, Blatt 55: Report for *Ers.-Batl. 2. Jäger Batl. Nr.* 13, 14 June 1918, in 'Berichte der Vertrauensleute 1918. Bd. 12'. The only problem with this system was that when a small state suffered disproportionate losses, as in the case of Württemberg, it was unable to maintain the strength of its units at the front. By the autumn of 1917, British intelligence was finding that company strengths in the Württemberg army were generally between 10 and 15 per cent lower than those of other contingents. See TNA, WO 157/ 24: Annexe to Advanced GHQ Summary of 1 September 1917.

At the lowest level of army organisations were companies, platoons and squads, in which soldiers provided each other with mutual support and loyalty, as well as peer pressure to conform. Modern sociological research has placed great emphasis on the importance of these 'primary groups' for armies' cohesion and combat efficiency.[91] Often, however, the ideal was not realised in reality. The historian Paul Knoch has gone so far as to suggest that 'the feeling and consciousness of comradeship represented more of an exception in the everyday experience of the soldier'.[92] Paul Plaut similarly described comradeship as 'only a professional solidarity' and believed that 'one looks after himself first'.[93] Certainly, combatants' diaries reveal that some men were not averse to stealing from their comrades.[94] Yet it is also clear that many soldiers derived huge benefit from the fraternal ethos which existed in some units: Richard Williams, for example, remarked of the war that 'it is only the spirit of brotherliness and mutual helpfulness that makes the thing tolerable'.[95] Gustav Klein was genuinely touched when his 'brave friend Lange' voluntarily offered to accompany him on a dangerous mission into no-man's-land.[96] Ludwig's analysis of combatants' essays, fifty-four of which mentioned *soziale Emotionen* (social emotions) as helpful in danger, also indicates that comradeship was widespread and particularly important in battle. Only two other factors, religious feelings and memories of home, received more mentions, justifying Ludwig's conclusion that 'the social emotions, in military life manifested especially in the form of comradeship, are without doubt one of the soldier's strongest supports in moments of danger'.[97]

Comradeship and 'primary groups' were in fact crucial to soldiers' ability and willingness to fight on. 'Social buffering' inhibits fear reactions, partly because, as the psychologist S.J. Rachman has argued, 'the presence of another person increases the possibility of control'.[98] In the

[91] The classic study is M. Janowitz and E.A. Shils, 'Cohesion and Disintegration in the Wehrmacht in World War II', in M. Janowitz (ed.), *Military Conflict. Essays in the Institutional Analysis of War and Peace* (Los Angeles: Sage Publications, 1975), pp. 177–220.

[92] P. Knoch, 'Kriegsalltag', in P. Knoch (ed.), *Kriegsalltag. Die Rekonstruktion des Kriegsalltags als Aufgabe der historischen Forschung und der Friedenserziehung* (Stuttgart: J.B. Metzlersche Versbuchhandlung, 1989), pp. 228–9.

[93] Plaut, 'Psychographie des Kriegers', p. 82.

[94] Ibid., pp. 84–5 and IWM, 85/51/1: A.E. Wrench, diary, 2 Sept. 1917.

[95] IWM, 82/26/1: A.R. Williams, letter to family, 24 Dec. 1915.

[96] BA-MA Freiburg, MSg 2/ 3788: G. Klein, letter to parents, 6 Feb. 1915.

[97] Ludwig, 'Psychologie der Furcht', p. 157. The importance of primary groups has been highlighted by research on desertion, which has found that poorly integrated men are more likely to go AWOL. See Jahr, *Gewöhnliche Soldaten*, p. 139 and Rose, 'Social Psychology of Desertion', p. 258.

[98] Rachman, *Fear and Courage*, p. 60.

chaotic and dangerous trench environment, where disempowerment was the prime stress on troops, the platoon, section or company, led by its officers and NCOs, represented security and order. As Charles Bird observed, men 'seek the protection of comrades by sinking their personality into the fighting unit' at times of danger.[99] Most sources agree that in attacks, soldiers ceased to operate on a conscious plane; men recorded that 'you lose all your senses' and could often describe only 'a mass of confused memories'.[100] Nonetheless, behind men's onward advance was probably the deep-seated desire for security. Forward movement meant escaping the enemy bombardment which would inevitably crash down on the attackers' jumping-off points and in no-man's-land. As Keegan has explained, a speedy advance provided the chance of capturing or killing enemy garrisons before they were able to climb out of shelter or operate their weapons. Above all, it was necessary for the individual because it kept him in touch with the imagined security of the group and its leaders; so important was this that even after armies had formally abandoned large closed-attack formations in favour of dispersed assault squad tactics, soldiers would endanger themselves by bunching up into groups, offering a perfect target for enemy machine-gunners.[101]

The organisation of men into self-supporting groups not only helped to propel them across no-man's-land during offensives but also more generally increased combat motivation. As one veteran observed, 'the greater losses a people has incurred in attempting to attain its war-aims, the more does their attainment appear to be worthy of further endurance'.[102] This was true also at the unit level, where casualties were rarely such that men were immediately forgotten. On the contrary, troops expended considerable effort on remembrance. One Bavarian Protestant pastor commented, 'it must touch every visitor and onlooker, when he sees the love with which our soldiers decorated the graves of their comrades'.[103] Numerous letters confirm his statement, recounting soldiers tending companions'

99 Bird, 'From Home to the Charge', 332. Cf. Plaut, 'Psychographie des Kriegers', p. 82.

100 IWM, P 317 Con Shelf: H.W. Yoxall, letter to mother, 24 Sept. 1917.

101 See Plaut, 'Prinzipien und Methoden', pp. 665–6, Stanford Read, *Military Psychiatry*, p. 11 and Keegan, *Face of Battle*, p. 284. 'Bunching up' was noted as a particular problem by American psychologists in the Second World War. See S.A. Stouffer, A.A. Lumsdaine, M.H. Lumsdaine, R.M. Williams Jr, M.B. Smith, I.L. Janis, S.A. Star and L.S. Cottrell Jr, *The American Soldier. Combat and its Aftermath* (2 vols., New York: John Wiley & Sons, 1949, 1965), II, pp. 283–4.

102 L.F. Richardson, *Mathematical Psychology of War* (Oxford: W.M. Hunt, 1919), p. 36.

103 LA Nuremberg, 3209: Bericht über Militärseelsorge im Felde from *Pfarrer* T. Niklas of *Ersatz-Infanterie-Regiment 28, bayerische Ersatz-Division* to *das königliche Oberkonsistorium*, Munich, 31 Jan. 1916. My thanks to Patrick Porter for bringing this source to my attention.

Plate 6. Comradeship: German troops at Lens, winter 1917–18. Under its officer and NCOs, the 'primary group' offered emotional support, a sense of safety and a modicum of control in the chaos and danger of the front line. From the album of a soldier serving in a *Reserve-Grenadier-Regiment*.

burial places, erecting crosses and writing memorial inscriptions.[104] Deaths generated a level of grief and guilt among survivors, however, which could not be quashed by laying flowers. In the short term, soldiers often felt a need to avenge fallen comrades. As Second Lieutenant E.H. Bennett explained, while 'you have only an impartial interest in strangers even though they are Englishmen, ... your own men downed, sets you cursing and throbbing with rage and hate'.[105] Sergeant A.J. Rixon's comrades clearly experienced similar emotions, for on the eve of the Battle of Loos in September 1915 he found them looking forward to the attack and 'all waiting for the time to come when one or two little accounts will be settled'.[106] In the longer term, the need to justify friends' and personal sacrifices reinforced men's will to endure. After many of his best friends had been killed, St Leger, far from becoming pacifist, comforted himself with the thought that 'my company is carrying on the work of Judge, Henry and Denis'.[107] The same mindset was encapsulated in the warning another officer sent to his family in 1916, 'remember that it is only by more sacrifices that we can save the sacrifices of the past two years from having been made in vain'. Casualties, far from sapping combat motivation, actually strengthened survivors' obligation to keep fighting.[108]

Combat did not only affect a man's relationship with his 'primary group' but also with the enemy. Hatred was probably most intense at the beginning of the war. In the British army, the emotion appears to have been a reaction to first-hand evidence of German atrocities in Belgium.[109] On the other side, German troops were convinced that dumdum bullets were being used against them and, after Neuve Chapelle, that treachery on the part of Indian prisoners had caused the British attack to be successful.[110]

104 See, for example, IWM, 82/3/1: J. Fowler, letter to niece and nephew, 2 May 1916; IWM, 69/25/1: G. Donaldson, letter to mother, 13 July 1916; BA-MA Freiburg, MSg 2/ 2735: H. Genscher, letter to father, 20 Dec. 1914; Staatsbib. Berlin, Ms. Germ. fol. 1651: C.F. Müller, diary, 6–7 May 1916 and DTA, 138b: G. Gruber, letter of Girlie to Gia, 18 June 1916.

105 IWM, 79/35/1: E.H. Bennett, letter to wife, 28 Apr. 1918.

106 IWM, 99/13/1: A. Rixon, diary, 23 Sept. 1915. For similar sentiments, see also Private 'Jack' Sweeney's account of bombing a German dugout on the Somme in 1916, reproduced in M. Moynihan (ed.), *Greater Love. Letters Home 1914–1918* (London: W.H. Allen, 1980), p. 79.

107 IWM, P 239: W.B. St Leger, diary, 21 Oct. 1917.

108 IWM, P 317 Con Shelf: H.W. Yoxall, 23 July 1916.

109 See WLHM, RAMC 699 Box 136: C. Chamberlain, diary, 7 Sept. 1914; IWM, 97/4/1: B.C. Myatt, diary, 17 Oct. 1914 and WLHM, RAMC 383 Box 41: H.J.S. Shields, diary, 25 Aug. and 25 Sept. 1914.

110 For dumdum bullets, see BZ, A. Bauer, letter to family, 12 Nov. 1914, BA-MA Freiburg, MSg 2/ 5254: E.W. Küpper, letter to wife, 21 Mar. 1915 and DTA, 262,1: A. Geyer, diary, 29 Aug. 1914. For Neuve Chapelle, see DTA, 262,1: A. Geyer, diary, 9–11 Mar. 1915 and BA-MA Freiburg, MSg 2/ 5254: E.W. Küpper, letter to wife, 23 Mar. 1915.

Under the anonymous conditions of trench warfare, hatred to some extent declined. Most commonly, it manifested itself as a temporary but intense emotion during and after an attack. Assault troops who braved the hail of machinegun fire to reach the enemy trenches were often disinclined to take prisoners. Georg Kirchner was horrified to see one of his men shoot a wounded Frenchman during an attack and Private C.M. Tames witnessed Royal Scots at Ypres in 1915 massacring 300 prisoners, shouting 'Death and Hell to everyone [*sic*] of ye s – '.[111] Howard Panton recorded numerous cases of prisoner killing at Loos later the same year:

> We came across three of our lads who had discovered some Huns in a cellar hiding. One man was fair mad and wanted to bayonet each one as they came up the stair. We held him back for a little but the fourth Hun was a huge chap and as he came up his brains were scattered along the wall by a shot from this chap. The others we eventually disposed of.[112]

In normal trench warfare, however, hatred was less common. As Ashworth has noted, sympathy and even fraternisation became possible between opposing troops.[113] Yet, although the anonymity of the combat was less likely to produce the feelings of animosity inspired by open warfare, it instead encouraged depersonalisation. The descriptions of killing in soldiers' letters rarely identify the enemy as a fellow human being.[114] Yoxall, for example, described in unemotional terms the death of a sniper, whom he located by bisecting the angle of his shots and whom he then dispatched with a mortar bomb. The point of his description lay not in the fact that he had killed a man but in the technical interest of the incident.[115] Howard Panton shot a German officer at Loos simply because he 'did not know what to do with him'.[116] Germans also experienced similar feelings of indifference to the enemy: 'As a soldier, it makes no difference to me whether an armed Russian, Englishman or Frenchman faces me,' observed one man. 'The feeling towards all enemies is the same: they must be annihilated'.[117] Under such

111 DTA, 9/II: G. Kirchner, letter to sister, 10 Nov. 1914 and IWM, 85/1/1: C.M. Tames, letter to sister, no date but probably 1915.
112 IWM, P 262: H. Panton, letter to brother, 29 Sept. 1915.
113 Ashworth, *Trench Warfare*, pp. 24–47 and 129–75.
114 Contrary to Bourke's argument that 'combatants insisted upon emotional relationships and responsibility' with and for their victims, the psychologist J.H. Schultz was told by numerous officers that it was most difficult to kill when the enemy could be identified as an individual human being. See Bourke, *Intimate History of Killing*, p. 6 and J.H. Schultz, 'Einige Bemerkungen über Feindschaftsgefühle im Kriege', *Neurologisches Centralblatt* 34, 11 (1 June 1915), 376.
115 IWM, P 317 Con Shelf: H.W. Yoxall, letter to mother, 5 Feb. 1917.
116 IWM, P 262: H. Panton, letter to brother, 29 Sept. 1915.
117 Volunteer 'H. Th'. quoted in Plaut, 'Psychographie des Kriegers', pp. 12–13.

circumstances, even the humanity of enemy corpses was denied: Ernst Vogt, for example, saw German troops playing around with dead Tommies during the 1918 spring offensive.[118] One of St Leger's brother officers possessed a German skull – 'when he found it it was wearing uniform, and he scraped off the flesh and hair'.[119]

Depersonalisation, especially when combined with the desire for revenge, resulted in prisoner killing becoming a habit for some men. As *Leutnant* Müller approvingly remarked, it was common knowledge that captured Englishmen often '"died" on the Ulan-led transports'.[120] British and Imperial soldiers were also not averse to prisoner killing. In 1917, German authorities compiled eyewitness testimonies of prisoner mistreatment by English and Scottish troops, including accounts of POWs being machinegunned, shot by officers and bayoneted by groups dispatched to kill German wounded lying on the battlefield.[121] Such actions were not only tolerated but sometimes even promoted by army authorities. As early as 21 August 1914, men of the German *58. Brigade* received a verbal order (renewed in writing on 26 August) not to take prisoners in Lorraine.[122] Arthur Wrench recorded that battalion orders before an attack at Third Ypres contained the words '~~NO PRISONERS~~', which, he explained, 'with the line scored through meant "do as you please"'.[123] The inevitable result of this prisoner killing was to further intensify the culture of vengeance at the front. Men of *Infanterie-Regiment Nr. 169*, for example, killed prisoners to avenge one of their wounded NCOs, whom they had seen the British throw into a canal.[124] Wrench and his comrades found the ambiguous order regarding prisoners a 'good joke' precisely because they believed that in a previous attack, surrendering Germans had picked up rifles and shot at Scottish troops from behind.[125] Moreover, the existence of such a culture meant that

[118] BA-MA Freiburg, MSg 1/ 3183: E. Vogt, diary, 5 Apr. 1918.

[119] IWM, P 239: W.B. St Leger, diary, 18 Apr. 1917. For an example of corpse-mutilation by German troops, see also G. Chapman, *A Passionate Prodigality* (Leatherhead: Ashford, Buchan & Enright, 1933, 1993), p. 272.

[120] Staatsbib. Berlin, Ms. Germ. fol. 1651: C.F. Müller, diary, 7 Apr. 1917.

[121] BA-MA Freiburg, PH 2/ 26: Kriegsrechtsverstöße englischer Truppen gegen deutsche Heeresangehörige in der Kampfzone. (Denkschrift über die von der deutschen Untersuchungsbehörde seit Ende des Jahres 1917 neu festgestellten Völkerrechtsverletzungen englischer Truppen), pp. 6–8, 15–16 and 20–1.

[122] Horne and Kramer, *German Atrocities*, p. 194.

[123] IWM, 85/51/1: A.E. Wrench, diary, 19 Sept. 1917. For further examples of prisoner killing see N. Ferguson, 'Prisoner Taking and Prisoner Killing in the Age of Total War. Towards a Political Economy of Military Defeat', *War in History* 11, 2 (April 2004), 157–9.

[124] BA-MA Freiburg, MSg 1/ 2970: H. Fuchs, 26 Jan. 1915.

[125] IWM, 85/51/1: A.E. Wrench, diary, 19 Sept. 1917.

for most of the war, surrender was not an attractive option for any individual who had tired of the fighting. Prisoner-killing stories were propagated by officers seeking to improve their men's combat motivation and some troops firmly believed that all prisoners were killed.[126] Private Jack Ashley, who accidentally walked into enemy lines at the Battle of the Somme, had an unpleasant discussion with a German soldier escorting him to the rear who asserted that the British shot all their prisoners and suggested that the Germans 'ought to do the same'.[127] One *Feldwebel* with whom Yoxall conversed asserted that he had fought until surrounded by six men because 'he had fully believed that the English killed all their prisoners'.[128] British prisoners interrogated by the Germans commonly expressed surprise at not being killed outright and being well handled.[129] In these circumstances, even individuals who were disillusioned with the war and wished to find an escape had little option at the front but to fight.

Active service thus actually strengthened men's will, if not their ability, to endure. The experience of combat could cause men to hate the enemy, seek vengeance or strengthen endurance through the belief that the sacrifices of one's friends had to be justified before fighting could stop. The unwilling were dragged along in the wake of the majority prepared to see the war through to its end. Discipline and personal pride hindered their retreat rearwards. The hatred, distrust or indifference of the enemy made surrender highly dangerous. Supported by living comrades, owing a debt to the dead and lacking any reasonable chance of escape, men continued to fight until death or exhaustion laid them low.

Disillusionment?

The men who fought during the four years of hostilities on the Western Front did so primarily in order to defend their homes and families from invasion by what they perceived to be a dangerous opponent. Army training inculcated obedience to orders and presented troops with new military loyalties, while service at the front gave them even more reason to distrust their enemy, who shot at them, killed their friends and

126 BA-MA Freiburg, PH 3/ 590: Gefangenen-Aussagen, AOK 4: Vernehmung von 3 Mann vom X/E. York R., 92 Brigade 31. Division, 5 Sept. 1918, p. 2.
127 Ashley, *War-Diary*, p. 66.
128 IWM, P 317 Con Shelf: H.W. Yoxall, letter to mother, 30 Sept. 1916.
129 BA-MA Freiburg, PH 3/ 585: Vernehmungsprotokolle, AOK 4: Vernehmung [of man from 20/Royal Fusiliers], 21 Aug. 1917, p. 2; ibid., Vernehmung [of one officer and seven men of 12th Comp. D. Batl., Tank Corps and one officer and three men of 18th Comp., F Batl., Tank Corps], 26 Aug. 1917, p. 6; ibid., Vernehmung [of deserter from 2/Yorkshire Light Infantry], 15 Sept. 1917, p. 3.

Plate 7. Disillusionment? A German protest – the placard reads: 'we didn't want the war'. The reference here may be to the Kaiser's pronouncement on 31 July 1915 'I didn't want the war' and the composition – including a donkey and an ox – suggests that the photographer's intention was not to flatter. Detail from a German photograph (anonymous).

sometimes even mutilated the dead. There are, however, good indications that in fact combat motivation decreased in the trenches. Tony Ashworth has drawn attention to the frequent 'live and let live' truces which took place in quieter parts of the line. In his opinion, only the machinations of high commands in organising raids and posting aggressive specialists to the line stopped these understandings from flowering into greater trust and sympathy between opponents.[130] Worse still, according to Eric Leed, 'familiarity with combat distanced the individual from the purpose and the significance of the project in which he was engaged'.[131] Men became disillusioned with their governments, war aims and, perhaps worst of all, the civilians whom they were protecting. Demands for peace increased during the war. How can this be squared

[130] Ashworth, *Trench Warfare*, pp. 160–70 and 176–203.
[131] Leed, *No Man's Land*, p. 132.

with the notion that experience of active service actually increased combat motivation?

Undoubtedly, a key factor undermining men's willingness to continue was fatigue. The physical demands of active service, the long periods away from home and the mental strain of taking constant risks and coping with the death of friends resulted in the increase of 'war-weariness'. The letters of men facing continuous strain at the front unsurprisingly demonstrate a gradually intensifying wish for relief. Heinrich Genscher, for example, after almost two and a half years of active service, had lost his earlier idealism and was asking resentfully, 'when will this world war come to an end? – I ask myself again once more!! Too stupid!!'[132] Kurt Reiter, who in 1915 had also entered the army enthusiastically, remarked cynically two years later that the average veteran 'no longer sees why one should die the "hero's death" (*Heldentod*)'.[133] Any enthusiasm for war felt by Wilhelm Lüthje had finally disappeared after four years at the front: 'now one does his duty for the sake of duty'.[134] And many other men would have agreed with Heinrich Anthes, who in May 1918 exclaimed, 'if only the war would finally finish; it's now already been four years, which is really rather a lot'.[135] Not only cumulative strain but also particularly stressful or horrible incidents could cause outbursts of frustration with the conflict or its causes. After watching the Germans shell one of their own military graveyards at Beaumont Hamel in November 1916, Private Arthur Wrench, a Territorial soldier, remarked that 'it strikes me there is not much glory these days in dying for your country'.[136] Dislike of the war did not need very long to develop: it only required one week of fighting the Russians in East Prussia to prompt Gustav Klein to remark, 'the war is terrible as the heaven-sent plague'.[137] After only two months at the front, Edward Chapman admitted, 'I hate all this war business from the bottom of my soul'.[138] For men who had not really wished to enlist, experience of active service simply made them more despondent. A good example of how their rejection of the war became more extreme the longer hostilities lasted can be seen in the letters of *Gefreiter* Kurt Beier. Already unenthused at the prospect of military service in August 1914, by October he was wondering, 'wie lange dieser Käse noch dauern wird' ('how long this cheese will

[132] BA-MA Freiburg, MSg 2/ 2735: H. Genscher, letter to father, 1 Feb. 1917.
[133] BA-MA Freiburg, MSg 1/ 161: K. Reiter, diary, 23 June 1917.
[134] BA-MA Freiburg, MSg 2/ 2797: W. Lüthje, diary, 26 Aug. 1918.
[135] Private Collection (Author): H. Anthes, letter to D. Anthes, 24 May 1918.
[136] IWM, 85/51/1: A.E. Wrench, diary, 16 Nov. 1916.
[137] BA-MA Freiburg, MSg 2/ 3788: G. Klein, letter to parents, 31 Aug. 1914.
[138] IWM, 92/3/1: E.F. Chapman, letter to mother, 27 Aug. 1916.

still last') and reporting that 'wir haben naturlich [*sic*] alle so satt bis obenrauf' ('we are naturally totally fed up with it all'). One year later, disgust with the war had become such that Beier and his comrades were referring to it as 'der alte Kotz' ('the old vomit'). By the winter of 1916 it had become a 'Trauerspiel' ('sorrow game') and Beier was complaining that 'diese[r] elend[e] Kotz . . . hangt einem so sehr zum Halse heraus das manns gründlich satt hatt [*sic*]' ('I'm utterly sick of this miserable vomit'). Finally, in early 1917 a further escalation in Beier's vocabulary took place when the war became an 'Elende Schwindel' ('miserable swindle').[139]

Beier's use of the word *Schwindel* was neither coincidental nor unique, but rather a reflection of the growing unpopularity of those perceived to be prolonging the war.[140] Not only the horror on the Western Front but also disillusionment with official war aims and the people they were protecting prompted men to hope for peace. The idealistic causes in which they had believed when they first entered the trenches lost their sheen under active service conditions. Contact with Belgian and French peasants robbed British wartime volunteers of their illusions of romantically wronged Gallic heroines. As one man remarked in February 1917, 'the people here don't half rob you. I reckon we would all join again if there was a war with France'.[141] On both sides, suspicion grew that politicians and profiteers were prolonging the war for their own benefit. Wrench complained in April 1917 about 'unscrupulous politicians and munition [*sic*] makers who urge on the war to their own profit and ends without the necessity of having to engage in it themselves'.[142] Bitterness against *Wucherer* and *Kriegsgewinnler* (profiteers) was still more widespread among German soldiers, particularly in 1917 and 1918.[143] Moreover, unlike in Britain, where criticism remained directed primarily against economic targets, political discontent also became manifest

139 Private Collection (Author): K. Beier, letters to wife, 5 Oct. 1914, 9 Sept. 1915, 11 Dec. 1916 and 25 Jan. 1917.

140 Indeed, according to Klemperer, the use of the word *Schwindel* to describe the war was widespread among German soldiers already at the beginning of 1916. See Klemperer, *Curriculum Vitae*, II, pp. 410, 426 and 448.

141 IWM, 84/46/1: M. Hardie, Report on Complaints, Moral, etc., 1 May 1917, pp. 3–4.

142 IWM, 85/51/1: A.E. Wrench, diary, 10 Apr. 1917. Cf. BA-MA Freiburg, PH 3/ 585: Vernehmungsprotokolle, AOK 4: Vernehmung [of man from 13/Royal Sussex], 2 Sept. 1917, p. 3.

143 See the letter of Richard Schiller dated 13 Oct. 1915 reproduced in Ulrich and Ziemann (eds.), *Frontalltag*, pp. 66–7 and BA-MA Freiburg, W-10/ 50794: Postüberwachung der *5. Armee*. 12 July 1917, p. 15, 28 Sept. 1917, p. 24 and Aug. 1918, p. 78. Also, A. Reimann, *Der große Krieg der Sprachen. Untersuchungen zur historischen Semantik in Deutschland und England zur Zeit des Ersten Weltkriegs* (Essen: Klartext, 2000), p. 281.

among sections of the German army. Countrymen were alienated from their leaders when their wives told them of compulsory food seizures from their farms, while class hostility increased among townsmen and industrial workers. As the Berliner Franz Brussig, for example, remarked with bitterness in the spring of 1916:

> Why are people still being led like flocks of sheep to the slaughter? We all know today that we are being sacrificed for the interests of a clique. We fight for the Prussian *Junker* economy, for the old nobility which has decided to stir up the entire world against us ... This clique has become the ruin of the German people.[144]

Discontent and suspicion grew to the extent that it was suggested that the war had been begun by crowned heads of state in order to annihilate troublesome and disloyal subjects. Annexationist ambitions on the part of the high command did little to alleviate the anger of soldiers who suspected that their lives were being placed in jeopardy by an irresponsible political elite intent on self-enrichment.[145]

Alienation also spread among soldiers due to perceived civilian insensitivity, selfishness or incomprehension of their ordeal. Newspapers aroused considerable ire when they presented soldiers living comfortably or portrayed useless loss as heroic sacrifice. Recounting the bombing of a munitions and petrol dump, in which eighteen men had lost their lives, Seligmann Scheer, for example, remarked bitterly, 'our newspapers write nothing about it; they write only what the German population wants to hear'.[146] Everth observed that propaganda showing soldiers leading easy lives had created 'much bad blood in the field' and Moran too considered the practice of 'cooking' news to have been 'a prime factor in unsettling opinion in France'.[147] Direct contact with civilians wishing to hear tales of heroism in the trenches from those that had experienced combat also aggravated soldiers: to Wrench such people were 'darned fools' who behaved 'as if I had no right to forget about [the front] for the time being'.[148] Although worried about his family when news of the

144 Staatsbib. Berlin, Ms. Boruss. fol. 1084: F. Brussig, diary, 29 Mar. 1916. For countrymen's anger at confiscations, see, for example, Private Collection (Author): K. Beier, letter to wife, 25 July 1917.

145 Staatsbib. Berlin, Ms. Boruss. fol. 1084: F. Brussig, diary, 29 Mar. 1916. For German soldiers' disapproval of annexations, see Ziemann, *Front*, p. 173.

146 BA-MA Freiburg, MSg 2/ 4470: S. Scheer, letter to friend, 20 Apr. 1915.

147 Everth, *Seele des Soldaten*, p. 17 and Moran, *Anatomy*, pp. 66–8. Cf. also IWM, P 317 Con Shelf: H.W. Yoxall, letter to father, 22 Sept. 1916 and IWM, 92/3/1: E.F. Chapman, letter to mother, 7 May 1917.

148 IWM, 85/51/1: A.E. Wrench, diary, 16 Dec. 1916. Cf. Everth, *Seele des Soldaten*, pp. 29–30.

bombing of his home town, Karlsruhe, reached him, *Leutnant* Albert Just was nonetheless of the opinion that:

It does quite a large number of stirrers, Philistines and armchair strategists a bit of good to hear how a mine sounds close up once in a while, so that they learn to control their impatience for new advances at the front and so that they get an idea of what it means to stand for months and years even in so-called 'quiet sectors', which still every single day get their portion of heavy and lighter shells, never mind rifle grenades and infantry fire.[149]

Anger that their sacrifice was not being adequately recognised by the home front grew among combatants. As Dr Karl Kießler, having survived service at Verdun, remarked bitterly in a letter home, 'when you write that no one could thank us enough for what we have been through, you are completely correct. No, one can't do it; but even if one could do it, one wouldn't do it'.[150]

The disgruntlement and war-weariness felt by soldiers, however, by no means automatically translated themselves into a rejection of the war. On the contrary, criticism on both sides was generally aimed not against the war itself but against those people who were perceived to be prolonging it unnecessarily or behaving inappropriately for wartime. It was for this reason that profiteers, newspapers and civilians trivialising the war were such widespread targets of aggression. This attitude is also implicit in much other rhetoric. Brussig, for example, condemned the *Junker* not because of their nationalist aggression but rather because he perceived them as unpatriotic: 'they have no feeling for the common wellbeing and they acknowledge a Fatherland only in so far that they as nobles can occupy the first place in the same'.[151] Graffiti found on leave trains in 1917 reflected similar sentiments, proclaiming 'down with the Kaiser who is guilty for the whole world war and has no notion of discipline'.[152] Although men expressed hatred of the war, they nonetheless continued to justify their participation in it. Despite his anger at politicians and profiteers and his severe doubts about the glory of dying for one's country, Arthur Wrench could still observe in April 1917 that 'we suffer ... willingly because we think we are doing a right thing in fighting for our country'.[153] Contrary to the popular

[149] Private Collection (Author): A.H. Just, letter to wife, 26 June 1916. Cf. BA-MA Freiburg, MSg 2/ 2797: W. Lüthje, diary, 3 Aug. 1918.
[150] BA-MA Freiburg, MSg 2/ 5460: K. Kießler, letter to family(?), 12 Nov. 1916.
[151] Staatsbib. Berlin, Ms. Boruss. fol. 1084: F. Brussig, diary, 29 Mar. 1916.
[152] GLA Karlsruhe, 456 F 8 /260: Eisenbahnüberwachungsreisen, Stellvertretendes Generalkommando des X. Armeekorps, 30 Mar. 1917.
[153] IWM, 85/51/1: A.E. Wrench, diary, 9 Apr. 1917.

Plate 8. Faith (1): 'Pals'. Far from having little idea of why they were fighting, many combatants possessed a very strong belief in the righteousness of their cause. From the diary of Arthur Wrench.

view that most soldiers had little notion of why they were fighting, the letters and diaries of men, and even more so officers, demonstrate that many were very aware. That Wrench remained certain of the justice of Britain's cause is indicated by a picture, drawn by him in November 1917, portraying the Kaiser linking arms with the devil paddling through a stream. The waves of the stream make the shapes 'Neutrality', 'Europe' and 'Treaties' and the Kaiser holds a bowl in which two fish marked 'Belgium' and Serbia' are imprisoned (see Plate 8).[154] On the other side, Hans Muhsal expressed discontent at 'the fantastic imbecility' of the war, yet left no doubt as to who he held responsible for the continuance of the conflagration, complaining that 'England leads the whole bunch around by the nose'.[155] In the second half of the war, British conscripts, whose combat motivation was often unfavourably compared with that of the earlier volunteers, still sang about 'a-marching and a-fighting in the good old British way'.[156] While the overblown patriotic language sometimes heard in 1914 became rarer, the fact that calls for an unconditional peace only became widespread in the German army during the second half of 1918 and never seriously affected the British army, confirms that for most of the war, the majority of soldiers believed their fight to be worthwhile.[157]

Propaganda played a crucial role in encouraging this perception. If the defence of Belgium was not the primary reason why British men had enlisted, it nonetheless remains true that the reports of German atrocities quashed liberal ambivalence about the war and spread fear of the consequences of an invasion. The adoption of idealistic war aims, namely, the restoration of Belgium, French security against aggression, guarantees of the independence of small states and the destruction of Prussian militarism, were actually more aggressive than Germany's officially defensive stance.[158] As such, they left little scope for anything other than complete victory, whereas Germany's more ambiguous goals prompted demands for compromise and a negotiated peace in the *Reichstag* and among soldiers. Moreover, while few soldiers could have necessarily recounted the aims exactly, knowledge that they were fighting for some sort of idealism provided men with, as Procter put it, 'the conviction that they were not being sold'.[159] The dissemination of atrocity propaganda playing on outrages such as German unrestricted submarine warfare and the sinking of the *Lusitania*, the naval bombardment

154 Ibid., cartoon, 8 Nov. 1917.
155 BA-MA Freiburg, H. Muhsal, diary, 11 Jan. 1917.
156 'The Last Long Mile' reproduced in R. Palmer, '*What a Lovely War*'. *British Soldiers' Songs from the Boer War to the Present Day* (London: Michael Joseph, 1990), pp. 122–3.
157 See BA-MA Freiburg, W-10/ 50794: Postüberwachung der *5. Armee*. 17 Oct. 1918, p. 106.
158 V.H. Rothwell, *British War Aims and Peace Diplomacy 1914–1918* (Oxford: Clarendon Press, 1971), p. 19.
159 Procter, 'Motives', 43

of British towns, Zeppelin raids on London, the executions of Nurse Cavell and Captain Fryatt and the 1917 reports of a 'corpse-conversion factory' all reinforced the stereotype of Germany's barbarity.[160] Procter recalled that 'stories of atrocities were propagated until the whole army … was aflame with indiscriminate hatred of everything German'.[161] Officers, in particular, whose grasp of political news was generally better than that of their men, maintained a deep distrust of the other side's intentions. Some British officers, for example, believed that the Germans were attempting to annex Calais in order to launch an attack on their homeland.[162]

Britain relied primarily on newspapers in order to send soldiers its propaganda message. Although troops did receive lectures on war aims from their officers from 1915, no systematic programme of propaganda was established before the final year of the war. Until March 1918, the BEF's official programme of propaganda consisted solely of twenty lecturers circulating behind the lines speaking to the troops. Thereafter, one full-time education officer was appointed to each army, divisional and base headquarters and a part-time officer was selected from the staff of each brigade.[163] German leaders had perhaps rather more explaining to do, having initiated the war and then turned a host of foreign powers against their country. Initially, the Kaiser and his government blamed Russia for the outbreak of hostilities, but as the war lasted longer, much of their venom was directed towards Britain, who, it was claimed, had willed the war due to Germany's growing economic dominance. A view of 'England' as the perfidious keystone of the Entente, bankrolling other countries in the attack on the *Kaiserreich*, was widely absorbed by

160 The 'corpse-conversion factory' was supposed to be a facility producing war commodities, such as soap, from the bodies of dead men. The idea derived from the misunderstanding of a Berlin newspaper article and a subsequent report in *The Times*. See Sanders and Taylor, *British Propaganda*, pp. 146–7. Not everyone was disgusted by it, as a note from Lieutenant St Leger's diary proves: 'Mumford said last night that the Irish [Guards] were arranging to write to the "Daily Mail" supporting the Huns' practice of making oil, glycerine and hog's food from human bodies . . ., saying that if their bodies could be of any use to England for munitions-making, and that each of their bodies could supply the ingredients to make a shell which would kill several Germans, they were quite willing for their bodies to be used for that purpose were they killed in action'. IWM, P 239: W.B. St Leger, diary, 25 Apr. 1917.

161 Procter, 'Motives', 42. German prisoner interrogations broadly confirm this statement. See BA-MA Freiburg, PH 3/ 556: AOK 2, 'Aus Unterhaltung mit gefangenen Engländern', 10 Sept. 1916.

162 BA-MA Freiburg, PH3/ 585: Vernehmungsprotokolle, AOK 4: Vernehmung [of one officer and seven men of 12th Comp. D. Batl., Tank Corps and one officer and three men of 18th Comp. F. Batl., Tank Corps]. 26 Aug. 1917, p. 6.

163 MacKenzie, 'Morale and the Cause', pp. 217–25.

middle-class men and officers.[164] The leitmotif of a defensive conflict was also continually emphasised and in the early war years seems to have been extremely successful, for throughout 1915 it stamped the fighting songs of the German army.[165] Failure to outline explicit war aims and, in particular, the government's ambiguity over the question of annexations later created unease, however. In order to contain the growing demands for a negotiated peace, the *OHL* set up a propaganda programme, *Vaterländischer Unterricht* (Patriotic Instruction), in mid-September 1917, which spent the rest of the war warning soldiers about the dreadful consequences of failing to obtain total victory.[166]

Debate has raged about the effectiveness of *Vaterländischer Unterricht*. Ziemann has suggested that it failed in the face of the organisers' incompetence and troops' apathy. Certainly, it is true that the dedication with which it was carried out varied between armies and the fact that compulsory lectures impinged on soldiers' badly needed rest periods did little to increase their popularity. However, it is clear that considerable thought was invested in the programme and it is rash simply to dismiss it out of hand. Soldiers were given the chance to discuss worries and grievances. Far from being rigid and official, company evenings were organised in which free beer helped to gain listeners' attention and goodwill. The message of the programme, that the only peace possible was that of total victory, was also relayed through innovative techniques: cinema pictures showing city and landscapes from Germany were particularly effective in reminding soldiers why they were fighting. Indeed, if the programme was successful, it was because from the beginning it identified the main source of its audience's combat motivation. As guidelines for organising the course emphasised in November 1917, 'everyone must hear time and again that in the case of an enemy victory not only the farther and nearer homeland but he himself and his relatives are lost'.[167] It thus seems reasonable to conclude that the programme in fact

[164] See, for example, BA-MA Freiburg, MSg 1/ 1383: F.O. Nawrath, letter to parents, 24 Jan. 1915; BA-MA Freiburg, MSg 1/ 161: K. Reiter, diary, 28 Aug. 1916; BA-MA Freiburg, MSg 1/ 3109: H. Muhsal, diary, 25 Aug. 1915, 11 Jan. 1917 and 16 Apr. 1917 and Staatsbib. Berlin, Ms. Germ. fol. 1651: C.F. Müller, diary, 26 Apr. 1917. For official and press hostility to England, see M. Stibbe, *German Anglophobia and the Great War, 1914–1918* (Cambridge University Press, 2001), particularly pp. 10–48.

[165] Schuhmacher, *Leben und Seele*, p. 29.

[166] See A.K. Rice, 'Morale and Defeatism in the Bavarian "Heer und Heimat" in the First World War (1916–18)' unpublished M.Phil. thesis, University of Oxford (2004), p. 55. For details of this programme, see also Ziemann, *Front*, pp. 128–33 and Lipp, *Meinungslenkung*, pp. 62–84.

[167] BA-MA Freiburg, PH 5 IV/ 2: Leitsätze für den Vaterländischen Unterricht der Armee-Abteilung A, 15 Nov. 1917, pp. 5–6. Cf. Rice, 'Morale and Defeatism', pp. 58–9. For the cinematic propaganda, see Lipp, *Meinungslenkung*, pp. 82–3.

'helped bring about the surprising successes in the spring offensive of 1918' and 'helped to keep a lid on the simmering troubles' in the German homeland.[168]

Perhaps more important in persuading soldiers that fighting was worthwhile, was that ultimately they had little choice and needed to justify both past sacrifices and future actions. L.F. Richardson, a veteran and amateur psychologist, attributed the ability of the two armies, each convinced of the justice of its cause, to fight for four years 'to the unifying attribute of the human mind, which tends to make people believe statements which harmonize with the course of action in which they are engaged'.[169] This notion is supported by modern psychological research, which has observed that humans 'seek information that is consistent with their own views, and discount disconfirming information'.[170] The death, horror and hardships at the front reinforced this tendency: men desperately declared that 'I really do feel that I am lucky to be here, and that after all it's something beside beastly slaughter'.[171] Under such circumstances, propaganda which could provide meaning to both past and future sacrifices was eagerly accepted. As Yoxall observed, 'one must at least believe that we are fighting for something or else the whole ghoulish business becomes so preposterously criminal that one couldn't carry on'.[172]

Finally, and crucially, the fear of invasion which had propelled most men towards recruiting officers or caused them to obey mobilisation orders did not cease to be emotive at the front. Families provided essential moral and emotional support for soldiers: 'You wouldn't believe how the consciousness of your love, of the harmony between our hearts and souls, strengthens me and makes me feel cheerfully confident in this dreaded war din,' wrote Eugen Küpper to his family.[173] 'I am always delighted to get your letters, far more so than ever before,' observed Rowland Owen from the front to his parents.[174] 'I really don't care about

[168] Respectively, J. Förster, 'Ludendorff and Hitler in Perspective. The Battle for the German Soldier's Mind, 1917–1944', *War in History* 10, 3 (July 2003), 326 and Rice, 'Morale and Defeatism', p. 64.

[169] Richardson, *Mathematical Psychology of War*, p. 14.

[170] This is known as the 'Confirmation Bias' heuristic. The 'Availability' heuristic, which affects memory, making pleasant memories easier to recall than unpleasant ones, may also have played a role in maintaining soldiers' conviction in their national cause. See W.A. Wagenaar, *Paradoxes of Gambling Behaviour* (London: Lawrence Erlbaum Associates, 1988), pp. 107–9.

[171] IWM, 87/8/1: R.P. Hamilton, letter to cousin, 5 June 1915.

[172] IWM, P 317 Con Shelf: H.W. Yoxall, letter to mother, 30 Jan. 1917.

[173] BA-MA Freiburg, MSg 2/ 5254: E.W. Küpper, letter to wife, 23 Mar. 1915.

[174] IWM, 90/37/1: R.H. Owen, letter to parents, 24 Sept. 1914.

general news very much just now, I am too busy. All I want to know is about what is going on at home,' Edward Chapman told his mother.[175] At all periods of the war, regardless of their disillusionment with political leaders, the thought of parents, wives, children or girlfriends strengthened soldiers' will to fight. In the survey of German soldiers' coping strategies undertaken by Ludwig during the conflict, patriotism was hardly mentioned but thoughts of home and family were cited no less than sixty-five times as a crucial source of support in danger.[176] Küpper was perhaps most explicit when he told his family, 'I live and fight for you' but other soldiers thought exactly the same way: *Leutnant* Müller, for example, reminded his troops at Christmas 1917 that they were still fighting in the fourth year of hostilities 'so that our homeland is preserved and our relatives are protected'.[177] Unlike more conventional patriotism, which could seem to lose its relevance in the horror of the trenches, the need to protect one's family never lost its appeal. Throughout the war, German soldiers, their own border only a short distance behind them, had only to look over the parapet to remind themselves why they were fighting: 'only one who knows the fate of the occupied territories and sees the ruins can grasp how much the homeland has to thank us field soldiers', was a commonly expressed sentiment.[178] Despite the relative safety of their families, British soldiers were also motivated by such thoughts. Even men who professed no longer to possess 'an ounce of what we call patriotism', nonetheless asserted to families and sweethearts that 'it's just the thought of you all over there – you who love me & trust me to do my share in the job that is necessary for your safety and freedom . . . that keeps me going & enables me to "stick it" '.[179] This simple thought lay at the heart of British and German combat motivation and it made both armies virtually indestructible.

Active service, therefore, did little to disillusion soldiers. On both sides most joined the army with the simple motive of defending their

[175] IWM, 92/3/1: E.F. Chapman, letter to mother, 13 Aug. 1916. For similar statements, see BA-MA Freiburg, MSg 1/ 1383: F.O. Nawrath, letter to parents, 11 Jan. 1915; IWM, 69/25/1: G. Donaldson, letter to parents, 13 July 1916; IWM, 82/26/1: A.R. Williams, letter to family, 17 Aug. 1916 and BA-MA Freiburg, MSg 2/ 5460: K. Kießler, letter to Sassner family, 27 Sept. 1916.

[176] Ludwig, 'Psychologie der Furcht', p. 163.

[177] BA-MA Freiburg, MSg 2/ 5254: E.W. Küpper, letter to wife, 25 Mar. 1915 and Staatsbib. Berlin, Ms. Germ. fol. 1651: C.F. Müller, diary, 13 Jan. 1918.

[178] BA-MA Freiburg, W-10/ 50794: Postüberwachung der *5. Armee*, 24 Feb. 1918, p. 65. Cf. Private Collection (Author): K. Beier, letter to wife, 26 Oct. 1914; DTA, 9/II: G. Kirchner, letter to sister, 2 Nov. 1914 and BA-MA Freiburg, MSg 1/ 161: K. Reiter, diary, 20 June 1916. Also TNA, WO 157/ 6: Annexe to [GHQ] Summary, 11 Apr. 1916 and Kruse, *Krieg und nationale Integration*, p. 189.

[179] IWM, 93/20/1: D.L. Rowlands, letter to girlfriend, 5 Feb. 1918.

homes and loved ones from an enemy they were told was ruthless. Combat did little to change this view: the wasted landscape of no-man's-land and the threat to personal safety presented by the men opposite did nothing except confirm that the enemy was highly dangerous. Friends' deaths could provoke hatred and revenge in the short term; over longer periods, they reinforced survivors' determination to endure in order to make the sacrifice worthwhile. War-weariness caused by physical exhaustion, homesickness and exposure to constant risk provoked soldiers to criticise profiteers and governments believed to be prolonging the war unnecessarily. On neither side, however, did talk of peace at any price set in while a chance of winning complete victory remained. The long duration of the conflict, the extreme hazards and discomforts endured by men and the dedication with which both armies fought, testify not only to the success with which armies were able to coerce and support their soldiers but above all to men's initial determination and continued conviction to see the fight through.

3 Self-deception and survival: mental coping strategies

Adaptation

Human resilience lay at the heart of the robustness displayed by the German and British armies on the Western Front between 1914 and 1918. Military institutions certainly enforced unit cohesion at the front, while societal and battlefield influences may have encouraged men to accept that fighting was necessary. Yet without individuals' innate ability to cope psychologically with the discomfort, danger and, above all, disempowerment of combat, armies would soon have become ineffective organisations full of mentally broken men. The low rates of psychiatric disorders and common displays of astounding endurance witnessed at the front testify, however, to men's success at overcoming unprecedentedly stressful conditions. As the psychiatrist Frederick Dillon observed, 'it was an impressive fact in the great war [*sic*] to note the extent to which the ordinary man was capable of adapting himself to active war conditions'.[1]

At the heart of men's adaptation lay the development of appropriate risk-assessment strategies. Soldiers who underestimated or were unable to recognise mortal threat could be overconfident and lose their lives through carelessness. Overestimation of danger could, however, be no less problematic, engendering unnecessary fear and anxiety which might result in panic or mental collapse. Troops new to the front were especially inclined to assess risk inappropriately. On both sides, wartime recruit training was short and often of poor quality.[2] Men consequently arrived in the line with an ignorance of the power of modern weaponry

[1] F. Dillon, 'Neuroses among Combatant Troops in the Great War', *British Medical Journal* (8 July 1939), 66.

[2] In the British army by the end of 1915, recruits received between twelve and fourteen weeks' training before being sent to a base camp in France. Wartime German training consisted of eight (twelve from February 1918) weeks' instruction at home followed by a period of at least one month in a recruit depot behind the lines. See Simkins, *Kitchener's Army*, p. 313, BA-MA Freiburg, W-10/ 50755: untitled *Reichsarchiv* historical work on training, pp. 18–19 and TNA, WO 157/ 197: Annexe to Fourth Army Summary, 17 Aug. 1918.

which today seems astounding. One British soldier, for example, described shells as being at first 'quite a novelty' and didn't feel frightened because 'I didn't know anything about them'.[3] Such naivety could lead to inappropriate or dangerous behaviour: another man recorded that on first coming under shellfire, he and his company 'didn't realise at first the danger we were in, and stood up and laughed at the thing'. Only when one shell burst over another company, killing two of his comrades, did the event become 'a very pannicky [*sic*] experience'.[4] Insufficient preparation was only one cause of recruits' complacency. Fear of being thought afraid and having their manhood questioned could prompt men to take unnecessary risks, often with fatal consequences. Officers were particularly prone to such behaviour: one of Lieutenant Edward Chapman's colleagues, for example, was a 'quite fearless' subaltern, who 'would not take any notice of flares or snipers, and was shot dead, the bullet going from ear to ear'.[5]

Other untried soldiers displayed intense fear. A study of British troops fighting in Salonika found that signs of nervousness, including 'palpitation, nightmare and broken sleep', were common even before the baptism of fire.[6] New men walked stooped in quiet sectors, ducked constantly and experienced great anxiety: Ernst Huthmacher described his first five days at the front as 'horrendous' and told his wife, 'I know now what mortal fear means'.[7] If the baptism occurred in heavy action, feelings of fear or panic were still more extreme. Private D.L. Rowlands, who had the misfortune to experience shellfire first during the Third Battle of Ypres, admitted to being 'absolutely frightened to death!' during the ordeal.[8] After such a scare, initial nervousness often receded slowly: the psychologist Charles Bird observed that 'for weeks the men suffer from intense fright as comrades are killed or horribly mutilated'.[9] Chapman admitted that this initial period 'nearly broke me'.[10] Some soldiers did indeed prove unable to cope. Robert Gaupp, a German psychiatrist attached to *XIII. Armeekorps*, observed that for some individuals, 'a single experience of horror ... cleared the way for psychotraumatic symptoms'.[11] Research undertaken on Bavarian

[3] IWM, Misc 99 Item 1515: Diary of unknown soldier, 21 Nov. 1915.
[4] IWM, 84/22/1: B.O. Dewes, 27 Nov. 1914.
[5] IWM, 92/3/1: E.F. Chapman, letter to mother, 27 Aug. 1916. Cf. the statement of Sir John Goodwin in *RWOCIS*, p. 13 and Scholz, *Seelenleben*, p. 128.
[6] See *RWOCIS*, p. 202.
[7] DTA, 930: E. Huthmacher, letter to wife, 12 Mar. 1915. Cf. Ludwig, 'Psychologie der Furcht', p. 137 and IWM, 92/3/1: E.F. Chapman, letter to mother, 20 Aug. 1916.
[8] IWM, 93/20/1: D.L. Rowlands, letter to girlfriend, 5 Feb. 1918.
[9] Bird, 'From Home to the Charge', 333.
[10] IWM, 92/3/1: E.F. Chapman, letter to mother, 14 Feb. 1917.
[11] Gaupp, 'Schreckneurosen', p. 72.

psychiatric casualties found that most men suffering from hysterical disorders had collapsed during their first experience of war.[12]

In order to survive the front both mentally and physically, soldiers thus had to learn to judge risk without being overwhelmed by it. Contemporaries reported that newly drafted troops often exhibited curiosity, indicative of an attempt to gather information about their environment and respond to it.[13] Gradually, they habituated to the frightening sights and noises of the front and developed what Franz Schauwecker, an ex-front officer turned amateur psychologist, termed *Dickfälligkeit* (thick-skinnedness).[14] Skills useful for survival were acquired, principally the ability to distinguish the size and direction of shells from their sounds, which according to the ex-officer and psychologist Paul Plaut normally took between one and two months to develop.[15] He also thought that men gradually learnt to view the landscape from the perspective of how it might help them survive: 'every depression or elevation is immediately considered from a utilitarian standpoint and afterwards used', he wrote.[16] Such skill not only provided soldiers with the knowledge necessary to counter imminent mortal threat but also increased their ability to operate effectively on the battlefield by raising their self-confidence. It was calmness and self-control in peril which, according to Plaut, distinguished the well-adjusted veteran from the naive recruit: 'even in the moment of direct, imminent danger', he wrote, 'an almost unexplainable sang-froid and emotional intransigence makes itself noticeable'. Soldiers' testimonies concur. In an emergency, as Private William Tait observed, 'only the old hands really kept their heads'. While other troops 'got the wind up a good bit', experienced soldiers would be 'watching each shell, predicting where it would fall & then scuttling'.[17]

As soldiers developed greater awareness of danger, they became more fatalistic about the possible consequences of their risk-taking. In a survey of German combatants' coping strategies undertaken by the psychologist Walter Ludwig, 44 of the 200 men questioned reported that they or their

[12] Weiler, *Nervöse und seelische Störungen*, p. 190.

[13] See Scholz, *Seelenleben*, p. 128 and Ludwig, 'Psychologie der Furcht', p. 155. For combatants' testimonies reporting curiosity see, for example, IWM, 69/25/1: G. Donaldson, letter to mother, 31 May 1916; IWM, 96/29/1: S.A. Knight, letter to girlfriend, 27 Feb. 1915 and IWM, P 239: W.B. St Leger, diary, 27 Sept. 1916.

[14] Schauwecker, *Im Todesrachen*, p. 12.

[15] Plaut, 'Psychographie des Kriegers', p. 31.

[16] Plaut, 'Prinzipien und Methoden', 650.

[17] Plaut, 'Psychographie des Kriegers', pp. 24–5 and IWM, PP/MCR/161: W.H. Tait, diary, 2 Nov. 1914. Second World War studies also support these observations. See Stouffer *et al.*, *American Soldier*, II, pp. 283–4.

comrades adopted this mindset at the front.[18] Letters and diaries also testify to the widespread adoption of fatalism, particularly in extreme adversity. 'One becomes a fatalist. If it comes, it comes,' wrote *Leutnant* Wilhelm Lüthje, serving in the German army's final traumatic retreat.[19] 'I think we are all Fatalists here believing in the preordained order of things,' observed Private Arthur Wrench on the other side one year earlier.[20] As *Leutnant* Hans Muhsal found, there were two routes to this state of mind: 'either one is completely dulled or he has just come to terms with the fact that the trouble must come again'.[21] Men noted that 'one seems to lose all depth of feeling and take things just as they come out here', yet they also attempted to cultivate fatalism by repressing disturbing thoughts or memories.[22] On both sides, soldiers agreed that 'if you did ruminate much on the real meaning of the things you do and the things that are done to you, your nerves would crack in no time' and correspondingly became 'determined to forget'.[23] They avoided 'telling the worst part of this war' in their letters and instead, particularly on the British side of the lines, used euphemisms such as 'knocked out' or a 'trying time' to avoid acknowledging traumatic or painful facts.[24]

Often fatalism was skewed: Plaut referred to the 'elation of being able to die in the middle of wanting to live' and Captain H.W. Yoxall similarly found that in the trenches 'while life becomes more desirable death seems less terrible'.[25] Under such circumstances, a certain amount of indifference to death could be a blessing, negating some fear which would otherwise have caused great mental strain. The middle path between excessive anxiety and total indifference was, however, difficult to maintain. As Ludwig observed, 'the impression [of fatalism] is often so strong or of such long influence that the will to live is crushed and makes way for a mindless apathy and resignation'.[26] Men could enter a state

18 Ludwig, 'Psychologie der Furcht', pp. 168–9 and 172.
19 BA-MA Freiburg, MSg 2/ 2797: W. Lüthje, diary, 3 Oct. 1918.
20 IWM, 85/51/1: A.E. Wrench, diary, 25 Oct. 1917.
21 BA-MA Freiburg, MSg 1/ 3109: H. Muhsal, diary, 5 Feb. 1917.
22 IWM, P 317 Con Shelf: H.W. Yoxall, letter to parents, 25 Dec. 1916. Cf. IWM, 87/56/1: O.H. Best, letter / diary, 2 Oct. 1914.
23 Respectively, IWM, P 317 Con Shelf: H.W. Yoxall, letter to family, 1 June 1916 and IWM, 82/26/1: A.R. Williams, letter to Dolly Gray, 31 Dec. 1915. Cf. IWM, 83/6/1: V.S. Braund, letter to brother, 2 July 1915.
24 IWM, 97/37/1: A. Cornfoot, letter to Winnie, 3 Sept. 1915. For euphemisms see IWM, Con Shelf: R.P. Harker, letter to Ethel, 16 Dec. 1914; IWM, P 317 Con Shelf: H.W. Yoxall, letter to mother, 18 June 1916; IWM, 85/51/1: A.E. Wrench, diary, 14 Nov. 1916 and 9 Apr. 1917 and IWM, 92/3/1: E.F. Chapman, letter to mother, undated but written between 28 and 30 April 1917. Also, Fussell, *Great War*, pp. 174–87.
25 Plaut, 'Psychographie des Kriegers', p. 66 and IWM, P 317 Con Shelf: H.W. Yoxall, letter to mother, 30 Jan. 1917.
26 Ludwig, 'Psychologie der Furcht', p. 168.

similar to that described by modern psychologists as 'learned helplessness'.[27] Soldiers worn down by mental or physical exhaustion became passive, indifferent and so 'callous' that they 'took very little trouble to protect [themselves]'.[28] Such a condition was highly dangerous: as Scholz remarked, 'he who does not fear death won't yearn long for it'.[29]

Alternatively, contemporaries also observed that veterans sometimes returned to a state of intense fear: 'some soldiers, and particularly officers, ... disappear ... as quickly as possible behind cover if the enemy happens to send over a few shots'.[30] Franz Brussig was surprised that in a bombardment, 'the men with most experience of shelling are in the most funk', while Yoxall similarly remarked that 'the people who have been out the longest like [shelling] least'.[31] Repression, although a useful immediate solution, was not an effective long-term coping strategy. Once out of danger, traumatic episodes could return to haunt soldiers as memories or nightmares; despite a determination to avoid thinking of painful events, men admitted to 'do it very often'.[32] According to the psychiatrist John MacCurdy, the failure of 'war sublimation' resulted in the soldier '[dwelling] obsessively on the difficulties which surround him ... and [being unable to] keep his mind away from the possibility of injury'.[33] Correspondingly, veterans 'sometimes became obsessed with fear'.[34] Loss of the ability to predict the fall of shells could follow and soldiers might become ultra-cautious, suffer breakdown or alternatively, seeking a way out of their misery, might actually wish for death, act recklessly and be killed.[35]

[27] A state of 'learned helplessness' is described as a situation in which there is non-contingency between the person's actions and outcomes, an expectation that future outcomes will not be contingent and passive behaviour. Individuals in this state suffer from 'low self-esteem, sadness, loss of aggression, immune changes and physical illness'. See C. Peterson, S.F. Maier and M.E.P. Seligman, *Learned Helplessness. A Theory for the Age of Personal Control* (Oxford University Press, 1993), pp. 8–9.

[28] J.F.C. Fuller in *RWOCIS*, p. 29. Cf. Moran, *Anatomy*, p. 71 and Scholz, *Seelenleben*, p. 128.

[29] Scholz, *Seelenleben*, p. 159.

[30] Ibid., p. 129. Cf. Fuller in *RWOCIS*, p. 29.

[31] Staatsbib. Berlin, Ms. Boruss. fol. 1084: F. Brussig, diary, 12 Jan. 1916 and IWM, P 317 Con Shelf: H.W. Yoxall, letter to mother, 1 June 1916.

[32] IWM, 82/3/1: J.P. Fowler, letter to niece and nephew, 2 May 1915. For nightmares behind the lines, see E.P. Frost, 'Dreams', *Psychological Bulletin* 13, 1 (15 January 1916), 13, Scholz, *Seelenleben*, p. 225 and chapter 1 above, pp. 33–4.

[33] MacCurdy, *War Neuroses*, p. 22.

[34] Fuller in *RWOCIS*, p. 29.

[35] MacCurdy, *War Neuroses*, p. 23 and Scholz, *Seelenleben*, p. 129. Cf. the explanation of soldiers' death prophecies in E. Schiche, 'Ueber Todesahnungen im Felde und ihre Wirkung', in W. Stern and O. Lipmann (eds.), *Beihefte zur Zeitschrift für angewandte Psychologie. 21. Beiträge zur Psychologie des Krieges* (Leipzig: Johann Ambrosius Barth, 1920), pp. 173–8.

As the psychiatrist W.H.R. Rivers found when treating men who had collapsed due to recurring painful memories or emotions, it was often better to reinterpret unpleasant experiences positively rather than attempt to repress them.[36] Abundant evidence shows that soldiers also recognised this, albeit subconsciously. Humour was widely used to reinterpret the environment positively, making it less threatening and thus less frightening. Mockery played a key role: while it was easy to be frightened of a machinegun or shellfire, a weapon thought of as 'chattering Charlie' or *die blauen Gurken* (the blue cucumbers) appeared less terrifying.[37] Brushes with death were similarly ridiculed: Sapper J.P. Fowler, recounting the discovery of a 'wee burned' hole in his tunic, joked about it by observing, 'never mind that as lang as the dinna nock any buttons off I will no say anything to them'.[38] Such levity not only made danger seem less threatening but, according to Ludwig, also sponsored 'a kind of climbing of the ego', which encouraged soldiers to believe in their own ability to overcome peril. The fact that German soldiers said *jetzt bist du groß* ('now you are big') to comrades who joked in danger surely supports this interpretation.[39] Finally, humour enabled men to cope with wishes as well as fear. In the British army, songs such as 'I Don't Want To Be a Soldier' or 'Far Far from Ypres I Want to Be' usefully, according to John Brophy and Eric Partridge, 'poked fun at the soldier's own desire for peace and rest, and so prevented it from overwhelming his will to go on doing his duty'.[40]

The historian J.G. Fuller has suggested that ridicule and irony were peculiarly British traits deriving from peacetime Edwardian culture. Noting their efficacy in averting strain, he argues that British humour was thus 'to many the war-winning quality', different from and advantageous

36 W.H.R. Rivers, 'An Address on the Repression of War Experience', *The Lancet* (2 February 1918), 173–7.

37 IWM, 69/25/1: G. Donaldson, letters to mother, 31 May 1916 and 6 July 1916 and BA-MA Freiburg, MSg 2/ 3788: G. Klein, letter to parents (from Eastern Front), 2 Nov. 1914. See also M.R. Habeck's argument that men anthropomorphised weaponry to make it appear less threatening. 'Technology in the First World War. The View from Below', in J. Winter, G. Parker and M.R. Habeck (eds.), *The Great War and the Twentieth Century* (New Haven: Yale University Press, 2000), pp. 112–16.

38 IWM, 82/3/1: J.P. Fowler, letter to niece and nephew, 2 May 1915.

39 Ludwig, 'Psychologie der Furcht', p. 161.

40 Brophy and Partridge, *The Long Trail*, p. 17. Psychologists also emphasise the uses of humour as a 'buffer' against stress. See, for example, S.M. Labott and R.B. Martin, 'The Stress-moderating Effects of Weeping and Humour', *Journal of Human Stress* 13, 4 (winter 1987), 163. Sense of humour is also one of the attributes associated with Flach's concept of 'resilience'. See R. Williams, 'Personality and Post-traumatic Stress Disorder', in W. Yule (ed.), *Post-traumatic Stress Disorders. Concepts and Therapy* (Chichester: John Wiley & Sons, 1999, 2000), p. 105.

to that of continental armies.[41] Examination of letters and diaries, however, reveals not only that Germans also valued humour as a coping strategy but that the genres they best appreciated were similar to those which Fuller sees as quintessentially British.[42] By April 1916, the German army's once patriotic war songs were giving way to satirical parodies mocking the war and the hardships of army life.[43] Like the British, who referred to 'tin hats' and 'tooth-picks' instead of 'steel helmets' and 'bayonets', the Germans undermined military pomp, downgrading their *Minenwerfer* (mine throwers) to *Marmaladeneimer* (jam buckets) and elevating the humble field kitchen to the status of *Gulaschkanone* (goulash gun).[44] Black humour was also not solely an English preserve. Even in the grim months after the opening of the 1918 spring offensive, German soldiers could still joke in a macabre way and according to one contemporary their 'pure gallows humour' became like that displayed 'by a sarcastic criminal who directly before his death can still laugh at the gathered public'.[45] Men learnt not only to treat the possibility of their own death with derision but also developed an increasingly dark sense of humour towards general misfortune. 'Something from the men in the 186th [Regiment] pleased me,' wrote Muhsal; 'namely, that they are still so war enthused that they even went so far as to mistake one of their own, who was sitting at night on the lavatory, for a Frenchman and stabbed him with a bayonet'.[46] Even hostile exchanges between opposing troops could take a black, almost sarcastic form, as Yoxall recounted:

> The Hun, too, is not without his sense of humour – grim enough, it is true, but everything out here is like that. We have a very clever machine gunner who can play tunes on his gun. the [*sic*] other night he fired a burst of fire with the 'Pom-tiddly-om-pom' cadence and Fritz replied with 'Pom-pom' and hit two men of ours who were on a working party. And so the game goes on.[47]

Rather than culturally specific, such humour may represent a human response to the situation confronting both sets of belligerents. Modern psychological research has found that humans demonstrate an increased

41 Fuller, *Troop Morale*, pp. 143–53.

42 For German views on the value of humour, see Neumann, 'Psychologische Beobachtungen', 1244 and Ludwig, 'Psychologie der Furcht', 160–1. Humour received thirty mentions in Ludwig's study, coming seventh on his list of coping strategies.

43 Schuhmacher, *Leben und Seele*, pp. 167–83.

44 Fuller, *Troop Morale*, p. 145, Plaut, 'Psychographie des Kriegers', p. 99 and BA-MA Freiburg, PH 3/ 93: Form der Propaganda und Soldatensprache. Feldpressestelle: letter to 'Chef IIIb', 16 Apr. 1916. Documents of Dr Bode.

45 BA-MA Freiburg, MSg 1/ 3183: E. Vogt, diary / memoir, 5 Apr. 1918. Cf. Ludwig, 'Psychologie der Furcht', p. 160.

46 BA-MA Freiburg, MSg 1/ 3109: H. Muhsal, diary, 9 Sept. 1915.

47 IWM, P 317 Con Shelf: H.W. Yoxall, letter to family, 10 June 1916.

liking for 'hostile' humour following uncontrollable experiences. Given the inability of the individual soldier on the Western Front to determine his own fate, it is thus not surprising that trench wit was similar on both sides and typified by ironic, black and gallows humour.[48]

Reinterpreting the front by considering it through the prism of the blackly absurd, ironic and ridiculous did not raise the objective chances of survival. Nor did it make soldiers' comparative powerlessness to influence their fates any less real. Rather, by humanising the horror of their situation, humour made it appear more manageable and thus protected men from becoming obsessed with fear or descending into an ultimately self-defeating, apathetic fatalism. It made the reality of death, mutilation and powerlessness at the front easier not only to accept but also to address and thus enabled men to maintain an optimal approach to risk, recognising but not becoming overwhelmed with it. So armed, they could endure the horror of the trenches.

Optimism, religion and superstition

Although humour undoubtedly helped men to confront the possibility of death and pursue a middle course between the two dangerous extremes of apathetic fatalism and overwhelming fear, there are nonetheless indications that most soldiers did not have a realistic grasp of the risks they faced. Both modern historians and contemporary psychologists studying soldiers of the First World War have observed an extremely widespread and in hindsight largely unjustified optimism with regard to personal chances of survival. Among the 200 men in Ludwig's study, 30 recorded that they found *allgemeine Hoffnung* (general hope) to be a useful coping strategy in danger. Still more surprising in warfare characterised as chaotic, unpredictable and intensely disempowering, 36 soldiers found that *Erwägungen über den Grad des möglichen Übels* (consideration of the degree of possible unpleasantness) helped to reassure them in danger. Perhaps most astounding, given the fact that on each side approximately half of all soldiers became casualties, no less than 17 claimed to have a firm belief in their own invincibility.[49] That these men were no exceptions is confirmed by Ziemann, who has found that German soldiers' letters and diaries betray a 'widespread illusion ... that one personally could not be killed or wounded'.[50] British soldiers appear to have been no less unrealistically optimistic than their opponents. Bird observed

48 A.D. Trice, 'Ratings of Humor Following Experience with Unsolvable Tasks', *Psychological Reports* 51, 2 (December 1982), 1148.

49 Ludwig, 'Psychologie der Furcht', p. 172.

50 Ziemann, *Front*, p. 174.

that most possessed an 'inner conviction that they themselves will not be killed' and the psychiatrist C. Stanford Read posited that 'each [soldier] mostly thinks that there is a good chance that he himself will be spared'.[51] Many a British soldier believed, like Lieutenant Chapman, that 'I'm a lucky sort of chap, I am'.[52]

Historians have explained away this unrealistic optimism as stemming from a human inability to imagine one's own demise. Ziemann suggests that men automatically repressed any notion that they might be killed, while Niall Ferguson quotes Freud's assertion that 'no instinct we possess is ready for a belief in [our own] death' to explain the phenomenon.[53] Psychologists, who (unlike Freud) had served in the front line, acknowledged that soldiers did have difficulty invoking concrete images of themselves no longer existing. However, they also observed that, in contrast, thoughts of dying were often extremely vivid:

> One can certainly think of death but not feel it. Death is quiet. In contrast, we suffer with the wounded man: we see his need and hear his complaints. And thus it is less the picture of death which makes even the brave tremble than that of dying; dying in pain.[54]

Repression or an inability to recognise the consequences of being hit is thus unlikely to have been at the root of men's confidence in their own survival. The results of Ludwig's study hint, however, at another explanation: among the coping strategies mentioned by his subjects, *religiöse Regungen* (religious feelings) were by some degree the most commonly named.[55] Could it be that in the absence of security, certainty or control in the natural world, men turned to the supernatural for reassurance?

Certainly, in the First World War German army in particular, religious belief was a great source of strength for many men. Although Ludwig Scholz reported that he was unable to find a single officer or man in his battalion who possessed a New Testament and there was only one believer in Pastor Paul Göhre's Saxon *Landsturm* platoon, to most German soldiers religion seems to have been important.[56] Göhre,

[51] Bird, 'From Home to the Charge', 336 and Stanford Read, *Military Psychiatry*, p. 10.
[52] IWM, 92/3/1: E.F. Chapman, letter to mother, 20 Aug. 1916.
[53] Ziemann, *Front*, p. 174 and Ferguson, *Pity*, p. 365.
[54] Scholz, *Seelenleben*, p. 153. Cf. Ludwig, 'Psychologie der Furcht', pp. 145–6. Modern research argues that 'the fear of death must be present behind all our normal functioning, in order for the organism to be armed toward self-preservation'. See E. Becker, *The Denial of Death* (London: Free Press, 1973, 1997), p. 16.
[55] Ludwig, 'Psychologie der Furcht', pp. 169–72. For Ludwig's results, see Appendix 1.
[56] Scholz, *Seelenleben*, p. 172 and P. Göhre, *Tat-Flugschriften 22. Front und Heimat. Religiöses, Politisches, Sexuelles aus dem Schützengraben* (Jena: Eugen Diederich, 1917), pp. 3–5. Both men served on the Eastern Front.

Plate 9. Faith (2): padre blessing German troops, October 1917. Religious belief was an important source of strength for many soldiers, particularly in the German army. Photograph taken by 'von Thoma *et al.*'

despite his own unit's secularism, thought that approximately 50 per cent of troops harboured some sort of belief, and the volunteer Friedrich Nawrath also observed that faith provided strength to many soldiers, although he emphasised that their creed was not that of the official army chaplains but rather an inner spirituality.[57] Ludwig saw embrasures on which men had scratched saints' names and holy verses, while Georg Pfeilschifter, an academic who undertook an examination of Catholic belief at the front, actually found cases of troops building altars and chapels in their reserve positions.[58] The fact that 'Wir treten zum Beten' ('We Go to Pray') was often heard sung by small groups of soldiers

[57] Göhre, *Front und Heimat*, pp. 9–11 and BA-MA Freiburg, MSg 1/ 1383: F.O. Nawrath, letter to parents, 8 Mar. 1915.

[58] Ludwig, 'Psychologie der Furcht', pp. 169–70 and G. Pfeilschifter, 'Seelsorge und religiöses Leben im deutschen Heere', in G. Pfeilschifter (ed.), *Deutsche Kultur, Katholizismus und Weltkrieg. Eine Abwehr des Buches La guerre allemande et la catholicisme* (Freiburg im Breisgau: Herdersche Verlagshandlung, 1916), p. 248.

directly before combat, and that among survivors, even those with minimal religious convictions, 'Nun danket alle Gott' ('Now Everyone Thank God') was the preferred anthem, illustrates how important religious faith was to the German army's ability to endure.[59]

Religion supported soldiers in various ways. For the pious but egotistical, it guaranteed survival: as Knoch has observed, 'a form of privatisation of divine help' took place in the trenches, with many interpreting their survival as evidence of godly favour.[60] Georg Kirchner, for example, having fought through the first two bloody months of the war and outlived most of his comrades, simply commented, 'I can only thank God that up to now he has spared me'.[61] *Gefreiter* Kurt Reiter interpreted a near miss by a shell as 'the dear God mercifully protected me' and *Grenadier* Franz Meier similarly attributed his survival through 'some difficult hours' to the fact that 'God's protection and help was with me and my comrades'.[62] For other, perhaps less naive souls, faith gave sense to an otherwise frightening and chaotic world. Gotthard Gruber, for example, noted in his diary that 'the thought which always put me personally back on my feet was that a God of Love stands behind everything'.[63] Many religious soldiers found that such a belief facilitated the acceptance of one's fate, regardless of its eventual form. Heini Weber, fighting in the Argonne, thought that in questions of mortality, 'one must just trust in God'. Arthur Meier, considering a possible transfer to the Somme battlefield in 1916, similarly fatalistically concluded, 'even in this case, I trust in our omnipotent and all-loving God, who guides everything for the best'.[64]

Religious faith was also important for many British troops, both as a reassurance of continued life and as a comfort in death. The Medical Officer of 1/Irish Guards, Hugh Shields, was heartened in September 1914 by the thought that despite the danger of his duties, 'somehow I don't feel that God means me to get killed yet'.[65] Lieutenant St Leger found solace in the idea that when a man achieved his earthly mission

59 Schuhmacher, *Leben und Seele*, pp. 152–5.

60 Knoch, 'Erleben und Nacherleben', p. 209. Cf. Reimann, *Große Krieg der Sprachen*, p. 97. One-third of the interviewees in Ludwig's study who mentioned religion testified that they or their comrades had some hope of divine assistance. See Ludwig, 'Psychologie der Furcht', p. 170.

61 DTA, 9/II: G. Kirchner, letter to sister, 2 Oct. 1914.

62 BA-MA Freiburg, MSg 1/ 161: K. Reiter, diary, 22 June 1916 and BA-MA Freiburg, MSg 2/ 5800: F. Meier, letter to *Fräulein* Dölker, 19 Mar. 1917.

63 DTA, 138a: G. Gruber, diary, 27 Feb. 1916 and Ludwig, 'Psychologie der Furcht', pp. 169–71.

64 DTA, 865: H. Weber, letter to friends, 7 Jan. 1915 and BA-MA Freiburg, MSg 2/ 5799: A. Meier, letter to *Oberpostsekretär* Dölker, 6 Sept. 1916.

65 WLHM, RAMC 383 Box 41: H.J.S. Shields, letter, 25 Sept. 1914.

'he is taken away by God to enjoy his rest', adding fatalistically, 'I wonder when I shall have fulfilled my parts'.[66] Britons were told to 'put their lives into God's keeping' so that they could 'shelve all responsibility and go forward with a quiet mind in the knowledge that God is at the helm and that nothing can happen without his sanction'.[67] In British trenches and dugouts, as in German, men could sometimes be seen 'reading scripture under the ugliest conditions of peril'.[68] Nonetheless, references to God are rarer in British correspondence than in German letters, a fact perhaps reflecting the lesser piety of English society in particular, when compared with that of the *Kaiserreich*.[69] Despite the widespread attendance of Sunday schools by British children, wartime investigations into soldiers' faith uncovered remarkable ignorance of Christianity. The Divisional Chaplain Philip Crick found that 'the [Anglican] Church has not succeeded in impressing upon the majority of them a sense of allegiance to her teaching and practices', and a study undertaken by the Bishop of Kensington estimated that 80 per cent of men from the Midlands had never heard of the sacraments.[70] Although recent research has highlighted the existence of extreme piety within some units and among certain individuals, the 'diffusive Christianity' widely agreed to have characterised Edwardian faith comprised little more than a vague belief in God and a practical attachment to the Church's moral teachings.[71]

66 IWM, P 239: W.B. St Leger, diary, 10 Oct. 1917.

67 Reverend M.S. Evers, letter to sister, no date, reproduced in P. Liddle, *Testimony of War 1914–1918* (Salisbury: Michael Russell, 1979), p. 61.

68 IWM, 82/26/1: A.R. Williams, letter to family, 26 Sept. 1916. Cf. Ludwig, 'Psychologie der Furcht', pp. 170–1.

69 While the hostility of Social Democracy towards religion had undermined faith among Protestant industrial workers in pre-war Germany, the churches there retained more influence over education than did those in England, and certain rituals, notably baptisms, remained more universally practised among German Protestants than English Anglicans, perhaps suggesting more ingrained religiosity. Still more important, Catholics, who were more resistant to secularisation than Protestants, comprised a larger percentage of Germany's population. See H. McLeod, *Secularisation in Western Europe, 1848–1914* (Basingstoke: Macmillan, 2000), pp. 264 and 285–9.

70 P.C.T. Crick, 'The Soldier's Religion', in F.B. MacNutt (ed.), *The Church in the Furnace. Essays by Seventeen Temporary Church of England Chaplains on Active Service in France and Flanders* (London: Macmillan & Co., 1917), p. 370 and D.S. Cairns (ed.), *The Army and Religion. An Enquiry and its Bearing upon the Religious Life of the Nation* (London: Macmillan & Co., 1919), p. 448.

71 For 'diffusive Christianity', see J. Cox, *The English Churches in a Secular Society. Lambeth, 1870–1930* (Oxford University Press, 1982), pp. 93–5. For its role in the British army of 1914–18, see M. Snape, *God and the British Soldier. Religion and the British Army in the First and Second World Wars* (London: Routledge, 2005), pp. 19–58 and R. Schweitzer, *The Cross and the Trenches. Religious Faith and Doubt among British and American Great War Soldiers* (London: Praeger, 2003), pp. 6 and 263–4.

The lesser prominence of God in British soldiers' correspondence did not necessarily indicate, however, that religion, as Private Rowlands asserted, 'hasn't a place in one out of a million of the thoughts that hourly occupy men's minds' at the front.[72] The Third Army's chief censor thought on the contrary that 'the Army is essentially religious – not necessarily in outward expression, but in the widest sense of an inward faith and trust in Divine guidance'.[73] Indeed, the desire to find meaning and security in the chaotic world of the trenches was such that even totally faithless troops on both sides were affected. As Pfeilschifter, observed:

> Even indifferent and in ordinary life so-called unbelievers are shaken up by the constant danger, renunciation of worldly things and suffering of the trench war and turn to the Almighty, as they feel and experience dozens of times that here blind chance does not prevail but that a friendly guide holds human fate in his hands.[74]

The supernatural protector to whom such men turned, however, was not necessarily a Christian God. For many, 'luck' became a form of *ersatz* personal deity controlling events. Both the religious and non-believers referred to it and it is not uncommon to find men hedging their bets when giving thanks for deliverance: Arthur Wrench, for example, attributed his 'repeated miraculous escapes' variously to 'luck', 'God' and 'Fate' at different points in his military career.[75]

Faith in an abstract omnipotent being was often supported by reliance on physical objects believed to possess supernatural powers. Often these were amulets of a religious nature, such as crucifixes, scapulars, *agnus dei* and consecrated coins.[76] Wrench recorded that many men carried a New Testament in their breast pocket in the hope that it might stop a bullet from entering their hearts. That metal objects might objectively have stood more chance of doing this was irrelevant; Wrench was emphatic that 'it has to be a bible even if its only other

72 IWM, 93/20/1: D.L. Rowlands, letter to girlfriend, 5 Feb. 1918.
73 IWM, 84/46/1: M. Hardie, Report on Complaints, Moral, etc., 23 Nov. 1916, p. 10.
74 Pfeilschifter, 'Seelsorge und religiöses Leben', p. 249.
75 IWM, 85/51/1: A.E. Wrench, diary, 22 Apr. 1917, 9 Sept. 1917, 28 Feb. 1918, 26 Mar. 1918 and 19 Apr. 1918. Cf. IWM, P 317 Con Shelf: H.W. Yoxall, letter to family, 29 May 1916; IWM, 76/121/1 & Con Shelf: C.S. Rawlins, letter to family, 12 Oct. 1915 and BA-MA Freiburg, MSg 1/3109: H. Muhsal, diary, 6 May 1917 and 31 May 1918.
76 Plaut, 'Psychographie des Kriegers', p. 78 and IWM, 96/29/1: J. McIlwain, memoir based on contemporary diary, p. 33.

use is for a convenient piece of paper to light a cigarette'.[77] So-called *Schutzbriefe*, letters with religious or magical formulae designed to protect their owner, were also widely carried. Some contained simple prayers or Bible quotations such as the comforting Psalm 91, which promised, 'A thousand may fall dead beside you, / ten thousand all round you, / but you will not be harmed'.[78] Others were more spiritualist in nature, naming protective ghosts or devils.[79] Lucky clover, coins and carp scales were all believed by German soldiers to avert danger, and Scottish soldiers of the 51st (Highland) Division wore as talismans 'little woolly golly-wogs' beneath their cap badges.[80] Objects of personal significance, such as letters and photographs, which linked men to their families and reminded them of why they were fighting, also often became charms. Such was men's need for security that, as Wrench observed, 'any little keepsake [the soldier] cherishes becomes a fetish and some will almost stake their lives on it'.[81]

Rituals also gave abstract religious beliefs and superstitions a more concrete, tangible and comforting character and, like amulets, took multifarious forms at the front. Scholz saw men uttering words and performing actions designed to deflect projectiles, and Plaut recorded the case of a serving student who, realising the day was the thirteenth of the month, suddenly decided that he would be killed unless he could appease the gods by offering a blood sacrifice of thirteen flies.[82] Another soldier, shocked by the bearded face of a fallen comrade, decided that salvation lay in shaving and obsessively removed the stubble from

[77] IWM, 85/51/1: A.E. Wrench, diary, 21 July 1917. Such beliefs may have been encouraged by wartime propaganda: newspapers on both sides ran features on bullets being lodging in Bibles as well as packets of razors, bullets etc. See, for example, 'Some Mascots and Trifles that have Saved Lives', *The War Illustrated. A Picture-Record of Events by Land, Sea and Air* 2, 28 (27 February 1915), 47 and Schmahl, 'Die Gewehre der europäischen Mächte', *Illustrierte Geschichte des Weltkrieges 1914/15. Allgemeine Kriegszeitung* 30 (n.d.), 100. *The B.E.F. Times* (a version of the infamous *Wipers Times*) also ran a spoof advert on 26 Feb. 1918 offering to supply 'bullets carefully fixed in Bibles'. See F.J. Roberts (ed.), *The Wipers Times. A Complete Facsimile of the Famous World War One Trench Newspaper Incorporating the 'New Church' Times, The Kemmel Times, The Somme Times, The B.E.F. Times, and the 'Better Times'* (London: Papermac, 1973), p. 286.

[78] Psalms xci.7.

[79] H. Bächtold, *Deutscher Soldatenbrauch und Soldatenglaube* (Strassburg: Karl J. Trübner, 1917), p. 17.

[80] Plaut, 'Psychographie des Kriegers', p. 78. IWM, 85/51/1: A.E. Wrench, diary, 21 July 1917. Carp was eaten at Christmas in Germany, and it was probably therefore the associations with home and family embodied in the scales which led soldiers to invest them with superstitious significance.

[81] IWM, 85/51/1: A.E. Wrench, diary, 21 July 1917. Cf. Scholz, *Seelenleben*, pp. 179–80.

[82] Scholz, *Seelenleben*, p. 180 and Plaut, 'Psychographie des Kriegers', p. 79.

his face twice daily.[83] Often rites took a more overtly Christian form: the quickly intoned 'Our Father' in danger was probably the single most common protective ritual used on the Western Front.[84]

The attraction of rituals and amulets lay not only in the apparent protection they offered or the fact that they provided something more tangible than abstract faith in an invisible God. Rather, their popularity stemmed primarily from their perceived ability to provide a clear set of unwritten instructions for survival in an unpredictable and frightening world. Woe betide the man who contravened these rules by forgetting his protective talisman, failing to pass on a *Kettenbrief* (chain letter) or who carried an 'unlucky' object, such as a pack of cards or wedding ring, into danger.[85] In contrast, the British dispatch rider who obeyed the self-imposed rules and turned back when he found he had forgotten his lucky rosary was rewarded by being spared a bombardment further along the road on which he had been travelling.[86] Moreover, not only did these rules provide security but they also returned responsibility for personal fate to the individual, negating the damaging feelings of disempowerment arising from the front's objective uncontrollability. It is significant, for example, that a British tank crewman, captured by the Germans in August 1917, attributed his deliverance from danger not directly to God but to the fact that he had prayed incessantly throughout combat.[87] Similarly, the German soldier who, wounded and captured by the French, blamed his fate not on the objective ineffectiveness of his *Schutzbrief* but on his own foolishness in losing faith in the letter for fifteen minutes and thus negating its protective powers, at least felt in control of his own fate.[88]

By looking beyond their own disempowering and dangerous world to the supernatural, soldiers were able to impose structure and certainty on the surrounding chaos. Belief that God, Providence or luck would shield them from death provided security and reassurance. Even faith that a loving deity was behind the bloodshed and destruction imposed some sense on an otherwise unpredictable and frightening world. Amulets and rituals, both Christian and pagan, became popular because they

83 Wittermann, 'Kriegspsychiatrische Erfahrungen', 1165–6.
84 For the forms of prayer used at the front, see Plaut, 'Psychographie des Kriegers', p. 74 and Ludwig, 'Psychologie der Furcht', pp. 170–1.
85 Bächtold, *Deutscher Soldatenbrauch*, p. 22 and Ulrich, *Augenzeugen*, pp. 45–6.
86 IWM, 85/51/1: A.E. Wrench, diary, 21 July 1917.
87 BA-MA Freiburg, PH 3/ 585: Vernehmungsprotokolle, AOK 4: Vernehmung [of one officer and seven men of 12th Comp. D. Batl., Tank Corps and one officer and three men of 18th Comp., F Batl., Tank Corps], 26 August 1917, p. 5. Cf. Ludwig, 'Psychologie der Furcht', p. 170.
88 Bächtold, *Deutscher Soldatenbrauch*, p. 19.

went further still in helping to satisfy the human need 'to predict the future and control events'.[89] Protected by a loving God, supplied with a set of rules which appeared to guarantee survival and imbued with a sense of power over their fate and their surroundings, it is perhaps unsurprising that many soldiers were able to remain highly optimistic about their ability to cheat death.

Positive illusions

Turning to the supernatural was, however, not the only means soldiers found to reassure themselves about the future. In attempting to understand men's experience on the Western Front, historians suffer from their own professional ethos, which encourages them to view the horrors there as objectively as possible. Soldiers, whose occupational demands were quite different, were far less keen to perceive their surroundings objectively. There is, in fact, considerable evidence in letters and diaries to suggest that the widespread belief in personal survival was not entirely based on fantasy but was rather grounded in a highly positively biased interpretation of the trench environment.

As Peter Bernstein has observed, 'the nature of risk is shaped by the time horizon'.[90] Although, as the conflict wore on, increasing numbers of soldiers wondered despairingly whether the war would ever end, many retained the hope that peace would soon break out. This was particularly so early in the war, when men found it 'extraordinary how all the Tommies seem to have a fixed idea in their heads that they will be home before Xmas'.[91] Once trench warfare became fully established, such concrete predictions became rarer. Monotony and routine probably helped to dull soldiers' consciousness of time, hindering consideration of the war's duration.[92] Nonetheless, hopes of an imminent end to the conflict never fully receded but were simply expressed in a different form, as peace rumours. In September 1916, Lieutenant O.P. Taylor heard gossip circulating the British trenches stating that 'the Kaiser wrote a private letter to King George asking him for an armistice to allow him to withdraw beyond the Rhine, which was

89 S. Joseph, 'Attributional Processes, Coping and Post-traumatic Stress Disorders', in W. Yule (ed.), *Post-traumatic Stress Disorders. Concepts and Therapy* (Chichester: John Wiley & Sons, 1999, 2000), p. 52.

90 P.L. Bernstein, *Against the Gods. The Remarkable Story of Risk* (Chichester: John Wiley & Sons, 1996), p. 197.

91 IWM, 84/22/1: B.O. Dewes, diary, 29 Nov. 1914. Cf. IWM, 78/4/1: T.H. Cubbon, diary, 29 Sept. 1914.

92 IWM, Con Shelf: R.P. Harker, letter to Ethel (probably his sister), 28 Dec. 1914 and BA-MA Freiburg, F.O. Nawrath, letter to parents, 24 Jan. 1915.

refused'.[93] Eleven months later, Arthur Wrench wrote excitedly of 'a great rumour that Austria has given Germany 24 hours to consider peace'.[94] Such hopes, although normally dashed, were probably important in reminding soldiers that the war was finite and that there was a chance to return home alive. Certainly, Plaut noted that soldiers continued to treat the conflict as a temporary interlude and argued that this attitude was important in their willingness to continue fighting.[95]

Hopes of temporary relief also helped soldiers cope with the stress of the trenches. Leave was joyfully anticipated both as a respite from danger and as a chance to see the loved ones for whom a man was fighting. To Yoxall, it was 'the best thing on earth' and 'the only thing which matters'.[96] Censorship reports on military morale indicate that most soldiers thought similarly:

> Nothing so cheers and heartens men as the prospect of leave; and, judging by the letters, it is impossible to emphasise too strongly the importance of leave as a factor in the moral of the Army. It is the constant 'lookforwardness' to eight or ten days of Blighty that, more than anything else, keeps them going ... The immediate prospect of leave, as something visible and tangible, seems to count for more to men's minds than the ultimate, visionary hope of Peace.[97]

Leave had two disadvantages, however. Firstly, it was seldom granted: at best, German soldiers were released from the army once a year, while British soldiers received ten days or, after November 1917, two weeks at home every fifteen months. Transport problems, manpower difficulties or security considerations often meant that the period between leaves was much longer.[98] Secondly, the hope and emotions invested in leave meant that when such release was finally granted, soldiers lost their fatalism and became terrified of being killed before their departure. Wrench recorded 'a rotten nervous feeling' on being told in December 1916 that he had been granted leave three days hence. 'I am almost afraid I will never survive till then,' he wrote. 'I am full of doubts and now that it seems years and years since I came out to France, at the moment it is only like yesterday while Sunday seems too far away to be real'.[99] Less

93 IWM, 92/3/1: O.P. Taylor, diary, 10 Sept. 1916.
94 IWM, 85/51/1: A.E. Wrench, diary, 30 Aug. 1917.
95 Plaut, 'Psychographie des Kriegers', p. 64.
96 IWM, P 317 Con Shelf: H.W. Yoxall, letters to mother, 30 Jan. and 1 Feb. 1917.
97 IWM, 84/46/1: M. Hardie, Report on Moral, &c. III Army, 1 Jan. 1917.
98 Ziemann, *Front*, pp. 84–5 and Fuller, *Troop Morale*, p. 72.
99 IWM, 85/51/1: A.E. Wrench, diary, 7 Dec. 1916. Other soldiers experienced similar feelings on being granted leave. See, for example, IWM, 96/29/1: S.H. Steven, letter to family, 10 Aug. 1915 and IWM, 92/3/1: E.F. Chapman, letter to mother, 18 Nov. 1916.

likely to interfere adversely with men's fatalistic attitudes and more common were the temporary rests allocated to units after periods at the front and in the reserve positions. British battalions could expect to spend only ten days per month in the line during normal trench warfare. Divisions too were rotated periodically from active to quiet sectors or taken out of the line altogether.[100] The recognition that combat, however awful, was only a temporary state did much to help soldiers through the more stressful periods of action. The rumour of relief after almost a month at Verdun in 1916, for example, strengthened Kurt Reiter's resolve to endure: 'Hurrah!', he wrote at the end of June, 'it is said that we will definitely be relieved on the 7 July. We are all looking forward to it! If only it were true. One must simply not lose hope.'[101]

Belief in an imminent end to the war, or at least the immediacy of rest, was helpful in maintaining both men's mental stability and army discipline because it encouraged soldiers to focus on short-term rather than cumulative risk. If such a perspective were adopted, then hopes for survival were by no means unjustified, for deaths on the Western Front usually came in a slow trickle rather than a flood. Analysis of casualties suffered by the 1/5 Durham Light Infantry, a typical Territorial battalion with an initial strength of 1,031 men, shows that outside 'battle' periods (as defined by the official history), a man was killed in action on average only once every six days. The risk of death rose dramatically during battles when, on average, six men per day were killed. However, such intense action was extremely rare: of the approximately 1,300 days in which the battalion was in France, only 63 were spent in a major battle.[102] Providing that a man ignored cumulative risk and concentrated on the short term, it was thus perfectly reasonable to believe that survival was highly likely. The benefits of this perspective were elucidated by Lieutenant-Colonel McTaggart in a military journal article after the war. Noting the increasing signs of mental strain exhibited by men employed on nightly carrying duties who feared their luck was running out, he suggested that they should be educated to think only of short-term

[100] G. Corrigan, *Mud, Blood and Poppycock. Britain and the First World War* (London: Cassell, 2003), pp. 89–91. Cf. also the chart in *A War Record of the 21st London Regiment (First Surrey Rifles), 1914–1919* (London: no publisher, 1928), p. 127, extrapolation from which reveals that the battalion spent approximately nine days per month in the line between March 1915 and November 1918. During the unit's 1,335 days of active service, 401 days were spent in the fighting line, 230 in brigade reserve, 326 in divisional reserve, 284 in corps reserve and 94 in army reserve.

[101] BA-MA Freiburg, MSg 1/ 161: K. Reiter, diary, 29 June 1916.

[102] Calculated from casualty lists in A.L. Raimes, *The Fifth Battalion, The Durham Light Infantry 1914–1918* (n.p.: Committee of Past and Present Officers of the Battalion, 1931), pp. 204–12. For the battalion's initial strength, see p. 222.

risk. Estimating the chance of being hit on such a carrying party at 3,000 to 1, he argued that 'if . . . men were taught to think of the chances in their favour each time they went up it would considerably lessen their apprehension'.[103]

Most commonly encountered in letters and diaries, however, are not estimations of one's own short-term chances of survival but rather of whether the next shell or bullet would hit; the extreme inefficiency of First World War weaponry in killing, although lost on most historians, was eagerly acknowledged by combatants.[104] Captain Geoffrey Donaldson marvelled at the 'little damage' the enemy did 'with his infernal instruments' while his opponents found consolation in the belief that 'Tommy appears to have a squint' and from the calculation 'that out of one hundred shells comes only one direct hit'. Private Jack Ashley thought it 'astonishing how harmless a really heavy coal-box can be' and H.W. Yoxall remarked in somewhat blasé fashion to his mother, 'it's wonderful how many shells it takes to kill a man. The expenditure of ammy. gives quite an exaggerated idea of the monetary value of human life'.[105] Bullets were similarly recognised as comparatively ineffective: Hugh Shields, for example, remarked on 'the minute number of casualties to bullets fired' and 'not every bullet hits' became a catchphrase among German troops.[106] Viewed in this way, and providing that the almost inexhaustible supply of enemy munitions was ignored, the chances of survival appeared reasonably good.

Even if contemporary weaponry did actually find a victim, permanent incapacitation was not certain: 64 per cent of British and 69 per cent of German wounded were healed and returned to the front during the war.[107] Realising this, many soldiers, particularly those fighting in active sectors where the quantity of ammunition being fired made the probability of unscathed survival seem slim, placed their redemptive hopes on comparatively minor injuries which would provide an exit from the trenches and preferably some time hospitalised at home. Thus, for

[103] M.F. McTaggart, 'Danger Values', *Journal of the Royal United Services Institution* 66, 462 (May 1921), 290.

[104] See chapter 1, p. 30.

[105] Respectively, IWM, 69/25/1: G. Donaldson, letter to mother, 5 June 1916, TNA, WO 157/ 23: Summary of Information (GHQ), 24 Aug. 1917, p. 4, Ludwig, 'Psychologie der Furcht', p. 165, Ashley, *War-Diary*, p. 9 and IWM, P 317 Con Shelf: H.W. Yoxall, letter to mother, 13 July 1916.

[106] WLHM, RAMC 383 Box 41: H.J.S. Shields, diary, 23 Oct. 1914; BA-MA Freiburg, MSg 2/ 2735: H. Genscher, letter to father, 24 Oct. 1914. Cf. Scholz, *Seelenleben*, p. 131 and Ludwig, 'Psychologie der Furcht', p. 165.

[107] *Medical Services*, p. 20. German figures calculated from *Sanitätsbericht III*, p. 64, *Übersicht 57*.

example, Sergeant T.H. Cubbon, lying exposed to rain and artillery fire after the heavy fighting of early September 1914, recorded in his diary, 'men wishing they were wounded to get taken away from here'.[108] One of Ludwig's soldiers similarly stated, 'I would be grateful to the Frenchman, if he would make me g.v.h. [fit for garrison service at home] for a few months'.[109] The failure to receive such a 'Blighty wound', *Tango-* or *Heimatschuß* could cause much disappointment: one German soldier, for example, writing in 1916 from the Somme battlefield, regretted that, 'I unfortunately could not get the much desired wound to send me home'.[110] For soldiers who did 'succeed' in getting such an injury, relief was often overwhelming. 'Praise God from whom all blessings flow! – I'm wounded,' wrote Arthur Wrench when a shrapnel splinter gave him a legitimate exit from the hell of the 1918 *Kaiserschlacht*.[111]

Less statistical but no less reasoned calculations also prompted soldiers to overestimate their chances of survival. Combatants sometimes adopted what modern psychologists might term 'a worse-off social comparison target' in order to feel better about their own plight. Thus, for example, after receiving news of his brother's death, Wrench consoled himself by comparing his situation to the experience of another man whose sibling had fallen dead into his arms while they served together at the front.[112] Hans Muhsal, serving on the comparatively calm but uncomfortable Vosges front in November 1916, reassured himself with the thought that whatever the hardships, his lot was better than that of his countrymen fighting on the Somme.[113] Similarly, it was not only to gain kudos that veterans told less experienced comrades that 'this here is alright. But once in front of Verdun, once at the Somme – that was something, there one could go mad'; such statements also reassured the speaker of the likelihood of his own future survival by placing the current danger in the context of much greater perils already overcome.[114] An analysis of contemporary letters and diaries suggests that this strategy had only limited application, most commonly being used by men in sectors with little or moderate violence rather than in areas where the full-scale *Materialschlacht* was raging; perhaps men embroiled in the

108 IWM, 78/4/1: T.H. Cubbon, diary, 17 Sept. 1914.
109 Ludwig, 'Psychologie der Furcht', pp. 166–7. Cf. Stanford Read, *Military Psychiatry*, p. 9. Five soldiers in Ludwig's sample expressed the wish for a *Heimatschuß*.
110 TNA, WO 157/ 13: Summary of Information (GHQ), 7 Sept. 1916.
111 IWM, 85/51/1: A.E. Wrench, diary, 24 Mar. 1918.
112 Ibid., 14 Dec. 1917.
113 BA-MA Freiburg, MSg 1/ 3109: H. Muhsal, diary, 16 and 24 Nov. 1916.
114 Schauwecker, *Im Todesrachen*, p. 49. Cf. Scholz, *Seelenleben*, p. 131 and Ludwig, 'Psychologie der Furcht', p. 165.

Kaiserschlacht or at the Somme were simply unable to imagine anything worse.[115]

When indeed the situation was truly hopeless, coping strategies did change. Objectively, when under very heavy bombardment, there was nothing a man could do except 'sit tight against the parapet, smoke cigarettes furiously, and trust in whatever gods there be'.[116] In such circumstances, rather than try to judge or rationalise the danger, soldiers simply ignored it by using avoidance and distraction strategies. As one of Ludwig's subjects observed, 'the soldier gets into the habit of using certain reflections in order to counter the thought of death in the moment of danger'.[117] Still more effective in averting fear and stress was the pursuit of some diversionary activity. Card playing was ubiquitous in shellfire and folk singing similarly provided a welcome distraction for some men.[118] Others preferred something more orchestral: when a bombardment opened on enemy lines close to Franz Brussig's dugout, 'all at once, Hoffmann began to play his concertina, Tuhnert & Decker gave a concert on the mandolin as well as they could and Hüb[ner] along with several other comrades let themselves be heard on harmonicas. Thus there was a concert until the bombardment came to an end'.[119]

In normal trench life, however, soldiers did possess a modicum of influence over their own fates. Mortar bombs could be dodged, enfiladed sections of trench could be identified and avoided and, as previously noted, men learnt to distinguish the direction and type of shells by sound. Interestingly, combatants tended to overestimate the control which these skills gave them, not just initially but even after they had become grizzled veterans. Thus, already after his first experience of trench warfare, Yoxall observed that 'barring the shells it's purely a contest of wits'. Seven months later, he had also learnt that artillery fire could be countered successfully, commenting that it was 'extraordinary' how men gained a 'sense of shelling – the knowledge where to go and where not to go, when to lie down and when to run, & c.'.[120] Other soldiers also emphasised that they were relatively safe from artillery fire providing that they could take adequate cover quickly. Ernst Berner, for

[115] Modern research has found that similar techniques are used by terminally ill cancer patients. See D.A. Armor and S.E. Taylor, 'When Predictions Fail. The Dilemma of Unrealistic Optimism', in T. Gilovich, D. Griffin and D. Kahneman (eds.), *Heuristics and Biases* (Cambridge University Press, 2002), p. 344.

[116] IWM, P 317 Con Shelf: H.W. Yoxall, letter to mother, 21 Dec. 1916.

[117] Ludwig, 'Psychologie der Furcht', p. 162.

[118] Ibid., p. 160.

[119] Staatsbib. Berlin, Ms. Germ. fol. 1084: F. Brussig, diary, 21 Feb. 1916.

[120] IWM, P 317 Con Shelf: H.W. Yoxall, letters to family, 1 June 1916 and to mother, 10 Jan. 1917 (mistakenly dated '1916').

example, derived comfort from the fact that although it was impossible to predict exactly where shells were going to land, 'mostly one has a trench or some hole into which one can throw himself'.[121] Donaldson actually took pride in his prowess at taking cover: 'I was well satisfied with the rapidity with which I got into that infernally muddy ditch when I heard the beggar coming,' he wrote of a shell that had just missed him.[122] Even actions objectively less likely to ensure survival could be interpreted by soldiers as part of their repertoire for cheating death. It is difficult, for example, to see how white-hot shrapnel falling from the sky could be dodged, yet on finding himself in this situation, Wrench recorded '[making] sure my tin hat was square on my head and my legs in good running order'.[123]

In the light of this evidence, it is reasonable to suggest that soldiers' unrealistic optimism about their personal chances of survival in the unpredictable, dangerous and disempowering world of the trenches did not stem solely from faith in an imagined supernatural order or confidence in a divine protector. Rather, men simply refused or were unable to recognise the high level of unresponsiveness and danger possessed by their surroundings. The environment they perceived, although not pleasant, offered a far greater likelihood of survival than the reality. Shells and bullets, it seemed, rarely found their targets and when they did, wounded instead of killed, thus providing a welcome rest from the trenches. Compared to previous experience or the ordeals which others were undergoing, sectors usually appeared to be 'cushy' with minimal risk. Moreover, a soldier's safety was assured by his own skill in avoiding danger and dodging death. Providing that the war ended soon, as it surely would, why should he doubt his ability to survive the conflagration?

Certainly, this unrealistic optimism was not without its pitfalls. The example of new recruits, whose overconfidence could often lead to unnecessary fatalities, implies that it was a highly dangerous mindset. However, other, more compelling factors indicate that actually it was an important strategy for coping with conditions on the battlefield. Firstly, the fact that soldiers themselves believed that optimism was crucial in the trenches does suggest that it was beneficial: contemporaries remarked on how the closer men were to the line, the more cheerful they became.[124] Moreover, the findings of this study echo those of modern

[121] BA-MA Freiburg, MSg 1/ 1941: E. Berner, letter to mother, 3 Apr. 1918.
[122] IWM, 69/25/1: G. Donaldson, letter to mother, 1 June 1916.
[123] IWM, 85/51/1: A.E. Wrench, diary, 28 Feb. 1918.
[124] BA-MA Freiburg, W-10/ 50794: Postüberwachung der 5. *Armee*, 12 July 1917, p. 13 and IWM, P 317 Con Shelf: H.W. Yoxall, letter to family, 23 July 1916.

psychological research carried out by Shelley Taylor and Jonathon Brown, who have found that individuals 'possess unrealistically positive views of themselves, an exaggerated belief in their ability to control their environment, and a view of the future that maintains that their future will be far better than the average person's'. Significantly, they argue that these 'positive illusions ... may be especially apparent and adaptive under circumstances of adversity, that is, circumstances that might be expected to produce depression or lack of motivation'.[125] A close examination of First World War soldiers' optimistic attitudes suggests that they were, indeed, highly adaptive. By imposing an imagined structure and order on the frightening and unpredictable environment in which they operated, soldiers made it seem less chaotic and threatening and provided themselves with a sense of security and empowerment crucial for mental health. Concentration on short-term risk not only gave a more positive prognosis for survival than did cumulative risk calculations but by encouraging soldiers to focus on immediate threat probably also raised the objective likelihood of leaving the trenches alive. Finally, overestimation of personal control was similarly beneficial as it discouraged men from sinking into a state of dangerous apathy by motivating them instead to interact with their environment and thus protect themselves. By lacking a truly objective sense of risk and of their surroundings, and instead embracing positive illusions, soldiers protected themselves from mental strain, probably prolonged their life expectancies and remained willing to risk their lives despite danger and disempowerment. Human faith, hope and optimism, no less than cultural traits, discipline, primary groups and patriotism, explain why and how men were willing and able to fight in the horrendous conditions of the Western Front for four long and bloody years.

[125] S.E. Taylor and J.D. Brown, 'Illusion and Well-Being. A Social Psychological Perspective on Mental Health', *Psychological Bulletin* 103, 2 (1988), 196 and 201.

4 Junior leadership: command, cohesion and combat motivation

Function and influence

Although patriotism, rational self-interest and natural resilience go far in explaining why and how Germans and Britons fought for so long, armies' impressive records of endurance cannot be understood without reference to junior officers. Examinations of troops' battlefield behaviour and discipline have erred by ignoring or underestimating the importance of these men: Tony Ashworth, for example, misinterprets command relations during the First World War as a direct struggle between other ranks and army staff rather than as a relationship mediated by junior officers.[1] Although identified with the army command in the rear by their commission or *Patent*, they were also united with combat soldiers by means of shared danger and deprivation. Psychological and sociological research has emphasised the great influence provided by this intermediary position. S.A. Stouffer's study of the American army between 1941 and 1945, for example, found that 'men's attitudes toward their officers had a real importance in determining whether men fought aggressively and stayed in the fight'. Morris Janowitz and Edward A. Shils similarly concluded from their examination of the Second World War *Wehrmacht* that soldiers' obedience and combat motivation 'depended upon the personality of the officer'.[2]

Like their successors, the junior officers of 1914–18 held huge sway over the behaviour and resilience of the common soldiery. As the contemporary psychologist Charles Bird explained:

> The leaders determine the morale of the troops who instinctively are imitators and who regard their officers as symbols of duty, discipline and the nation. At times the loss of an officer may terrorize a company and cause disaster to a regiment.[3]

[1] Ashworth, *Trench Warfare*, pp. 32–9.

[2] Stouffer *et al.*, *American Soldier*, II, pp. 126–7 and Janowitz and Shils, 'Cohesion and Disintegration', p. 196.

[3] Bird, 'From Home to the Charge', 343.

Combat narratives confirm this observation. A German intelligence analysis of a raid on 1/Royal Irish Rifles in April 1916, for example, highlighted the pivotal role of a British officer, Lieutenant Hill, in the defence. While 3 Platoon, lacking leadership, was quickly overwhelmed and surrendered, the soldiers in 1 Platoon, inspired by Hill, fought almost to the last man: 'the majority had to be shot down or bayoneted', noted the report. 'Only four men were taken prisoner'.[4] Another German intelligence study, this time investigating British performance at Loos in September 1915, similarly emphasised officers' crucial role in this attack. 'The lack of junior leadership was clearly revealed in the fighting at Loos,' asserted the report. Well-trained Regular officers and NCOs were acknowledged as having made an 'excellent impression' but were too few to influence the battle. The more numerous and inexperienced Kitchener officers, in contrast, lost control of their men with the result that 'at all points of the active front, troops of Englishmen were observed who ran around often aimlessly and purposelessly and through their behaviour offered our artillery and infantry the best possible target'.[5] Although single deserters did appear in enemy lines and isolated men did sometimes surrender, in closed formations of any nationality it was usually the officers who decided whether to fight or capitulate.[6] Even the psychological health of other ranks could depend greatly upon the resilience of their officers. William Tyrrell, a Regular MO, recorded an incident in October 1914 when an officer's mental collapse had catalysed breakdowns among a number of his men. Two years later, Captain Geoffrey Donaldson, explaining why he had allowed a broken officer but no men to go back during action on the Somme, argued that 'an officer is a different thing, because on him depends so largely the nerves of the men'.[7] As the war clearly revealed, 'the competence of the officers forms the gauge of the army's efficiency'.[8]

A number of factors account for officers' disproportionate influence on the battlefield. Simply the symbolic authority deriving from their rank

4 BA-MA Freiburg: PH 3/ 546: Eingangene Meldungen, AOK 2, pp. 92–8: Vernehmung der [twenty-two] Engländer die bei der Unternehmung des RIR 110 am 11.4.16 abends gefangen genommen wurden. 13 Apr. 1916, see particularly point 14.

5 BA-MA Freiburg, PH 5 II/ 64: OHK 6, Die September Offensive, 11 Oct. 1915.

6 For examples of German, British and French officers' pivotal role in surrender, see, respectively, letter of Second Lieutenant A.C. Young to aunt, 16 Sept. 1916, reproduced in L. Housman (ed.), *War Letters of Fallen Englishmen* (Philadelphia: Pine Street Books, 1930, 2002), p. 316, BA-MA Freiburg: PH 3/ 556: Interrogations undertaken in the Cambrai POW Camp: Vernehmung eines Mannes des X. West York Ba[taill]ons, 50. Brig. XVII Division. 17 Sept. 1916 and BA-MA Freiburg, MSg 2/ 1247: P. Seese, memoir, p. 2.

7 *RWOCIS*, p. 36 and IWM, 69/25/1: G. Donaldson, letter to mother, 18 July 1916.

8 HStA Munich/IV, MKr 4751: Order of the *bayerisches Kriegsministerium* regarding officer training, 8 Oct. 1918.

played an important role in gaining men's compliance; as the dramatic experiments carried out by the psychologist Stanley Milgram in the 1960s demonstrated, people possess a strong propensity to obey those whom they regard as legitimate authorities. Bird explicitly noted this factor and it was also recognised by officers themselves: E.F. Chapman, for example, remarked on hearing of his promotion in 1917, that it would be 'a great help to have Captain's rank while I have the Company, to give me more authority'.[9] Officers' rank was, however, not solely symbolic but also conferred considerable power upon its wearer. As has already been seen, coercion was sometimes used by officers to stiffen their men's resistance or maintain order. Yet still more important was their ability to reward men who were loyal, obedient and performed well in battle. As Chapman also recognised, officers could 'make a difference to people. A man works well, and you can get him promoted, which means extra pay. He behaves badly, or shirks his work, and if you think fit you can have him doing pack drill until he curses the day you were born'.[10]

On the battlefield, however, officers' power derived primarily from their ability to provide the sense of order, empowerment and safety sought so desperately by soldiers in the midst of chaos and danger. As the British psychiatrist Charles Myers observed, officers were able to reduce 'the ill-effects of expectancy and want of control' on men. The modern psychologist S.J. Rachman has similarly found that 'effective, calm leaders [make] important contributions to the control of fear'.[11] To Lord Moran, 'phlegm', which he described as 'a supreme imperturbability in the face of death which half amused [men] and half dominated them', was the primary quality needed by officers.[12] Outward displays of confidence and composure by leaders provided a comforting sense of control for subordinates, thus reducing the subjective impact of danger: as *Leutnant* Lüthje noted, 'if one is himself calm, this has a good effect on the men'.[13] Leaders who failed to provide soldiers with a reassuring example in combat were unpopular and viewed as serious liabilities. Bavarian soldiers sung mockingly of the *Hendenaber* (artillery colonel) cowering in the rear 'because it appears to him safer there', while British troops' *bête noire* was the

[9] S. Milgram, 'Behavioural Study of Obedience', in R.D. Gross (ed.), *Key Studies in Psychology* (London: Hodder & Stoughton, 1990), pp. 116–29 and IWM, 92/3/1: E.F. Chapman, letter to mother, 24 Mar. 1917.

[10] IWM, 92/3/1: E.F. Chapman, letter to mother, 3 Aug. 1916.

[11] Myers, *Shell Shock*, p. 39 and Rachman, *Fear and Courage*, pp. 50 and 59–63.

[12] Moran, *Anatomy*, p. 188.

[13] BA-MA Freiburg, MSg 2/ 2797: W. Lüthje, diary, 7 Aug. 1918.

CO 'down in a deep dugout'.[14] *Hauptmann* Helmuth Fuchs, a capable company commander in *Füsilier-Regiment Nr. 40*, condemned one of his *Fähnriche* as 'a bad example for the men' on precisely this ground: 'folded up like a pocket knife when a shell landed nearby while I was speaking with him. We can do without such officers,' he concluded.[15]

Not only fortitude and courage but also competence was essential if officers were to reassure men that their leadership guaranteed safety and control. The widespread recognition that fighting was necessary meant that most other ranks went willingly into battle, but once there, none wished to be sacrificed needlessly. Officers devoid of military skill or knowledge were thus distrusted by their subordinates. The war volunteer August Bauer, for example, wrote a bitter but relieved letter to his family in the autumn of 1914, explaining thankfully that his utterly inept CO 'luckily for us, if I might say so, has now been wounded for 14 days'. The man had caused Bauer's artillery unit heavy casualties, on one occasion by driving straight into enemy infantry fire and on another by allowing it to be outflanked.[16] Irrational displays of bravery which endangered men's lives were also looked on unfavourably and any officer who attempted to coerce subordinates into following him on such an adventure ran the risk of receiving a bullet from behind. British prisoners captured near Ypres in August 1917 after an unsuccessful attack claimed that a captain who had tried to force them through an artillery barrage by threatening them with a revolver would have been disposed of in this way, had he not been killed by a sniper.[17] In October 1917, British intelligence did actually find the body of a German officer whose men had tied his hands behind his back and shot him when he had refused to allow them to surrender.[18]

While fortitude, courage and military skill were all crucial as immediate reactions to battlefield danger, good leadership also depended on the establishment of mutual trust and liking between ranks. As the psychologist and former front officer Paul Plaut confirmed, the soldier 'goes through fire for [his officer] as soon as he has the feeling: that is a "good chap"'.[19] In the long periods of inactivity which defined trench warfare, the best method by which an officer could establish a good relationship with his men was by demonstrating paternalistic affection. In the

[14] See Schuhmacher, *Leben und Seele*, p. 169 and Palmer, *Lovely War*, pp. 118–19.
[15] BA-MA Freiburg, MSg 1/ 2965: H. Fuchs, diary, 14 Sept. 1915.
[16] BZ, A. Bauer, letter to family, 8 Nov. 1914.
[17] BA-MA Freiburg, PH 3/ 585: Vernehmungsprotokolle, AOK 4: Vernehmung [of eight men from 10/Royal West Kents, six men from 11/Royal West Surreys, one man from 23/ Middlesex and twenty-three men from 20/Durham Light Infantry], 3 Aug. 1917.
[18] TNA, WO 157/ 25: Summary of Information (GHQ), 23 Oct. 1917.
[19] Plaut, 'Psychographie des Kriegers', p. 88.

Plate 10. Officers (1): British officers of the Royal Engineers on the Somme, 1 July 1916. The bravery and paternalism of the BEF's junior leadership was an important factor in its formidable resilience. Official British photograph.

opinion of the historian Gary Sheffield, this was 'possibly the most important factor in determining a soldier's attitude to his officer'.[20] It was also crucial in ensuring loyalty and compliance when officers did have to lead their men into danger. As an order issued by the headquarters of *Armee-Abteilung von Strantz* in June 1916 explained:

> The officer who does not timidly separate himself from the men, but rather shows himself to be constantly concerned for them, who shares joy and sorrow with his men and who does not scorn the field kitchen rations given to them, who at the right moment finds a word of recognition and of humour; he will find every man at his side.[21]

Soldiers who knew that an officer had cared for their welfare during periods of inactivity would also trust him not to throw their lives away needlessly in battle. In contrast, officers who alienated their men

[20] Sheffield, *Leadership*, p. 104.

[21] Reproduced in M. Hobohm, *Soziale Heeresmißstände als Teilursache des deutschen Zusammenbruches von 1918. Die Ursachen des Deutschen Zusammenbruches im Jahre 1918*. Part 2: *Der innere Zusammenbruch* (12 vols., Berlin: Deutsche Verlagsgesellschaft für Politik und Geschichte, 1929), XI.1, p. 16 (doc. 2).

through poor treatment were less likely to be followed or respected, regardless of their bravery or military prowess. Discipline outside battle might suffer: according to deserters' statements, insensitive handling by superiors was often a major factor in prompting men to abscond.[22] Alternatively, units could be subverted by bad leadership, rendering them unmanageable and militarily worthless. One company commander of *bayerisches Infanterie-Regiment Nr. 16*, for example, who was captured in October 1917, told interrogators of the mutinous spirit in his unit, explaining that the soldiers had threatened to shoot their battalion commander if he came up to the front line and had nearly killed a *Leutnant*.[23]

Numerous opportunities existed for officers to demonstrate paternalism in the endurance warfare of 1914–18. A few examples from the British army suffice to illustrate the forms and effects of officers' care for their men. Small gifts were very common: officers in the 2/7 Warwickshires pooled their funds in 1916 to buy cigarettes for their soldiers. Sometimes, subordinates' wellbeing was safeguarded by bending the letter of military law: the dispatch rider William Tait recorded, for example, how his major ordered him to report sick, not because he was ill but because the officer had realised that he was in urgent need of a rest. Even cheering men up was considered by many officers to be part of their duty: Lieutenant St Leger, for example, recorded how one officer in his unit had encouraged another to put in his eyeglass during a parade, 'so that the men could laugh'.[24] Such gestures were appreciated greatly by soldiers. At Arras in April 1917, for example, Wrench was genuinely touched on waking up soaking wet to find that an unknown benefactor had left him a dry pair of socks.[25] Chapman, who plied his men with mouth organs, clothes and cigars and once declared that 'my heart and soul are in C coy', received a letter of thanks and condolence from the company cook after he was wounded, revealing the great respect and affection which his concern had elicited:

Sir may I say, that the Company were proud of you, we admired you for your coolness, it seemed danger was never in your thoughts, I can assure you, then I

[22] See the interrogation report in TNA, WO 157/ 1: Summary of Information (GHQ), 28 Aug. 1915 and also GLA Karlsruhe, 456 F 8 /231: Tätigkeitsbericht der Militärpolizeistelle Karlsruhe (Oktober 1917–März 1918), 1 Mar. 1918, p. 7.

[23] TNA, WO 157/ 25: Summary of Information (GHQ), 12 Oct. 1917.

[24] IWM, 69/25/1: G. Donaldson, letter to mother, 13 July 1916; IWM, PP/MCR/161: W.H. Tait, diary, 13 Sept. 1914 and IWM, P 239: W.B. St Leger, diary, 14 Feb. 1917. Officers' paternalism and, in particular, their attempts to keep their men cheerful were satirised by Bruce Bairnsfather in his cartoon 'The Conscientious Exhilarator'. See B. Bairnsfather, *More Fragments from France* (8 vols., London: *The Bystander*, 1916), II, p. 15. For more examples, see Sheffield, *Leadership*, pp. 82–3.

[25] IWM, 85/51/1: A.E. Wrench, diary, 17 Apr. 1917.

should have perhaps have put this first as no doubt it won the mens [*sic*] hearts for you, you studied & understood us. I feel I speak for the Company apart from my own personal feelings.[26]

Crucially, such behaviour not only ensured good discipline and unit cohesion on the battlefield, but it also limited the stress of active service and thus protected men from mental collapse. As the psychiatrist Edward Mapother observed, 'neurosis was rarest in units whose officers showed real interest in securing for their men any possible comfort or mitigation of hardship and when out of the line knew how to insist on discipline and fitness without annoying men about eyewash'.[27] Both the investigation into 'shellshock' undertaken by the Southborough Committee shortly after the war and more recent research on military endurance concur that the presence of 'good officers, especially as regards leadership and the care of their men' is a key factor protecting soldiers from psychiatric disease.[28]

Junior officers possessed immense influence over the combat performance and resilience of First World War armies. Although their symbolic rank and real powers of punishment and reward brought them respect and obedience, it was above all the ability to provide direction and some sense of order and safety which lent officers such authority. Steadfastness, skill and reasoned bravery were all officer qualities respected by other ranks because they reduced the subjective impact of danger and uncontrollability. Trust was also crucial for effective command, and in the long periods of low-intensity, stressful trench warfare, was most successfully created by officers who behaved paternalistically. Leaders who looked after their men both on and off the battlefield attracted considerable loyalty, commanded more effectively and were, therefore, the keystones of any army's disciplinary and supportive structures and the ultimate arbiters of military resilience and performance.

Privilege and paternalism

Modern research into the British and German armies of 1914–18 has diverged nowhere more starkly than in its judgements of their respective junior officer corps. Whereas British junior leadership has been praised

26 IWM, 92/3/1: E.F. Chapman. Letter of Private W. Wheeler to Chapman, 15 June 1917. For examples of Chapman's concern for his men, see ibid., E.F. Chapman, letters to mother, 3 Aug. 1916, 16 Jan. and 2 Mar. 1917.

27 Mapother in United Services Section with Section of Psychiatry, 'Discussion on Functional Nervous Disease', 863.

28 *RWOCIS*, p. 151. Cf. A.D. English, 'Leadership and Operational Stress in the Canadian Forces', *Canadian Military Journal* (Autumn 2000), 33–8.

as being 'of higher quality and greater military significance in the First World War ... than before or since', German officers' performance has been considered far less successful.[29] Historians have blamed the corps' social elitism for impeding its ability to carry out its military duties. Martin Kitchen asserts that the refusal to liberalise the army 'was a significant factor determining Germany's inability to achieve a political equilibrium that might have given the nation reserves of strength to withstand defeat'.[30] Heiger Ostertag has similarly suggested that 'the special social character of the army hindered a successful consciousness of the real area of responsibility of an armed force: the military component'.[31] Wolfgang Kruse also supports this view, arguing that at the front the social segregation of officers and men led inevitably to harsh discipline, insensitive handling and minimal understanding. Lacking the paternalistic protection from which British other ranks benefited, German soldiers became disconsolate, bitter and even revolutionary.[32]

The German officer corps was indeed a self-consciously socially elite institution. Despite a large influx of upper middle-class men in the years before hostilities, its character and ethos were quintessentially aristocratic: 30 per cent of the 33,036 professional (or 'active') officers in pre-war service came from the nobility, but tradition and their disproportionate share of the upper ranks (52 per cent of officers between the ranks of *Oberst* and *General* were aristocrats) ensured that they maintained overweening influence.[33] Strict entry criteria were used to protect the corps' distinctive 'sense of caste identity' or *Standesbewußtsein*. Only men who had been educated at a *Kadettenanstalt* (cadet school) or spent nine years at a *Gymnasium*, *Realgymnasium* or *Oberrealschule* (elite secondary schools) were eligible to become professional officers. Regiments set financial conditions, commanders interviewed candidates in order to assess their social and moral qualities and, once training had been completed, the acceptance of the prospective officer had to be confirmed by his future colleagues through a so-called *Offizierswahl* (officer election).[34] The

29 Keegan, *Face of Battle*, p. 277. Cf. Sheffield, *Leadership*, pp. 178–9.
30 M. Kitchen, *The German Officer Corps 1890–1914* (Oxford: Clarendon Press, 1968), p. 227.
31 Ostertag, *Bildung*, p. 214.
32 Kruse, 'Krieg und Klassenheer', 532–3.
33 For the strength of the professional corps, see Gothein, *Warum verloren wir den Krieg?*, p. 80. His figure is supported by the army's medical history, which quotes an establishment strength of 33,804 professional officers (including medical and veterinary officers) in 1913–14 (see *Sanitätsbericht III*, p. 12). For the social composition (1913 figures), see Ostertag, *Bildung*, p. 45.
34 Ostertag, *Bildung*, pp. 56–7, Samuels, *Command or Control?*, pp. 80–1 and A. Teicht, 'Die Offiziersausbildung in Bayern während des 1. Weltkriegs' unpublished Pädagogik Diplomarbeit, Hochschule der Bundeswehr Munich (1978), pp. 20–2.

reserve corps, numbering approximately 40,000 officers on the outbreak of war, was hardly less socially exalted: in 1905, 45 per cent of the Prussian reserve corps were higher officials, and businessmen and landowners each comprised around 13 per cent.[35] Entry criteria were only marginally less demanding than for the professional corps, candidates being expected to have completed the sixth class of a *Gymnasium* and passed the *Einjährig-Freiwillige* examination. Proof of financial suitability and class was provided by the fact that these men were obliged to pay for their year-long training themselves and, like active officers, their morals were subject to scrutiny by an *Offizierswahl*.[36] Through this careful selection and also rigorous training, reserve officers were inculcated with the same aristocratic ethos as their professional counterparts.[37]

Far from being exceptional, however, the elite social composition of the German army's leadership was common to most European officer corps in the early twentieth century and by no means foredoomed them to failure. As comparison with the much-praised British corps indicates, theories asserting that such social segregation between ranks was inevitably destabilising are too simplistic. Comprising 12,738 Regulars, 5,759 reservists and 9,563 Territorials, the pre-war British corps was much smaller than its future opponent but similarly 'characterised by social and financial exclusiveness'.[38] Forty-two per cent of its generals and one-third of its colonels hailed from the nobility or gentry, while lower commissioned ranks came predominantly from the upper

[35] For reserve officers' occupations, see H. John, *Das Reserveoffizierkorps im Deutschen Kaiserreich 1890–1914. Ein sozialgeschichtlicher Beitrag zur Untersuchung der gesellschaftlichen Militarisierung im Wilhelminischen Deutschland* (Frankfurt am Main: Campus, 1981), p. 264. In 1913, the German army possessed 23,000 reserve and 11,000 *Landwehr* officers according to British intelligence, which reached this conclusion by adding up the names in that year's published army lists. Additional to this figure were perhaps 6–7,000 commissioned reserve medical and veterinary personnel. No definitive estimate for these men exists, but it is known that the army required a little more than 10,000 such men on mobilisation in August 1914, approximately 3,000 of whom were probably active officers. See General Staff, *German Army Handbook April 1918*, ed. D. Nash (London and New York: Arms and Armour Press and Hippocrene Books, 1977), p. 24, *Sanitätsbericht III*, pp. 4* and 8* and C. von Altrock (ed.), *Vom Sterben des deutschen Offizierkorps* (Berlin: E.S. Mittler & Sohn, 1922), p. 54.

[36] Teicht, 'Offiziersausbildung', pp. 23–5 and John, *Reserveoffizierkorps*, pp. 54–9 and pp. 261–6.

[37] E.-O. Volkmann, *Soziale Heeresmißstände als Mitursache des deutschen Zusammenbruches von 1918. Die Ursachen des Deutschen Zusammenbruches im Jahre 1918*. Part 2: *Der innere Zusammenbruch* (12 vols., Berlin: Deutsche Verlagsgesellschaft für Politik und Geschichte, 1929), XI.2, pp. 23–4.

[38] K. Simpson, 'The Officers', in I.F.W. Beckett and K. Simpson (eds.), *A Nation in Arms. A Social Study of the British Army in the First World War* (Manchester University Press, 1985), p. 65. For officer numbers, see Sheffield, *Leadership*, p. 30.

middle class.[39] Entry criteria were similar to those of the German corps. A public school education, although not a formal requirement, was in practice a *sine qua non* for acceptance. Financial criteria were also stipulated by individual regiments, the most prestigious demanding that their officers possess minimum independent means of 400 pounds per year. Some ideological differences did exist: whereas the German corps drew its ethos from the hereditary nobility, the British emphasised 'gentlemanliness', a concept more closely related to education and upbringing than blood. Theoretically, this made the British corps more open to the promotion of lower-class men from the ranks; in practice, however, it made little difference in the pre-war period, when only 2 per cent of officers were accepted through this route.[40]

Not only was the British corps no less socially elite than its German counterpart but recent research has actually emphasised the beneficial effects of this composition on officer–man relations. As Gary Sheffield has explained, upper-class officers were preferred by the British army precisely because their background and education provided them with useful leadership skills. 'Chivalric influences', he argues, 'ingested via the public school, pulpit and sports-field, left the young men . . . with little doubt as to the standards expected of gentlemen placed in command of men who were fighting for their country'. Heroism, self-sacrifice, team spirit and duty were all encouraged by the sport, popular literature and study of classics which featured so prominently in the lives of upper-class youth. Moreover, the 'gentlemanly' principle that privilege was accompanied by responsibility to social inferiors was firmly ingrained in the country's social elite through the paternalism–deference exchange characterising peacetime class relations. The deep-rooted acceptance of this doctrine, known as *noblesse oblige*, ensured that when upper-class men such as Chapman entered the army, they automatically cared for their subordinates, with excellent results for unit cohesion and combat performance.[41]

39 For generals and colonels, see Spiers, 'Regular Army', p. 40. For the lower commissioned ranks, see the table in Simpson, 'Officers', p. 91. This shows the occupations of fathers of entrants into the Sandhurst officer training academy: in 1910, military professionals comprised the largest group with nearly 43.8% of the total, 23% were 'civilian professionals', 9.3% were 'businessmen and managers' and 20.5% were classified simply as 'gentlemen'.

40 Simpson, 'Officers', p. 64.

41 Sheffield, *Leadership*, pp. 4–6, 43–53 and 178–9. For a summary of the argument, see also G. Sheffield, 'Officer–Man Relations, Discipline and Morale in the British Army of the Great War', in H. Cecil and P.H. Liddle (eds.), *Facing Armageddon. The First World War Experienced* (London: Leo Cooper, 1996), pp. 413–24.

A closer examination of the German army's preference for upper-class men suggests that it was motivated similarly by military considerations rather than simply snobbery. Since the early 1890s, education at *Gymnasien* and *Realgymnasien* had cultivated fierce patriotism and a strong sense of loyalty to the Hohenzollerns; qualities which fitted very well with the officer corps' own direct fealty to the Kaiser.[42] Honour (*Ehre*), the aristocratic concept which lay at the heart of officers' identity, was also valued by upper-class youths, as proven by the pledges, mock duels and quasi-medieval customs of German student fraternities.[43] Far from being irrelevancies in modern war, such attitudes were believed to be essential for leading troops through the hail of fire on the modern battlefield: just as officers imbued with the aristocratic moral code could be expected to defend their personal honour by duelling in peace, so, too, in war they could be relied upon to suffer the hero's death (*Heldentod*) to inspire their soldiers and defend the honour of King and Kaiser.[44] Moreover, contrary to the impression given by current historiography, the corps' *Standesbewußtsein* was impeccably paternalist. The necessity for officers to take an interest in their soldiers had been recognised by the Prussian army since the promulgation of its liberalising 'Order on Military Punishment' in 1808, leading to the metamorphosis of the unit *Hauptmann* into the *Kompagnievater* (company father) during the nineteenth century.[45] By the First World War, paternalistic responsibilities had been codified as an integral part of the officer's position. Point Six of the 1908 *Felddienst-Ordnung*, the service manual of the Prussian army, stated, 'never resting care for the welfare of his men is the good and rewarding privilege of the officer'.[46] Point Five reminded officers that 'it is not enough that one orders, nor that one has right in mind; much more influential on subordinates is the way in which one orders'.[47] Given the aristocratic heritage of these ideas, it was only natural that the officer

42 M. Kraul, *Das deutsche Gymnasium 1780–1980* (Frankfurt am Main: Suhrkamp, 1984), pp. 120–3.

43 See K.H. Jarausch, 'German Students in the First World War', *Central European History* 17, 4 (December 1984), 310–15 and G.L. Mosse, *Fallen Soldiers. Reshaping the Memory of the World Wars* (Oxford University Press, 1990), pp. 53–69.

44 M. Funck, 'In den Tod gehen. Bilder des Sterbens im 19. und 20. Jahrhundert', in U. Breymayer, B. Ulrich and K. Wieland (eds.), *Willensmenschen. Über deutsche Offiziere* (Frankfurt am Main: Fischer Taschenbuch, 1999), p. 231.

45 See K. Demeter, *The German Officer-Corps in Society and State 1650–1945* (London: Weidenfeld and Nicolson, 1962, 1965), pp. 174–82 and HStA Munich/IV, Gen.-Kdo I. AK 52: Order from *Chef des Generalstabes des Feldheeres* concerning physical and verbal mishandling, 18 Sept. 1916.

46 Kriegsministerium, *Felddienst-Ordnung (F.O.)* (Berlin: Ernst Siegfried Mittler und Sohn, 1908), p. 10.

47 Ibid., pp. 9–10.

corps should turn to upper-class men to implement them: the tradition of *noblesse oblige* was no less integral to German nobles' identity than it was to that of their cousins across the Channel, and by the late nineteenth century, its philanthropic values had also been adopted by burgeoning urban elites.[48]

Despite the belief that upper-class men would possess a natural affinity to command, pre-war German officer training did not neglect to reinforce paternalistic values. The controversial *Kadettenanstalten* which prepared boys for life as active officers may have provided little intellectual stimulus but did place their pupils within a 'mild and paternal' model of discipline and encouraged them to take responsibility for younger peers.[49] Whether previous cadets or graduates of civilian *Gymnasien*, men who sought a professional military career all personally experienced life in the ranks, practised command as NCOs and were themselves subject to the army's paternalistic impulses, a young *Leutnant* being nominated as their guiding *Fähnrichsvater* (Ensign Father).[50] Training for prospective reserve officers was organised along similar principles: as barrack-room seniors, *Einjährig-Freiwillige* were held responsible for their conscripted comrades' hygiene and tidiness and expected to set an example of loyalty, obedience and efficiency.[51] Such instruction was designed to create paternalistic officers not only concerned for men's physical wellbeing but also capable of guiding conscripts away from the perceived malign influences of Social Democracy and instilling in them feelings of loyalty and duty towards the Kaiser.[52] Modern critics might question its success, given contemporary scandals

[48] For the aristocracy, see S. Malinowski, *Vom König zum Führer. Sozialer Niedergang und politische Radikalisierung im deutschen Adel zwischen Kaiserreich und NS-Staat* (Berlin: Akademie, 2003), pp. 111–13. For the urban upper classes' adoption of similar values, see H. Jaeger, 'Der Unternehmer als Vater und Patriarch', in W. Faulstich and G.E. Grimm, eds., *Sturz der Götter? Vaterbilder im 20. Jahrhundert* (Frankfurt am Main: Suhrkamp, 1989), pp. 105–6.

[49] This description is that of the American general Emory Upton, who visited the schools in the 1870s. Quoted in S.E. Clemente, *For King and Kaiser! The Making of the Prussian Army Officer, 1860–1914* (London: Greenwood, 1992), p. 123. The quality of life and education provided by the *Kadettenanstalten* continue to be debated. For criticism (especially of the low intellectual standards and bullying that the system could encourage), see ibid., pp. 81–135. For a more positive view, see J. Moncure, *Forging the King's Sword. Military Education between Tradition and Modernization. The Case of the Royal Prussian Cadet Corps, 1871–1918* (New York: P. Lang, 1993), especially, for details of leadership training, pp. 179–84 and 199–202.

[50] See Clemente, *For King and Kaiser!*, pp. 72–3, Ostertag, *Bildung*, pp. 99–100 and Teicht, 'Offiziersausbildung', p. 21.

[51] Frevert, *Nation in Barracks*, pp. 167–9 and John, *Reserveoffizierkorps*, pp. 119–23.

[52] See Frevert, *Nation in Barracks*, pp. 194–5, Clemente, *For King and Kaiser!*, p. 162 and also BA-MA Freiburg, PH 3/ 62: Order of *Generalquartiermeister* on combating leftist propaganda, 25 July 1917.

about the verbal and physical mishandling of recruits. Yet the significance of these cases should not be overestimated; the 800 plaintiffs who came before the courts annually in Prussia were a tiny proportion of the 800,000 men serving in the peacetime army, and the overwhelming majority of accusations seem to have been directed at NCOs rather than officers.[53] A useful corrective to the popularised view of professional German officers as upper-class brutes may be found in the experience of Wilhelm Lüthje, who on arrival at a Nuremberg regiment for officer training in 1909 was barked at by the active *Hauptmann* who received him: 'first come the horses, then the men, then you yourself!' As Lüthje had not been greeted and was still standing in civilian clothes this surprised him. Yet it clearly made a deep impression, for nine years later, as a veteran *Leutnant*, he criticised a superior in his diary but then rehabilitated him with the words, 'he does however understand something; he interests himself in the men and horses, and that is the main thing'.[54] Such concern for the wellbeing of subordinates was unlikely to have been exceptional. As another officer remembered after the war, 'the young officer was taught to understand the characteristics of the man from his earlier civilian occupational activity and to be thoroughly concerned with his personal relationships, in order to support him with advice and help if necessary'.[55]

During the war, both armies underwent huge expansion. At first, new officers were drawn from traditional recruiting grounds. The British army stipulated in April 1915 that officer candidates should possess 'adequate military knowledge', 'a public school education or its equivalent' and be under twenty-seven years of age.[56] The German corps, although it reduced some of its educational requirements (the Bavarian corps, for example, dropped its demand that professional officers should possess the *Abitur* exam qualification in December 1914), also maintained its high social standards during the first half of hostilities.[57] The constant demand for new leaders to replace casualties or command new units, however, eventually forced both officer corps to adopt a more

[53] Kitchen, *German Officer Corps*, pp. 182–4. Evidence that most of the accused were NCOs comes from Saxon army figures, which record that between 1909 and June 1914, only seven officers were sentenced for mishandling, in contrast to 109 NCOs. See Volkmann, *Soziale Heeresmißstände* XI.2, p. 123. German NCOs had a particular propensity to resort to unofficial means of maintaining discipline due to fear of themselves accumulating bad reports and being denied a civil service post at the end of their career. See Samuels, *Command or Control?*, p. 80.

[54] BA-MA Freiburg, MSg 2/ 2797: W. Lüthje, memoir section of diary, p. 8 and diary, 3 Sept. 1918.

[55] F. Altrichter, *Die seelischen Kräfte des Deutschen Heeres im Frieden und im Weltkriege* (Berlin: E.S. Mittler & Sohn, 1933), p. 57.

[56] Sheffield, *Leadership*, pp. 30 and 39.

[57] Teicht, 'Offiziersausbildung', pp. 31 and 36.

Plate 11. Officers (2): German officers at Verdun, March 1916. The youth of many German junior leaders is particularly evident in this photograph. From the album of *II/Feldartillerie-Regiment Nr. 84*.

flexible approach towards recruitment. In the British army, which awarded 247,061 new commissions during the conflict, 39 per cent of officers came from the lower middle and working classes by the end of the war.[58] Many of the 220,000 wartime officers (*Kriegsoffiziere*) recruited by the German army also came from less prestigious backgrounds as first educational standards were lowered and then, from June and December 1917, the old financial and social criteria were discarded.[59] Unlike in the British army, however, the continued

[58] Sheffield, *Leadership*, pp. 30–2.

[59] Due to the fragmentary nature of the sources, this figure is necessarily an estimate. Volkmann (*Soziale Heeresmißstände* XI.2, p. 33) states that 272,053 active and reserve officers served during the war. Subtracting the approximately 30,000 active and 34,000 reserve officers appointed in peacetime (see notes 33 and 35 above) leaves 208,000 (non-medical or veterinary) wartime commissions. A further 10–11,000 medical and veterinary officers (excluding the perhaps 10–15,000 emergency *Feldhilfsärzte* and *Feldhilfsveterinäre*) were also promoted during hostilities (see von Altrock (ed.), *Vom Sterben*, p. 54), making a total of about 220,000 wartime commissions. For entry standards, see Teicht, 'Offiziersausbildung', pp. 31, 36, 54 and 85.

requirement that officers possess a good secondary education meant that working-class soldiers remained effectively barred from promotion. NCOs who proved themselves in battle but lacked the academic qualifications needed for reserve officer training were rarely made full officers but instead promoted to the lesser rank of *Feldwebelleutnant*, 21,608 of whom were created by the Prussian army during the war.[60]

The greater openness of the wartime British officer corps to working-class men was emphatically not an attempt to democratise the army but rather a pragmatic solution to officer shortages. Far from surrendering its pre-war ethos of exclusivity, the army attempted to maintain a veneer of class distinction between ranks and ensure that new, lower-class officers were fully imbued with the traditional values of paternalism and leadership. In particular, Officer Cadet Battalions were established in February 1916 to provide the new lower-class officers not only with military training but also with an introduction to the gentlemanly mores of the traditional officer class.[61] In this respect, the British hardly differed from their opponents, who also sought to inculcate lower middle-class wartime officers with the chivalrous pre-war 'caste consciousness'. The necessity of leading from the front continued to be promulgated by the German corps: as training guidelines observed in November 1916, 'the officer is the model for his men; his example pulls them forward with him'.[62] The overriding importance of paternalism also continued to be emphasised, official guidelines for officer training ordering in 1917 that 'it is to be stressed in the instruction that the care for the wellbeing of the man is one of the foremost leadership duties'.[63] Once commissioned, the new officers were constantly reminded that, 'the longer the war lasts, the greater must be the care and personal sympathy of the superior for his subordinate'.[64] As

60 For the promotion of lower middle-class men, see Altrichter, *Seelischen Kräfte*, p. 232. For an example of a man who benefited from the reduced criteria of wartime, see BA-MA Freiburg, MSg 2/ 3788: Papers of G. Klein. Klein's father was a master carpenter, a profession which would not have satisfied the high standards maintained by the corps in the pre-war period. For *Feldwebelleutnants*, see Volkmann, *Soziale Heeresmißstände*, XI.2, p. 36. Theoretically, NCOs lacking the *Befähigung zum Einjährig-Freiwilligen Dienst* could be promoted to *Leutnant* if they distinguished themselves before the enemy. As only eighty-two and ninety-one *Feldwebel* were commissioned in the Prussian and Bavarian armies respectively on these grounds, the condition was virtually irrelevant.

61 Sheffield, *Leadership*, pp. 54–60.

62 BA-MA Freiburg, PH 3/ 28: Zum Exerzier-Reglement. Kampfschule. Allgemeines. Nov. 1916. Modern research agrees: see Stouffer *et al.*, *American Soldier*, II, p. 124.

63 HStA Munich/IV, MKr 1857: *Bestimmungen für die Lehrgänge der Anwärter zu Offizieraspiranten des Beurlaubtenstandes der Infanterie, Jäger und Schützen einsch. Maschinengewehr-Truppen auf Truppenübungsplätzen des Inlandes* (Berlin: Reichsdruckerei, 1917), p. 8.

64 HStA Munich/IV, Gen.-Kdo I. AK 52: Order from *Chef des Generalstabes*, 18 Sept. 1916.

Heeresgruppe Deutscher Kronprinz bluntly warned at the end of the war, 'an officer who does not care for his men, does not belong in his place'.[65]

Not only admonitions but also practical tips were issued in order to help the new German reserve officers to act paternalistically. A 1917 booklet produced for divisions being transferred to the west after the cessation of fighting in Russia reminded officers that not only should they know their subordinates' names but also their attitudes, characters and familial relations. It advised that efforts should be made to amuse men outside hours of instruction with sport, competitions, music and the cinema.[66] An array of booklets written by professional soldiers in order to help the quickly trained front-line officers to adapt to their new role reinforced this message. That written by *Major* Georg Wintterlin echoed and bettered the *Felddienst-Ordnung* when it observed, 'care for the man [is] the greatest privilege for the officer'.[67] Wintterlin emphasised the importance of allowing men to sleep undisturbed after battle and the need to provide good food and warm quarters. Singing should be promoted, sporting competitions organised and, ambitiously, he suggested that the men should be encouraged to become teetotal. The guide produced by *Oberst* Eckart von Wurmb echoed Wintterlin's advice on rations and accommodation and paid particular attention to the importance of ensuring men's feet were in good condition.[68] *Oberst* Schaible, in his 1917 manual, more generally warned against dishonourable behaviour towards subordinates and recommended that demonstrations of trust would help to form a good relationship between the young officer and his men.[69]

By offering this advice, these professional officers were attempting to pass on the ethos of the pre-war army to the young recruits, on whose leadership at the front the fate of Germany depended. While the traditional *Standesbewußtsein* or 'caste consciousness' of the officer corps was

[65] HStA Munich/IV, Gen.-Kdo I. AK 52: Order from *Heeresgruppe Deutscher Kronprinz*, 7 Nov. 1918. Cf. Hobohm, *Soziale Heeresmißstände*, XI.1, pp. 13–78. Such orders are generally interpreted as proof of neglect by officers, but they may more accurately reflect the deeply ingrained paternalistic concern of the General Staff.

[66] BA-MA Freiburg, PH 3/ 33: Maasgruppe West (Generalkommando VII AK), *Richtlinien über die Ausbildung von Offizieren und Mannschaften des östlichen Kriegsschauplatzes in der westlichen Kriegsfuehrung*. 22 Nov. 1917, pp. 3 and 19.

[67] G. Wintterlin, *Kriegsgemäße Ausbildung der Kompagnie. Eine Anleitung für Kompagnie- und Zugführer* (Berlin: Ernst Siegfried Mittler & Sohn, 1917), pp. 68 and 70.

[68] E. von Wurmb, '*Zum Offizier befördert!*' *Kameradschaftlicher Ratgeber für junge Offiziere und den Offizierersatz der Linie und des Beurlaubtenstandes* (Berlin: R. Eisenschmidt, 1917), pp. 43–4.

[69] C. Schaible, *Standes- und Berufspflichten des deutschen Offiziers. Für angehende und jüngere Offiziere des stehenden Heeres und des Beurlaubtenstandes* (Berlin: R. Eisenschmidt, 1917), pp. 24–5.

certainly designed to distinguish leaders from the led, one of its central tenets was that position entailed responsibility. Aristocratic culture had a long history of paternalism, and it was partly for this reason that social exclusivity was considered so important not only for the peacetime but also for the military functions of the officer corps. When heavy casualties and the requirements of a nation in arms necessitated the loosening of social criteria for recruitment into the corps, efforts were made to inculcate the new lower middle-class reserve officers with the paternalistic ethos. Far from being encouraged to be indifferent, condescending or even brutal towards their subordinates, officers in the peace- and wartime German armies, as in their British opponent, were given every encouragement to support, care for and build relationships with the men under their command.

Deficiencies and disadvantages

Despite the German officer corps' attempts to inculcate its members with paternalistic ideals in both peacetime and during war, relations between ranks in the Kaiser's force were indeed less harmonious than those of its opponent. During hostilities, a widely attested 'officer hate' (*Offiziershaß*) swept through German units. One of the earliest, most detailed and best known accounts of this emotion was a tract written by an NCO, Hermann Kantorowicz, in September 1916, which warned of an 'irreconcilable hatred against one's own officer'. Unfairness in the distribution of rations, pay and awards were, in his opinion, the primary grounds for the bitterness.[70] Independent confirmation of the causes and extent of resentment among the rank and file can be found in a postal censorship report of July 1917 which observed that 'disparaging criticisms of officers are the order of the day' and listed inequalities in pay, rations and leave as being particularly divisive.[71] After the war, the leftist liberal *Reichsarchiv* historian Martin Hobohm collected an impressive array of official documents referring to the abuses and discontent within the army. Besides the factors mentioned by the censor and Kantorowicz, he identified severe discipline, insensitive handling, corruption and shirking on the part of officers, unfair promotion, inadequate leave and rest and inequitable quartering as further causes of tension. For him, it was not the leftist extremists at home who had undermined the army, as the high command claimed, but the poor behaviour of a selfish, elitist officer

[70] Kantorowicz, *Offiziershaß*, pp. 11 and 15–21.
[71] BA-MA Freiburg, W-10/ 50794: Postüberwachung der 5. *Armee*, 12 July 1917, p. 15.

corps: 'What was the *Spartakus* movement', he asked, 'against the gluttonous, rancorous, haughty fraction among the officers?!'[72]

Hobohm sought to blame the pre-war officer corps for the discontent, arguing that the segregation of ranks by class had created an 'obsolete model of army'.[73] Certainly, as pre-war scandals demonstrated, young upper-class men, when placed in positions of authority, were not immune from victimising their social inferiors.[74] The corps ethos may also have inadvertently encouraged such tendencies. In the BEF, particularly in its Regular units, officers were no less exalted than their German counterparts but were united with their subordinates by devotion to the regiment, 'the cornerstone of the relationship between officers and other ranks'.[75] In contrast, the keystone of German officers' ideology, the maintenance of the *Standesbewußtsein*, provided no such vertical links; concern to uphold the honour and standing of their caste provided only horizontal loyalty to other officers, shutting off leaders from their men. Nonetheless, the intense promotion of paternalistic impulses within the corps should have worked to discourage insensitive or arrogant behaviour towards subordinates and indeed, during the early war years, there do seem to have been few problems. Although Kantorowicz recorded hearing rumours of a 'widespread officer hate' in 1915, he himself did not believe them until the following year.[76] Hobohm's own evidence also indicates that the resentment was not a major feature of the earlier period of the war: among the impressive collection of documents that he produced illustrating military abuses, only one dated from before mid-1916, and this dealt with the minor issue of officers flirting with women in public.[77] An independent examination of the Bavarian army's papers uncovered no warnings about the verbal or physical mishandling of subordinates in 1914, although some from 1915 and early 1916.[78] In general, however, the paternalistic ethos of the original upper-class officers seems to have successfully lubricated command relations. Active

[72] Hobohm, *Soziale Heeresmißstände*, XI.1, p. 364.

[73] Ibid., p. 373.

[74] See, for example, HStA Munich/IV, MKr 4751: Order of *bayerisches Kriegsministerium* warning that *Fähnriche* and *Fahnenjunker* had been mishandling subordinates, 20 July 1912.

[75] Baynes, *Morale*, p. 169.

[76] Kantorowicz, *Offiziershaß*, p. 4.

[77] See the documents reproduced in Hobohm, *Soziale Heeresmißstände*, XI.1, pp. 13–79 and 377–421. Document 1 (p. 14) dates from the end of 1915.

[78] The Bavarian War Ministry issued warnings against mishandling on 12 May, 7 Sept. and 9 Nov. 1915 and 20 Apr. 1916. Similar orders were promulgated by the Acting Command (*stellvertretendes Generalkommando*) of *I. bayerisches Armeekorps* on 17 Nov. and 31 Dec. 1915, 31 Jan. 1916 and 19 Feb. 1916. See HStA Munich/IV, Gen.-Kdo I. AK 52 (Akt. 4); Stellv. Gen.-Kdo I. AK 591 and MKr 11254.

officers were usually praised, not despised, by contemporaries. Genscher, for example, commented admiringly on the 'purposeful appearance of a professional officer, behind which in most cases is concealed knowledge and understanding for the common soldier' and complaints against officers made late in the war often referred nostalgically to the professionals' exemplary behaviour in 1914 and 1915.[79]

Defenders of the professional corps argued that discontent stemmed not from its aristocratic 'caste consciousness' but rather from the failure of the less socially elite, wartime-recruited officers to internalise its paternalistic precepts. For the *Reichsarchiv* historian and former staff officer Erich-Otto Volkmann, the heavy casualties of the first fifteen months of war, which in fatalities alone totalled 17 per cent of active officers and 9 per cent of the reserve, irrevocably damaged the corps' ability to transmit its ethos and expertise.[80] Expansion had also simply been on too great a scale: the *Kriegsoffiziere* and *Feldwebelleutnants* appointed during hostilities had numbered almost eight times the strength of the original active officer corps. While these arguments tally with the chronology of discontent, they do not stand scrutiny. British wartime officers were often of lower class than their German counterparts, outnumbered the Regular corps of 1914 by twenty to one, yet, as Sheffield has demonstrated, were thoroughly imbued with its paternalistic ethos.[81] Any failure on the part of the *Kriegsoffiziere* to internalise the *Standesbewußtsein* cannot be blamed on their numbers but was rather the result of inadequate training. Whereas British wartime officers' instruction lasted between three months and one year, active officers in the German army were commissioned after an eight- (later twelve-) week programme and reserve officers were taught within their regiments before being sent on brief courses, often lacking suitable teaching personnel.[82] Although partly offset by the considerable period spent by most *Kriegsoffiziere* in the ranks and as NCOs, during which they often acquired battlefield skills and leadership experience, the decentralised nature and poor quality of much of their training may have hindered

79 BA-MA Freiburg, MSg 2/ 2735: H. Genscher, letter to father, 20 Mar. 1915. For praise of peacetime-trained officers serving early in the war, see Hobohm, *Soziale Heeresmißstände*, XI.1, pp. 45 (doc. 16b) and 67–71 (doc. 26) and Gothein, *Warum verloren wir den Krieg?*, p. 81. Also, cf. Volkmann, *Soziale Heeresmißstände*, XI.2, p. 101.

80 Volkmann, *Soziale Heeresmißstände*, XI.2, pp. 34 and 89. Cf. Altrichter, *Seelischen Kräfte*, p. 213.

81 For statistics, see above, pp. 115–16 and 121–2. Calculations exclude medical and veterinary personnel.

82 Simpson, 'Officers', p. 69 and Teicht, 'Offiziersausbildung', pp. 58, 81, 83–4 and 86.

Plate 12. Hunger: German military kitchen in France. Note the empty shelves: an inadequate and inequitable food supply did much to unsettle German officer-man relations. From a German airman's album.

their absorption of the professional officers' consciousness of honour and the paternalistic responsibility which accompanied it.[83]

Most importantly, however, the conditions in which these new *Kriegsoffiziere* operated were far more difficult than those faced either by their peacetime-trained predecessors in 1914 and 1915 or by British officers serving during the war. It was above all the food shortages which beset the German army from the spring of 1916 that catalysed protests against officers' privileges. According to the official *Reichsarchiv* history, the

[83] Letter and diary evidence suggests that the period of probation could be as much as two years. See BA-MA Freiburg, MSg 2/ 3788: G. Klein, letters and BA-MA Freiburg, MSg 2/ 2735: H. Genscher, letters. Cf. also French, *Military Identities*, p. 177, who suggests that the pre-1914 system of unit-based training in the British army was inferior to the school-based methods used to instruct German active officers. If correct, the inversion of this situation during the war, when the British instituted home courses for all prospective officers, whereas the Germans relied heavily on regiment-based teaching for the majority of wartime-commissioned (reserve) officers, therefore implies a corresponding downgrade in the uniformity and quality of German leadership training.

calorific content of soldiers' rations decreased from 3,100 in August 1914 to 2,500 during the winter of 1917–18.[84] Already from early April 1916, men on leave trains could be heard to complain that officers 'indulged to excess, while the soldiers don't even have the bare necessities'.[85] By August, officers belonging to the General Command of *I. bayerisches Armeekorps* were aggrieved that other ranks had apparently forgotten the comradeship forged in the shared danger outside Verdun and were complaining that 'the officers live like lords in the field and the soldier has nothing to eat!'[86] The army attempted to respond in December 1916 by establishing so-called *Menagekommissionen*, boards of officers and men whose job was to ensure that food was distributed fairly, and also by issuing constant warnings to officers not to flaunt their better rations. Complaints did not abate, however.[87] Only when officers ate with the men and shared their food did criticism cease but the enforcement of such a policy was steadfastly refused by the high command in the belief that separation between officers and men was a precondition of good discipline. This was certainly a mistake: officers who did eat with their subordinates often gained respect. It is significant, for example, that a captured NCO of the elite *4. Sturm-Bataillon* who 'spoke in glowing terms' about his officer mentioned specifically that he messed with the unit's NCOs behind the lines.[88]

More could, of course, have been done by the officer corps to allay criticism. The notional equality in food could have been enforced with much more vigour. Other benefits of rank, such as wartime pay rates, were unnecessarily generous compared with relative scales in the British army and could have been reduced.[89] Yet not only would such measures have demoralised officers, but it is also questionable whether all

[84] Reichsarchiv, *Der Weltkrieg 1914 bis 1918. Die Kriegsführung an der Westfront im Jahre 1918* (14 vols., Berlin: E.S. Mittler & Sohn, 1944), XIV, p. 31, footnote 1. Cf. Offer, *First World War*, p. 60, who nonetheless maintains that the army successfully supplied 'an energy ration' throughout the conflict.

[85] HStA Dresden, 11352 Stellv. Gen.-Kdo XIX AK Nr. KA(P) 24139: Kriegsakten betr. Eisenbahnüberwachungsreisen, p. 67, report dated 13 Apr. 1916.

[86] HStA Munich/IV, Gen.-Kdo I. AK 104: Order of *Generalkommando, I. Bayer AK*, 27 Aug. 1916.

[87] HStA Munich/IV, Gen.-Kdo I. AK 52: Order of the *Generalquartiermeister*, 26 Dec. 1916.

[88] TNA, WO 157/ 192: Summary of Information. Fourth Army. 1 Mar. 1918. For the belief that discipline could be damaged if men and officers ate together, see Hobohm, *Soziale Heeresmißstände*, XI.1, p. 51 (doc. 19).

[89] Thus, for example, while a Second Lieutenant in the field received almost 10 shillings per day, ten times more than the lowest paid private, a German *Leutnant* was given 310 marks per month, almost twenty times the pay earned by his men. See Hobohm, *Soziale Heeresmißstände*, XI.1, pp. 111–13, Simpson, 'Officers', p. 77 and General Staff, *Field Service Pocket Book. 1914* (London: HMSO, 1914), p. 179.

complaints would have ceased. Such was the sensitivity caused by material hardship that it was not unknown for even NCOs' much lesser privileges to be challenged by 1917, ditties such as 'Fünf Mark dreissig, / Immer fleißig, / Dreizehn Mark, / Faul und stark' ('Five Marks thirty, / Always busy, / Thirteen Marks / Lazy and strong') becoming widespread.[90] Contrary to the assertions of post-war socialists, it was not selfishness and exaggerated privilege generated by an elitist and outmoded aristocratic ideology which caused inter-rank tension but the simple fact that Germany was not in a position to satisfy its soldiers' basic needs. It was, no doubt, fortunate for the continued success of the paternalism–deference exchange between ranks and good reputation of the British officer corps that the BEF's troops were so well supplied that, as one German prisoner-interrogation report noted enviously, cheese and bully beef could be thrown away and biscuits burnt *en masse*.[91]

Undoubtedly, the composition of the *Kriegsoffiziere* exacerbated other ranks' feelings of bitterness. Casualties were such that many new officers were middle-class men who had only just reached military age, and whose youth and inexperience hindered their ability to win their subordinates' loyalty. Far from the 'officer hate' being a consequence of class divisions between ranks, in many units it was therefore a generation gap which caused conflict. The army, ever desperate for more soldiers, drew in one-third of its replacement drafts from men over thirty-five by 1917. Numerous orders testify to the difficulties experienced by young *Kriegsoffiziere* in relating to and commanding such troops.[92] Middle-aged men condemned an army which commissioned 'boys of 19 years', who 'understand nothing of the world, already have big mouths and pocket large salaries'.[93] Moreover, rather than easing this criticism, the social expansion of the wartime corps sometimes actually encouraged it, soldiers lambasting newly promoted officers of inferior social status, 'who

90 GLA Karlsruhe, 456 F 8 /260: Report on graffiti in toilets of *Schnellzug* D 32 and 33 Metz–Würzburg–Metz issued by *stellvertretendes Generalkommando*, Karlsruhe, 17 Nov. 1917 (p. 748).

91 BA-MA Freiburg, PH 3/ 585: Vernehmungsprotokolle, AOK 4: Vernehmung [of men from 6/Somerset Light Infantry], 22 Aug. 1917. For British soldiers' general contentment with food, see IWM, 84/46/1: M. Hardie, Report on Complaints, Moral, etc., 23 Nov. 1916, p. 1.

92 See, for example, HStA Munich/IV, MKr 1857: Memoranda on officer training from *Oberkommando der 6. Armee* to *preußisches Kriegsministerium*, 28 Dec. 1916 and 30 June 1917 and HStA Munich/IV, MKr 1858: Memorandum on officer training of *11. bayerische Infanterie-Division* to *bayerisches Kriegsministerium* of 18 Dec. 1917. For the composition of drafts, see Ziemann, *Front*, pp. 64–5.

93 BA-MA Freiburg, W-10/ 50794: Postüberwachung der 5. *Armee*, 12 July 1917, p. 20. See also Kantorowicz, *Offiziershaß*, pp. 17–19.

never saw so much money in their lives'.[94] Not simple class tension but rather the thought that some men were unfairly benefiting from the war was the primary factor behind the 'officer hate'.

Wartime alterations in the German army's command structure probably also inflamed criticism. Partly due to its exclusive recruitment, the peacetime corps was only large enough to fill two-thirds of the fully mobilised army's 119,754 officer posts.[95] Heavy losses combined with the corps' continued intransigence in lowering its entry conditions exacerbated the shortfall in officers during the first two years of war, a low point being reached in July 1916, simultaneous with the army's food crisis.[96] These shortages, combined with an ongoing reluctance, possibly motivated by the desire to preserve the structure of the peacetime corps, to promote officers raised to new positions of responsibility, resulted in a process of 'rank appreciation', whereby middle- and junior-ranking commissioned leaders were gradually distanced from the soldiery. An examination of one unit, *bayerisches Reserve-Infanterie-Regiment Nr. 23*, sheds light on this development. On its departure for the front in mid-January 1915, the regiment was led by an *Oberstleutnant*. Its three battalions were commanded by another *Oberstleutnant* and two *Majore* and, in the first battalion, one *Major*, two *Hauptleute* and an *Oberleutnant* acted as company commanders.[97] By September 1916, heavy casualties had resulted in the lowest officer ranks being given much more responsibility. Although the same *Oberstleutnant* continued to command the regiment, its battalions were now led by two *Hauptleute* and a *Major*. Most significantly, the company commanders of *I. Battalion* now consisted of three *Leutnants* and an *Oberleutnant*. In February 1918, these ranks continued to lead the companies. Alterations had taken place further up the hierarchy, however, with a *Major* now commanding the regiment and *Hauptleute* leading each of the battalions. Thus, after four years of war, each rank had effectively received a promotion: *Majore* filled posts which had belonged to *Oberstleutnants* at the outbreak of

94 Staatsbib. Berlin, Ms. Boruss. fol. 1084: F. Brussig, diary, 1 Feb. 1916. Cf. the similar complaints quoted in BA-MA Freiburg, W-10/ 50794: Postüberwachung der *5. Armee*, 12 July 1917, pp. 18–19 and also Klemperer, *Curriculum Vitae*, II, p. 373.

95 See C. Jany, *Geschichte der Preußischen Armee vom 15. Jahrhundert bis 1914* (5 vols., Osnabruck: Biblio, 1933, 1967), IV, pp. 329–30. Retired officers and NCOs appointed to *Offizierstellvertreter* were used to fill empty command positions. See L. Rüdt von Collenberg, *Die deutsche Armee von 1871 bis 1914* (Berlin: Ernst Siegfried Mittler und Sohn, 1922), p. 118.

96 According to establishment figures, the ratio of officers to men in the Field Army stood at 1:44.31 in July 1916, in contrast to 1:38.75 in August 1914.

97 For German ranks, see Appendix 3, Table 6.

hostilities, *Hauptleute* replaced *Majore* as battalion commanders and *Leutnants* commanded not just platoons but also companies.[98]

Not only did this process create the unfortunate impression of an officer corps gradually withdrawing from danger, but it also made it more difficult for front-line officers, the *Leutnants*, to fulfil their paternalistic duty to their subordinates: whereas before the war these men had led platoons of 80 soldiers, by 1916, the low officer establishment of many units meant that inexperienced men were placed in command of companies numbering 150 or 200 other ranks. In stark contrast to British battalions, which habitually went into the line with twenty-five officers and by the end of the war possessed forty-three officers each, as well as a few spare, German battalions rarely reached their entitlement of twenty-three officers and sometimes fielded less than half this number.[99] Although establishment figures suggest that German officer numbers

98 K. Roth, *Das K.B. Reserve-Infanterie-Regiment Nr. 23* (Munich: Max Schick, 1927), pp. 219–29. For comparison, see Raimes, *Fifth Battalion*, p. 216. The 1/5 Durham Light Infantry was led by a Lieutenant-Colonel and possessed companies commanded by three Captains and a Major in April 1915.

99 For British officer strengths, see Samuels, *Command or Control?*, p. 226 and Simpson, 'Officers', p. 87. Examination of regimental diaries broadly confirms these figures: the 7/Middlesex began its active service with 30 officers in March 1915 and during the following two years their numbers fluctuated between 24 and 36, according to quarterly strength returns. At the end of 1917, however, commissioned personnel suddenly increased to 48 and during the course of the following year the number of officers fluctuated between 43 and 53 (E.J. King, *The History of the 7th Battalion Middlesex Regiment* (London: Harrison & Sons, 1927), p. 368). German battalions, in contrast, had an officer establishment of 23 (see General Staff, *German Army Handbook April 1918*, p. 44), but examination of Prussian and Bavarian regimental diaries reveals that the total officer strength of individual battalions was often well below this figure: *I/ bayerisches Reserve-Infanterie-Regiment Nr. 23* possessed only 15 officers on departure for the front in January 1915 and only 12 in September 1916. Fighting strengths would, of course, have been even lower and in such circumstances, as British intelligence confirmed in 1918, *Offizierstellvertreter* or *Vizefeldwebel* rather than *Leutnants* generally commanded platoons (see ibid). The only exception to this rule may have been Württemberg regiments, which some evidence suggests fielded more officers than average. It is noticeable, for example, that while the Prussian, Saxon and Bavarian armies suffered one officer fatality for every 33.52, 35.75 and 37.98 other rank deaths respectively, in the Württemberg army, the ratio was 1:31.30. Examination of Württemberg's *Reserve-Infanterie-Regiment Nr. 121* shows that in this unit the number of officers in each battalion increased from 22 in 1914 to 35 in July 1917, a complement far larger than that reported in Prussian regimental histories. Whether this greater command base might partly account for the elite reputation of Württemberg units is debatable, but seems possible. See Roth, *K.B. Reserve-Infanterie-Regiment Nr. 23*, pp. 219–29, vom Holtz, *Reserve-Inf.-Regiment Nr. 121*, pp. 83–8 and von Altrock (ed.), *Vom Sterben*, p. 68 (for casualty figures). Cf. also H. von Selle and W. Gründel (eds.), *Das 6. Westpreußische Infanterie-Regiment Nr.149 im Weltkriege* (Berlin: Tradition Wilhelm Kolk, 1929) and M. Bierwagen, *Zwischen Somme und Pripjet. Geschichte des Res. Infanterie-Regiments Nr. 271 im Weltkriege 1914 bis 1918* (Oldenburg: Gerhard Stalling, 1927).

recovered by the end of 1917, tactical innovations in assault methods and 'elastic defence' ensured that young front-line officers continued to receive more responsibility.[100] According to one regimental historian, by the beginning of 1917, 'the former tasks of the battalion commanders now lay in the hands of junior leaders'.[101] Rather than carry out duties themselves, they were forced to delegate to NCOs, whose numbers and importance increased: whereas in August 1914 there was nominally one officer to 3.72 NCOs, the ratio had become one to 4.32 by July 1918.[102] Officers in all arms found that they could rely on this capable and experienced body of veterans. *Leutnant* Lüthje, for example, serving in the transport, considered it unnecessary to accompany small supply columns personally to the front, instead sending *Unteroffiziere* to supervise.[103] Infantry commanders were probably particularly prone to such behaviour. Already by March 1916, British intelligence believed that NCOs were commanding sections of the German front line alone. 'The officer,' one report observed, 'probably under orders from the higher authorities, usually keeps in a position of comparative safety'.[104]

From a purely operational perspective, the policy of delegating much responsibility at the front from young *Kriegsoffiziere* to hardened NCOs was probably sensible. From the viewpoint of morale, however, it was extremely dangerous. Janowitz and Shils found when investigating cohesion and disintegration in the Second World War *Wehrmacht* that any reduction in face-to-face contact between officers and their men 'sometimes tipped the balance of the submissiveness–rebelliousness scale, in the successful manipulation of which lay the secret of the effective control of the German army'.[105] The apparent withdrawal of middle-ranking officers from the line and the greater reliance on NCOs for battlefield

[100] According to official establishment figures, the proportion of officers to men gradually recovered from mid-1916, although only in December 1917 did it reach the level of August 1914. See *Sanitätsbericht III*, pp. 3*–4*. Even then, however, Bavarian army statistics suggest that the infantry remained short of junior officers: while the artillery, technical troops and the train all possessed more than their entitlement of *Leutnants*, in the infantry, they remained 12 per cent below establishment in August 1917 and just under 9 per cent in August 1918. See Teicht, 'Offiziersausbildung', pp. 63 and 122.

[101] Graf von der Schulenburg (ed.), *Das Infanterie-Regiment Keith (1. Oberschlesisches) Nr. 22 im Kriege 1914–1918* (Berlin: Mars-Verlag Carl Siwinna, n.d.), p. 144. For command decentralisation, see Samuels, *Command or Control?*, pp. 158–97 and Gudmundsson, *Stormtroop Tactics*, particularly, pp. 94 and 101–2.

[102] Calculated from *Sanitätsbericht III*, p. 4*.

[103] BA-MA Freiburg, MSg 2/ 2797: W. Lüthje, diary, 25 May 1918.

[104] IWM, K.85/ 3374: First Army, *German Methods of Trench Warfare*, 1 Mar. 1916. Cf. also Graves, *Goodbye to All That*, p. 136, who claimed that by the autumn of 1915, NCOs rather than officers usually led German front-line patrols.

[105] Janowitz and Shils, 'Cohesion and Disintegration', p. 198.

leadership also called into question the right of the officer corps to privileges, already contested in a period of intense shortage. Under the strain of greater demands, junior officers could also vent their frustration verbally or physically on their subordinates: behaviour highly damaging for unit morale.[106]

The junior officers who led the German army during the second half of the war carried out their duties under extremely difficult circumstances. Not only were they comparatively poorly trained but they were also often expected to shoulder more responsibility than pre-war officers. Many were very young, a fact which made their privileges even more difficult to accept for the older men in the ranks. The gradual distancing of the officer corps from its subordinates and from the front, the growth in war-weariness and hunger and the inexperience of front-line officers presented the potential for discontent and rebellion in the German army during the final years of the war.

Performance

Despite the problems caused by wartime conditions, the German army functioned extremely successfully on the Western Front for four years. Although outnumbered, it brought numerous major Allied offensives to a standstill and, according to the battle analyses undertaken by Trevor Dupuy, constantly outperformed all of its enemies.[107] Its resilience and operational excellence are surprising, given the influence of junior officers in these realms and the historiographical consensus that officer–man relations within the force were poor. The question of how the army continued to function successfully when inter-rank hostility was allegedly so high has not yet been satisfactorily answered.

A close analysis of the army's 'officer hate' suggests one reason for the maintenance of its ability to fight well. Despite their shortcomings and difficulties, Kantorowicz was quite clear that other ranks' discontent was aimed neither primarily at the high command, who ensured Germany's continued survival, nor junior officers leading troops at the front:

> It is especially the middle officers – *Hauptleute* and staff officers – whom [the man] targets, because these, unlike the *Leutnant*, do not even stake their lives as the price of their supposedly comfortable living, while the restraint of the generals and General Staff away from the firing line naturally meets with approval.[108]

106 See Gaupp, 'Schreckneurosen', p. 101.
107 Dupuy, *Genius for War*, pp. 330–2.
108 Kantorowicz, *Offiziershaß*, p. 13.

Combatants' letters and diaries support this observation: the artilleryman Heinrich Genscher, for example, was favourably disposed to most of his own officers but referred contemptuously to those in the rear areas as 'lacquer-shoed masters'.[109] Another soldier, Ernst Vogt, remarked more explicitly that 'the high officers, who almost all keep down in the rear areas at others' expense and lead a good, lazy life ... are held by the front troops in deepest contempt – yes, great hatred'.[110] Even front-line officers participated in this 'officer hate': *Leutnant* Hans Muhsal of *Landwehr-Infanterie-Regiment Nr. 119* spent much time complaining about staff officers' crassness and ignorance of front-line conditions.[111]

In this light, the 'officer hate' appears to be less the distinctively German phenomenon portrayed by historians than an extreme example of the front–rear tension normal in wartime armies. This emotion had little to do with class hostility; even as egalitarian and meritocratic an army as that of America in the Second World War experienced what the sociologist Samuel Stouffer termed 'a smoldering resentment' against officers in rear areas and inactive theatres.[112] It was certainly present among front-line officers and men in the British army. Lieutenant Yoxall, for example, considered it as much a combat soldier's job to 'spoof the fools behind' as it was to 'beat the Bosch'.[113] General Smuts similarly remarked on the cynical disillusionment of British soldiers against 'the Staff' at the beginning of 1918.[114] Far from damaging battle performance, however, Sheffield argues that dislike of generals and staffs in the rear could actually raise combat formations' *esprit de corps* by providing soldiers of all ranks with an enemy against which to unite.[115]

Junior officers were not left entirely unscathed by the 'officer hate'. A study of combatants' letters undertaken by the *Reichsarchiv* historian Hermann Cron found considerable inter-rank tension in some units. Crucially, however, he emphasised that these were rear-line formations; in combat units, relations between officers and men remained reasonable and were often actually good right up until the end of the war.[116] Partly,

109 BA-MA Freiburg, MSg 2/ 2735: H. Genscher, letter to father, 13 Mar. 1915.
110 BA-MA Freiburg, MSg 1/ 3183: E. Vogt, diary / memoir, 5 Apr. 1918.
111 BA-MA Freiburg, MSg 1/ 3109: H. Muhsal, diary, 27 and 29 Mar. 1915, 13 Jan. 1916, 24 Aug. 1917, 24 Feb. and 12 Apr. 1918.
112 S.A. Stouffer, E.A. Suchman, L.C. DeVinney, S.A. Star and R.M. Williams Jr, *The American Soldier. Adjustment during Army Life* (2 vols., New York: John Wiley & Sons, 1949, 1965), I, p. 369.
113 IWM, P 317 Con Shelf: H.W. Yoxall, letter to mother, 1 June 1916.
114 See Wilson, 'Morale and Discipline', p. 271.
115 Sheffield, *Leadership*, p. 98.
116 Volkmann, *Soziale Heeresmißstände*, XI.2, pp. 135–7. Cf. Schuhmacher, *Leben und Seele*, p. 173.

the divergence in attitudes may have been the result of differing material conditions between front and rear. Troops along the lines of communication received smaller rations than those at the front and were thus more likely to resent their officers' privileges.[117] Moreover, they were often older than combat troops: after April 1917, it was decided that no soldier over thirty-five was suitable for infantry service in the *Materialschlacht*, with the result that many were withdrawn to the rear or sent to *Landwehr* units in Russia.[118] Nonetheless, the most likely explanation for the better inter-rank relations at the front was that despite the considerable difficulties faced by combatant officers, they were able to perform their duties successfully and, in doing so, won the respect of their subordinates.

Front-line junior officers were less exposed to the 'officer hate' than their senior and rear-line colleagues for two reasons. Firstly, as Kantorowicz indicated, the shared experience of combat was a major factor limiting conflict between junior officers and their men. Active service reduced the distance between ranks. As the 5. *Armee* censor observed:

> A not to be underestimated factor [affecting morale] is also that among ... combat troops, the common soldier and officer are subject to the same dangers, same deprivations etc. If the soldier sees that the leaders have shortages – especially of food – if he sees that the leader has no better sources than are accessible to him, then he bears his hardships more easily and willingly and often with humour.[119]

Combat not only allowed officers to demonstrate that they were prepared to endure the same dangers and hardships as their subordinates but it also provided them with the opportunity to justify their privileges by leading from the front and risking their lives. Only when officers exploited the benefits of their position without undergoing the commensurate risk or danger did men feel bitter. The connection between rank and responsibility was clearly expressed by Franz Brussig, who was outraged when his officers reported sick after the unit was ordered to Verdun: 'Yes, those are heroes. Until now they've lived like the Lord God in France and now, when it's off to Verdun and time to throw one's life into the ring, they creep away'.[120] Casualty statistics indicate, however, that Brussig's experience was exceptional; most German junior officers were particularly conscientious in the execution of their leadership

[117] See *Military Effort*, p. 586 and TNA, WO 157/ 13: Reductions in the Scale of Rations in the German Army, 18 Sept. 1916.
[118] Ziemann, *Front*, pp. 62–4.
[119] BA-MA Freiburg, W-10/ 50794: Postüberwachung der 5. *Armee*, 12 July 1917, p. 15.
[120] Staatsbib. Berlin, Ms. Boruss. fol. 1084: F. Brussig, diary, 18 Mar. 1916.

duties. In the British army, 11.7% of men and 13.6% of officers were killed. In the German army, despite the fact that it fielded a lower proportion of its officers at the front, and in contrast to the 13.3% of NCOs and men killed, 15.7% of reserve officers and a frighteningly high 24.7% of active officers fell during the First World War.[121]

Secondly, junior officers were less vulnerable to criticism precisely because their proximity to their men enabled them to act paternalistically. As Dr Neter, one of the veterans who testified at the post-war investigation into the German army's collapse, observed, even officers' privileges could be accepted by troops, providing that their own welfare had been assured:

> I always had the impression that the men willingly acknowledged the operational privileges of the officer (better rations and accommodation), but only under the condition that the officer showed himself worthy of these privileges ... Where the officer provided first for his men and only then for himself, I never saw particular envy or bitterness.[122]

The good combat performance of the army reflects the fact that, contrary to current historiographical consensus, many officers took advantage of this opportunity and acted paternalistically. Numerous examples recounted in letters record how such behaviour manifested itself and how it eased men's hardship, strengthened inter-rank ties and encouraged good discipline. Genscher, for example, recorded in October 1914 that pipes sent as gifts to his regiment were distributed by his *Oberleutnant* by means of a race. Such a competition was not only fun for the men but was fair and probably encouraged unit cohesion.[123] Three years later, *Kanonier* Konstantin Kramer recorded that after he and two comrades won the Iron Cross for bravery, his battery commander appeared at their barracks with a box of fine cigars under his arm – a rare luxury in late 1917. He and his unit spent a pleasant evening talking and smoking in, as Kramer put it, 'real comradeship'.[124] Helmuth von Obergassel, an *Oberleutnant* serving at the opening of the Verdun Offensive in February 1916, contravened regulations and sent men back to fetch a 25-litre barrel of rum for his company in the front line. Significantly, when his battalion commander heard of this action,

[121] British percentages calculated from figures in Beckett, 'Nation in Arms', p. 8, *Military Effort*, pp. 234–5 and Winter, *Great War*, p. 91. For the German percentages (which probably, understate the army's losses), see Volkmann, *Soziale Heeresmißstände*, XI.2, p. 35. German officer fatalities outnumbered those of other ranks in every month between August 1914 and July 1918 except for November and December 1915, January 1916 and January 1917. See *Sanitätsbericht III*, p. 132*.

[122] Quoted in Hobohm, *Soziale Heeresmißstände*, XI.1, p. 129.

[123] BA-MA Freiburg, MSg 2/ 2735: H. Genscher, letter to father, 24 Oct. 1914.

[124] DTA, 506: K. Kramer, diary, 6–7 Dec. 1917.

far from admonishing the *Oberleutnant* he praised him for his independence.[125] Officers' generosity also helped to ease the considerable material shortages suffered by German soldiers. In September 1915, for example, *Hauptmann* Fuchs gave a pair of his socks to a man who had attempted to make good a shortage by cutting his own from sandbags.[126] Food, the key problem in the second half of the war, was also an area in which officers could do good work. Tasting his men's rations was one of the prescribed duties of the company commander, allowing him to keep in touch with his men's needs effectively. One soldier, whose letter was read by the censor, complained that 'the hunger is always greater' but also recorded significantly that 'the officers see that the men can't hold out any more, so we should get more to eat'.[127] Similarly, the artilleryman Kurt Reiter was impressed when a new *Hauptmann* expressed astonishment at the paucity of his men's rations and ordered warm food to be sent up to the trenches. When the officer was severely wounded by shellfire one month later, Reiter once again praised his kindness and recorded the genuine regret felt by the men.[128]

Letters and diaries confirm that the combination of conscientiously dispensed paternalism and good battle leadership did bring German soldiers of all ranks together. Officers often evinced considerable affection for their men and many were deeply distressed when they were killed. *Leutnant* Lüthje, for example, knew the soldiers in his artillery column well and the death of one particularly brave man left him grieving.[129] After Ernst Huthmacher's death in action, his *Hauptmann* wrote a letter of condolence to his wife, referring to the *Gefreiter* in glowing terms and admitting, 'his death touched me very deeply'.[130] Perhaps the best refutation to the charges of universal selfishness and callousness among officers appears in Kurt Reiter's diary. In his entry for 16 June 1916, Reiter recorded that his unit had received notification that morning that one of its NCOs had died in hospital and that this news had hit his *Hauptmann* hard. When, an hour later, an artillery driver reported that a shell had landed in the company positions, killing two NCOs and wounding a further five men, the officer found that he could no longer cope. As Reiter continues:

With the words 'My men, my men' he collapsed into a faint. As indeed known, he was very nervous and anxious. He then lay unconscious for some time and lapsed

[125] BA-MA Freiburg, MSg 1/ 805: H. von Obergassel, diary, 24 Feb. 1916.
[126] BA-MA Freiburg, MSg 1/ 2965: H. Fuchs, diary, 7 Sept. 1915.
[127] BA-MA Freiburg, W-10/ 50794: Postüberwachung der 5. *Armee*, 12 July 1917, p. 21.
[128] BA-MA Freiburg, MSg 1/ 161: K. Reiter, diary, 12 July and 8 Aug. 1916.
[129] BA-MA Freiburg, MSg 2/ 2797: W. Lüthje, diary, 15 and 16 May 1918.
[130] DTA, 930: E. Huthmacher, letter from *Hauptmann* Fischer to *Frau* Huthmacher, 4 Aug. 1915.

into spasms often during this period. As he came to after an hour, he was no longer able to speak and looked absently in front of him. Our *Hauptmann* had become a psychiatric casualty.[131]

Given the concern evinced for their subordinates by many officers, it is perhaps unsurprising that nervous breakdowns were reportedly more common among junior officers than other ranks.[132]

None of this is to deny that abuses of authority took place, or that poor training and greater responsibilities in the second half of the war had an effect on inter-rank relations. As has been seen, the elitist 'caste consciousness' of the corps did indeed sometimes encourage arrogance and disrespect towards subordinates. In third-rate units such as Brussig's labour battalion officership was sometimes very poor, making service for the ordinary soldiers extremely unpleasant. Brussig recorded that in his battalion discipline was so harsh that there was 'absolutely no difference between us and galley slaves'.[133] The men were not protected from bullying or insults by the NCOs and their self-confidence was undermined by harsh and insulting treatment. 'We are so disrespectfully handled', wrote Brussig, 'that we are ashamed to be before the French civilian population'. An attempt to write home about his grievances resulted in persecution by officers and punishment.[134]

Nonetheless, the balance of evidence supports Cron's opinion that inter-rank relations at the front were often good, soldiers returning their officers' affection. Graffiti in leave-train lavatories, for example, not only criticised but also defended officers. Underneath the ubiquitous ditty, 'den Offizieren Mannschaftsbrot und Mannschaftsessen, / dann wäre der Krieg schon lang vergessen' ('If officers got men's bread and men's food, / The war would already be long forgotten'), scribbled in one toilet, police found the comment, 'Is that a real German heart? With God for King and Fatherland'. The demand, 'Soldiers, shoot your officers,' was met with the words 'rogue, traitor, miserable rascal'.[135] Diaries also reveal that some men were fond of their officers. Genscher

[131] BA-MA Freiburg, MSg 1/ 161: K. Reiter, diary, 16 June 1916.

[132] Scholz, *Seelenleben*, pp. 221–3. The larger number of reported breakdowns among officers probably principally reflected contemporary armies' greater willingness to acknowledge psychiatric disease in commissioned ranks than in their subordinates. However, some research conducted during the Vietnam War does suggest that officers are indeed placed under more stress than other ranks in battle. See P. Watson, *War on the Mind. The Military Uses and Abuses of Psychology* (London: Hutchinson, 1978), pp. 209–11.

[133] Staatsbib. Berlin, Ms. Boruss. fol. 1084: F. Brussig, diary, 3 Feb. 1916.

[134] Ibid., 4 Sept. 1915. Cf. also entries for 20 and 22 Aug., 10, 11 and 16 Sept. 1915.

[135] GLA Karlsruhe, 456 F 8 /260, Blatt 575 and Blatt 748: Reports of *Eisenbahnüberwachung* on graffiti found in leave-train lavatories, dated 30 Mar. 1917 and 17 Nov. 1917.

hero-worshipped his professional officer, the twenty-year-old *Leutnant* von Horstig.[136] The company commander, *Leutnant* Muhsal, who closely identified with the soldiers under him, was pleasantly surprised in 1916 when fifteen who were being transferred to active regiments sent him a goodbye card: 'pleased me very much; there is more recognition in that than in the best regimental dispatch', he noted in his diary.[137]

The fact that good inter-rank relations survived in combat units indicates that, despite its disadvantages, the German officer corps' aristocratic *Standesbewußtsein* continued to be highly relevant for leadership on the battlefields of the Western Front. While the code may have been applied too rigidly, wasting much potential leadership talent, it was above all wartime material shortages which excited criticism. The withdrawal of officers above the rank of *Oberleutnant* from front service was a particularly inept response to recruitment difficulties, as it encouraged other ranks, already bitter about food shortages, to view the officer corps as shirking the responsibilities that justified its privileges. The structural reorganisation of the army and the formulation of new tactical doctrines emphasising independence and delegation also exacerbated the problems of the comparatively poorly trained *Kriegsoffiziere* in providing adequate paternalistic care for their men. The fact that the 'officer hate' had only a minimal impact on inter-rank relations at the front is partly a reflection of how combat reduced the distance between ranks but also a testament to how well, despite their difficulties and disadvantages, these officers executed the corps' traditional functions. Although relations were perhaps never so good as in the BEF, the self-sacrifice and paternalism of these young, overstretched officers played a crucial role in ensuring the survival of the German army in a gruelling war of endurance for four years.

[136] BA-MA Freiburg, MSg 2/ 2735: H. Genscher, letter to father, 28 Jan. 1915.
[137] BA-MA Freiburg, MSg 1/ 3109: H. Muhsal, diary, 25 Nov. 1916.

5 Morale and military endurance

Morale in the British Expeditionary Force, 1914–17

The question of what constitutes 'morale', the common shorthand for military resilience and combat motivation, lies not only at the heart of this book but also at the centre of twentieth-century literature on battlefield performance. Scholars and soldiers have generally defined the quality by outlining its component parts. The psychiatrist Frederick J. Manning, for example, has argued that a range of individual and group factors, including on one hand, the satisfaction of biological and psychological needs, and on the other, high *esprit de corps*, together produce good 'morale'.[1] Shelford Bidwell similarly contends that culture, psychological constitution, commitment to war aims, training and conditioning, integration into 'primary groups' and confidence in leaders are the main ingredients of the quality.[2] An even more thorough but diffuse explanation of the term was provided by the veteran, journalist and historian S.L.A. Marshall:

> Morale is the thinking of an army. It is the whole complex body of an army's thought: The way it feels about the soil and about the people from which it springs. The way that it feels about their cause and their politics as compared with other causes and other politics. The way that it feels about its friends and allies, as well as its enemies. About its commanders and goldbricks. About food and shelter. Duty and leisure. Payday and sex. Militarism and civilianism. Freedom and slavery. Work and want. Weapons and comradeship. Bunk fatigue and drill. Discipline and disorder. Life and death. God and the devil.[3]

While it is undoubtedly true that very many factors do contribute to the formation of good 'morale', these explanations provide no understanding of *why* they influence soldiers to keep fighting or *how* they function in

[1] F.J. Manning, 'Morale, Cohesion, and Esprit de Corps', in R. Gal and A.D. Mangesdorff (eds.), *Handbook of Military Psychology* (Chichester: John Wiley & Sons, 1991), pp. 467–8.

[2] S. Bidwell, *Modern Warfare. A Study of Men, Weapons and Theories* (London: Allen Lane, 1973), p. 127.

[3] S.L.A. Marshall, *Men Against Fire. The Problem of Battle Command* (Norman: University of Oklahoma Press, 1947, 2000), p. 158.

order to ensure that men, and therefore armies, endure terrible conditions willingly and successfully.

The investigation of individuals' combat motivations and psychological coping strategies undertaken in previous chapters does, however, shed some light on how the factors comprising 'good morale' functioned in maintaining soldiers' willingness to accept risk and death for extended periods. At the heart of combat motivation lay confidence in ultimate victory and in personal survival. The tremendous resilience of First World War armies was to a large extent a reflection of the fact that men were 'hardwired' to believe firmly in both. Yet the argument that 'morale' is confidence also explains why the military-institutional factors emphasised in traditional literature functioned so well to support men. Training, the inculcation of 'primary group' solidarity, regimental *esprit de corps*, good leadership and propaganda were all designed to instil in soldiers confidence in personal survival and in their ability to execute military tasks effectively. Nor does it conflict with the important role attributed by censorship reports and military commentators to basic necessities, such as food, protection from the elements and rest, in the formation of military morale. Without physical wellbeing, psychological contentment and self-assuredness were impossible. As the battalion doctor and psychologist Ludwig Scholz asked rhetorically, 'who can be brave with toothache or stomach pain?'[4]

An analysis of morale in both the British and the German armies is really a history of the peaks and troughs in their men's confidence to win the war and return home unscathed. Scholars concentrating on the traditionally emphasised factors in morale – discipline, regimental pride, training and 'primary group' solidarity – have generally assumed that the original professional BEF, 247,432 men strong, was of higher quality and greater resilience than the mass force of (eventually) almost 2 million citizen-soldiers which succeeded it.[5] In part, this view has been heavily influenced by the work of the official historian, J.E. Edmonds, who constructed a legend of heroism around the Regulars' 1914 exploits, while complaining that 'the awful slaughter and pitiably small results of the battles of 1915 were the inevitable consequences of using inexperienced and partly trained officers and men to do the work of soldiers'.[6]

4 Scholz, *Seelenleben*, p. 140. For the censorship reports, see particularly IWM, 84/46/1: M. Hardie, Report on Complaints, Moral, etc., 23 Nov. 1916, pp. 1–4 and BA-MA Freiburg, W-10/50794: Postüberwachung der 5. *Armee*, 12 July 1917, pp. 13–15.

5 Sheffield, *Forgotten Victory*, p. 95.

6 J.E. Edmonds, *History of the Great War based on Official Documents. Military Operations. France and Belgium, 1915. Battles of Aubers Ridge, Festubert, and Loos* (London: Macmillan & Co., 1928), p. ix.

It also reflects the continuing impact of the tragic first day of the 1916 Somme Offensive, when 20,000 British soldiers lost their lives, and the memory of the disastrous retreat in the spring of 1918, when on the first day of the attack alone the army lost almost 100 square miles.[7] Finally, it also appears to be confirmed by one of the earliest and most thorough assessments of military morale in the First World War, John Baynes' examination of the Scottish Rifles, which concluded that it was above all regimental loyalty, a quality far less developed among citizen-soldiers than in their professional forbears, which prompted this unit to fight so hard at Neuve Chapelle in March 1915.[8] Although research by Paddy Griffith has demonstrated that the New Armies underwent a 'learning curve' between 1916 and 1918, the initial shortages in arms and equipment, poor preparation and the military inexperience of the troops seem to have been ill-suited to provide the confidence necessary to overcome the stressful conditions on the Western Front.[9]

Curiously, however, most indicators suggest that not 1916 or 1918 but rather 1914 was the British army's year of crisis. Self-inflicted wounds were more prevalent in the autumn and winter of 1914 than at any other point during the war, some officers even seeking an exit from the front via this method.[10] Equally significantly, desertion also reached record levels while most of Britain's troops were still professionals. Already in September, orders had to be issued to stop soldiers using the railheads to abscond from the front. Prosecutions for desertion rose rapidly from November 1914 and peaked in February 1915, when at 0.044 per cent the rate was more than three times the wartime average.[11] Although the total number of men attempting to leave the army remained tiny, the comparatively very high rate of desertion in the winter of 1914–15 was

[7] The notion that British citizen-soldiers were insufficiently robust to cope and became 'disillusioned' by these events appears particularly strongly in older literature such as A.J.P. Taylor, *The First World War. An Illustrated History* (London: Penguin, 1963, 1966), p. 140 and Middlebrook, *Kaiser's Battle*, pp. 337–9.

[8] Baynes, *Morale*, pp. 253–4.

[9] Griffith, *Battle Tactics*, pp. 192–200. For the poor training conditions experienced by many New Army units in Britain, see Simkins, *Kitchener's Army*, pp. 296–7.

[10] For self-inflicted wounds, see IWM, 78/4/1: T.H. Cubbon, diary, 3 Oct. 1914 and IWM, 95/31/1: N.L. Woodroffe, letter to mother, 30 Sept. 1914. For the official concern and reaction to these cases, see WLHM, RAMC 380/1/10 Box 40: Major General Sir Maurice Holt, field message book containing orders, notes etc., p. 40 (diary entry of 26 Sept. 1914). Cf. also TNA, WO 95/ 1320: 2nd Division. Assistant Director of Medical Services. War Diary, vol. IV, appendix XXXIII containing order of 14 Nov. 1914.

[11] For desertion from the railheads, see TNA, WO 95/ 1242: Diary of Deputy Assistant Director of Medical Services, 1st Division, 5 Sept. 1914. For desertion figures, see Jahr, *Gewöhnliche Soldaten*, pp. 169–74. Desertion may have been a substitute for psychiatric breakdown.

symptomatic of a wider malaise. Officers worried about their units' discipline and isolated instances of severe insubordination were reported: one sergeant at First Ypres, for example, recorded that Special Reservists of the Connaught Rangers mutinied and had to be 'put in trenches with another Line [*sic*] behind them to fire on them if they attempt to come out'.[12]

Above all, however, it is the high surrender rate which indicates a lack of confidence among professional soldiers in their own ability to carry out their military tasks. Even during the major tactical defeats during the first half of 1918, the British army demonstrated more willingness to fight to the death than in August 1914, when the ratio of soldiers captured and missing to killed was more than 8:1 (see Figure 3).[13]

Taken as a whole, 1914 witnessed the highest proportion of men surrendering rather than fighting to the death of any war year (see Table 2). The mythologising of the early clashes between British and German forces by the official historian ignored this fact. 'In the British battalions which fought at the Marne and Ypres', he wrote, 'there scarcely remained with the colours an average of one officer and thirty men of those who had landed in August 1914'.[14] Yet not bloody vainglory or heroism but rather capitulation and imprisonment was the principal but unspoken reason behind the destruction of the Regular Army by the end of November 1914.

Indeed, the only major indicator suggesting that professional troops were more resilient and motivated than their citizen-soldier successors are psychiatric disorder statistics, which indicate that the share of the wounded accounted for by such afflictions in 1914 was between only half and one-third of that in later war years.[15] These figures, however, are unreliable, probably better reflecting military medical personnel's greater ignorance of nervous diseases at the beginning of the war than the relative resilience of the soldiery. Although professional officers at

[12] IWM, 78/4/1: T.H. Cubbon, diary, 11 Nov. 1914. Cf. Wilson, 'Morale and Discipline', pp. 67–8 and 91.

[13] The ratios of British captured and missing to killed in September and October 1914 were 1.6:1 and 2:1 respectively. In March 1918, the comparable ratio was 4.8:1, but for most of the war the ratio rarely rose above 1:1. In this light, Sir John French's much criticised wish to withdraw the BEF after the Mons retreat and refit becomes more comprehensible. See Strachan, *First World War*, I, pp. 248–50.

[14] J.E. Edmonds, *History of the Great War based on Official Documents. Military Operations. France and Belgium, 1914. Antwerp, La Bassée, Armientières, Messines, and Ypres. October–November 1914* (London: Macmillan & Co., 1925), p. 465.

[15] See Appendix 2, Table 5. The impression given by the statistics is also supported by the statements of professional officers. See, in particular, the eulogy to the Regular Army in Edmonds, *History of the Great War ... October–November 1914*, pp. 460–6 and *RWOCIS*, pp. 4, 35, 45, 56 and 73.

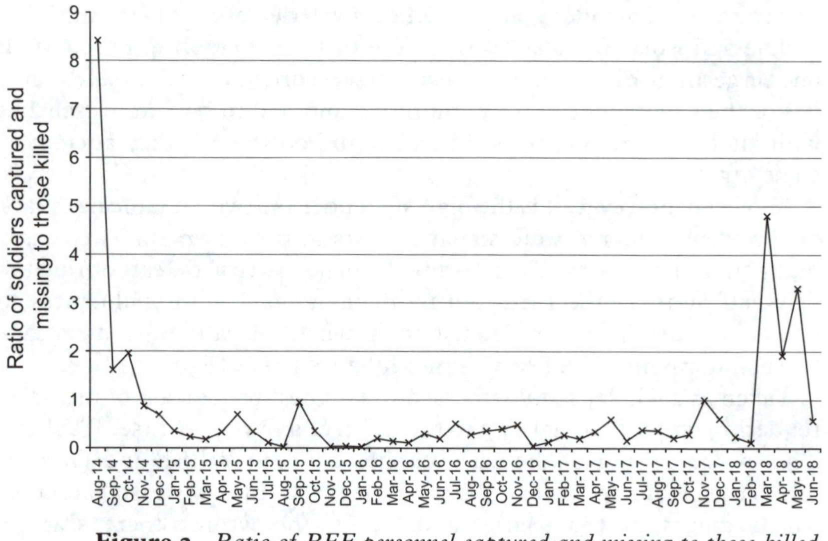

Figure 3. *Ratio of BEF personnel captured and missing to those killed, August 1914–June 1918*
Source: *Military Effort*, pp. 253–68

the Southborough Committee's 1922 investigation into shellshock testified that psychiatric collapse was virtually unknown in the Regular Army, private diaries demonstrate otherwise. In the 9th Field Ambulance during September, Captain A.H. Habgood, for example, encountered one young soldier 'in hysterics' and Corporal C. Chamberlain mentioned a bugler who had been evacuated because 'the shelling had been too much for him' and an officer casualty who 'was not injured but suffering from shock'.[16] Dispatch rider Herbert Best recorded in October the case of two motorcyclists 'sent home "dotty" from the front' and, at Ypres in November, Lieutenant G.A. Loyd witnessed 'some very pitiable sights, officers and men broken and incoherent from the terrific shell fire'.[17] The unexceptional nature of these examples is confirmed by the official medical history, which states that between 3 and 4 per cent of the men and 7 to 10 per cent of officers admitted to Boulogne hospitals in 1914 were sent back to Britain suffering from nervous disorders.[18]

[16] IWM, P 115 & Con Shelf: A.H. Habgood, diary, 14 Sept. 1914 and WLHM, RAMC 699 Box 136: C. Chamberlain, diary, 22 and 23 Sept. 1914.

[17] IWM, 87/56/1: O.H. Best, letter / diary, 2 Oct. 1914 and IWM, 98/2/1: G.A. Loyd, diary, 1 Nov. 1914.

[18] *J&R*, p. 2. Cf. Aldren Turner, 'Remarks on Cases of Nervous and Mental Shock', 833–4.

Table 2. *BEF personnel captured and killed, 1914–18*

Year	Prisoners	Killed	Ratio of prisoners to killed
1914	19,915	13,009	1 : 0.65
1915	8,621	48,604	1 : 5.64
1916	15,516	107,411	1 : 6.92
1917	23,227	131,761	1 : 5.67
1918	107,647	80,2476	1 : 0.75

Source: Medical Services, pp. 122, 136, 149, 158 and 168.

Circumstantial factors undoubtedly played a role in the Regular Army's high dropout rates. The fighting in 1914 was bloodier than in subsequent years and the winter in the trenches was extremely harsh.[19] The fluidity of the combat also contributed to losses from desertion and surrender. Mobility meant that the army was less able to supervise all its personnel than in static warfare, with the result that desertion appeared more attractive to some individuals. Similarly, constant movement resulted in troops or even units becoming separated from the main body of the army, trapped behind enemy formations and forced to surrender. The high ratio of killed to prisoners and missing in the years 1915–17 reflected not only the high combat motivation of the soldiers in this period but also the fact that the dynamics of trench warfare usually left men with little option other than to stand and fight.

Differences in personnel's preparedness were more important in determining the resilience of the army, however. Historians have overestimated professionals' readiness for the conditions of the First World War. The Regular Army was designed and trained for small-scale colonial fighting, not the terrifying combat against well-equipped conscript forces which it encountered in 1914. Confidence in its ability to carry out its duties was damaged by its heavy reliance on reservists, who formed 61.8 per cent of its personnel on mobilisation and were given no chance to readapt to army life.[20] Poorly prepared 'Special Reservists', civilians with six months of training, and large drafts of physically

[19] See *Medical Services*, pp. 122, 136, 148–9, 158 and 167–8. For weather, see Wilson, 'Morale and Discipline', p. 74.

[20] Samuels, *Command or Control?*, p. 79. 1/Somerset Light Infantry, for example, absorbed 400 reservists in four days on mobilisation. See Strachan, *First World War*, I, pp. 205–6.

inferior men incorporated as replacement troops were scarcely better.[21] Professional soldiers were also arguably naturally less well equipped than their wartime successors to withstand intense strain. The taboo on joining the peacetime army had resulted in the recruitment of British society's most disadvantaged men, some of whom were, in the harsh words of the psychiatrist Edward Mapother, 'wasters and half-wits who broke down easily'.[22] Particularly important was the low average intellect of other ranks: by October 1913, no less that 65 per cent had not attained the educational standard expected of contemporary eleven-year-olds. For these men, the biased reasoning which characterised successful coping in the trenches may have been more difficult than for more intelligent and better educated wartime recruits, exposing them to collapse; certainly, as has been seen, modern psychological research indicates that high IQ acts as a 'buffer' against stress.[23] The ill-preparedness of the soldiers to deal with the unexpectedly fierce fighting quickly made itself known in the demoralisation which swept through some units. Already by mid-September, for example, Sergeant Cubbon of 15/King's Hussars remarked in his diary that, 'troops are beginning to get downhearted here, as the Germans have proved themselves to be a better army than we thought'. On 19 September, his entry read 'never felt so cold, wet + miserable in my life as I do now' and mentioned that a man had shot himself through the foot to escape the trenches. Despite the strict discipline imposed by the unit's CO, Cubbon recorded that demoralisation at the unexpected length of hostilities, self-inflicted wounds and poor combat performance dogged the unit throughout the autumn of 1914.[24]

Not only many other ranks but also some officers of the Regular Army seem to have been unable to cope with the exertion and stress of modern warfare in 1914. Their failure to overcome the shock of battle resulted in some large capitulations at the beginning of the war. For example, on 27 August, during the gruelling retreat from Le Cateau, the weary and demoralised commanders of 1/Royal Warwickshires and 2/Royal Dublin

[21] For Special Reservists, see Samuels, *Command or Control?*, p. 119. For drafts, see TNA, WO 95/ 1242: Confidential War Diary of ADMS 1st Division from 1 Dec. to 30 Dec. 1914 (vol. II.), respectively 16 and 20 Dec. 1914 and Wilson, 'Morale and Discipline', pp. 79–81.

[22] Mapother in United Services Section with Section of Psychiatry, 'Discussion on Functional Nervous Disease', 863. For reservists, see Samuels, *Command or Control?*, p. 78.

[23] War Office (ed.), *The General Annual Report on the British Army for the year ending 30th September, 1913, with which is incorporated the Annual Report on Recruiting, prepared by command of the Army Council. Presented to both Houses of Parliament by Command of His Majesty [Cd. 7252.]* (London: HMSO, 1914), p. 95. For intelligence's role in proofing men against stress, see chapter 1 above, p. 37.

[24] IWM, 78/4/1: T.H. Cubbon, diary, 17, 19 and 29 Sept., 25 Oct. and 11 Nov. 1914.

Fusiliers were prevailed upon by the mayor of St Quentin to surrender their men to approaching Germans unconditionally, in order to save the town from destruction. Only the timely arrival of a cavalry officer, who successfully organised the exhausted men to withdraw, stopped the capitulation from taking place.[25] Poor leadership did actually result in the surrender of more than 500 men from 1/Gordon Highlanders, 2/Royal Scots and 2/Royal Irish on the night of 26–27 August. Although a post-war investigation exonerated the commanders of this column, it also revealed that considerable confusion and some loss of nerve had taken place, both officers at one point abandoning the force and attempting to escape by cutting through fields.[26]

Despite the serious demoralisation and disciplinary problems which it experienced, the Regular Army nonetheless managed to stabilise the line, stopping a German breakthrough at Ypres during the autumn of 1914 and again in the spring of 1915. The army sent out to replace it was composed partly of pre-war trained Territorial soldiers but mainly of citizen-soldiers with no peacetime military experience. Many problems were encountered in raising this force. Inundated with recruits at the outbreak of war, the army's system of medical inspections collapsed, allowing men to enter who would not even have passed muster in the peacetime army.[27] According to Lord Moran, 'doctors were asked to pass as many as two hundred recruits in a single day, so that their examination was perfunctory or worse; the machinery collapsed, there was chaos'.[28] The result was that both the physically disabled and the mentally unstable were accepted. The psychiatrist C. Stanford Read recalled that one of his patients had volunteered directly on being released from the 'imbecile ward of an asylum', while another had come from 'an institution for mentally defective children'.[29] Mapother similarly recorded encountering a soldier who had consistently failed in his

[25] For details of this attempted surrender, see P.T. Scott, *'Dishonoured'. The 'Colonels' Surrender' at St Quentin, the Retreat from Mons, August 1914* (London: Tom Donovan, 1994), particularly pp. 49–59.

[26] See TNA, WO 141/ 38: 'Enquiry into Circumstances of Surrender of 1st Gordon Highlanders in August 1914' and also the rough drafts of this document (which give a slightly different version of the event) in TNA, WO 141/ 37.

[27] TNA, WO 95/ 2834: War Diary of 1/4 Battalion East Yorks, 5 Aug. 1914.

[28] Moran, *Anatomy*, p. 156. Cf. TNA, WO 95/ 2834: War Diary of 1/4 Battalion East Yorks, 5 Aug. 1914. Also, Simkins, *Kitchener's Army*, p. 179 and C. Hughes, 'The New Armies', in I.F.W. Beckett and K. Simpson (eds.), *A Nation in Arms. A Social Study of the British Army in the First World War* (Manchester University Press, 1985), p. 102, who suggests that not only time but also pecuniary considerations militated against proper medical examination: until May 1915, doctors were paid 2*s* 6*d* per man and some thus hurried recruits through.

[29] Stanford Read, *Military Psychiatry*, p. 108.

trench duties and who, on examination, turned out to be 'a schizophrenic who within five minutes was telling me about the women that seduced him at night'.[30] Such men were unable to cope with the strain of the front for long: it was unsurprising that Charles Myers, the army's 'Specialist in Nervous Shock', found that cases of 'undoubted insanity … rapidly grew in number' when the New Armies landed in France in 1915.[31]

Particular difficulty was found in equipping the wartime force recruited in 1914 and 1915 due to the time required by British industry to switch its production to military needs. Some units received their full complement of kit only shortly before embarkation for France. This naturally impacted on training, forcing units lacking rifles or munitions to spend unnecessary amounts of time drilling. According to Denis Winter, the instruction was correspondingly often stamped with an 'air of unreality' and indeed, as has already been seen, some soldiers did arrive at the front with little notion of the power of modern weaponry.[32] Shortages of suitable instructors or experienced soldiers in the ranks lowered the standard of military knowledge in the new units. The men of the battalions raised as part of Kitchener's fourth 'hundred thousand', who received the fewest professional officers and NCOs, were still, in the opinion of John Keegan, 'bands of uniformed innocents' when they went over the top on the first day of the Somme Offensive on 1 July 1916.[33] The particularly high rate of 'shellshock' suffered during the battle was certainly partially attributable to this poor preparation.[34]

Nonetheless, the wartime citizen army endured not only the Somme Offensive but also the Battles of Arras and Passchendaele and the *Kaiserschlacht*, as well as long periods of stressful trench warfare. There were a number of reasons for the army's impressive resilience, particularly *vis-à-vis* the quick demoralisation of Regular troops in 1914. Firstly, as Adrian Gregory has demonstrated, the Kitchener volunteers who enlisted at the outbreak of war were not naive boys but men expecting a long and hard fight. Despite the ignorance of some individuals regarding the power of modern weaponry, plenty of information about

30 United Services Section with Section of Psychiatry, 'Discussion on Functional Nervous Disease', 863.
31 Myers, *Shell Shock*, pp. 76–7.
32 D. Winter, *Death's Men. Soldiers of the Great War* (London: Allen Lane, 1978, 1979), p. 39.
33 Keegan, *Face of Battle*, p. 226.
34 See Appendix 2 below, *J&R*, p. 4 and statements of A.B. Soltau and W. Johnson (both attached to field ambulances during the battle) in *RWOCIS*, pp. 73 and 82 respectively. J.F.C. Fuller asserted that desertions to the enemy were also widespread on the Ancre, although surviving 'prisoner and missing' statistics provide little support for this claim. See ibid., pp. 28–9 and Figure 3 above.

the front was available through popular newspapers and magazines throughout 1915, giving these soldiers some idea of what to expect in modern war.[35] Although some official training was of low quality, it was at least aimed at preparing soldiers for the fighting on the Western Front and was by no means always as poor as historians have suggested. The wartime 30th Division, for example, organised in October 1915 what must have been one of the earliest examples of the 'realism training' popularised in the Second World War. Thousands of men took part in a mock battle involving trenches, wire entanglements and blank ammunition for machineguns and rifles. When they were sent against the German lines on 1 July 1916, the men of the division were thus by no means 'uniformed innocents' but rather had a reasonable idea of the noise and nature of modern warfare.[36] Although not all units benefited from such advanced means of instruction, the average time spent by New Army battalions training in Britain, at 9.4 months, was adequate to enable strong primary group bonds and feelings of *esprit de corps* to form.[37] Often forgotten is also the fact that unlike the Regulars and reservists in 1914, most Kitchener units were not sent straight into the horror of a major battle but were first allowed to spend at least six months hardening and training in quiet sectors of the front. The result, according to the former subaltern and Somme Offensive participant Charles Edmund Carrington, was that 'the troops who went over the top on 1 July were very different from the greenhorns who had landed in France a year earlier'.[38] Finally, although unfit and unstable men were allowed into the ranks of the wartime army, the average standard of recruit was probably far higher than that of the Regular Army, particularly among the volunteers, who were composed predominantly of the skilled working class, together with a high proportion of middle-class men, who comprised the best fed, best educated, probably most intelligent and therefore most resilient members of British society.[39]

35 See, for example, the weekly magazine, *The War Illustrated. A Picture-Record of Events by Land, Sea and Air*. For Gregory's work, see chapter 2 above, pp. 44–5 and 49.

36 P. Liddle, *The Soldier's War 1914–18* (London: Blandford Press, 1988), pp. 18–19.

37 Samuels, *Command or Control?*, p. 120.

38 C.E. Carrington, 'Kitchener's Army. The Somme and After', *Journal of the Royal United Services Institute for Defence Studies* 123, 1 (March 1978), 17. The New Army began to arrive in France in May 1915, when the 9th, 12th and 14th Divisions landed. Eighteen further divisions were sent during the course of 1915, leaving only five to arrive during the first half of 1916. See I.F.W. Beckett and K. Simpson (eds.), *A Nation in Arms. A Social Study of the British Army in the First World War* (Manchester University Press, 1985), appendix I.

39 For volunteer composition, see Winter, *Great War*, pp. 34–5. Cf. Major General Ivor Maxse's opinion of the high quality of volunteers, quoted in Simkins, *Kitchener's Army*, p. 316. Maxse was commander of 18th (Eastern) Division.

Not naivety, but rather the long training and high quality of the volunteers account for the high level of confidence many evinced at the opening of the Somme Battle. As the artilleryman Richard Downing wrote excitedly to his parents a fortnight before the beginning of the offensive, 'the time has come for us to show our best & I am glad of it, eager & longing for it. We shall have all our work cut out to smash the Germans, but we can do it'.[40] Despite the fact that the offensive failed to be the hoped-for decisive breakthrough, instead costing 419,654 men for the gain of only 98 square miles of land, the army did not suffer any demoralisation similar to that experienced by the Regulars in 1914. On the contrary, men retained the confidence that, as one officer put it, 'they can beat the Bosche when and where they like'.[41] Partly this optimism reflected the difficulty of judging relative casualties combined with men's natural tendency to see events as positively as possible. This is clear from Downing's letters, which even when they admitted that 'our infantry have suffered terribly', immediately passed over this negative thought by insisting 'it is nothing to the German losses'.[42] Henry Mountifort Dillon, second in command of 1/West Yorkshires, similarly believed that 'this battle is being run on the right lines I am sure, i.e. for every man we lose we out more than one German'.[43] Yet as in other cases of optimistic reasoning, these judgements were not based solely on fantasy or wishful thinking but did have some factual basis. Above all, the vast increases in the number of prisoners captured during the Somme Battle impressed men. Downing remarked that 'it is nice to see so many prisoners passing our Batteries' and the machine-gunner Richard Williams also consoled himself for the lack of territorial gain by claiming that 'the German infantry can't stand what we have been giving them, and they give themselves up where they get a safe opportunity'.[44] A few months later, H.W. Yoxall similarly asserted that Württembergers, the best troops in the German army, were also 'deserting in large numbers down on the Somme'.[45] Prisoner statistics confirm these subjective opinions: not only were 40,207 Germans captured in the second half of 1916, in contrast to only 1,101 during the first half of the year, but the statistics also show that they did indeed display an increasing propensity to surrender rather than fight to the death during the Somme Campaign (see Figure 4). The

40 IWM, 88/7/1: R. Downing, letter to parents, 14 June 1916.
41 IWM, P 317 Con Shelf: H.W. Yoxall, letter to mother, 26 Sept. 1916. Cf. IWM, 84/46/1: M. Hardie, Report on Complaints, Moral, etc., 23 Nov. 1916, pp. 6–8.
42 IWM, 88/7/1: R. Downing, letter to family, 'Sunday', July 1916.
43 IWM, 82/25/1: H.M. Dillon, letter to 'G.F-G', 14 Aug. 1916.
44 IWM, 88/7/1: R. Downing, letter to family, 'Sunday', July 1916 and IWM, 82/26/1: A.R. Williams, letter to brother, 12 Aug. 1916.
45 IWM, P 317 Con Shelf: H.W. Yoxall, letter to mother, 19 Feb. 1917.

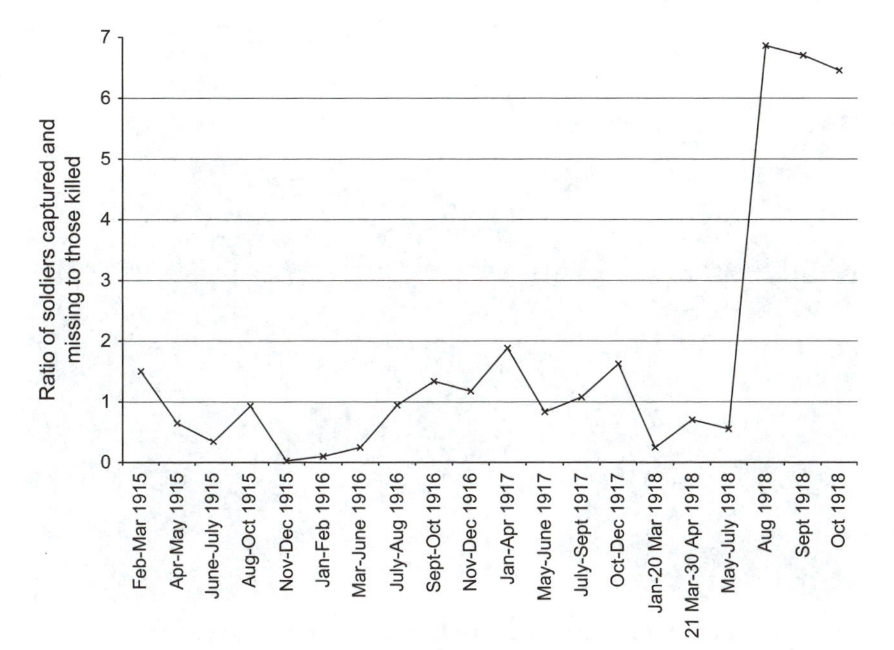

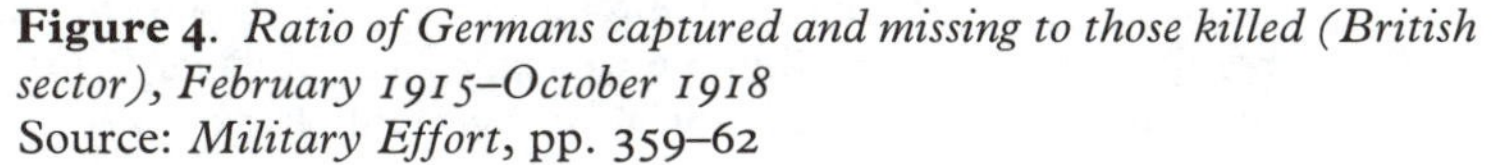
Figure 4. *Ratio of Germans captured and missing to those killed (British sector), February 1915–October 1918*
Source: *Military Effort*, pp. 359–62

recognition of this fact provided troops with something positive on which to focus and served as compensation and justification for the heavy British losses.

Not only the first sight of large numbers of German prisoners provided British troops with hope but also the evidence of material superiority possessed by the Entente convinced them that they were winning. Downing was particularly impressed by what he termed 'our H-lish shell-fire'. 'Our supply seems unlimited', he wrote, '& we have Batteries galore around here with all sizes of guns of different calibres'.[46] The British Third Army's censor found in November that 'the spirit of confidence in the superiority over the enemy, of our troops in the trenches, and of our artillery and aircraft, is everywhere noticeable'.[47] Even British prisoners expressed this opinion. A German intelligence report concluded from interviews with men captured during

[46] IWM, 88/7/1: R. Downing, letter to family, 'Sunday', July 1916
[47] IWM, 84/46/1: M. Hardie, Report on Complaints, Moral, etc., 23 Nov. 1916, p. 6.

Plate 13. Material might (1): British 6-inch howitzer and crew, 1 July 1916. Despite its tactical ineffectiveness, the ferocity of the BEF's bombardment on the Somme did much to convince British soldiers that they were winning. Official British photograph.

the autumn of 1916 that 'the typical Englishman is of the opinion that the superior forces arrayed against us will vanquish Germany'.[48]

Events during the first half of 1917 did nothing to dispel this confidence. The German withdrawal to the Hindenburg Line during February and March convinced even men demoralised by the heavy casualties of the Somme Battle that the fighting 'was worth while after all'.[49] Despite its higher rate of attrition and unnecessary prolongation, the initial success of the offensive around Arras in the spring brought the army further cause to hope for victory. The postal censor of the Third Army, which carried out the attacks, observed in May that 'the consciousness of success and of effective progress has undoubtedly served to exhilarate our troops, filling them with the promise of a speedier conclusion of the War'.[50] Improved

48 BA-MA Freiburg, PH 3/ 556: Aus Unterhaltungen mit gefangenen Engländern, 10 Sept. 1916.

49 IWM, 92/3/1: E.F. Chapman, letter to mother, 20 Mar. 1917. This was a typical response to the German withdrawal: see HStA Dresden, *Militärbevollmächtigter* 4210, Bl. 122: Mitteilungen Nr. 7 über die britische Armee, 16 Jan. 1918.

50 IWM, 84/46/1: M. Hardie, Report on Moral, &c., 1 May 1917, p. 1.

infantry tactics developed from experience gained on the Somme were instrumental in both making battlefield advances possible and maintaining good morale. Promoting initiative, individual specialisation and cooperation between different weapons groups, the new doctrine empowered soldiers, raising men's trust in their own abilities both to protect themselves and to reach assigned objectives.[51] Moreover, as industry completed its war mobilisation, the all-important flow of weapons and material became such that, in the words of the historian Ian Malcolm Brown, 'a superabundance of ammunition was the norm' by mid-1917. From this point onwards, the army's primary logistical difficulty became the replacement of guns worn out through too much firing.[52]

The opening of Field Marshal Haig's great Third Ypres Offensive was thus greeted as the final push by the troops who, as German intelligence remarked, entered the battle with unprecedented confidence in victory.[53] Poor planning, horrendous weather conditions and the discovery that the expectations of success were overblown quickly brought about demoralisation, however. Men taken prisoner on 31 July west of Zandvoorde told their captors that they had been confident of success and were 'now very depressed'.[54] As the battle wore on and conditions worsened, this mood also spread to units not directly involved in the offensive. The Third Army's censor warned in late August that talk of peace had become common in troops' correspondence. 'There is a feeling of uncertainty as to the progress of our arms to an ultimate victory, and a growing inclination to believe that military enterprise must give place to political ingenuity,' he observed.[55] The generals were held responsible for the debacle; trust declined so severely that German interrogators reported prisoners declaring, 'we

[51] For the new tactics, see Griffith, *Battle Tactics*, pp. 76–9 and Lee, 'Some Lessons of the Somme', pp. 79–87. This literature convincingly challenges Martin Samuels' argument that initiative was rejected in favour of rigid obedience at the lower levels of British command. Still, it should be noted that not all British training espoused independent action; recruit training at Étaples base seems in particular to have been defined by its emphasis on rigid discipline. See Gill and Dallas, 'Mutiny at Etaples Base', 89–90 and Samuels, *Command or Control?*, pp. 123 and 224.

[52] I.M. Brown, *British Logistics on the Western Front, 1914–1919* (London: Praeger, 1998), pp. 164 and 167. For the Arras Offensive, see Sheffield, *Forgotten Victory*, pp. 159–66.

[53] HStA Dresden, *Militärbevollmächtigter* 4210, Bl. 122: Mitteilungen Nr. 7 über die britische Armee, 16 Jan. 1918.

[54] BA-MA Freiburg, PH 3/ 585: Vernehmungsprotokolle, AOK 4: Vernehmung [of eight men from 10/Royal West Kents, six men from 11/Royal West Surreys, one man from 23/Middlesex and twenty-three men from 20/Durham Light Infantry], 3 Aug. 1917.

[55] IWM, 84/46/1: M. Hardie, Report on Moral, &c., 25 Aug. 1917, p. 3.

must have French general staff officers'.[56] The army's self-confidence was seriously shaken. The Third Army's censor recorded in October that its men had 'arrived at a state of bewildered anxious doubt as to whether our high command or our politicians at home see any definite issue from an apparent impasse' and feared that 'they are drifting into an endless destruction and sacrifice'.[57] German intelligence arrived at similar conclusions, reporting in early 1918 that 'great confidence in victory and the feeling of superiority in military matters have, as a result of the events of the last year of hostilities, been replaced by a pronounced war-weariness'.[58]

The demoralisation caused by the Ypres fighting had serious implications for the BEF's discipline and combat performance. Given the anger and distrust of the upper leadership at the time, it was not coincidence that the only serious group disobedience of the war, that at the Étaples base camp in September 1917, took place while the battle was raging. The exhaustion caused by the heavy fighting and appalling conditions also led to one of the most severe battlefield routs of the conflict, when the 55th Division dissolved in the face of a German counterattack at Cambrai on 30 November. Enquiries set up to establish the causes of the disaster listed a number of contributory factors: the division had lost 7,000 officers and men in Flanders who had been replaced by improperly trained drafts; the new system of elastic defence was not properly understood; the novel and overwhelming form taken by the German attack had terrorised the defenders with low-flying aircraft and used stormtroops to infiltrate their lines. As even Haig admitted, however, the root of the problem was that due to the strenuous and indecisive fighting of previous months, 'many of the men were very tired and unable to resist the enemy's blow'.[59]

The key reason why neither panics nor mutinies spread, however, was that despite the weariness and distrust of the staff catalysed by the Third Ypres Offensive, British soldiers remained confident of their ability to win the war. Reference to peace actually declined in the Third Army's letters during September and October, and even the men of the Second

[56] See BA-MA Freiburg, PH 3/ 585: Vernehmungsprotokolle, AOK 4: Vernehmung [of 2 officers, 13 NCOs and 258 men from 33, 29 and 23 Divisions], 28 Sept. 1917. Cf. ibid., Vernehmung [of one man from 13/Royal Sussex Regiment], 2 Sept. 1917.

[57] IWM, 84/46/1: M. Hardie, Report on Peace, 19 Oct. 1917, p. 2.

[58] HStA Dresden, *Militärbevollmächtigter* 4210, Bl. 122: Mitteilungen Nr. 7 über die britische Armee, 16 Jan. 1918.

[59] See, respectively, Gill and Dallas, 'Mutiny at Etaples Base', 88–112 and TNA, WO 158/ 53: Cambrai Enquiry File No. 1, 29 Jan. 1918, p. 10 and TNA, CAB 24/ 37: War Cabinet. Cambrai Inquiry. Memorandum by General Smuts. G.T.-3198, particularly pp. 3, 9 and 13.

Army, whom the censor found to be most demoralised and war weary, still expressed the feeling that 'only one kind of peace is possible and that the time is not yet come'.[60] Prisoners, who were liable to be depressed on capture and in at least some cases may have felt they could talk more candidly to interrogators than families back home, also evinced no defeatism, even when they doubted that a victory by military means alone was possible:

> War-weariness and a lack of confidence are voiced quite openly in prisoners' statements. The British soldier no longer believes in the military defeat of Germany. Nonetheless, he is still ready to hold out, for a British victory, even without a military decision, is still regarded as certain. Shortages in rations and war material have not yet made themselves noticeable. The Englishman considers a German victory impossible ... The expectation that Germany will be forced by economic or internal political causes to give in is still generally held. From this, the view is taken in the army that a negotiated peace will come about. That this will mean an English victory and bring Great Britain advantages is taken as self-evident.[61]

Ultimately, the British army survived the debacle of Third Ypres because its troops continued to believe in their ability to outlast the Germans. Although disillusionment with the BEF's upper leadership grew, there is no evidence to suggest that British soldiers ceased to trust their junior leaders or doubted their own martial prowess. Consciousness of material superiority played a crucial role in supporting this confidence, encouraging soldiers in the belief that even if decisive breakthrough was impossible in the conditions which existed on the Western Front, Germany would eventually be forced to capitulate. The readiness to endure and certainty of victory would serve troops well in the spring of 1918 when, overstretched and still physically weary, they faced the full strength of the German army's best troops.

Morale in the German Field Army in the west, 1914–17

As Niall Ferguson has observed, 'to the economic historian, the outcome of the First World War looks to have been inevitable from the moment the majority of Asquith's Cabinet swallowed their Liberal scruples and opted for intervention'.[62] At the outbreak of war, the Triple Entente and its allies had far greater resources at their disposal than those available to

60 IWM, 84/46/1: M. Hardie, Report on Peace, 19 Oct. 1917, p. 2 and a censor report of the Second Army quoted in Gill and Dallas, *Unknown Army*, p. 82.
61 HStA Dresden, *Militärbevollmächtigter* 4210, Bl. 122–3: Mitteilungen Nr. 7 über die britische Armee, 16 Jan. 1918.
62 Ferguson, *Pity*, p. 248.

the Central Powers. Even excluding the much larger colonies of the Entente, the rival populations respectively numbered 258,500,000 and 118,000,000. The Entente's national income was 60 per cent greater than that of its enemies and already on mobilisation its armies numbered 5,726,000 men, 2 million more than those possessed by the Central Powers.[63] The German army's failure to defeat its French opponent decisively in 1914 condemned it to a difficult two-front war. Although the tactical advantage lent by contemporary weapons provided it with the ability to ward off superior forces, the longevity of the static warfare was ultimately a severe disadvantage, as it provided the time needed by Russia and Britain to train and equip huge armies. Almost continual numerical inferiority in the west limited the German army's opportunities to attack decisively and placed great pressure on its troops (see Table 3).

In order to survive against its numerically superior enemies, Germany had to mobilise its manpower on an unprecedented level. The Field Army expanded from a peacetime strength of 808,280 to a highpoint of 5,380,637 soldiers in June 1917. In contrast to the comparatively modest 49 per cent of British military-aged males who served during the war, the German army recruited no less than 13,387,000 men, representing 86 per cent of its eligible manpower.[64]

A high level of mobilisation was alone not sufficient to compensate for the army's inferiority, for although the measure increased numbers, it also resulted in a qualitative decline in manpower. This process was not smooth or regular. The first major lowering of standards took place at the end of 1914, when in order to find the 1.3 million troops required to build new units and replace the heavy losses inflicted in the mobile fighting, the army recruited many older men. Some of these soldiers suffered from physical impairments such as deafness or even partial paralysis.[65] Others were psychologically disturbed, psychiatrists complaining that 'in

63 Ibid., pp. 92–3 and 248.

64 Strachan, *New Illustrated History*, p. 140, *Sanitätsbericht II*, p. 1 and *Sanitätsbericht III*, pp. 12 and 7*. Figures given in the literature vary slightly: Rüdiger Overmans, for example, suggests that Germany and France both mobilised 81 per cent of eligible manpower (men aged fifteen to forty-nine in 1914), while the United Kingdom mobilised 53 per cent. See Overmans, 'Kriegsverluste', in G. Hirschfeld, G. Krumeich and I. Renz (eds.), *Enzyklopädie Erster Weltkrieg* (Paderborn: Ferdinand Schöningh, 2004), pp. 664–5. Part of the reason for the United Kingdom's lesser mobilisation was that men in Ireland were less willing to volunteer than their peers in Britain and were never conscripted: whereas 58 per cent of Englishmen, Welshmen and Scotsmen aged fifteen to forty-nine in 1911 served in the war, the figure in Ireland was only 15 per cent. See Winter, 'Britain's "Lost Generation"', 450.

65 See BA-MA Freiburg, PH 3/ 582, Bl. 19: Summary of Information (5th Corps). No. 23, 21 May 1915.

Table 3. *Field strength of major armies on the Western Front, 1914–18*

Army	August 1914	July 1916	November 1918
French	1,421,000	2,234,000	1,554,000
British	118,000	1,462,000	1,202,000
Belgian	177,000	*c.* 150,000	115,000
American	N/A	N/A	1,175,000
Allies	1,716,000	3,846,000	4,046,000
German	1,318,000	2,943,000	2,912,000
Allied advantage	398,000	903,000	1,134,000

Sources: Strachan, *First World War*, I, p. 206 (French active army only), A. Clayton, *Paths of Glory. The French Army 1914–18* (London: Cassell, 2003), p. 162, M. Huber (ed.), *La population de la France pendant la Guerre* (Paris and New Haven: Les Presses Universitaires de France and Yale University Press, 1932), p. 115, *Military Effort*, p. 628, J. Ellis and M. Cox, *The World War I Databook. The Essential Facts and Figures for all the Combatants* (London: Aurum Press, 1993), p. 245 and *Sanitätsbericht III*, p. 6*. German figures for 1918 include the small Austrian contingent serving on the Western Front, and may also be inflated by non-combatant troops securing Belgium. Other figures (in Altrichter, *Seelischen Kräfte*, p. 192) suggest that the Field Army numbered only 2,563,107 men at the end of the war.

the speed of the mustering …, some mentally ill, some epileptics, some imbeciles entered the army'.[66] These men may well have contributed to the army's losses from psychiatric disorders, which reached their highest rate of the war during the winter of 1914–15.[67] Thereafter, the army experienced a temporary improvement, as fit eighteen-, nineteen- and twenty-year-olds were recruited in early 1915 and a new, more comprehensive gradation system and stricter physical criteria were introduced.[68] Already in September 1915, however, the need to counter the expansion of Entente forces forced the army to turn back to

66 K. Singer, 'Wesen und Bedeutung der Kriegspsychosen', *Berliner Klinische Wochenschrift* 8 (22 February 1915), 177.

67 Calculated from *Sanitätsbericht III*, pp. 6* and 42*.

68 Ibid., pp. 15–16. Prospective recruits were divided into *kriegsbrauchbar* and *kriegsunbrauchbar*, the former of which was subdivided into the *Kriegsverwendungsfähigen*, *Garnisonverwendungsfähigen* und *Arbeitsverwendungsfähigen*. The instructions explaining the new system were issued as the 'Anleitung für die militärärztliche Beurteilung der Kriegsbrauchbarkeit beim Kriegsmusterungsgeschäft, bei den Bezirkskommandos und der Truppe'. For improved physical criteria, see BA-MA Freiburg, W-10/50755: Anonymous *Reichsarchiv* historical work, p. 12.

substandard recruits: 821,051 men who had been rejected for service in peacetime were reinspected, 184,142 of whom were reclassified as *kriegsverwendbar* (fit for combat service) and 286,137 were considered fit for non-combatant posts. The greatest qualitative decline took place in the winter of 1916–17, however, when in order to replace the heavy losses of the *Materialschlachten* the army was forced to comb out fit men in the Home Army and in the rear areas of the Field Army and send them to the front.[69] Regular and ruthless inspections by commissions aware of the urgent need for more fighting troops won combat units more than 38,000 nominally fit but often extremely resentful officers and men.[70] Worse still, the eighteen-year-olds recruited in the winter of 1916–17 were widely reported as being inferior to classes recruited in previous years. German officers noticed that they were despondent about army service. *Leutnant* Müller, for example, ascribed their lack of enthusiasm to the length of the war and the fact that 'everyone has already heard much about it all from men on leave etc.'.[71] It may also have resulted from hunger and poor physique: British prisoner interrogators noticed that many drawn from the towns showed 'signs of underfeeding' due to the naval blockade. Whatever the reason, the presence of large numbers of these men in a unit was judged to '[militate] against its steadiness and morale'.[72]

The decline in the quality of its recruits forced the German army to seek methods to maximise their potential in order to maintain combat performance. From the summer of 1916, the army began to pay increasing attention to the composition of its units. Already in the pre-war period, it had been organised according to age, the youngest men serving in *Aktive* and *Reserve* units, while older men were allocated to the *Landwehr* and *Landsturm*. In 1914, *Landwehr* men of between twenty-eight and thirty-eight had been placed on the defensive in Alsace-Lorraine, while their younger, fitter peers in *Aktive* and *Reserve* regiments had undertaken the exhausting offensive marches through Belgium and into France.[73] Thereafter, drafts had been allocated indiscriminately, but in August 1916,

[69] *Sanitätsbericht III*, p. 16.

[70] See ibid. for information on mustering and also Volkmann, *Soziale Heeresmißstände*, XI.2, p. 128. Figures refer to the period up to 31 Dec. 1917.

[71] Staatsbib. Berlin, Ms. Germ. fol. 1651: C.F. Müller, diary, 25 Apr. 1917.

[72] TNA, WO 157/ 24: 'Notes on German Prisoners Recently Captured in Flanders', in Annexe to Advanced GHQ Summary of 1 September 1917 and TNA, WO 157/ 190: Summaries of Information. Fourth Army, 2 Jan. 1918. Cf. Camena d'Almeida, *L'armée allemande*, p. 275.

[73] See the introduction by T. Cave in United States War Office, *Histories of Two Hundred and Fifty-One Divisions of the German Army which Participated in the War* (London: London Stamp Exchange, 1920, 1989), p. iii.

Plate 14. Human decline: 'The Guard once and now', 1917 and 1914. Clearly a joke, but with a serious point behind it: by the war's third year, the German army's supply of fit manpower was running low. From the album of a soldier serving in a *Reserve-Grenadier-Regiment*.

segregation by age was once more introduced, the youngest drafts being sent to divisions intended for the most demanding tasks, while older troops serving in these units were exchanged for youths in *Landwehr* and *Landsturm* formations. The extreme demands of the *Materialschlacht* prompted the *OHL* to rule in April 1917 that men older than thirty-five were not suitable for service with Western Front infantry or pioneers and many were transferred to serve instead with units in Russia.[74] The advantages of this system were twofold: firstly, it raised the physical standard of combat divisions in the *Materialschlacht* to a level above that of their British opponents, which recruited regardless of age. The second benefit was psychological: older men, less able to stand front conditions and more inclined to complain, were separated from their younger counterparts, thus preventing them from having a demoralising influence. The units they formed were of minimal military value but capable of garrisoning inactive sectors, of which the German army, unlike its British opponent, had a plentiful supply.[75]

Although age remained the most import selection criterion, efforts were also made to examine other individual qualities, in order to slot men into posts best fitting their skills and capabilities. Recruiting guidelines issued at the end of 1917 ordered that men's background, physique and peacetime occupation should all be taken into account when allocating men to units. The mountain artillery was logically sent natives of Alpine regions or men who in peacetime had been mountaineers, while well-built individuals were transferred to the heavy artillery. The pioneers, who comprised some of Germany's crack troops, were allocated 'powerful, strong-nerved people who from peacetime are used to demanding activity'.[76] Personnel needed for the particularly dangerous positions of tank- and aircrew were specially selected.[77] By the end of the war, scientific procedures had been introduced in order to assess candidates' suitability for certain posts: prospective artillery spotters, for example, underwent tests in 1918 designed to assess eyesight, hearing

[74] Ziemann, *Front*, pp. 62–4. See also BA-MA Freiburg, MSg 1/ 3109: H. Muhsal, diary, 11 and 24 Nov. 1916.

[75] Allied military intelligence gave all but five of the forty-six *Landwehr* divisions the lowest possible of its four combat efficiency ratings in 1918. See United States War Office, *Histories*. This figure includes as *Landwehr* divisions the *35. Reserve-Division* and the *88., 89., 91., 92., 95., 224., 226., 227.* and *255. Divisionen* which all contained a majority of *Landwehr* units.

[76] GLA Karlsruhe, 456 F 8 /106, p. 214: Order issued by the *stellv. Generalkommando, XIV AK* in accordance with instructions from the *preußisches Kriegsministerium*, 1 Dec. 1917.

[77] Hofmann, 'Die deutsche Nervenkraft', p. 449.

and concentration.[78] Probably the most complex examination was that designed to test the concentration, reactions and nervousness of prospective lorry drivers, in whose charge were placed the most precious vehicles of the German army. The candidate sat in a fake cab and counted the flashes made by a number of white lights while a horn, searchlight and noise generator were turned on and off as distractions. Any variation in an engine sound played had to be noted by the driver and three red lights in front of him and to his left and right warned him to brake or avoid imaginary hazards.[79]

Scientific testing was a novel method of ensuring that personnel would be both capable and confident of fulfilling their military tasks. A more traditional method designed with the same purpose was training. Already in the pre-war period, the German army had sought to balance its material inferiority against Russia and France by providing a very high level of instruction for its conscripts. The rush to mobilise as many men as possible and quickly win a decisive victory over France in 1914 led to the abandonment of this principle. Training was cut drastically from two years to two months and declined greatly in quality as active officers were sent to the front.[80] The greatest losers were the units of volunteers and *Ersatzreservisten* (conscripts lacking pre-war training) given two months instruction and then thrown into the fierce fighting around Ypres in the desperate hope that they would break through British lines. Almost 15,000 men were lost by the *XXIII.*, *XXVI.* and *XXVII. Reserve-Armeekorps* between 19 October and 18 November in failed attacks, and the rate of psychiatric loss suffered by these formations was, unsurprisingly, far higher than that experienced by units composed of peacetime-trained conscripts.[81] Other units also found the standard of replacement troops' battlecraft unsatisfactory during this period, but despite constant complaints, soldiers who had been given almost no shooting or entrenching practice and did not know how to take cover were still being captured by the British army in May 1915. Lacking confidence in their own abilities to cope with the front, these

[78] O. Klemm, 'Eignungsprüfungen an meßtechnischem Personal', in E. Abderhalden (ed.), *Handbuch der biologischen Arbeitsmethoden*. Part VI: *Methoden der experimentellen Psychologie*. Part C/I (Berlin: Urban & Schwarzenberg, 1928), p. 565.

[79] B. Herwig, 'Psychotechnische Methoden im Verkehrswesen', in E. Abderhalden (ed.), *Handbuch der biologischen Arbeitsmethoden*. Part VI: *Methoden der experimentellen Psychologie*. Part C/I (Berlin: Urban & Schwarzenberg, 1928), pp. 722–5.

[80] BA-MA Freiburg, W-10/ 50902: Denkenschrift über die Ersatzstellung für das Deutsche Heer von Mitte September bis Ende 1914, p. 31 and BA-MA Freiburg W-10/ 50755: Anonymous *Reichsarchiv* historical work, p. 11.

[81] See Watson, 'For Kaiser and Reich', 62–6. For casualties, see Edmonds, *History of the Great War ... October–November 1914*, p. 467. No figures exist for the *XXII. Reserve-Armeekorps*, which was also heavily engaged.

Plate 15. Preparation: inspection at a German recruit training depot behind the lines. The German army attempted to compensate for its numerical inferiority by raising the standard of its training. From an album belonging to the Adjutant of *14. Reserve-Division*.

men were reported to exhibit 'not only despondency, but a real hatred against those who sent them to fight under these conditions'.[82]

The decline in troops' military skill and the recognition that the war would last for a long time did eventually bring about a change in German attitudes to training. In April 1915, it was finally acknowledged that the instruction in home depots was mediocre and Field Recruit Depots were established behind the lines in order to allow recruits to benefit from the experience of veteran instructors. Henceforth soldiers spent eight weeks learning basic field craft in home units and were than transferred to a depot for a more advanced course usually lasting four weeks.[83] Further improvements were implemented by the Third *OHL* after August 1916, when

[82] For the combat units' complaints, see BA-MA Freiburg, W-10/ 50755: Anonymous *Reichsarchiv* historical work, p. 11 and, for the prisoners, see the captured British intelligence document in BA-MA Freiburg, PH 3/ 582, Bl. 19: Summary of Information (5th Corps). No. 23, 21 May 1915.

[83] TNA, WO 157/ 13: 'Note on the Recruitment of German Classes during the War', in Annexe to GHQ Summary, 28 Sept. 1916 and TNA, WO 157/ 197: Annexe to Fourth Army Summary, 17 Aug. 1918.

tactical reforms forced the army to emphasise the development of individual skills and initiative. By November 1917, when divisions were being given offensive training in preparation for the *Kaiserschlacht*, instruction was operating on the principle that 'the most careful individual training is the most important basis for all further battle schooling. The instilling of independence has won a heightened meaning in the present fighting conditions'.[84]

For Ferguson, this emphasis on individual initiative benefited the German army principally by raising its combat performance. He calculates that during the course of the war, the Central Powers inflicted losses of 10.3 million on their enemies, while suffering 'only' 7.1 million permanent casualties themselves. 'Between August 1914 and June 1918', he argues, 'the Germans consistently killed or captured more British and French soldiers than they lost themselves'.[85] Certainly, superior killing power helped the German army to avoid being overwhelmed by its more numerous enemies. Yet arguably training played a less important role in the army's ability to inflict heavy casualties than high quality staff-work, superior operational doctrine and its predominantly defensive stance in the west, which maximised the effectiveness of its weaponry.[86] German recruits actually received less instruction than their British counterparts; only in February 1918 was basic training extended to twelve weeks and by the end of the war many units believed that this was insufficient, arguing instead that fifteen or sixteen weeks would be more suitable.[87] The special courses designed to raise troops' tactical skill later in the war were also by no means always of a high quality. One veteran *Landwehr* officer who attended a company leadership course in October 1917 was disgusted to find himself being taught obviously outmoded tactics: 'the drill was that of thirty years ago', he grumbled in his diary, 'firing lines which were straight as an arrow'.[88]

While training played a crucial role in strengthening the resilience of the German army, its effect was often more psychological than practical.

[84] BA-MA Freiburg, PH 6 V/ 6: Order from *Chef des Generalstabes des Feldheeres* regarding 'Ausbildung der Truppe', 20 Nov. 1917. Cf. also Gudmundsson, *Stormtroop Tactics*, pp. 147–51.

[85] Ferguson, *Pity*, pp. 296–8, 300–3, 308–9 and 445.

[86] See Samuels, *Command or Control?*, pp. 283–4. While the relative merits of German and British infantry tactics at different points in the war remain controversial, there is evidence to support Samuels' argument that the German emphasis on delegation and decentralisation at upper and middle command levels did indeed prove more operationally effective than British traditions of 'umpiring' and 'restrictive control'. Cf. particularly Travers, *How the War Was Won*, pp. 27–31 and 175–6.

[87] BA-MA Freiburg, W-10/ 50755: Anonymous *Reichsarchiv* historical work, pp. 18–20.

[88] BA-MA Freiburg, MSg 1/ 3109: H. Muhsal, diary, 8 Oct. 1917. The poor standard of training described was not exceptional. See also chapter 6 below, p. 186 for examples of units in the *Kaiserschlacht* adopting outmoded tactics.

As Hew Strachan has argued, the principal purpose behind the extensive training programmes preceding the *Kaiserschlacht* was not to upgrade troops' tactical prowess but rather to raise their morale after the stagnation of four years of trench warfare. The army recognised that self-confidence alone improved resilience and combat performance: as Ludendorff himself observed, 'a body of troops, which is rested, confident of its training and conscious of a moral and physical superiority over the enemy will be equal to all tasks'.[89]

Although selection and training enabled the German army to counter the qualitative decline of its manpower, inferiority in men and material nonetheless had an impact on its morale. Food shortages played an important role in demoralising men during the second half of the war. Troops worried about their families not having enough to eat and were outraged when turnips were issued in place of potatoes at the end of 1916 and the bread ration reduced in 1917.[90] The consequences of the shortages on inter-rank relations have already been discussed. Equally important, however, was their effect on soldiers' confidence that the war could be won. Men linked the army's ability to supply food directly with its capacity to achieve victory: Franz Brussig, for example, recovering from illness in a field hospital outside Verdun, recorded that the distribution of a thin soup without meat among his fellow patients at the end of March 1916 prompted a wave of disgust against the war. 'Why is no peace concluded, if there is nothing to eat?', they asked.[91] One year later, a man serving in *8. Armee* similarly remarked that 'it is high time that the swindle comes to an end, otherwise we will drop dead on the street due to hunger'. Another letter read by the *5. Armee* censor declared in July 1917, 'At midday there was a meal which was impossible to enjoy. If it continues this way, we cannot win'.[92]

German troops' powers of endurance were strained not only by hunger but also by fatigue. In contrast to the BEF, which only launched its first

89 BA-MA Freiburg, PH 6 V/ 6: Order from *Chef des Generalstabes des Feldheeres* regarding 'Ausbildung der Truppe', 20 Nov. 1917. Cf. Strachan, 'Ausbildung, Kampfgeist und die zwei Weltkriege', p. 277.

90 For outrage at reductions in the quality and quantity of soldiers' own rations, see BA-MA Freiburg, W-10/ 50794: Postüberwachung der *5. Armee*, 12 July 1917, p. 14. British interrogation reports also registered a drop in morale among prisoners as soon as the food shortages began in 1916. See TNA, WO 157/ 5: Summary of Information (GHQ), 20 and 27 Mar. 1916 and TNA, WO 157/ 6: Summary of Information (GHQ), 2 Apr. 1916. For worry about the home front, see BA-MA Freiburg, MSg 2/ 5290: W. Dietl, letter to family, 30 Apr. 1916 and BA-MA Freiburg, MSg 1/ 3109: H. Muhsal, diary, 23 Dec. 1917–12 Jan. 1918.

91 Staatsbib. Berlin, Ms. Boruss. fol. 1084: F. Brussig, diary, 5 Mar. 1916.

92 See the censor report of *8. Armee* for letters sent between 25 June and 13 July 1917 reproduced in Hobohm, *Soziale Heeresmißstände*, XI.1, pp. 30–6 (doc. 11) and BA-MA Freiburg, W-10/ 50794: Postüberwachung der *5. Armee*, 12 July 1917, p. 22.

major offensive at the Somme in mid-1916, the German army was involved in heavy fighting from the first days of the war. Exhaustion and feelings of hopelessness were increased by inept official policy regarding unit rotation: whereas the BEF sensibly relieved divisions in active sectors regularly throughout the war, the German army kept them at the front until they were no longer capable of holding the line. Soldiers' diaries testify to the unnecessary stress caused by this policy, which had the dual disadvantages of denying men a comforting deadline for relief at which they could aim and risking such casualties that the transmission of *esprit de corps* to new recruits would be endangered. Only in the autumn of 1917 was a similar system to that used by the British adopted.[93] Adequate provision was made for relaxation behind the lines. Field libraries and reading rooms were organised and, as in the British army, divisions formed their own concert ensembles and screened films. Yet manpower shortages meant that soldiers' chances to take advantage of these facilities were limited. To give one, possibly extreme example, the *183. Division* received only three months' rest between March 1917 and the end of the war.[94]

While the shortage of basic necessities slowly eroded German resilience, it was the advent of the *Materialschlacht* which dealt the Kaiser's soldiers their greatest psychological blow. Soldiers' letters and diaries testify to the tremendous strain caused by the sustained and bloody fighting around Verdun in 1916. Here, however, they were at least on the attack, experienced some major initial successes, most notably the almost bloodless capture of Fort Douaumont, and were fighting on equal or even advantageous terms against the French.[95] In contrast, from its

[93] See TNA, WO 157/ 25: Summary of Information (GHQ), 25 Oct. 1917. *Reserve-Infanterie-Regiment Nr. 121*, for example, served on the Somme front from June until 7 November 1916 and was again sent back for heavy fighting in the middle of that month. See vom Holz, *Reserve-Inf.-Regiment Nr. 121*, p. 39. For the stress caused by the lack of rotation, see the diary of Kurt Reiter (BA-MA Freiburg, MSg 1/ 161: K. Reiter, diary), who served from the beginning of June until mid-August at Verdun with his unit, *Feldartillerie-Regiment Nr. 204*.

[94] For an example of a German concert party, see BA-MA Freiburg, PH 5 IV/ 42: Wander-Theater, Armee-Abteilung A Programme, Nov. 1916 and for other measures relating to relaxation in the rear, see Lipp, *Meinungslenkung*, pp. 82–7. For similar British recreation, see Fuller, *Troop Morale*, pp. 174–80, and particularly 96–109. Finally, for the *183. Division*, see Volkmann, *Soziale Heeresmißstände*, XI.2, p. 72.

[95] For the strain caused by the fighting at Verdun, see BA-MA Freiburg, MSg 2/ 2735: H. Genscher, letter to father, 30 Mar. 1916 and BA-MA Freiburg, MSg 1/ 161: K. Reiter, diary, 31 May–16 Aug. 1916. For Fort Douaumont's capture, see Horne, *Price of Glory*, pp. 105–25. See also von Selle and Gründel (eds.), *Das 6. Westpreußische Infanterie-Regiment Nr.149*, pp. 226–7 for the lesser demands of attacking at Verdun, as compared with the exhausting defensive battle fought under disadvantageous material conditions on the Somme.

Plate 16. Material might (2): British tank. Although not tactically decisive, the appearance of the tank in 1916 was yet another manifestation of Allied industrial superiority – and a terrifying machine to have to confront. From a French soldier's album.

seven-day opening bombardment, in which 1.5 million shells were fired, the Somme Offensive presented German troops with the first clear evidence of their material inferiority. Despite its ineffectuality in terms of killing or disabling the defenders, the experience of sheltering under this prolonged artillery fire entered German military folklore as a uniquely traumatic event.[96] The huge weight of metal fired shook the defenders' confidence in their ability to resist: the historian of the *Reserve-Infanterie-Regiment Nr. 121*, who himself who been wounded on the Somme, remembered that 'one immediately had the impression that the enemy was vastly superior to us in terms of material'.[97] Nor, despite British

[96] See Staatsbib. Berlin, Ms. Germ. fol. 1651: C.F. Müller, diary, 7 Apr. 1917 and Ziemann, *Front*, p. 183.

[97] Vom Holz, *Reserve-Inf.-Regiment Nr. 121*, p. 33. Cf. the similar statement in Roth, *K.B. Reserve-Infanterie-Regiment Nr. 23*, p. 78.

troops' serious losses and failed attacks, did the subsequent struggle evoke much sense of triumph among the Kaiser's soldiers. On the contrary, most were simply horrified at the prolonged and brutal nature of the heavy fighting:

> I am incapable of giving an account of the battle on the Somme. You could not imagine it. It is perhaps enough if I give you some figures. I don't know the exact number of dead. The company's total casualties amount to between 150 and 160 men . . . The troops had done well and fought bravely. Nonetheless, the strain was too immense. The men were completely exhausted and the English exploited this on the last day before the relief. They surprised us in a manner never seen before. They came on unstoppably in front of us. Behind came numerous armoured automobiles armed with machineguns, flamethrowers etc. In addition, the greatest part of the trench garrison was certainly killed or buried alive by the preceding bombardment. What remained wanted to surrender but was mostly killed.[98]

It is unsurprising that, under such circumstances, combatants should manifest signs of severe stress. The commander of *bayerisches Reserve-Infanterie-Regiment Nr. 5* noted in August 1916 that his troops were becoming increasingly jittery and warned that 'this state of terror on the Somme front must be dispelled, and calm must take its place'.[99] Other units also displayed evidence of severe demoralisation. Examinations of prisoners taken by the British from the *XIII. (württembergisches)* and *XIX. (sächsisches) Armeekorps*, for example, revealed that 'shelling has considerably affected their moral'.[100] Men of *Garde-Regiment Nr. 5* captured in early September were even more depressed, expressing 'the hope that [the BEF] would attack soon and make an end of the war'.[101] In other cases, however, the experience of fighting on the Somme battlefield actually increased the resolve to keep enemy troops out of Germany. 'One hears far less criticism than in previous months,' observed the author of a Railway Police report in September 1916. 'The soldiers do not of course

[98] BA-MA Freiburg, MSg 2/ 4563: Letter of Hans Frimmel describing the British attack of 15 Sept. 1916, reproduced in H. Ullrich, 'Auszüge aus Kriegsbriefen Unterthaler Soldaten, 1914–1917'.

[99] Regimental order of 5th Bavarian Reserve Regiment [*sic*], 30 Aug. 1916, reproduced and translated in IWM, 84/46/1: Papers of M. Hardie: 'Extracts from Letters found on Germans during the Somme Battle'. Intelligence / propaganda sheet.

[100] TNA, WO 157/ 12: Summary of Information (GHQ), 21 Aug. 1916. Cf. TNA, WO 157/ 16: Summary of Information (GHQ), 26 Dec. 1916; IWM, 84/46/1: Papers of M. Hardie: 'Extracts from Letters found on Germans during the Somme Battle'. Intelligence / propaganda sheet; BA-MA Freiburg, MSg 2/ 5458: J. Kohler, letter to parents, 3 July 1916 and BA-MA Freiburg, MSg 2/ 2735: H. Genscher, letter to uncle, 6 Nov. 1916.

[101] TNA, WO 157/ 13: Summary of Information (GHQ), 2 Sept. 1916.

conceal the fact that their work at the front demands superhuman strength, but they are very content and when questioned express cheerful confidence'.[102]

The first half of 1917 brought little to raise German soldiers' morale. Although the defeat of Romania at the end of 1916 was greeted with enthusiasm in some quarters, the entry of America into the war on 6 April 1917 depressed the men. Some worried that the necessity of fighting a new, major opponent would prolong hostilities further. Others, more realistically, were frightened that it made Germany's defeat certain. *Leutnant* Heinrich Genscher, wartime volunteer and one-time enthusiast of the conflict, feared what he termed an American 'mass murder' if the war did not end in 1917: 'if we emerge from this war with *one* black eye, we will have had damn good luck!'[103] Despite the increasingly bleak strategic situation, men fought on because they had little choice other than to protect their families. Nonetheless, the prolonged strain and absence of any clear war aims other than *durchhalten* ('hold out') led many to hope for a negotiated peace: by the middle of the year, the postal censor of the *5. Armee* was reporting that 'everyone wishes an end to the war as soon as possible'.[104] While unconditional capitulation was not considered to be an option by the vast majority of soldiers, the fear that Germany's leaders were continuing the war for their own benefit caused increasing resentment. Requests for war-loan contributions were treated with contempt as cynical confidence tricks designed by the upper classes and officers to prolong the war: 'don't be so stupid as to sign something; if the officers don't get any more pay, the war will be finished'.[105]

It was at the Third Battle of Ypres that the fatigue and demoralisation felt by German soldiers first broke out into group disobedience and mutiny. As in the previous year's fighting on the Somme and at Verdun,

[102] GLA Karlsruhe, 456 F 8/ 260: Report regarding *Eisenbahnüberwachungsreisende* to *stellvertretenden Generalstab der Armee IIIb*, 1 Sept. 1916.

[103] BA-MA Freiburg, MSg 2/ 2735: H. Genscher, letter to father, 20 Mar. 1917. For the fear that the war would be prolonged by America's entry, see BA-MA Freiburg, MSg 1/ 3109: H. Muhsal, diary, 12 Mar. 1917. For Romania, see Private Collection (Author): K. Fritsche, letter to mother, 7 Dec. 1916. Cf. also BA-MA Freiburg, W-10/ 51507: Entwicklung der Stimmung im Heere im Winter 1916/17. Forschungsarbeit von Obkircher (1936).

[104] BA-MA Freiburg, W-10/ 50794: Postüberwachung der *5. Armee*, 12 July 1917, p. 14.

[105] HStA Dresden, 11352 Stellv. Gen.-Kdo XIX AK KA(P) 24135: Letter to *königlich[es] sächsische[s] Kriegsministerium* from anonymous member of the public reporting an overheard conversation among soldiers, *c.* April 1917. Cf. BA-MA Freiburg, W-10/ 50794: Postüberwachung der *5. Armee*, 28 Sept. 1917, pp. 27 and 31–2.

the battle was defined by heavy and intensely disempowering artillery fire. The chaplain of the *9. bayerische Reserve-Division*, stationed behind the lines without shelters between 30 July and 19 August, recalled that it 'had not only claimed many victims but above all had also placed the highest demands on the nerves of our men'.[106] Already during the fifteen-day opening bombardment, in which British guns fired 4.3 million shells, German troops began to break. Men of *Infanterie-Regiment Nr. 104* lost their nerve and fled up to five miles behind the front, soldiers of the *49. Reserve-Division* abandoned their positions in similar disorder, while members of *111. Division* deserted their units when ordered to man the line on 31 July.[107] The heavy fighting of the following months engendered more panics and insubordination. In August, soldiers of *79. Reserve-Division* were found to have 'fled in batches to the rear' during a British attack, while *Reserve-Infanterie-Regiment Nr. 49*, *Nr. 51* and *Nr. 212* and the pioneer companies of the *233. Division* all experienced cases of collective disobedience during the battle.[108] Even the elite *26. Division* suffered dissension, when three companies of the *III/Infanterie-Regiment Nr. 125* abandoned the line south-west of Poelcappelle after their relief had been continually postponed.[109] Units facing French troops also exhibited similar indiscipline: in mid-August, 102 men of the *206. Division*, stationed near Verdun, deserted to the enemy, while the *80. Reserve-Division* was alleged at the same place and time to have suffered from both desertions and mutinies. Still more seriously, units of the *13. Division* were reported in October to have surrendered *en masse* under their officers on the Chemin des Dames.[110]

The disorder within the German army during the summer and autumn of 1917 bore some similarity to the indiscipline preceding the famous French mutinies earlier that year. As in the Kaiser's army, these incidents, according to Guy Pedroncini, had been small scale, limited in intent and had often taken place in the front line.[111] Allied intelligence records, the main surviving evidence for the trouble in the German

106 LA Nuremberg, 3209: Report by Hermann Kornacher, Protestant chaplain of the *9. bayerische Reserve-Division*, 29 July 1918. My thanks to Patrick Porter for bringing this source to my attention.

107 United States War Office, *Histories*, pp. 444, 487 and 602. For the bombardment, see Prior and Wilson, *Passchendaele*, pp. 82 and 87.

108 TNA, WO 157/ 23: Summary of Information (GHQ), 14 Aug. 1917, p. 5; United States War Office, *Histories*, pp. 85 and 217; TNA, WO 157/ 25: Summary of Information (GHQ), 4 Oct. 1917, p. 2 and ibid., 14 Oct. 1917, p. 3.

109 TNA, WO 157/ 23: Summary of Information (GHQ), 30 Aug. 1917, p. 2.

110 Camena d'Almeida, *L'armée allemande*, p. 283 and United States War Office, *Histories*, pp. 542 and 227.

111 Pedroncini, *Mutineries de 1917*, pp. 102–7.

army, rarely reveal whether initial command collapses at the front were followed by more substantial insubordination behind the lines. Fragmentary German documentation from the *26. Division* is suggestive, however. After the mutiny of *III/Infanterie-Regiment Nr. 125* in August, further indiscipline took place in September, when four soldiers serving in *Infanterie-Regiment Nr. 121* were condemned for 'Meuterei und erschwerten Ungehorsam' (mutiny and aggravated insubordination) after they had refused to march up to the line. Whether this incident was independent or resulted from cross-fertilisation by the unit's previously mutinous sister regiment – a common event during the French mutinies – is unclear. What is certain, however, was that it was only one manifestation of wider disciplinary trouble within the division. The CO's order which mentioned this incident also condemned one of the formation's battalions for a further unspecified but clearly serious upset during the rail journey away from Flanders.[112] Even after transfer to Italy at the end of the month, indiscipline does not appear to have abated completely; a further order in November warned of 'a series of mainly alcohol-driven crude excesses and anarchy', including brawling, plundering, disobedience and theft.[113]

The sustained indiscipline in the *26. Division* indicates that, in common with the French and Russian armies before it, the German military was experiencing the effects of cumulative strain. By the opening of Third Ypres, it had suffered 1,129,414 fatalities and lost 585,575 men missing and a further 2,822,292 wounded.[114] Like its continental opponents, the army had been fully engaged in the war since 1914, it was suffering severe shortages and its troops were more disillusioned with their political leadership than were British soldiers. Nonetheless, even the disorder reported in *26. Division* was not comparable in scale or seriousness to the mutinies in the Tsar's army in the autumn of 1916 and in the French army during the following spring and summer, let alone to the widespread collapse of Russian military authority in 1917. No reports of whole divisions refusing to march to the front or issuing demands for peace exist for the Kaiser's army, as

112 HStA Stuttgart, M38/ 17, vol. II: *26. Infanterie-Division, Divisions-Tagesbefehl Nr. 149*, 21 Sept. 1917. For details of the men who mutinied see HStA Stuttgart, M 461/ 25: *Kriegsstammrolle der 8. Kp., Inf.-Reg. Nr. 121*, entry nos. 1193, 1195, 1202 and 1235. Each was sentenced to between six and fifteen years in prison but no record of their trials appears in the surviving military tribunal documents of the Württemberg army.

113 HStA Stuttgart, M38/ 17, vol. V: Order issued by officer commanding *26. Infanterie-Division*, 20 Nov. 1917.

114 BA-MA Freiburg, PH 3/ 446: Denkschrift der Obersten Heeresleitung über die deutsche Volks- und Wehrkraft, pp. 17–18.

they do for its enemies.[115] Partly, the lack of such actions may have been circumstantial: while discontent with a failed offensive strategy comprised a major motive for French and Russian soldiers, German troops were on the defensive in the west in late 1917, their high command lacked the strategic initiative and any sustained refusal to fight could only result in an Entente breakthrough and defeat. Yet it may well also indicate that the German indiscipline was fundamentally different from the Entente mutinies. Intelligence reports imply that the majority of incidents were panicky reactions by small units to conditions on the Western Front. In at least seven cases, it was the extremely heavy Entente artillery fire which sparked indiscipline. Elsewhere, the rain, mud and claustrophobic pillboxes, which restricted movement and vision even more than did trenches, broke men's mental resistance. Even in the *26. Division*, the initial August mutiny was blamed on these factors and it is noticeable that, despite the continued poor behaviour behind the lines, troops' fighting spirit returned once they had been removed from Flanders, the formation performing very well against the Italians at Caporetto.[116] Thus, whereas the French and Russian indiscipline developed into organised mutinies fuelled by general grievances about basic necessities or strategy, most German disorder appears to have been primarily spontaneous mental and physical collapses under extreme duress. While not offering the same threat to the army's command structure, these numerous, small-scale outbreaks of panics and disobedience were ultimately no less ominous, for they signified that many German troops were becoming mentally and physically incapable of coping with the heightened demands of the *Materialschlacht*.

Nonetheless, although by the end of the Ypres Offensive the German army's confidence had been shaken, the bulk of the force was not yet ready to collapse. Troops were sufficiently well trained and rested and officers good enough not only to halt the British offensive but also to

[115] For comparison, see particularly the accounts of mutinies in the French 5e *Division d'Infanterie* in May and June 1917 and the Russian 56th Infantry Division at the end of 1916 in, respectively, Smith, *Between Mutiny and Obedience*, pp. 175–214 and A.K. Wildman, *The End of the Russian Imperial Army. The Old Army and the Soldiers' Revolt (March–April 1917)* (2 vols., Princeton University Press, 1980), I, pp. 115–20. For Russian indiscipline in 1917, see A.K. Wildman, *The End of the Russian Imperial Army. The Road to Soviet Power and Peace* (2 vols., Princeton University Press, 1987), II, pp. 73–111 and 224–61.

[116] See United States War Office, *Histories*, p. 363. It is also noticeable that a prisoner-interrogation report emphasised short-term factors, such as heavy artillery fire and terrible front-line living conditions in prompting the initial August mutiny, rather than more general grievances such as the conduct of the war or shortages. See TNA, WO 157/ 23: Summary of Information (GHQ), 30 Aug. 1917, p. 2.

launch a highly successful counterattack after the famous Cambrai tank offensive. Men continued to recognise the necessity of protecting their families and homes: as the *5. Armee* censor remarked at the end of September 1917, complaints on being ordered to the front continued to be rare: 'it simply "must" be done, as the majority report home'.[117] What the offensive did reveal, however, was the severe strain under which German troops were fighting. The battlefield indiscipline in the second half of 1917 was testimony to the decline in the quality of the army's manpower and the difficulty of fighting against overwhelming Entente material superiority. The desperate hopes of peace almost universally expressed in soldiers' letters indicate that many were coming to the end of their endurance, and the fact that the desertion rate of 1917 was three times that of the previous year demonstrates that some were seeking their own exit.[118] Although it still possessed many very good combat formations, the accumulated strain of more than three years of fighting, material shortages and numerical inferiority was making a resolution to the war increasingly urgent for the German army by the end of 1917.

The Kaiserschlacht, March–July 1918

The German army's much needed opportunity for respite came in the form of the Russian Revolution in October 1917. The rapid disintegration of the Russian army after the Bolshevik *coup d'état* and the subsequent cessation of hostilities in the east reopened the possibility of a decisive German victory on the Western Front. The material preconditions for an offensive were met as troops gradually became available: from 1 November 1917, 48 divisions were redeployed to France and Belgium, so that on the eve of the *Kaiserschlacht* in March 1918, 191 German divisions faced the 178 of the Allies.[119] No less important, the defeat of the Russians also rejuvenated morale among Germany's tired troops, who temporarily regained their confidence in victory and looked forward to one last decisive attack which would allow them to return home. As the postal censor of the *5. Armee* observed in January 1918:

117 BA-MA Freiburg, W-10/ 50794: Postüberwachung der 5. *Armee*, 28 Sept. 1917, p. 27.
118 Jahr, *Gewöhnliche Soldaten*, p. 150.
119 See G. Fong, 'The Movement of German Divisions to the Western Front, Winter 1917–1918', *War in History* 7, 2 (April 2000), 229–30 and (for Allied strength) H.H. Herwig, *The First World War. Germany and Austria-Hungary 1914–1918* (London: Arnold, 1997), p. 401. It should be noted that although forty-eight divisions were transferred to the German western Field Army during this period, its net gain was forty-four, as four of its own divisions were redeployed to other theatres.

> The majority of the letter writers [are] convinced that the final peace must first still be bought through a 'great' blow in the west. The men have the entirely correct feeling where Germany's most stubborn enemy can be found. 'The English must first still be beaten' and similar are read daily.[120]

The German experience of the *Kaiserschlacht* will be the subject of the next chapter. Of interest here is the success with which the BEF survived the onslaught, the initial strength of which was unprecedented on the Western Front. By the end of 1917, the British army was exhausted, still somewhat depressed after the failure of Third Ypres and its infantry was suffering from a shortage of men. Between January and March 1918, divisions were reduced from twelve to nine battalions, the surplus manpower being used to bring the remaining units up to strength.[121] Worse still, this diminished force was stretched along a line one-third longer than that of 1917, extending 123 miles.[122]

The area which the Germans attacked on 21 March 1918 was the weakest part of the newly elongated British line. Haig positioned most of his army in the north, in order to protect the crucial channel ports. His southernmost force, the Fifth Army commanded by General Gough, was allocated only twelve divisions to defend 43 miles of front, much of which was composed of notoriously poorly fortified trenches built by the French. Lack of labour and the need to repair the Fifth Army's lines of communication meant that little work could be done on the defences, with the result that when the German offensive began only the Army's foremost defensive 'Forward Zone' was complete. The 'Battle Zone' was provided with strong points and artillery positions, but construction of the rearmost Brown Line, to which the Army was to retire in case of emergency, had only just begun.[123] Haig, despite the incomplete preparation, was nonetheless confident by early March that the defences were more than adequate: 'I was only afraid', he recorded in his diary on 2 March, 'that the enemy would find our front so very strong that he will hesitate to commit his Army to the attack with the almost certainty of losing very heavily'.[124] Some of the more experienced soldiers under his command did not, however, share his optimism. Sent to the front on 13 March in order to repel the expected attack, Lieutenant St Leger

120 BA-MA Freiburg, W-10/ 50794: Postüberwachung der 5. *Armee*, 10 Jan. 1918, p. 35.
121 Samuels, *Command or Control?*, pp. 221–2.
122 *Military Effort*, p. 639.
123 J. Keegan, *The First World War* (London: Pimlico, 1999), pp. 425–7.
124 R. Blake (ed.), *The Private Papers of Douglas Haig 1914–1919. Being Selections from the Private Diary and Correspondence of Field-Marshal the Earl Haig of Bemersyde, K.T., G.C.B., O.M., etc.* (London: Eyre and Spottiswoode, 1952), p. 291 (entry for 2 Mar. 1918).

recorded in his diary that 'I felt that I could understand the feelings of prisoners of the 16th century who had been sentenced to have their heads chopped off at dawn'.[125]

St Leger was right to be nervous, for when the German attack materialised, it was overwhelming. During the initial five-hour bombardment, 6,473 guns and 3,532 trench mortars fired 1,160,000 shells into British lines. The BEF's heavy artillery was outnumbered in the battle area by a ratio of five to two and was effectively neutralised by poison gas.[126] Contemporary reports testify to the very damaging effect which the bombardment also had on the BEF's infantry: the commander of 2/York and Lancs recorded that during the hour in which it was concentrated most heavily on the British forward trenches, 'the barrage killed & wounded practically the whole of the front line Coy., only 15 O[ther] R[anks] surviving and eventually getting back to the Reserve line'.[127] Under cover of fog, the German infantry attacked in overwhelming numbers, overrunning the British forward defences and much of the British 'Battle Zone' and in the process capturing 98½ square miles of ground. Given the static nature of the Western Front for the previous three and a half years this was an impressive and dramatic achievement. Five hundred guns were taken and approximately 38,500 casualties were inflicted on the British army.[128] During subsequent German pushes, this pattern was repeated, although on an ever decreasing scale. By the end of the *Michael* Offensive on 5 April, the ninety divisions involved in the attacks had penetrated almost 40 miles into Allied lines, captured more than 1,300 artillery pieces and inflicted on the Allies approximately 212,000 casualties.[129] A new offensive, launched in Flanders on 9 April, caused further British losses and prompted Haig to issue his famous Order of the Day, explaining to his troops that 'with our backs to the wall and believing in the justice of our cause each one of us must fight on to the end. The safety of our Homes and the Freedom of mankind alike depend upon the conduct of each one of us at this critical moment'.[130]

It was the failure of many British troops to 'fight on to the end', however, which made the defeat so serious. On the first day of the

[125] IWM, P 239: W.B. St Leger, diary, 13 Mar. 1918.
[126] J.E. Edmonds, *History of the Great War based on Official Documents. Military Operations. France and Belgium, 1918. March-April: Continuation of the German Offensives* (London: Macmillan & Co., 1937), p. 460, Middlebrook, *Kaiser's Battle*, p. 52 and Sheffield, *Forgotten Victory*, p. 188.
[127] TNA, WO 95/ 1610: 'Report on Operations 21st March', in War Diary of 2/York and Lancs, Mar. 1918.
[128] Middlebrook, *Kaiser's Battle*, p. 322.
[129] Reichsarchiv, *Weltkrieg*, XIV, p. 254.
[130] Quoted in Sheffield, *Forgotten Victory*, p. 192.

offensive, 21,000 of the 38,500 casualties were prisoners. Some units had made minimal attempts to repel the enemy: according to the 2/York and Lancs' CO, in the battalion's reserve lines, 'no resistance was offered . . . & . . . the garrison surrendered without fighting, being plainly visible leaving the trench with their hands up as the enemy approached'.[131] By 5 April, 90,000 Allied troops, 75,000 of whom were British, had surrendered to the German army. The Battle on the Lys, which began on 9 April, cost the Allies a further 112,000 men, 30,000 of whom were prisoners.[132] Disorderly retreats, panics and routs also contributed to the defeat. Battalion diaries are often reluctant to admit that such incidents took place among their own men but do record other units fleeing in the face of the enemy. Thus, for example, the diary of the 20/Middlesex mentioned that its neighbouring unit, 8/Sherwood Foresters, were seen 'running away in disorder' on 22 March and had to be led back into action by the Middlesex's second in command. On 26 March, the same diary records that the Lancashire Fusilier Brigade situated near Ablainzeville 'left their trenches and retired in a very disorderly manner, the men streaming all over the country, & making the situation even more critical and acute'.[133] Retirement by units on their flanks forced battle-ready troops to withdraw, creating a ragged rearward movement along much of the front. This took place extremely quickly, so that already by 23 March Haig was concerned to find that the Fifth Army was behind the Somme and at a loss to explain why it had 'gone so far back without making some kind of a stand'.[134]

Historians have debated the causes of the British collapse at length. Martin Middlebrook has emphasised the role played by thick fog in the initial German assault, arguing that its presence 'completely distorted the outcome of the fighting'.[135] Yet the effects of the weather were not entirely one-sided, for the fog hampered German artillery observation and caused the infantry to lose their way and waterlogged ground further hindered the advance.[136] The BEF's defensive organisation certainly played a major role in the German success. Martin Samuels has shown that the imperfect understanding of defence in depth which contributed to the rout on 30 November 1917 was an important contributory factor in the disaster on 21 March 1918. By deploying too many of its troops in

131 TNA, WO 95/ 1610: 'Report on Operations 21st March', in War Diary of 2/York and Lancs, Mar. 1918.
132 M. Kitchen, *The German Offensives of 1918* (Stroud: Tempus, 2001), p. 122.
133 TNA, WO 95/ 2615: War Diary of 20/Middlesex, 22 and 26 Mar. 1918.
134 Blake (ed.), *Private Papers of Douglas Haig*, p. 296.
135 Middlebrook, *Kaiser's Battle*, pp. 329–32.
136 Reichsarchiv, *Weltkrieg*, XIV, p. 131.

the static, isolated posts of the Forward Zone, GHQ removed the possibility of quick reinforcement with the result that many soldiers surrendered prematurely.[137] While agreeing that the British system of defence was deeply flawed, Tim Travers also argues that poor performance at the middle and upper levels of the BEF's command structure contributed to the defeat. Generals Gough and Byng made errors in their responses to the offensive, resulting in a gap opening between Fifth and Third Armies. Corps commanders and staff retreated unnecessarily, contributing, as the official history noted, 'to the general dislocation of the machinery of command, and to considerable sarcasm, if not despondency, among the troops'. According to Travers, 'the March retreat in its first six or seven days was a command failure, starting at the top'.[138]

There remains, however, also the possibility that the legacy of despondency and war-weariness from Passchendaele had eroded the lower ranks' will to fight. Already in March, there were some indications of a disciplinary breakdown: one man, whose unit had been ejected from Albert, was told that 'many of our troops had to be left in the town, dead drunk on the wine, etc., left by the fleeing civilians. Most of those left like that were "Jocks", or Scotch troops'.[139] Middlebrook compares the performance of the 1918 citizen-soldiers unfavourably to that of the Regulars in 1914 and argues that many of the former surrendered prematurely.[140] After the attack on Mount Kemmel at the end of April 1918, in which 7,000 prisoners, 53 guns and 233 machineguns were captured, the Germans also claimed to have noticed a change in the British soldiers' attitude. 'For the first time, the Briton had visibly set aside his arrogant pride and from his statements made evident that the collapse of the English army was severe and our operation worthy,' observed a report on the fighting.[141] There are also indications that the morale of already exhausted British units attacked by the Germans on the Aisne in the following month was similarly poor, most notable among which is the infamous request by the commander of 19th Division to 'confirm and have carried out' death sentences on stragglers.[142]

Most evidence suggests, however, that when properly led, combat motivation among British soldiers remained high. As has already been

[137] Samuels, *Command or Control?*, pp. 214–21.

[138] Travers, *How the War Was Won*, p. 90 and Edmonds, *Military Operations. France and Belgium, 1918. March–April*, p. 533.

[139] IWM, 86/32/1: S.T. Fuller, diary, 1 Apr. 1918.

[140] Middlebrook, *Kaiser's Battle*, pp. 332–9.

[141] BA-MA Freiburg, PH 3/ 53: Chef des Generalstabes des Feldheeres, Tägliche Lageberichte von den Kriegsschauplätzen Jul. 1914–Sept. 1918. No. 102, 27 Apr. 1918.

[142] See Travers, *How the War Was Won*, p. 105 and Sheffield, 'British Military Police', 38.

Plate 17. Prisoners (1): British soldiers captured in the German spring offensive, 1918. Note the grimaces: most BEF personnel did not welcome captivity. From a German airman's album.

demonstrated, in terms of surrender the Fifth Army's performance in March and April 1918 was actually superior to that of the Regular army in 1914. Heavy casualties were inflicted by British troops in what one combatant described as 'cold-blooded murder and mass slaughter'; the Germans, he explained in his diary, 'get it from our Lewis and machine guns'. Casualty statistics confirm this subjective impression, recording that the attackers' losses numbered nearly 1 million men by July 1918.[143] The German attacks created considerable disorganisation and confusion in the British army's battle-zone and rear areas but, as Gary Sheffield has shown, most stragglers in the first days of the *Kaiserschlacht* were not

[143] IWM, 85/51/1: A.E. Wrench, diary, 22 Mar. 1918 and Deist, 'Military Collapse', 202–3.

combat troops but rather rear-line labour personnel.[144] Far from succumbing to despair, soldiers separated from their commanders in the fighting of March and April often demonstrated extreme resilience and bravery. To give just one example, thirty-two other ranks belonging to the 20/Middlesex, separated from their unit in mid-April, simply joined other parties of men and 'were in the forefront of the action for a total of 13 days, or 8 days after the Battalion had been withdrawn from the line. When they rejoined they brought with them 3 Lewis Guns ... These guns had been in action continuously & were in perfect condition when the men rejoined the Battalion'.[145]

When surrenders did take place, it was usually because the unit had been surrounded and overwhelmed by the enemy: Second Lieutenant Robert Railton, for example, decided to capitulate at Reige Bailleul on 9 April only when his company came under attack from the rear by Germans using the nearby village as cover. 'On account of enemy being able to approach too near without being seen we were soon overcome and compelled to follow the enemy,' he wrote, explaining his capture.[146] Sometimes other ranks took the initiative in the process of capitulation. Major Francis Hill, trapped with nine men and a group of officers, claimed that he was forced to capitulate 'when an orderly met me & said "The Boch [*sic*] are here they wish to see the Major." ... I found our men were surrendering to about 40 of the enemy and more of the latter were coming up. I handed my revolver to the German officer'.[147] More often than not, however, it was officers who determined the duration of their isolated outposts' resistance. On 21 March, for example, it was a Second Lieutenant who inspired the men of the 15/Royal Irish Rifles to hold out at Racecourse Redoubt for almost nine hours. Only once he had been killed did the post capitulate. Similarly, it was the death of their Colonel which precipitated the surrender of survivors from the 168 soldiers of the 16/Manchesters defending Manchester Hill on the same day. In other cases, the German advance was speeded by the capitulation of officers who realised that their isolated units had little hope of rescue and every chance of annihilation at the hands of vastly superior forces. After satisfying his honour by demanding a document stating that he had

144 Sheffield, 'British Military Police', 39. Sheffield suggests that during the March retreat there were well over 25,000 stragglers, including 11,214 in XIX Corps alone, but shows that these men were efficiently collected and returned to the battle.

145 TNA, WO 95/ 2615: War Diary of 20/Middlesex, April, Appendix B.

146 TNA, WO 339/ 115371: R. Railton, 'Statement Regarding Circumstances which Led to Capture', 28 Dec. 1918.

147 TNA, WO 339/ 12350: F.R. Hill, 'Statement Regarding Circumstances which Led to Capture', 15 Jan. 1919.

fought hard, the CO of the 2/Royal Inniskilling Fusiliers, Lord Farnham, surrendered himself, his 10 officers and 241 men to the Germans without resistance on the first day of the *Kaiserschlacht*. Elsewhere, a Captain of the same unit gave himself and his 30 men up to a single NCO.[148] According to Brigadier-General Home of the Cavalry Corps, it was primarily officers' inability to deal with the fluid combat which retarded the fighting efficiency of British units. 'There is no doubt that our tired-out Divisions do not stand well now,' he noted in his diary on 10 April. 'It is owing to the lack of training of the Officers. The men are all right but want to be led, now they have no trench to stay in. Once they get out into the open, they are lost'.[149]

Why did the Germans fail to break the British army during their temporary period of material superiority? Firstly, despite the operational and tactical errors made by the British command, the army's logistical services continued to support combat troops effectively. British soldiers remained able to endure and fight because, as Ian Malcolm Brown has shown, food and ammunition continued to reach them in abundant quantities. Despite the disruption caused by the retreat, already by 28 March the quantity of rations coming forward for the Fifth Army was satisfactory and by 1 April the situation was considered generally good. This success was reflected in soldiers' letters during March and April, which, according to the censor, contained almost no complaints about food.[150] Munitions supply also, in Brown's words, 'remained excellent throughout the offensive'. Although the Germans had some success in neutralising and capturing artillery pieces on the first day of the *Kaiserschlacht*, losses were quickly replaced by stockpiled weapons and the British army fired almost 5.5 million 18-pounder and 1.5 million 4.5-inch howitzer shells.[151] In contrast, as the German army moved away from its railheads, it experienced increasing difficulty in keeping its troops supplied. Lacking motorised transport, it had often to rely on exhausted horses pulling wagons over shattered ground. The diary of Wilhelm Lüthje, an officer serving in *Etappe-Munitions-Kolonne Nr. 303*, gives some idea of the difficulties encountered by

148 For these examples from the *Kaiserschlacht*, see Middlebrook, *Kaiser's Battle*, pp. 263–8 and 337 and Samuels, *Command or Control?*, pp. 262–3.

149 A. Home, *The Diary of a World War I Cavalry Officer* (Tunbridge Wells: Costello, 1985), p. 163. Cf. the identical opinion of the XVIII Corps training school's commander, Lieutenant-Colonel William Fraser in D. Fraser (ed.), *In Good Company. The First World War Letters and Diaries of the Hon. William Fraser, Gordon Highlanders* (Salisbury: Michael Russell, 1990), pp. 246–7 (diary entry for 16 April 1918).

150 Brown, *British Logistics*, p. 188 and TNA, WO 256/ 33: The British Armies in France as gathered from Censorship, 12 July 1918 in *Lord Haig's Diary*, XXXI, p. 12.

151 Brown, *British Logistics*, p. 189.

Plate 18. Material might (3): British shells being unloaded, 23 March 1918. Allied logistical superiority was crucial in providing the BEF's soldiers with both the physical means and psychological will to keep fighting. Official British photograph.

German supply troops trying to bring ammunition through wasted territory up to the front:

At Illies, I have the feeling that we have been marching in the wrong direction; . . . We ask on several occasions but don't receive any useful information and in the meantime Tommy begins to shoot and not at all badly . . . I thus ride on ahead and come upon two recently shot up carts and two dead horses. Through a miracle, the driver remains unhurt. They warn that we should not drive past, for [in front] it's hell. But what can you do? . . . Therefore forwards. Now, however, the way begins to get bad. Thick mud makes forward progress difficult and soon we have a supply column stuck fast in front of us . . . A Saxon mobile bridging unit cannot go any further, it approaches us and gets stuck. We therefore harness the horses, push, make room, unload the bridging unit's stuff etc. All in deepest darkness and with the least possible noise. In addition, the shells crash around but one no longer worries about them. After much effort the wagons are got back on the road and we think: 'Now the comrade and his column – who missed their way – can go on.' But no! Just then a narrow-gauge train comes rushing along. Irresponsible chaps have thrown munitions on the rails. One jolt and the train is derailed – on exactly that street, along which we have to pass! What to do? With unspeakable effort, the munitions which are jammed at the front are removed, the derailed carriage is lifted by means of a winch, then the route is free. Now the vehicles can get through and they start up again. We then come to the worst part of the road . . . Thick clay allows us to go forward only gradually, at every moment a wagon and its driver gets stuck, reserve teams are sent forward, bridges over streams are especially difficult to cross and on top of that we are under heavy fire.[152]

As the official *Reichsarchiv* history acknowledged, the army simply lacked the number of supply columns and the quality of horse necessary to overcome the difficulties of bringing up badly needed provisions over broken land.[153] As early as 25 March, one German corps was forced to halve its ammunition consumption due to a shell shortage.[154] Although not lacking in stockpiled munitions, transport difficulties meant that on a number of occasions during the subsequent months attacking German troops were inadequately supported by their artillery.[155] This was a principal reason why, as Martin Kitchen has observed, 'the German army had a number of brilliant initial successes, but . . . [was] unable to maintain the momentum of [its] offensives for more than five to ten days'.[156]

Secondly, the BEF was well supplied with reinforcements. Between 24 and 28 March, 39,384 men were sent to France as replacement drafts, followed by a further 73,618 in the first week of April. By the end of August 1918, drafts received by the BEF since 21 March totalled 544,005 men. In order to find these reinforcements, the numbers of men normally conscripted were doubled during the crucial months of April to June 1918. Simultaneously, the minimum age for front service was reduced to eighteen and a half years, on the proviso that these recruits received at least three months' training.[157] Although forced to commit fifty-five of its sixty divisions to the battle, including twenty-nine twice and six three times, the BEF, with the support of French and

152 BA-MA Freiburg, MSg 2/ 2797: W. Lüthje, diary, 8 Apr. 1918.
153 Reichsarchiv, *Weltkrieg*, XIV, p. 256.
154 Brown, *British Logistics*, p. 196. Cf. vom Holtz, *Reserve-Inf.-Regiment Nr. 121*, p. 71 and K. von Einem, *Ein Armeeführer erlebt den Weltkrieg. Persönliche Aufzeichnungen des Generalobersten v. Einem*, ed. J. Alter (Leipzig: v. Hase / Koehler, 1938), p. 389, the latter of whom (the commander of the *3. Armee*) claims in a diary entry of 20 April 1918 that on 25 March the *18. Armee* found itself without ammunition, its supply columns having become completely disorganised in the advance.
155 Kitchen, *German Offensives*, pp. 121, 146–7, 152, 155 and 164. An indication that transport rather than material was the Germans' main problem is given by the fact that the opening barrage of Operation *Blücher* on 27 May was of greater intensity than that which had heralded the beginning of the *Kaiserschlacht* on 21 March. See ibid., p. 136.
156 Ibid., p. 236.
157 Edmonds, *Military Operations. France and Belgium, 1918. March–April*, pp. 10–11 and *Military Effort*, p. 364.

American units, thus possessed enough troops to repel Ludendorff's offensive. Losses were heavy: the army had suffered 250,000 casualties by the end of April, yet it was not until May that the 'critical manpower crunch' took place, by which time the German attacks had been redirected towards the French.[158]

Finally, in this war of endurance, the *Kaiserschlacht* ultimately failed because it did not break British troops' confidence in their ability to win. Not only the material but also the psychological benefits of adequate logistical support were crucial in enabling troops to keep fighting. Self-assurance was also important. By July, German intelligence noted that British prisoners rated their divisional commanders and brigadiers poorly, hardly surprising given that their failures had contributed greatly to the initial defeats suffered by the BEF during the German offensive. Significantly, however, the captives did express confidence in both Haig and Foch and, still more importantly, possessed complete faith in their own military prowess: 'in the English army', noted the report, 'the opinion is widespread that under German leadership English soldiers could conquer the entire world'.[159] After the depressing senselessness of the bloodletting at Third Ypres, the German attacks injected meaning and a sense of mission back into the war. As the British postal censor observed, 'the ruin and loss of towns and villages where they had so often been welcomed, the streams of refugees with their pathetic burdens, the vision of their homes and families in like circumstances, steeled [British soldiers'] determination to render impossible the recurrence of such horrors'. German prisoners' boasts of ravishing French women in towns they had captured hardly endeared them to BEF personnel and well-publicised atrocities such as the bombing raids on the hospitals at Étaples and the sinking of the *Llandovery Castle* also reinforced troops' resolve.[160] Indeed, perhaps due to the heavy casualties, a note of hatred crept into the letters and diaries of some British combatants during the intense fighting. Arthur Wrench, for example, who had formerly been relatively well disposed towards individual Germans, remarked in July 1918 that 'my personal opinion of the German soldiers is they are brave enough so long as they can fight shoulder to shoulder

[158] See Kitchen, *German Offensives*, p. 250 and Brown, *British Logistics*, p. 192. For a full discussion of the methods used to replenish Britain's armies in 1918, see K. Grieves, *The Politics of Manpower, 1914–18* (Manchester University Press, 1988), pp. 181–99.

[159] BA-MA Freiburg, PH 3/ 589: NO 4 Gefangenen-Aussagen: Vernehmung [of three men from 8/Royal Highlanders, 26 Brigade, 9 Division], 21 July 1918.

[160] TNA, WO 256/ 33: The British Armies in France as gathered from Censorship, 12 July 1918 in *Lord Haig's Diary*, XXXI, p. 3 and Home, *Diary of a World War I Cavalry Officer*, p. 168 (entry for 17 Apr. 1918).

and outnumber their enemy by great odds. Then they are bullies and hard masters but otherwise they are not so hot'.[161] The result was that far from encouraging despondence or feelings of subjection, the heavy fighting actually increased most British soldiers' self-confidence and sense of purpose. Illustrative of this attitude is a story told by Sydney Fuller, a signaller serving in the Suffolk Regiment during the heavy fighting around Ypres in April 1918. Forced to retreat from a position enfiladed by a machinegun, Fuller recorded that 'before leaving, "Nutty" [a comrade], pinned up on the side of the Sig's funk-hole a paper, on which he had written – "He who fights and runs away, will live to fight another day."'[162] As a censorship report on the Fifth Army's morale during this period concluded, 'the will to boat [*sic*] the enemy is as firm and definitely expressed as ever'.[163]

The key factor in armies' resilience was their troops' confidence in their own ability to win the war and return home unscathed. The self-assuredness of British and German soldiers, their belief in themselves and in their organisations, carried them through four years of extremely frightening and bloody warfare. Partly, this confidence stemmed from natural human qualities, most importantly the optimistic view that most men took of their surroundings. Psychological factors, such as intelligence and mental stability, were extremely influential in maximising men's natural resilience. Military institutions which encouraged men to feel secure and able to execute their tasks were, however, also very important. This was particularly so in the cases of selection and training, which were used by the German army to good effect in order to counter its material and numerical inferiority during the war. Ultimately, however, it was not enough. Despite its powerful onslaught on 21 March 1918, the German army did not possess the strength to impose the continuous pressure needed to break the BEF. In contrast, British soldiers, secure in the knowledge that they were supported by vast material reserves, confident of their own personal superiority and more conscious than ever before of the consequences of defeat, refused to be cowed, despite the temporary paralysis of their command structure. Not 'better nerves' but superior supplies and a lower level of exhaustion allowed the British army not only to survive the *Kaiserschlacht* but ultimately to counterattack and win the war.

161 IWM, 85/51/1: A.E. Wrench, diary, 20 July 1918.
162 IWM, 86/32/1: S.T. Fuller, diary / memoir, 17 Apr. 1918.
163 TNA, WO 256/ 33: The British Armies in France as gathered from Censorship, 12 July 1918 in *Lord Haig's Diary*, XXXI, p. 4.

6 The German collapse in 1918: strike, mutiny or an ordered surrender?

Morale and the *Materialschlacht* – 1918

After fifty-two months of fighting, blockade, near total mobilisation and 2 million deaths, the German army finally capitulated on 11 November 1918. Outgunned and outnumbered by its enemies, whose forces were rapidly increasing due to the massive influx of fresh American troops into France, the army stood little chance of significantly delaying, let alone permanently halting, the retreat towards its own borders. Stretched to the limit of its powers of endurance during the course of its own offensives earlier in the year, in the summer of 1918 it broke. Although some troops continued to fight bravely, the willingness and ability of most to resist the Allied offensive disappeared. While, in the estimation of no less a distinguished soldier than Field Marshal Sir Douglas Haig, the German army possessed enough material resources to prolong the war into 1919, its men lacked both the inclination and energy to do so. Matters of morale, which had been decisive in determining the conflict's longevity, were also pivotal in bringing about its termination. As Ludendorff himself acknowledged two and a half weeks before the armistice, at the end of the war it was not primarily the number (*die Zahl*) but rather the spirit of the troops (*Geist der Truppe*) which was decisive.[1]

At the beginning of 1918, German prospects had appeared much brighter. Despite the exhaustion and rumbles of discontent caused by the previous year's heavy fighting, the Kaiser's army remained in remarkably good condition for a force which had held off four major powers, as well as numerous minor ones, for three and a half years. Its principal opponents had also suffered grievously during 1917: the failure of the Third Ypres Offensive had left the BEF despondent and lacking manpower, while the French army was still recovering from its spring

[1] Blake (ed.), *Private Papers of Douglas Haig*, pp. 332–3 and HStA Dresden, *Militärbevollmächtigter* 4216, Bl. 114–15: Report of the Saxon *Militärbevollmächtigter* to the War Minister of a speech given by *General* Ludendorff, 24 Oct. 1918.

and summer mutinies. With only 300,000 men in France by March 1918, the Americans posed little immediate threat to the Germans. Crucially, as already discussed, Russia's exit from the war had materially improved Germany's strategic position and raised her army's flagging morale. Already in December the armistice announced by Lenin had provided what one front officer referred to as 'a ray of hope for the common man' and by mid-January most soldiers believed that Russia was 'finished'.[2] The signing of the final peace treaty at Brest-Litovsk on 3 March 1918 was greeted with enthusiasm by troops who calculated, in the words of *Gefreiter* Kurt Reiter, 'now there is at least the possibility of still coming to a general peace this year'.[3] Thorough preparations began for one last great offensive. Divisions were transferred from the eastern Field Army, munitions stockpiled, new artillery positions dug and camouflaged, streets repaired and fascines for trench crossing made ready for use. Rumours of new and terrible gases, 'special small infantry-cooperation aircraft', tanks and Turkish and Bulgarian troops circulated in German units. Suspense mixed with hope and confidence as soldiers viewed the preparations. Yet, as diary entries show, underneath these emotions lay a despair born of the knowledge that, if Germany was to win and the war to end soon, the offensive must succeed: 'God, give us Germans victory, don't place the people under still greater tests,' was not an unusual sentiment.[4]

Operation *Michael* began at 4.20 a.m. on 21 March with a five-hour bombardment. Infantry attacks in thick fog followed and by the evening the British Expeditionary Force had suffered what John Keegan has referred to as 'its first true defeat since trench warfare had begun', having lost most of its forward defensive zone, 500 guns and 38,500 men killed, wounded, missing or taken prisoner.[5] The Germans too had suffered heavily, leaving over 10,000 dead behind them and incurring 29,000 wounded. They had also failed to reach their objectives, a fact which led some junior officers to reason that the attack had already failed.[6]

2 Staatsbib. Berlin, Ms. Germ. fol. 1651: C.F. Müller, diary, 7 Dec. 1917 and BA-MA Freiburg, W-10/ 50794: Postüberwachung der 5. *Armee*, 10 Jan. 1918, p. 35.

3 BA-MA Freiburg, MSg1/ 161: K. Reiter, diary, 4 Mar. 1918. Cf. also Private Collection (Author): H. Hausbalk, letter to family, 3 Mar. 1918 and Staatsbib. Berlin, Ms. Germ. fol. 1651: C.F. Müller, diary, 11 Feb. and 12 Mar. 1918.

4 Staatsbib. Berlin, Ms. Germ. fol. 1651: C.F. Müller, diary, 18 Mar. 1918. Cf. von Einem, *Armeeführer*, p. 375 (letter of 10 Mar. 1918).

5 Keegan, *First World War*, pp. 429–30 and Sheffield, *Forgotten Victory*, pp. 185–9.

6 See Middlebrook, *Kaiser's Battle*, p. 340 and the interview of an officer from the German 221 Mountain MG Detachment in TNA, WO 157/ 192: Summary of Information, No. 96 (Fourth Army), 24 Mar. 1918, p. 1. For casualty figures see Middlebrook, *Kaiser's Battle*, pp. 322 and (for captured guns) 341.

These men, however, were very much in the minority and the German army continued to apply pressure over the following days, pushing their enemies back and threatening to split the British and French armies. When the offensive was broken off on 5 April, however, the Germans had managed only to create a salient 40 miles deep rather than a decisive breakthrough. Subsequent offensives against the British in Flanders (Operation *Georgette*, 9–11 April) and then against Amiens (24 April), on the Aisne (27 May) and the Matz (9 June) captured more territory but failed to cause an Allied collapse. The final German attack was launched with fifty-two divisions at Rheims on 15 July but was terminated by a French counterattack at Villers-Cotterêts three days later.[7]

It is not necessary to examine the strategic mistakes that resulted in the ultimate failure of the spring and summer offensives here. What is important is that despite its impressive advances and the serious losses inflicted on Allied forces, the strength and morale of the German army were in unstoppable decline by mid-1918. Attacks over open ground made by the German army in the spring and summer had been costly, especially as assaulting units often used obsolete tactics. Although fifty-six specially designated attack divisions had been given three weeks of special instruction before the offensive began, British soldiers still reported facing enemy attacking in 'the usual German close formation' who were 'mowed down like corn'.[8] Losses were particularly heavy in the infantry: already by 30 March this arm of the *1. Garde-Reserve-Division*, for example, had lost two-thirds of its strength, according to the formation's intelligence officer.[9] Companies, which in March 1918 had numbered 120 men, averaged only between 70 to 90 by mid-July.[10] Already by 10 April, one-fifth of the original 1.4 million-strong attacking force

[7] Middlebrook, *Kaiser's Battle*, p. 438 and Sheffield, *Forgotten Victory*, p. 195.

[8] IWM, 85/51/1: A.E. Wrench, diary, 21 Mar. 1918. Cf. IWM, 86/40/1: G.R. Barlow, letter to Alice, 6 Apr. 1918. These reports are confirmed by German sources: in a diary entry of 22 April, the commander of *3. Armee*, Karl von Einem, blamed the heavy losses on the fact that 'the infantry appear to have rushed forward in masses' and an order issued by Ludendorff in early May specifically warned against wild advances without reconnaissance directly into machinegun nests. See von Einem, *Armeeführer*, pp. 390 and 393. For pre-*Kaiserschlacht* training see Samuels, *Command or Control?*, pp. 246–7.

[9] BA-MA Freiburg, MSg 1/ 2968: H. Fuchs, diary, 30 Mar. 1918. Cf. *Sanitätsbericht III*, p. 57 which records that between 21 and 31 March, the division lost 3,118 out of 12,500 men (one-quarter of its entire complement) due to wounds alone. Missing and killed totalled a further 1,000 men.

[10] *Why Germany Capitulated on November 11, 1918. A Brief Study Based on Documents in the Possession of the French General Staff* (London: Hodder and Stoughton, 1919), pp. 28–9.

had become casualties, and by the end of July, manpower wastage in the Field Army since March numbered 977,555 men.[11] Moreover, this figure excludes lightly wounded and ill, whose numbers increased to frightening levels once the influenza epidemic began in June: in that month, 135,002 badly needed men were taken ill with influenza and in July a further 374,524 had to be temporarily excused from duty due to the same cause. The crisis was further heightened by the fact that members of combat units, living in the worst conditions and suffering the greatest stress, were most vulnerable, the disease depriving them of up to 30 per cent of their effectives at any one time in mid-July.[12] Stretched out across a largely unfortified front 75 miles longer than in March, the much-reduced army available to Ludendorff had little chance of defending effectively against an Allied onslaught.[13]

It was, however, not only the quantity of soldiers available to *OHL* but still more their quality which gave cause for concern by mid-1918. As part of the preparation for the offensive, German divisions had been categorised as 'mobile', 'attack' or 'position' units and the former two types had received the best equipment and contained the most accomplished and reliable soldiers. Once the offensive began, these elite troops were sent into the assault and suffered disproportionately heavy casualties. In contrast, the inferior, defensive 'position' units, which had been ordered to exchange their younger personnel for men over thirty-five, lost far fewer soldiers.[14] Worse still, junior leaders suffered particularly heavily: during the attacks of March and April, officer fatalities were proportionally double those of their men and already by mid-April, *Landwehr* divisions were being ordered to transfer officers to active units.[15] Such casualties could not fail to affect both the combat efficiency and confidence of the army. As the professional officer Friedrich Altrichter observed in the interwar period, 'the large, irretrievable loss of officers and veteran soldiers led to a severe fall in the army's morale'.[16]

The reserves which were available as replacements for losses suffered in spring and early summer 1918 did little to raise the quality of the army. As the conscript class of 1900 would only be available for service

11 Deist, 'Military Collapse', 197, *Sanitätsbericht II*, table 6 and *Sanitätsbericht III*, p. 143*.
12 *Sanitätsbericht III*, p. 28* and TNA, WO 157/ 196: Weekly Appreciation. For Period July 6th to July 12th (inclusive). Fourth Army, 13 July 1918, p. 5.
13 Deist, 'Military Collapse', 200 and H. Strachan, 'The Morale of the German Army, 1917–18', in H. Cecil and P.H. Liddle (eds.), *Facing Armageddon. The First World War Experienced* (London: Leo Cooper, 1996), p. 390.
14 Ziemann, *Front*, pp. 64–5 and Deist, 'Verdeckter Militärstreik', p. 149.
15 *Sanitätsbericht III*, p. 132* and BA-MA Freiburg, MSg 1/ 3109: H. Muhsal, diary, 17 Apr. 1918.
16 Altrichter, *Seelischen Kräfte*, p. 136.

in the autumn, Ludendorff was forced to rely on unpromising soldierly material to fill the ranks of his depleted units. Bolshevik unionists who had led the January strikes in Berlin were punished by recruitment into the army, as were convicted criminals.[17] Scarcely more useful as additions to combat strength were soldiers retrieved from well-paid war industries or from rear-line units. The brusque manner and liberal interpretation of the term *kriegsverwendbar* adopted by the ironically nicknamed 'hero seeking commissions' (*Heldensuchkommissionen*) in the army's back areas gave rise to considerable resentment, especially among the often old and unfit men whom they ordered out to the front.[18] Probably the most difficult reinforcements were, however, former prisoners of war returned from Russia. These men were placed in quarantine for six to eight weeks after their arrival in Germany and then also assigned to combat units. Resentful at being returned to the front after their ordeals and in some cases influenced by Bolshevik ideology, they were usually reluctant soldiers and often mutinous.[19] Moreover, heavy fighting during the Allied advance, in which the Germans lost approximately 800,000 more men, ensured that these reinforcements were insufficient to close the gaps in German ranks.[20] Despite reducing 40 per cent of its battalions from four to three companies and disbanding twenty-nine divisions, the army was unable to stop its infantry all but disappearing: generals reported that divisions with a nominal fighting strength of 8,000 men possessed a mere 1,000 and company strengths had sunk to an average of 50 men by the time of the armistice.[21] Due to the rapid growth of the American Expeditionary Force in France, Allied forces increased over the same period, with the result that by the end of the war 3,527,000

[17] Reichsarchiv, *Weltkrieg*, XIV, p. 524.

[18] See, for example, BA-MA Freiburg, MSg 1/ 2968: H. Fuchs, diary, 25 July 1918 and the letter extract in BA-MA Freiburg, W-10/ 50794: Postüberwachung der *5. Armee*, 31 Aug. 1918, pp. 80–1. Also, Ziemann, *Front*, pp. 176–7.

[19] Altrichter, *Seelischen Kräfte*, pp. 160–2 and Reichsarchiv, *Weltkrieg*, XIV, p. 523. For cases of mutiny and demoralisation in which former Russian prisoners played a major role see, for example, the document referring to the mutiny of the *5. Landwehr-Bataillon* in *Why Germany Capitulated*, p. 55 and also the entry for *94. Division* in United States War Office, *Histories*, p. 557.

[20] Deist, 'Military Collapse', 203

[21] For divisional infantry, see von Einem, *Armeeführer*, p. 446 (diary entry for 7 Oct. 1918) and also pp. 420, 426, 442 and 448. Additionally, Kronprinz Rupprecht von Bayern, *In Treue fest. Mein Kriegstagebuch* (3 vols., Munich: Deutscher National Verlag A.-G., 1929), III, pp. 26, 352 and 361. Estimates of company strengths appear in *Why Germany Capitulated*, pp. 28–9 and BA-MA Freiburg, W-10/ 51921: *Reichsarchiv* historical work. Incomplete manuscript, p. 25. For unit disbandment, see Altrichter, *Seelischen Kräfte*, p. 189 and for nominal divisional strengths, see the introduction by Cave in United States War Office, *Histories*, pp. iii–iv and TNA, WO 157/ 197: Summary of Information, No. 230 (Fourth Army), 5 Aug. 1918.

German and Austrian soldiers faced an Allied army numbering 6,432,000 men on the Western Front.[22]

The dire manpower situation of the German army was exacerbated by its vastly inferior supplies of war *matériel*. Particularly important was the disparity between the artillery arms of the belligerents. By the armistice, the Kaiser's forces possessed only 16,181 artillery pieces, many of which were worn out; in contrast, Allied armies were able to field 21,668 guns on the Western Front.[23] Moreover, German economic and logistical problems, as well as the loss of irreplaceable stockpiled shells in the retreat at Villers-Cotterêts in mid-July, meant that their guns were increasingly short of ammunition while the Allies' superior industrial base provided them with an ample munitions supply. Ever more stringent restrictions were placed on munitions expenditure from the end of August, just as Allied bombardments were becoming increasingly effective; by late September, the British had enough guns and stockpiled munitions to fire 943,847 shells into the Hindenburg Line within a period of twenty-four hours.[24] This situation naturally had repercussions for the morale of the German infantry, with German prisoners complaining about the weakness of their own artillery fire in comparison to the accurate and heavy bombardment put down by the Allies.[25]

Besides their advantages in men and artillery, the Allies also made good use of a number of new weapons in their final advance. Large tank formations played an important role in the Allied advance, 750 such machines being used by the French at Villers-Cotterêts and 552 by the British at Amiens on 8 August.[26] Ludendorff attributed the initial French success on 18 July to their impact and by September was blaming them for the German inability to stop the Allied advance, claiming that 'due above all to the effect of the tanks, command on the Western Front has now taken the character of a game of chance. The *OHL* can no longer reckon on definite factors.'[27] Aircraft also played a significant role in both supporting Allied advances and demoralising the German army.

22 *Military Effort*, p. 628.

23 Ibid. Cf. *Why Germany Capitulated*, pp. 35–6, which suggests that the Germans possessed only 13,500 guns (9,000 field guns and 4,500 heavy and long-range pieces) by early November.

24 *Military Effort*, p. 482.

25 TNA, WO 157/ 197: Summary of Information, No. 254 (Fourth Army), 29 Aug. 1918, pp. 6–7.

26 Herwig, *First World War*, p. 418 and Sheffield, *Forgotten Victory*, p. 201.

27 HStA Dresden, *Militärbevollmächtigter* 4221: Report of speech given by Ludendorff to the *Militärbevollmächtigten*, 30 Sept. 1918, p. 159. For Ludendorff's explanation of the French success on 18 July, see BA-MA Freiburg, PH 3/ 293: Order entitled 'Ausbildung', 4 Aug. 1918.

Hardly a diary or letter collection exists which does not express the fearsome effect of this weapon on German morale at the end of the war. The impossibility of predicting the fall of aerial bombs, the difficulty of defending oneself against such attack and the knowledge that even rest areas were now no longer safe, made uncontrollability at the front still greater and prompted many soldiers to rate the weapon as worse than artillery. The psychologist Walter Ludwig acknowledged the great morale effect of air attack, even arguing that the increasing effectiveness of raids behind the lines and on rest areas had resulted in a noticeable growth in the adoption of fatalistic attitudes among German soldiers.[28]

Fatalism which, as already discussed, was not a mindset conducive to fighting efficiency, was accompanied by an equally debilitating condition of extreme exhaustion and apathy in the last months of the war. Towards the end of the German offensives, combatants' diaries began to complain that 'everyone is weary of the war' and Altrichter noted that by summer, 'the army humour so important for the mood had totally disappeared'.[29] The censor characterised the troops' frame of mind at the end of August as being stamped by 'war exhaustion, moroseness and depression'.[30] The fatigue and sense of hopelessness became more intense as the German army was forced to retreat in the face of unstoppable Allied attacks. Rest became increasingly rare as the army expended its reserves in trying to stop this onslaught; French intelligence estimated that the number of fresh divisions which *OHL* was able to keep in reserve decreased from forty-three to two between July and November. During September and October, 60 per cent of divisions remained continually at the front, while others fought without respite for twenty to thirty days.[31] The

[28] Ludwig, 'Psychologie der Furcht', p. 168. British intelligence also remarked on the substantial damage to material and morale inflicted by low-flying aircraft. See TNA, WO 157/ 197: Summary of Information, No. 238 (Fourth Army), 13 Aug. 1918, p. 9. For soldiers' opinions on this mode of attack see BA-MA Freiburg, MSg 1/ 3183: E. Vogt, diary / memoir, 5–24 Apr. 1918; BA-MA Freiburg MSg 1/ 161: K. Reiter, diary, 24 Sept. 1918; BA-MA Freiburg, MSg 2/ 2797: W. Lüthje, diary, 28 Sept. 1918; Staatsbib. Berlin, Ms. Germ. fol. 1651: C.F. Müller, diary, 21 Oct. 1918 and BA-MA Freiburg, MSg 2/ 1291: E. Ahrend, 'Die letzte Schlacht', letter to parents, p. 10, 6 Nov. 1918.

[29] BA-MA Freiburg, MSg 1/ 161: K. Reiter, diary, 1 May 1918 and Altrichter, *Seelischen Kräfte*, p. 152.

[30] BA-MA Freiburg, W-10/ 50794: Postüberwachung der 5. *Armee*, 31 Aug., p. 75.

[31] *Why Germany Capitulated*, pp. 27–30. According to French intelligence documents, on 15 July the German army possessed 207 divisions in total of which 81 were in reserve. Among this latter figure, 43 were 'fresh' (having had at least one month's rest), 26 had been 'reconstituted' (having had two to four weeks' rest) and 12 were classified as 'worn-out' (having had less than fifteen days' rest). On 11 November the army possessed 184 divisions of which 17 were in reserve. 2 of the reserve units were fresh, 5 reconstituted and 10 worn-out. Cf. Altrichter, *Seelischen Kräfte*, p. 192.

unfortunate men of the *220. Division* wrote to the Prussian War Ministry in September to complain that they had spent nine uninterrupted months at the front.[32] Even when units were lucky enough to be relieved, lack of transport and the constant retreat meant that they were often expected to march long distances to their rest areas: for example, the *3. Marine-Division*, its infantry strength reduced to 700 men after ten days of intense fighting at the beginning of October, was ordered to march 30 kilometres (just under 19 miles) to reach new rest areas.[33] Logistical difficulties left men with inadequate food and clothing, both of which were inevitably contrasted to the plentiful supplies which German soldiers had seen in Allied depots during the spring offensives. Material need became so great that soldiers began selling pieces of uniform, equipment and even rifles to the civilian population in the occupied zone in order to buy food.[34] The extreme psychological and physical strains destroyed the German army's pugnacity: as one man put it, the war 'is no longer any fun for us'.[35] In the estimation of the psychiatrist Robert Gaupp, during the last months of fighting most men were suffering from a condition of 'neurasthenic exhaustion'.[36]

A brief examination of a sample unit, the *241. Division*, provides an insight into the development of this intense mental and physical exhaustion and its effect on units' combat efficiency. The division had been transferred from Russia in order to take part in the spring offensive and had at first attacked enthusiastically, winning thanks from the King of Saxony for its conduct near Coucy in early April. However, the heavy fighting in this engagement and the subsequent two-month period spent in the line inflicted heavy losses on the division, which were replaced on 23 June by a draft 1,500 strong. Given less than one month to absorb this large reinforcement, the unit was returned to the front near Villers-Cotterêts and was there when the French attacked on 18 July. The large influx of new men and the absence of a period for rest and retraining clearly demoralised the division drastically, for Allied intelligence records state that it lost 42 officers and 2,074 men as prisoners in this engagement. As in other formations, conditions during the following counteroffensive declined still

[32] See the memorandum dated 13 Sept. 1918 from the *preußisches Kriegsministerium* to *OHL* reproduced in Hobohm, *Soziale Heeresmißstände*, XI.1, pp. 403–4 (doc. 48).

[33] HStA Munich/IV, Gen.-Kdo I b. AK Bund 52 Akt 12: Memorandum from *3. Marine-Division, Div. St. Qu*, reproduced 10 Oct. 1918.

[34] See the August 1918 statement of a captured Bavarian officer to *Temps* in Hobohm, *Soziale Heeresmißstände*, XI.1, pp. 396–7 (doc. 44) and also see Altrichter, *Seelischen Kräfte*, p. 153. For an early disgruntled comparison of German and Allied rations see BA-MA Freiburg, W-10/ 50794: Postüberwachung der *5. Armee*, 23 June 1918, p. 72.

[35] BA-MA Freiburg, W-10/ 50794: Postüberwachung der *5. Armee*, 31 Aug. 1918, p. 87.

[36] Gaupp, 'Schreckneurosen', p. 91.

further. Fully trained recruits now being unavailable, the division was forced to replace the losses of two of its three regiments with men reclaimed from rear-line units who lacked adequate battle training and were resentful of being used as combat troops. Replacement officers were drawn from *Landwehr* divisions in the east and had no experience of the western *Materialschlacht*. Despite these deficiencies, military conditions required that the division be returned to the front within days of most drafts arriving, where it stayed for much of September, effectively making any training impossible. Morale was hardly improved by logistical problems which meant that it was possible neither to delouse the soldiers nor to supply many with basic necessities such as shirts, coats and mess tins. This situation persisted until the beginning of October, when the division was called upon to face a major Allied attack. Soaking wet, its men marched up to the line north of St Quentin on the evening of 29 September and the following day they were bombarded and then assaulted by an Allied force supported by massed tanks. Lacking artillery support due to the munitions shortage and overwhelmed by the speed and numerical superiority of the attack, the division's infantry quickly surrendered. By 10 October, the division had lost 1,900 men as prisoners, the majority of whom, according to British intelligence, made little attempt at resistance. A report investigating the disaster described the division's personnel as 'completely apathetic' due to the extreme exertions of previous months. 'The troops are no longer adequate; not only in the 241st [Division], but also in other divisions,' observed the report. 'Lacking are training, unit bonds and – worst of all – it appears to me that in the German army the spirit of resolute endurance to the end is frequently missing.'[37]

The speed with which this mood developed varied among different groups in the German army. The first to demonstrate unwillingness to make further sacrifices for German victory were those men who had always had the least personal interest in it: the army's national minorities. Due to their discriminatory handling by the army, Alsace-Lorrainers had already been irreconcilably alienated from the German cause during 1917 and were poorly motivated even before the beginning of the spring offensive. Indeed, Christoph Jahr, having examined the desertion figures

[37] HStA Dresden, *Militärbevollmächtigter* Nr. 4216, Bl. 62–3: Report of *Generalmajor* von Oeeletz[?] to the *königlich sächsischer Militärbevollmächtigter*, 14 Oct. 1918. The above account is based on this report, that of *Generalleutnant* Fortmüller, 7 Oct. 1918, in HStA Dresden, *Militärbevollmächtigter* Nr. 4216, Bl. 69–74, United States War Office, *Histories*, pp. 737–8 and TNA, WO 157/ 199: Summary of Information, No. 289 (Fourth Army), 3 Oct. 1918, p. 3.

for *Heeresgruppe Albrecht* in 1918, has convincingly argued that the military situation had relatively little influence on the behaviour of Alsace-Lorrainers, whose desertion rate, unlike that of their German comrades, remained relatively constant between December 1917 and September 1918.[38] Nonetheless, this rate was extremely high: according to the *Reichsarchiv* about one-third of the German army's approximately 1,000 deserters in the first half of 1918 were Alsace-Lorrainers, a proportion far above those provinces' share of the army's manpower.[39] The *31. Division*, which contained a large number of Alsace-Lorrainers, appears to have been particularly unreliable: in early February 1918, British intelligence had received a report that fifty men from this division and their Alsatian officer had fled across the Dutch border. Five months later rumours of a mass desertion to the enemy involving 260 men and 3 officers from the same division were circulating on the German side of the lines.[40] By early summer, Alsatians in other units were beginning to seek an escape from combat. At the beginning of May 1918, British intelligence files reported how thirty armed Germans, chiefly Alsatians, had forced an unarmed British stretcher-bearer to take them prisoner 'against his will'. The prisoners, the report notes almost comically, 'were a source of obvious alamm [*sic*] to the stretcher bearer ... [and] were following him about wherever he went'.[41] Still more serious was the attempt by Alsatians and Poles to organise a large-scale mutiny at the Beverloo training camp later in the same month. Although this was discovered and thwarted, it appeared to have involved several hundred men. An order issued by the camp authorities and captured by the Allies demanded help in seeking out the ringleaders and directed all Alsatians to be distributed evenly between companies and platoons.[42]

38 Jahr, *Gewöhnliche Soldaten*, p. 278.

39 Reichsarchiv, *Weltkrieg*, XIV, p. 523.

40 Respectively, TNA, WO 157/ 191: Summary of Information (Fourth Army), 1 Feb. 1918, pp. 4–5 and BA-MA Freiburg, MSg 2/ 2797: W. Lüthje, diary, 30 July 1918. A reserve officer from Alsace-Lorraine was also held responsible for forewarning the French about the German offensive against Rheims in mid-July 1918. See A. von Thaer, *Generalstabsdienst an der Front und in der O.H.L. Aus Briefen und Tagebuchaufzeichnungen 1915–1919*, ed. S.A. Kaehler (Göttingen: Vandenhoeck & Ruprecht, 1958), pp. 213–14, letter of 16 July 1918.

41 TNA, WO 157/ 194: Summary of Information, No. 134 (Fourth Army), 1 May 1918, pp. 4–5.

42 See TNA, WO 157/ 196: Annexe to Fourth Army Summary dated 27 July 1918 and A. Kramer, '*Wackes* at War. Alsace-Lorraine and the Failure of German National Mobilization, 1914–1918', in J. Horne (ed.), *State, Society and Mobilization in Europe during the First World War* (Cambridge University Press, 1997), pp. 118–19. The plotters intended to desert to Holland. While British intelligence believed that many of the camp's 10,000 men took part, Kramer's examination of German documents suggests that several hundred were involved, twenty-four of whom actually attempted to escape and were court-martialled.

If Alsatians' motivation to fight was decreasing well before the end of *OHL*'s spring and early summer offensives, the hiatus for the majority of the German army is usually identified with the opening of the Allied counterattacks in mid-July and August. Certainly, these offensives were experienced as major blows by the army's leaders: Crown Prince Rupprecht of Bavaria, commanding an army group on the German right wing, saw the French attack on the Marne as being a 'turning point of the war', while Ludendorff famously described the Allied attack on 8 August as 'the black day of the German army'. According to the General Staff officer Albrecht von Thaer it was this offensive, resulting in an 8-mile Allied advance and a German loss of 27,000 men, which prompted the army commander to recognise that 'our troops are more or less finished'.[43] After the unexpected assault, many less prestigious soldiers serving at the front reached similar conclusions:

> One looks into the future with great concern. Will the German army be successful in averting the impending danger? Yes, if German soldiers were still those of 1914, full of enthusiasm and love for their Fatherland. But now, after four years of fighting, a certain depression is taking hold of the soldiers; they know that they must die for a hopeless cause. To them, better peace today at any respectable price rather than tomorrow.[44]

Among prisoners captured by the British, 'the universal wish expressed was that the war should come to an end in some way . . . None of those examined expressed the belief that Germany could win the war, but a number thought she could not be beaten in the field.' Surviving censorship reports similarly remark on the grave effect of the Allied military victories on German morale. 'The letter writers', noted that of the *6. Armee* for 4 September, 'have come to terms with what for them is the plain fact: "We cannot win" and in some cases even add to this the view that Germany will inevitably be defeated.'[45]

However, while the Allied victory at Amiens undoubtedly unnerved Ludendorff and sent shockwaves through the German high command, its effect on other ranks' morale was probably far less decisive. It was not the Battle of Amiens but rather the French attack on the Marne

43 Rupprecht von Bayern, *Kriegstagebuch*, II, p. 424, E. Ludendorff, *My War Memories. 1914–1918*, 2nd edn (2 vols., London: Hutchinson & Co., 1923), II, p. 679 and von Thaer, *Generalstabsdienst*, p. 222 (diary entry for 15 Aug. 1918). For the results of the 8 August attack, see Sheffield, *Forgotten Victory*, p. 198.

44 BA-MA Freiburg, MSg 1/ 161: K. Reiter, diary, 10–14 Aug. 1918.

45 TNA, WO 157/ 197: Summary of Information, No. 242 (Fourth Army), 17 Aug. 1918, p. 3 and report of the *Postüberwachungsstelle der 6. Armee*, 4 Sept. 1918 reproduced in Ulrich and Ziemann (eds.), *Frontalltag*, p. 203.

which began the Allied counteroffensive, and evidence from prisoner interrogations shows that the units attacked on 8 August were already demoralised by news of this previous defeat.[46] Indeed, Ludendorff himself felt obliged to address an order to the entire western Field Army after the French assault, noting that 'in many places a certain apprehension for enemy attack holds sway' and attempting to reassure his shaken troops with claims that the success had been of minor tactical importance.[47] Moreover, the sudden collapse of the German front both on 18 July and on 8 August is highly suspicious, particularly because of the large number of men surrendering in both battles. After only three days attacking on the Marne, the French captured 17,000 prisoners.[48] The British encountered a similar phenomenon at Amiens. Before 6 August, an average of 472 Germans had been captured per week in 1918 but in the week of the Amiens Offensive 20,145 men were captured, of whom just over 12,000 were taken on 8 August.[49] These figures may partially reflect the effect of improved Allied tactics and firepower, yet, as in the case of the *241. Division*'s mass surrenders in July and early October, it seems likely that war-weariness and exhaustion had already eroded German units' combat motivation to a very great extent.

In fact, as the interwar commentator Friedrich Altrichter rightly observed, far from being a turning point, the Battle of Amiens simply exposed the psychological exhaustion and physical fatigue which had already taken hold of German other ranks.[50] As Hew Strachan has pointed out, the decline in German morale and discipline did not begin in summer 1918 but had already begun to make itself apparent at least one year earlier.[51] The good mood discernible after the armistice with Russia and at the beginning of the *Kaiserschlacht* was in fact a blip in a downward trend and most evidence suggests that it did not last very long. No censor reports survive for the period March to July, but other sources give an indication of how morale developed during the Germans' own offensives. A report compiled by *Militär-Polizeistelle Leipzig* for the period 1 March to 30 April 1918 found that soldiers travelling on the railways in its area of jurisdiction were confident of a successful end to the western offensive but also more ominously noted a rise in general

[46] See TNA, WO 157/ 196: Summary of Information, No. 224 (Fourth Army), 30 July 1918, p. 2
[47] BA-MA Freiburg, PH3/ 293: Ludendorff's order entitled 'Ausbildung', 4 Aug. 1918.
[48] Reichsarchiv, *Weltkrieg*, XIV, pp. 502–3.
[49] *Military Effort*, p. 632 and TNA, WO 157/ 197: Summary of Information, No. 234 (Fourth Army), 9 August 1918, p. 1.
[50] Altrichter, *Seelischen Kräfte*, p. 157.
[51] See Strachan, 'Morale', pp. 387–8 and also chapter 5 above, pp. 168–71.

war-weariness.[52] Behaviour in the initial attacks of the *Kaiserschlacht* also reveal how far discipline had loosened in the German army by early 1918, for even in elite assault divisions infantrymen forgot their objectives and slowed the advance by stopping to plunder Allied supply depots. Pneumatic tyres, bicycles, pieces of clothing and footwear, white bread, meat, coffee and tobacco were all pillaged from depots and villages by German troops.[53] Alcohol, too, was discovered in large quantities, causing major disciplinary problems: Reiter saw soldiers streaming back in mid-April with tinned food and wine bottles under their arms, and British intelligence reports record the case of a naval division which delayed a German attack by becoming intoxicated and pillaging Albert. According to Altrichter, such incidents were not exceptional during the offensive.[54]

Alcohol-induced insubordination, although serious, was nonetheless not as important in shaking German discipline as signs that the offensive would not bring the decisive victory hoped for by German soldiers. According to Altrichter, morale was still high by the time the initial offensive, Operation *Michael*, was closed down on 5 April. However, the subsequent pause in offensive action shook soldiers' confidence in imminent victory, and the launching by the enemy of some successful counterattacks, most notably that at Villers Bretonneux on 24 April, prompted a mood swing into depression and despair.[55] By May, reports of disobedience among combat troops in the German army began to multiply. Unlike the large-scale mutiny organised by the Alsatians at Beverloo, however, most incidents appear to have been aimed at securing a temporary relief from the hardships of battle rather than escaping from military service altogether. For example, on 4 May, prisoners of the *20. Reserve-Jäger-Bataillon* (a light infantry battalion) reported that they had been sent to the front early, as *Infanterie-Regiment Nr. 74*, which was still recovering from heavy losses, had mutinied and threatened to desert if forced to go forward. Five days later, a prisoner belonging to *Infanterie-Regiment Nr. 97* told his captors that ration carriers in his regiment had refused to go up the line after suffering heavy casualties, and the captured personal papers of a soldier in *Infanterie-Regiment Nr. 419* mention on 14 June that the

[52] HStA Dresden, 11352 Stellv. Gen.-Kdo XIX AK KA(P) 24158: Bericht der Militär-Polizeistelle Leipzig über die Eisenbahnüberwachung im Bereich des stellv. Generalkommandos XIX. AK für die Zeit vom 1.3.–30.4.18, p. 251.

[53] See BA-MA Freiburg, MSg 1/ 2968: H. Fuchs, diary, 26 Mar. 1918, DTA, 758: P. Keppeler, letter to Lina [sister?], 1 May 1918 and BA-MA Freiburg, MSg 2/ 2797: W. Lüthje, diary, 10 Apr. 1918.

[54] BA-MA Freiburg, MSg 1/ 161: K. Reiter, diary, 13 Apr. 1918 and Altrichter, *Seelischen Kräfte*, p. 136.

[55] Altrichter, *Seelischen Kräfte*, p. 137.

unit's *III. Bataillon* refused to go to the front and that men from *II. Bataillon* had deserted. That these incidents, although small scale, were not exceptional is confirmed by a command issued on 12 June by the *2. Armee*, noting that 'cases of soldiers openly refusing to obey orders are increasing to an alarming extent'.[56] Reports from July mention that platoons of *Infanterie-Regiment Nr. 148* had refused to stay in line and record the attempt of Prussian troops at Albert to fraternise with their opponents.[57]

The decline in morale before the beginning of the Allied counter-offensive was not uniform within the German army but probably varied according to units' quality, combat experience, losses and exhaustion. Throughout the first half of 1918, soldiers' letters reveal that men were by no means united in their assessments of the military situation.[58] Nonetheless, the above examples of indiscipline do suggest that the German defeats of 18 July and 8 August did not represent a turning point but rather catalysed a quickly growing mood of disillusionment and hopelessness. War-weariness and sullenness continued to predominate in September and the level of trust in the country's leadership declined to the extent that most soldiers believed that the Austrian peace proposal at the end of the month was simply a device to prepare them for a new war loan.[59] Instead, many looked to the Allies to bring about a quick end to the war: 'unfortunately, the retreat has not gone far because the English are too thin on the ground to bring it further', wrote Josef Kollendorfer of *bayerisches Infanterie-Regiment Nr. 16*, and many other men shared his mixture of hope and despair. In mid-September, men of the *2. Garde-Division* not only expressed joy at being captured but, according to British intelligence, had 'actually urged our men to go on attacking, and to capture as many Germans as possible so that the war might quickly end. Each fresh batch of prisoners brought into the Cage

56 For the order referring to indiscipline in the *2. Armee*, see TNA, WO 157/ 196: Summary of Information, No. 202 (Fourth Army), 8 July 1918, p. 5. Otherwise, see respectively TNA, WO 157/ 194: Summary of Information, No. 137 (Fourth Army), 4 May 1918, p. 5 and No. 142, 9 May 1918, p. 5. Also, TNA, WO 157/ 195: Summary of Information, No. 185 (Fourth Army), 21 June 1918, p. 4.

57 TNA, WO 157/ 196: Summary of Information, No. 210 (Fourth Army), 16 July 1918, p. 5 and No. 212, 18 July 1918, p. 5.

58 Thus, for example, Ernst Vogt, serving near Amiens, had already concluded by the end of April that at most Germany could force a draw. Kurt Reiter, who took part in Operation *Georgette* in Flanders only came to a similar conclusion in June. *Leutnant* Hans Muhsal, far removed from the main battle theatre, reported in late July from the Vosges that among his comrades were still optimists claiming that *OHL* retained the initiative. See BA-MA Freiburg, MSg 1/ 3183: E. Vogt, diary / memoir, 5–24 Apr. 1918; BA-MA Freiburg, MSg 1/ 161: K. Reiter, diary, 19–26 June 1918 and BA-MA Freiburg, MSg 1/ 3109: H. Muhsal, diary, 28 July 1918.

59 BA-MA Freiburg, W-10/ 50794: Postüberwachung der *5. Armee*, 28 Sept. 1918, p. 92.

[*sic*] was greeted with open delight at our success'.[60] The German peace offer of 3 October was seen by the majority of soldiers as an admission of defeat, and by the middle of the month, rumours of an imminent armistice were circulating and some men surrendered, claiming that they believed peace had already been declared.[61] Among those who remained out of enemy hands, the demand for peace at any price became explicit. 'We can't [do] any more, we don't want [to do] any more, we want [to go] home' was the main sentiment expressed in their letters.[62]

But what was it that allowed demoralisation to turn into outright indiscipline? Were not structures of military organisation designed to deal with such symptoms of weakening? Previous accounts have failed to lay adequate stress on the breakdown of morale among officers as well as the other ranks. They had shared with their men the physical hardships of the offensives earlier in the year and had suffered proportionally almost twice as many casualties in March and April. Already during the offensives in early and mid-1918, isolated examples of demoralisation began to appear in the officer corps, most especially in the *237. Division* in the Argonne, where during the spring, officers encouraged their men to fraternise with the French.[63] Less serious but still significant was the widespread decline in standards of dress and behaviour within the corps during the early summer.[64] It was, however, the advent of the Allied counteroffensive which finally shattered the front officer corps' will to keep fighting. According to the former company and machinegun officer Hermann Schützinger, 'after all the failures of the years 1916 and 1917 and after the defeat of the "offensive" of the year 1918 despair ate deep into the officer corps'.[65] The morale of officers captured at the end of July was said to have been 'seriously lowered' by the French victory at Villers-Cotterêts, and officers taken at the Battle of Amiens were also

60 Respectively, BA-MA Freiburg, MSg 2/ 5458: J. Kollendorfer, letter to parents, 9 Oct. 1918 and TNA, WO 157/ 198: Summary of Information, No. 266 (Fourth Army), 10 Sept. 1918, p. 6.

61 See HStA Stuttgart, M 30/ 1 Bü 337, Bl. 80: Order of *Armee-Oberkommando 19* entitled 'Gerüchte von Waffenruhe u. Dergl.', 15 Oct. 1918 and TNA, WO 157/ 199: Summary of Information, No. 296 (Fourth Army), 10 Oct. 1918, p. 6.

62 BA-MA Freiburg, W-10/ 50794: Postüberwachung der *5. Armee*, 17 Oct. 1918, p. 106.

63 United States War Office, *Histories*, p. 730.

64 See HStA Stuttgart, M30/ 1 Bü 336, Blatt 201: Order of *Oberkommando der Heeresgruppe Herzog Albrecht* warning officers to improve their behaviour and standards of dress, 18 June 1918 and also TNA, WO 157/ 197: Summary of Information, No. 228 (Fourth Army), 3 Aug. 1918, p. 5, which reproduces an order from the *6. Armee* dated 8 May 1918 ordering officers and men to salute.

65 Letter of H. Schützinger to M. Hobohm, 30 Mar. 1927 reproduced in Hobohm, *Soziale Heeresmißstände*, XI.1, p. 424.

very depressed. According to a special intelligence report produced on the subject, many acknowledged that 'Germany was in practically a hopeless condition', although they believed that the war would continue if the Allies aimed to crush the country entirely. In contrast to their confidence in total victory in March 1918, few officer prisoners in August thought that the war could be ended any more favourably for Germany than by a negotiated peace, perhaps at the cost of Alsace-Lorraine. The report concluded that 'the moral[e] of the officers, owing to the recent German reverses seems universally deteriorating'.[66]

The events of the following months were not conducive to promoting an improvement in morale. The autumn of 1918 was, as *Leutnant* Müller put it, 'a difficult time for every patriotic man'.[67] The *5. Armee* censor characterised officers' letters at the end of August as serious but giving no cause for complaint, but most other sources present a gloomier view of morale in the corps.[68] Schützinger, running a machinegun instruction course for officers in September, observed that the mood of his pupils was 'extremely dejected' and considered them 'mentally broken' by the failure of Ludendorff's strategy.[69] A special examination of officers' post in the *17. Armee* during the same month found that most believed that the war could last no longer than late autumn or winter.[70] Many were reaching a stage of mental paralysis due to exhaustion: a Bavarian officer, captured by the French in August, remarked that the lack of rest had made his colleagues apathetic and indifferent.[71] Other officers openly expressed their misgivings about Germany's future, further depressing those around them. 'What sort of victory prospects should one give an army, in which even officers consider the game to be up, e.g. when each day at the table a battalion commander moans about his despair to his officers?', asked one heavy-artillery officer in a letter to a friend.[72] This behaviour clearly became widespread, particularly after the German peace offer, for on 7 October, the headquarters of *19. Armee* issued an order noting the rise in defeatist remarks among officers and warning

[66] TNA, WO 157/ 196: Weekly Appreciation. For Period from July 27th to Augt. 2nd (inclusive). Fourth Army, 3 Aug. 1918, pp. 1–2 and TNA, WO 157/ 197: 'Report on Moral of Officers captured on August 8th & 9th in the third battle of the Somme', in Annexe to Fourth Army Summary, 23 Aug. 1918.

[67] Staatsbib. Berlin, Ms. Germ. fol. 1651: C.F. Müller, diary, 30 Aug. 1918.

[68] BA-MA Freiburg, W-10/ 50794: Postüberwachung der *5. Armee*, 31 Aug. 1918, p. 79.

[69] Letter of H. Schützinger to M. Hobohm, 30 Mar. 1927 reproduced in Hobohm, *Soziale Heeresmißstände*, XI.1, p. 424.

[70] Rupprecht von Bayern, *Kriegstagebuch*, II, p. 443.

[71] Hobohm, *Soziale Heeresmißstände*, XI.1, p. 396 (doc. 44).

[72] Reproduced in HStA Dresden, *Militärbevollmächtigter* Nr. 4216, Bl. 3–3a: 'Anlage zur Z.St.412 vom 29.9.18: Brief eines Frontoffiziers an einen Kamerad [8 Sept. 1918]'.

them to cease expressing such views in front of comrades, subordinates and the enemy population.[73] *General* Groener, in a speech to the military plenipotentiaries of Germany's states on 1 November actually went so far as to blame the officer corps for the poor mood of the men. 'Morale, determination and self-sacrifice are being eroded,' he wrote. 'There lacks the inner fire of enthusiasm, the steadfastness.'[74]

By the armistice, demoralisation had spread throughout the German army, sapping its ability to fight further. The first to be affected were non-German soldiers serving in the Kaiser's forces, who were already engaged in acts of mass disobedience by early summer 1918. German other ranks' morale, which had risen briefly after the peace with Russia, also quickly declined once *OHL*'s offensive began to be checked in April. Among them too, acts of collective indiscipline increased in the early summer, although at this point they arose less from a rejection of the war than from extreme exhaustion. At least until the summer of 1918 the German army remained a formidable fighting force and, given a respite, its morale might have somewhat improved. The Allied advance, however, shattered any remaining illusions of an imminent German victory and further increased the pressure on German soldiers by exhausting *OHL*'s strategic reserve and making it impossible for men to be given adequate rest. The army now found itself facing a crisis of morale, which peaked after the Peace Note of 3 October had effectively admitted German defeat. Despite the lack of attention paid to them by modern historiography, it is important to recognise that German front officers were not unaffected by the increasingly gloomy events on the Western Front in 1918. They suffered more heavily than the rank and file during the spring offensive and were dismayed by the opening of the Allied counteroffensive. Exhaustion, apathy and demoralisation quickly took hold of the officer corps during the retreat, just as they had among the men. Extreme physical fatigue and the knowledge that victory was no longer possible were responsible for the erosion of fighting spirit by the autumn. As a Scottish soldier accurately observed of German prisoners taken in the fighting of September 1918, 'the weariness of the mind along with the weariness of the body stamps them with the hall-mark of a beaten enemy'.[75]

[73] HStA Stuttgart, M30/ 1 Bü 337, Bl. 76: Order from *Armee-Oberkommando 19* entitled 'Stimmung in Offizierskorps', 7 Oct. 1918.

[74] HStA Dresden, *Militärbevollmächtigter* Nr. 4221, Bl. 226: Report of the Saxon *Militärbevollmächtigter* to the War Minister of a speech given by *General* Groener, 1 Nov. 1918.

[75] Letter of Sergeant J. Duncan to D. MacArthur, 5 Sept. 1918, reproduced in Housman (ed.), *War Letters*, p. 97.

Indiscipline?

The unprecedented mental and physical strain placed on German soldiers in 1918 inevitably translated itself into an increasingly widespread reluctance to fight further. Already by the end of the spring and early summer offensives, utterly exhausted soldiers were beginning to mutiny in order to avoid undergoing further exertion and risk. Before the opening of the Allied counterattack, however, these acts of collective indiscipline remained small in scale and limited in number. When the onslaught was finally unleashed on the Marne and at Amiens, German troops were driven to new levels of exhaustion and a number of frightening scenarios became possible. Revolution, such as took place in the Russian army, was certainly a worry entertained by some contemporaries. Large organised mutinies, like those in the French army in 1917, were another method by which soldiers might have demonstrated their exhaustion and unwillingness to fight. As has already been discussed, most historians favour Deist's notion of a 'covert strike' and believe that men simply expressed their unwillingness to fight further by 'shirking' and deserting in enormous numbers at the end of the war. Alternatively, apathy and indifference may have inhibited any form of protest, numbing men and making them vegetative and uninterested in either their own fate or that of Germany.

For the German army's Field Police, the fear that Bolshevik revolution might flare up within the ranks appeared very real. Some evidence exists to suggest that this trepidation was not entirely groundless; as early as January 1918, some troops were remarking in their correspondence that the 'misery swindle' would end only when the people took matters into their own hands, 'just as in Russia'.[76] The desire among the soldiers for a republic grew according to Ziemann, and in Kruse's opinion many had embraced extremist politics by the end of the war and were actively hoping for revolution.[77] Information picked up by the German security services in October 1918 suggested that these aspirations were finally coming to fruition and that soldiers were being incited to disobey orders and prepare for revolt: rumours of men on leave being encouraged to desert by mysterious figures at train stations and of Rhinelanders bringing home weapons 'for later' were

[76] BA-MA Freiburg, MSg 2/ 5458: J. Kohler, letter to parents, 27 Jan. 1918.

[77] Strachan, 'Morale', pp. 395–6, B. Ziemann, 'Enttäuschte Erwartung und kollektive Erschöpfung. Die deutschen Soldaten an der Westfront 1918 auf dem Weg zur Revolution', in J. Duppler and G.P. Groß (eds.), *Kriegsende 1918. Ereignis, Wirkung, Nachwirkung. Beiträge zur Militärgeschichte. Herausgegeben vom Militärgeschichtlichen Forschungsamt.* Vol. LIII (Munich: R. Oldenbourg, 1999), p. 177 and Kruse, 'Krieg und Klassenheer', 559.

reported.[78] Officers' diaries refer to train lavatories overflowing with anti-war leaflets.[79] During the final months of the conflict, a German version of The Internationale was circulating in the Field Army and anthems of the 1848 Revolution expressing the belief that 'Blood must flow . . . for the German Republic!' could be heard.[80] In some divisions this actually took place as group disobedience broke out. Allied intelligence files mention three mutinies in which left-wing influences may have played some part: in October, *232. Division* was 'influenced by Bolsheviks' and refused to fight, *45. Reserve-Division* may have been prompted to revolt by men of a draft 'with decidedly Bolshevik tendencies' and 'revolutionary agitation' was experienced by the *25. Landwehr-Division.* A further mutiny in the *18. Landwehr-Division*, recently transferred from the east, merited mention by *General* Groener in a speech to the military plenipotentiaries on 1 November.[81] Smaller acts of group indiscipline demonstrating social grievances or revolutionary sympathies were also reported behind the front line. On the night of 26–27 October, for example, *Hauptmann* Fuchs, the intelligence officer of the *1. Garde-Reserve-Division*, heard men outside his billet shouting 'thrash the officers' but recorded that when a colleague had grabbed one of them by the scruff of the neck, the rest had run off.[82] Other soldiers were less timid, particularly after the outbreak of the revolution at home on 9 November: *Leutnant* Berner of the *1. Garde-Division* was nearly attacked by soldiers without cockades on 10 November. Two days later, *Leutnant* Muhsal recorded seeing young, insubordinate machine-gunners carrying red flags in Alsace.[83]

However, despite these manifestations of apparent revolutionary fervour, it is clear that no Bolshevik revolt was brewing in the army by late 1918. Closer inspection of the evidence cited above suggests that

[78] For subversive figures at stations, see HStA Dresden, 11352 Stellv. Gen.-Kdo XIX AK KA(P) 24159: Report issued by the *stellvertretendes Generalkommando*, 22 Oct. 1918 and for the Rhinelanders, see HStA Stuttgart, M30/ 1 Bü 49: Report of *Feldpolizeistelle Colmar*, 18 Oct. 1918. Cf. also the August letter from the Acting Command of the *XIV. Armeekorps* speculating that troops on leave in the Westphalian Rhineland and Saar areas were being incited to mutiny: GLA Karlsruhe, 456 F 8 / 106. Blatt 381: *Stellvertretendes Generalkommando, XIV. Armeekorps* to *Kommandeure sämtlicher Ersatztruppenteile*, letter, 29 Aug. 1918.

[79] BA-MA Freiburg, MSg 1/ 2968: H. Fuchs, diary, 27 Oct. 1918.

[80] Schuhmacher, *Leben und Seele*, p. 181.

[81] United States War Office, *Histories*, pp. 467, 720 and 360 respectively and HStA Dresden, *Militärbevollmächtigter* Nr. 4221, Bl. 225: Report of the Saxon *Militärbevollmächtigter* to the War Minister of a speech given by *General* Groener, 1 Nov. 1918.

[82] BA-MA Freiburg, MSg 1/ 2968: H. Fuchs, diary, 27 Oct. 1918.

[83] BA-MA Freiburg, MSg 1/ 1941: E. Berner, 10 Nov. 1918 and BA-MA Freiburg, MSg 1/ 3109: H. Muhsal, diary, 12 Nov. 1918.

preconceptions about the form disorder would take encouraged both German and Allied intelligence to exaggerate the revolutionary impetus behind the mutinies. As Christoph Jahr has explained, Bolshevism had been a bugbear of German intelligence throughout the second half of the war and vague rumours of revolution and conspiracy were collected obsessively.[84] The indistinct nature of the references to Bolshevik agitation in the three small mutinies mentioned in Allied reports and the fact that at least one officer was involved in the disorder among men of the *25. Landwehr-Division* also indicate that their revolutionary nature was overstressed.[85] In fact, as Altrichter observed in his study of the German army's collapse at the end of the war, the Field Army itself remained largely free of Bolshevism. Only among drafts travelling to the front did he find any evidence of revolutionary agitation.[86] Most combat soldiers were uninterested in or, as *Hauptmann* Fuchs observed in his diary on 11 November, 'completely against the revolutionaries', probably because the chaos of a rebellion threatened their quick return home.[87] Revolutionaries had actually never been able to convert any other than a small minority of soldiers in the Field Army to their political creed. Kruse's argument that Bolshevism had come to the army through extremist munitions workers and troops transferred from the east is unconvincing. As Strachan points out, the former, who had spent most of the war behind the lines, were more likely to be a source of resentment to veterans than potential leaders of a revolution.[88] The latter may well have been accepted as comrades or leaders, yet there is little evidence to suggest that most were adherents of Bolshevik ideology; their troublesome behaviour and reluctance to fight in the west was primarily a reflection of war-weariness and the feeling that they had won 'their' war, not a result of extreme political views.[89] To be sure, German prisoners in Russia did fraternise with the Bolsheviks, yet as the report of an escaped German officer makes clear, the majority were motivated less by revolutionary fervour than by the improved material conditions offered to collaborators.[90] For their

[84] Jahr, *Gewöhnliche Soldaten*, p. 163.
[85] See United States War Office, *Histories*, pp. 720, 467 and 360 respectively.
[86] Altrichter, *Seelischen Kräfte*, pp. 148–9.
[87] BA-MA Freiburg, MSg 1/ 2968: H. Fuchs, diary, 11 Nov. 1918.
[88] Strachan, 'Morale', p. 394. Most of the munitions workers were conscripted as a punishment after the Berlin strikes of January and February 1918. These strikes were extremely unpopular at the front. See BA-MA Freiburg, W-10/ 50794: Postüberwachung der *5. Armee*, 24 Feb. 1918, p. 44.
[89] Altrichter, *Seelischen Kräfte*, pp. 160–2. Cf. TNA, WO 157/ 26: Annexe to GHQ Summary [of Information], 8 Dec. 1917.
[90] HStA Dresden, *Kriegsamtstelle Leipzig* KA(P) 24159, Bl. 11–14: *Leutnant* Andreas Werner, 'Bericht über das Verhalten der deutschen Kriegsgefangenen in Sibirien dem russischen Revolutionsgedanken und der Roten Garde gegenüber', 19 June 1918.

comrades who had witnessed the advent of the Russian Revolution from the safety of the German trenches in 1917 and early 1918, there was even less reason to sympathise with the Bolsheviks. For most men, especially those with agricultural backgrounds, its chaos did not offer an attractive model in conflict termination.[91] Lack of interest, not, as Kruse suggests, disciplinary measures, explains the absence of any revolutionary organisation within the Field Army. As the historian Ulrich Kluge observed, 'a revolutionary movement never caught hold of the western army; the confrontation between men and officers, which the home army had on all sides experienced, failed to materialise here'.[92] Indeed, when *Soldatenräte* (soldiers' councils) did finally appear in the army during early November, they were not developed from the bottom but rather imposed on soldiers by *OHL* and organised by company officers. Often they contained a mixture of officers and men and their demands were distinctly non-revolutionary. To take one probably not atypical case, the soldiers in Alfred Volquartz's company of *Infanterie-Regiment Nr. 425* used their newly acquired power to request that all ranks be given the same food and that some unpopular officers be sent home. They were quite content to follow Volquartz, still an officer but now wearing a red armband, across the border into Germany.[93]

Far from taking the form of a Bolshevik revolution, or even open anti-war protest, 'overt' indiscipline on the Western Front after the early summer of 1918 was in fact predominantly spontaneous, motivated by material needs or self-preservation rather than political goals, late in appearance and surprisingly small in scale. Although rumours of regiments refusing to fight circulated the Western Front during the second half of 1918, it is remarkably difficult to find instances of mutiny, especially before October. Reports of group indiscipline at the front actually drop in frequency in the files of British intelligence from mid-1918. In contrast to the numerous small-scale mutinies it reported early in the summer of 1918, the intelligence staff of the BEF's Fourth Army, for example, found evidence of only two such incidents after the beginning of the British counteroffensive on 8 August. On 23 September, a first-class unit, the *III/Infanterie-Regiment Nr. 153*, had mutinied when ordered to counterattack owing to previous heavy losses. The second case, which

[91] See BA-MA Freiburg, MSg 1/ 571: A. Volquartz, 'Die Russische [*sic*] und die deutsche Revolution, 1917–18' (*c.* 1970), p. 6.

[92] U. Kluge, *Soldatenräte und Revolution. Studien zur Militärpolitik in Deutschland 1918/19* (Göttingen: Vandenhoeck & Ruprecht, 1975), p. 104.

[93] BA-MA Freiburg, MSg 1/ 571: A. Volquartz, 'Die Russische [*sic*] und die deutsche Revolution, 1917–18' (*c.* 1970), pp. 6, 17–18. This case was not untypical. See the examples cited in Kluge, *Soldatenräte und Revolution*, p. 397, notes 420–1.

also took place at the end of September, was similar, involving a company of an unspecified *Garde-Grenadier-Regiment* which also disobeyed a command to counterattack.[94] Other examples of disorder reported on the Western Front also indicate that soldiers were more concerned with self-preservation and basic living necessities than political grievances. Although largely ignored by historians concerned primarily with soldiers' attempts to escape or protest against the war, German documents indicate that the most common form of group disobedience to take place in or directly behind the lines in 1918 was the looting of provision trains and depots. As has already been noted, during the spring offensive German troops had wantonly plundered Allied supplies in search of food and alcohol. When the attacks began to fail and opportunities for such action receded, they instead turned on their own army's stockpiles. As early as 17 April, the Quartermaster-General at the headquarters of the *17. Armee* was forced to issue a warning after a bread train had been repeatedly plundered by troops marching on the Cambrai–Bapaume road.[95] This early incident appears to have been motivated by opportunism, but during the following months, perpetrators became increasingly organised. In May, the *3. Reserve-Division* decided that it was necessary to equip personnel on supply trains with light machine-guns in order to defend themselves against attack from German soldiers, and towards the end of the war some fatalities were caused by fighting between would-be plunderers and train or depot guards.[96] Two aspects of these attacks made them particularly ominous. As a complaint made in August 1918 against the entire *7. Batterie* of *Feldartillerie-Regiment Nr. 36* testifies, this looting was undertaken not only by isolated stragglers or ill-trained rear-echelon soldiers but also by combat units.[97] The second and still more worrying aspect was the role played by junior officers and senior NCOs in these robberies. In most reported cases, they appear to have been present but lacked either the authority or the will to intervene; in the April incident mentioned above, officers were

[94] TNA, WO 157/ 199: Summary of Information, No. 287 (Fourth Army), 1 Oct. 1918, p. 7 and ibid., No. 289, p. 5. For the rumours, see, for example, BA-MA Freiburg, W-10/ 50794: Postüberwachung der *5. Armee*, 31 Aug. 1918, p. 81 and BA-MA Freiburg, MSg 1/ 3109: H. Muhsal, 19 Sept. 1918.

[95] HStA Stuttgart, M38/ 17 Bü 5, Bl. 43: order of *Oberquartiermeister*, *Armee-Oberkommando 17*, 17 Apr. 1918.

[96] Order of *3. Reserve-Division* dated 18 May 1918 translated and reproduced in TNA, WO 157/ 196: Summary of Information, No. 198 (Fourth Army), 4 July 1918, p. 5. For fatalities caused by plundering see BA-MA Freiburg, MSg 1/ 2968: H. Fuchs, diary, 7 Nov. 1918.

[97] Order dated 30 Aug. 1918 issued by the officer commanding *10. Division*. Translated and reproduced in *Why Germany Capitulated*, pp. 53–4.

nearby but failed to stop their men from robbing the bread train. However, it is also clear that in other cases they were actually complicit in the plundering. An order issued by the *7. Armee* in mid-June 1918 regretted that 'some officers have not been ashamed to interfere with the guard [of supply depots] in the execution of their duty and to insult the officials to whose charge the provisions have been entrusted'.[98]

Most historians follow Wilhelm Deist in arguing that the stringency of military discipline at the front retarded most attempts at 'overt' group protest. Instead, they argue, soldiers committed 'covert' acts of indiscipline. Lipp suggests that *unerlaubte Entfernung* (absence without leave) became the main method by which soldiers avoided combat during the second half of 1918, but according to Deist, many adopted more innovative ways of 'shirking'. Soldiers returning to combat units from hospital, for example, dumped their equipment on the journey and were thus sent back for more when they arrived at the front.[99] Not only the army's logistical organisation but even its disciplinary mechanisms could be exploited as a way out of the trenches. Ludendorff complained that the practice of punishing soldiers with suspended sentences encouraged 'shirking' because it allowed men to commit crimes in the knowledge that they would not be immediately punished but instead removed from the front to await trial.[100] Military medical provision was also abused by soldiers wishing to escape combat duty. Kits designed to produce leg boils were being sold to front soldiers as early as May 1918 and for the poor and thrifty the deliberate inhalation of small amounts of gas provided a cheap, if dangerous, way of escaping the trenches.[101] The influenza epidemic of mid-1918 also supplied men with a welcome pretext to go sick and it is noticeable that venereal disease rates were far higher in 1918 than during previous war years, despite the fact that much of the army was stationed on the old Somme battlefield, an area devoid of civilians.[102]

98 Extract from order dated 14 June 1918 issued by the *7. Armee* in TNA, WO 157/ 196: Summary of Information, No. 217 (Fourth Army), 23 July 1918, pp. 4–5. See also Volquartz's account of helping his men to plunder a depot shortly after the armistice in BA-MA Freiburg, MSg 1/ 571: A. Volquartz, 'Die Russische [*sic*] und die deutsche Revolution, 1917–18', p. 6.

99 Lipp, *Meinungslenkung*, p. 145 and Deist, 'Military Collapse', 201.

100 HStA Stuttgart, M30/ 1 Bü 337: Order from Ludendorff entitled 'Aufrechterhaltung der Manneszucht in der Armee', dated 1 Aug. 1918.

101 For boil kits, see Ulrich and Ziemann (eds.), *Frontalltag*, p. 200, doc. 56c. Order of the *bayerischen Kriegsministerium* of 29 May 1918. For gas, see the order issued by *1. Reserve-Division* dated 1 Sept. 1918 in *Why Germany Capitulated*, p. 60.

102 See Strachan, 'Morale', pp. 394–5 and *Sanitätsbericht III*, pp. 28*–9* and 66*–7*.

In a theory which has become an established part of the literature on the First World War, Deist posits that in the last months of the conflict between 750,000 and 1 million men 'shirked' their duty or deserted, together forming a 'covert strike', the purpose of which was to cripple the German army and bring about peace.[103] The lack of evidence of any central organisation or direction, however, has prompted Lipp and Ziemann to argue that the decision to 'shirk' or strike was usually an individual one and that far from wishing to find a 'political answer' to the problem of irresponsible military leadership, most men avoiding combat duty were primarily concerned with issues of self-preservation.[104] The non-political and material- or survival-focused nature of group indiscipline at the front, outlined above, supports this interpretation. By late 1918, combat troops were under so much pressure that political calculations hardly influenced them: most were occupied simply with staying alive and finding the next meal.

If, however, Lipp and Ziemann are correct in their belief that 'shirking' and desertion were primarily individual matters rather than organised forms of disobedience, why was the German army's disciplinary organisation powerless to stop so many men committing these crimes? Throughout the war, armies on the Western Front had been extremely good at wringing obedience from individuals; only when large groups or whole units of men mutinied, as had happened in the French army in 1917, did they face real difficulties.[105] One possible answer is that the credence given to Deist's estimate of between 750,000 and 1 million 'shirkers' is exaggerated. Deist took this figure from the historian and former staff officer Erich-Otto Volkmann, who presented it in a tract written for the 1920s' commission investigating the German army's collapse of 1918. As Volkmann's express purpose in penning this work was to rebut the thesis of another historian, Martin Hobohm, who argued that the army's disintegration had been primarily the fault of its officer corps, it was in his interests to minimise the contribution made by that body of men in the breakdown and instead concentrate on and even exaggerate the role played by the other ranks. Close examination of the method by which he reached his figure of between 750,000 and 1 million shirkers reveals that his calculations were seriously flawed. Arguing against Hobohm, who had reasoned that 'shirkers' in the last

103 Deist, 'Military Collapse', 202.

104 See ibid., 207, Lipp, *Meinungslenkung*, p. 146 and Ziemann, 'Enttäuschte Erwartungen', pp. 180–1. In a later article, Deist himself also placed more emphasis on self-preservation and exhaustion as motivating factors for the strike. See Deist, 'Verdeckter Militärstreik', pp. 156–7 and 160.

105 See Smith, *Between Mutiny and Obedience*, pp. 175–214.

months of the war could have totalled no more than 300,000, Volkmann reached his estimate by adding to this number a further 340,000 prisoners and missing. Unfortunately, this figure not only included many men who had surrendered legitimately to the Allies but it also came from the same source which Hobohm had used in order to arrive at his estimate of 'shirking'. Without presenting any evidence, Volkmann then added a further 100,000 to 350,000 men, who, he claimed, had left the line temporarily in order to avoid battle and then afterwards returned to their units. When analysed, the source cited by Deist as a reliable estimate of 'shirking' in the second half of 1918 thus consists of the figure for German prisoners and missing added to itself, plus a highly arbitrary estimate for men who temporarily absconded.[106] In fact, there is no definitive figure for 'shirkers'; contemporary estimates of their numbers vary wildly between 200,000 and 1.5 million men.[107]

Responsibility for the widely differing estimates for 'shirking' lies largely with the vagueness of the term, for its definition can encompass everything from laziness to permanently decamping. Deist himself is ambiguous in his use of the expression: he argues that 'it was rarely a case of straightforward desertion', yet his evidence refers predominantly to men absconding from troop transports and storming medical trains in order to escape the front. Other historians have thus concluded that there were 'up to a million shirkers lurking in the rear and making their way back to Germany'.[108] In the light of contemporary evidence, however, indiscipline on such a scale can be discounted. Certainly, the disorder caused by the Allied advance from the summer of 1918 did loosen the cohesion of the German army. Some soldiers became separated from their units in the fierce fighting, while others took advantage of the disarray in the army's disciplinary mechanisms to abscond. Already by late August, orders were issued warning that 'the number of stragglers and shirkers wandering about the rear has increased to an alarming extent'.[109] Yet the German figure for missing and prisoners does not

[106] See Volkmann, *Soziale Heeresmißstände*, XI.2, p. 66, Hobohm, *Soziale Heeresmißstände*, XI.1, pp. 183–4, particularly note 1 and Deist, 'Military Collapse', 202. The source which both men were using was *General* von Kuhl's testimony to the *Münchener Dolchstoßprozeß*.

[107] Reichsarchiv, *Weltkrieg*, XIV, p. 760.

[108] Deist, 'Military Collapse', 201–2 and Strachan, 'Morale', p. 395.

[109] See the extract from the order issued by *9. Armee* on 22 Aug. 1918 reproduced in *Why Germany Capitulated*, p. 53 and cf. *7. Armee* order of 14 June 1918 reproduced in TNA, WO 157/ 196: Summary of Information, No. 217 (Fourth Army), 23 July 1918, pp. 4–5 and the interrogation report referring to 'versprengte Leute' (scattered men) in TNA, WO 157/ 197: Summary of Information, No. 254 (Fourth Army), 29 Aug. 1918, p. 6.

support the notion of large groups of men milling behind the lines. Both Hobohm and Volkmann agreed that 340,000 German soldiers went missing or were taken prisoner in the period 18 July to 11 November. According to the *Reichsarchiv*, 233,200 soldiers were captured by the British, Belgian, French and American armies in August and September 1918. British statistics show further that between the beginning of October and the armistice a further 68,217 men surrendered to Haig's armies. It is unlikely that the remaining Allies captured much fewer than 40,000 prisoners and, indeed, they may have taken more; Altrichter states that the total number of German prisoners taken during the Allied offensive was 385,000 men.[110] These figures thus suggest that there were, in fact, very few deserters or 'shirkers' escaping rearwards and that the vast majority of missing were prisoners of the Allies.

Other evidence also supports this conclusion. In an army numbering 3,582,203 men in July 1918, it would be surprising if over one-quarter of its complement managed to desert or continually 'shirk' without raising some comment in the letters and diaries of officers.[111] Curiously, however, commanders' writings hardly mention either phenomenon during the Allied counterattacks: while Crown Prince Rupprecht, for example, expressed concern about his men's intense fatigue and increasing tendency to panic, worry about absconders only creeps into his diary from mid-October.[112] *Generaloberst* von Einem was similarly anxious about the condition of the army, yet primarily because of its substantial prisoner losses: 'if this continues, the German army will die of exhaustion', he wrote. 'No war can be won with men who give themselves up.' Like Rupprecht, however, only in the very last weeks of the conflict does he mention shirkers and deserters as a problem.[113] Statistics for *unerlaubte Entfernung* in his *3. Armee* indicate that there was, indeed, little cause for

[110] Reichsarchiv, *Weltkrieg*, XIV, p. 612, *Military Effort*, p. 632 and Altrichter, *Seelischen Kräfte*, p. 157. These figures are by necessity approximate and contain some minor discrepancies. Thus, for example, contrary to the *Reichsarchiv* figure of 123,600 German prisoners captured by British forces during August and September 1918, British statistics give the slightly lower figure of 118,190 men.

[111] *Sanitätsbericht III*, p. 6*.

[112] Rupprecht von Bayern, *Kriegstagebuch*, II, pp. 459 (entry for 12 Oct. 1918) and 468 (entry for 28 Oct. 1918), both referring to shirkers or deserters. For panics and exhaustion, see ibid., pp. 441–2 (entry for 5 Sept. 1918), 452 (entry for 29 Sept. 1918) and 465 (entry for 23 Oct. 1918).

[113] Von Einem, *Armeeführer*, pp. 434–5 (letter of 14 Sept. 1918). For other evidence of von Einem's concern about the heavy prisoner losses, see ibid., pp. 428–9 (letters of 23 and 31 Aug. 1918). For indiscipline and shirking, see pp. 451 (letter of 15 Oct. 1918) and 460 (entry for 2 Nov. 1918). The former entry is a vague reference to loosened discipline but the latter does refer more specially to large numbers of soldiers circulating in the rear areas outside military supervision.

concern: in the whole force, which contained over 200,000 men, only 79 cases were registered in September and a further 162 in October.[114] Such figures also agree with impressions gleaned from the sample of junior officers' letters and diaries examined for this study, in which references to men deserting or continually shirking during the Allied counteroffensive are universally absent. In contrast, a report issued in late September by the Acting General Staff in Berlin did remark on an increase in the number of men going AWOL in the operational area, yet, suspiciously, it also observed that the number of deserters apprehended on leave trains had noticeably decreased.[115] The report explained this discrepancy away by stating that the numbers of men on the trains made identity checks difficult, but Christoph Jahr's research suggests another explanation. Having examined the collection points set up to gather shirkers and stragglers, he argues that although the German retreat caused some disorganisation, only in the last three or four weeks of the war is there evidence of large numbers wandering in the army's rear areas.[116] Supporting his results is also the fact that it was not until the beginning of October, once the issue of the German Peace Note made clear that an armistice was imminent, that *OHL* found it necessary to reinforce the military police with five cavalry squadrons.[117] It would thus seem more likely that the real reason for the failure of the Railway Police to apprehend the expected number of deserters was simply that they did not exist. 'Shirking' and deserting were not so 'covert' that they could escape the notice of experienced company NCOs, officers or even the *OHL*, as witnessed by the fact that most evidence on manifestations of 'shirking' derives from divisional and army orders countering it.[118] Although the mobile warfare and retreat of the last months of 1918 caused confusion and disrupted military cohesion, not until after the October Peace Note does it appear that the German army's disciplinary mechanisms ceased to function.

If 'shirking' did have an effect on the combat efficiency of the German army, it was not as an 'overt' or 'covert strike' which threatened to pull apart the force by intentional and calculated indiscipline but rather as a deepening apathy which came about due to soldiers' intense fatigue. This was no new phenomenon; 'swinging the lead', as 'shirking' was

[114] See Lipp, *Meinungslenkung*, p. 147, note 236. The strength of *3. Armee* in July 1918 (the last figures available) was 241,154 men. See *Sanitätsbericht III*, p. 6*.

[115] HStA Dresden 11352 Stellv. Gen.-Kdo XIX AK KA(P) 24140: Report issued by the *stellvertretenden Generalstab der Armee, Abteilung IIIb*, 23 Sept. 1918.

[116] Jahr, *Gewöhnliche Soldaten*, pp. 166–7.

[117] Cron, *Imperial German Army*, p. 229.

[118] See above and also Deist 'Military Collapse', 201–4, particularly footnotes. Much of Deist's evidence comes from generals' diaries and memoirs.

colloquially referred to in the British army, had been practised by tired and lazy soldiers on all sides throughout the war. Most such behaviour was extremely temporary and a man who 'shirked' once could, if given rest and good leadership, become a fine fighter. However, the inability of the *OHL* to provide its troops with adequate respite from battle in the second half of 1918 inevitably brought about rising exhaustion and a corresponding decline in combat motivation throughout the army. Officers noted that fatigue had left their men demoralised and that they had little wish to fight on: 'our men [are] mostly rather timid', wrote *Leutnant* Müller, for example, at the beginning of October. 'If no officer is present, they quickly go back.'[119] So intense was soldiers' fatigue during the summer and autumn of 1918 that it not only lowered their willingness and ability to fight but probably also inhibited dissent and indiscipline. Although resentment against the Kaiser's army and state was felt by some troops, constant fighting and long periods in the line meant that they had neither the time nor the energy to organise mutinies. The heavy casualties inflicted by the Allies during both the spring offensive and the autumn counteroffensive undermined the primary group solidarity which was a precondition of group indiscipline. Large drafts of men, such as those received by the *241. Division*, were given little chance to get to know veterans or each other but were thrown straight into combat. Most importantly, as contemporaries observed, apathy and indifference, not anger and defiance, were the main emotions generated by exhaustion. Until the German Peace Note in October, most soldiers doubted that their own leaders would terminate the conflict, as witnessed by their cynical reaction to the earlier Austrian peace offer. Some, as has already been noted, looked to the Allies to bring about a quick end to hostilities. Few appear to have considered the possibility that they themselves could play a part in finishing it. Their long submission to the state of war and the extreme exhaustion brought about by constant combat and little rest militated against such thoughts. In many units a kind of 'learned helplessness' set in: as one soldier observed in September 1918, 'Humanity is so zombified, smitten and suppressed by the war that it feels too weak to do anything against it.'[120]

The different form the collapse at the front could have taken had troops been less exhausted and the army's disciplinary organisation destroyed is shown by an examination of the one place where insubordination and disorder were widespread in 1918: the lines of

[119] Staatsbib. Berlin, Ms. Germ. fol. 1651: C.F. Müller, diary, 6 Oct. 1918. Cf. also his comments on 19 Oct., 22 Oct. and 2–3 Nov. 1918.

[120] BA-MA Freiburg, W-10/ 50794: Postüberwachung der *5. Armee*, 28 Sept. 1918, p. 105.

communication. Particularly problematic was the situation on troop transports, where, as Deist rightly pointed out, desertion did become endemic. Already in the autumn of 1917, it had not been uncommon for troop transports from Russia to arrive on the Western Front having lost 10 per cent of their strength *en route*, and by late May 1918, according to the army group commander, Crown Prince Rupprecht of Bavaria, the proportion of men missing was often as high as 20 per cent.[121] During the summer and autumn of 1918, this behaviour spread to fresh drafts being sent to the Field Army from Germany. Assuming that desertion among these men was similar to that encountered on transports from Russia, then it is possible that in the final five months of the war between 130,000 and 180,000 men absconded from trains travelling to the front.[122] Although it is worth noting that 80 per cent of reinforcements did choose to remain on the transports and were absorbed into combat units, this nonetheless represented a serious loss for an army which was already in the middle of a manpower crisis. Moreover, far from simply being, in Deist's phrase, a 'covert strike' against the war, men on the transports not only deserted but openly challenged authority, doing everything possible to draw attention to their disillusionment with the war and reluctance to fight. As Walter Giffenig, the former Chief of Staff in the Seventh Military District, remembered, their behaviour was highly disruptive whenever their troop train halted at a station:

> Then the train emptied quickly and about 500 people poured noisily into the waiting room. It soon became routine that in the darkness they raged and shouted. The provocative call 'light out! Knife out! Let him have it!' soon became habit. If the signal to re-entrain was given, hardly anyone took any notice. Gradually the practice was developed whereby the train very slowly started up. Only then did the waiting rooms empty more or less quickly, and when everyone had climbed in, the train accelerated.[123]

[121] R. Bessel, 'Die Heimkehr der Soldaten. Das Bild der Frontsoldaten in der Offentlichkeit der Weimarer Republik', in G. Hirschfeld, G. Krumeich and I. Renz (eds.), *Keiner fühlt sich hier mehr als Mensch . . . Erlebnis und Wirkung des Ersten Weltkriegs* (Essen: Klartext, 1993), p. 225 and Rupprecht von Bayern, *Kriegstagebuch*, II, p. 402.

[122] These estimates have been extrapolated from figures in Herwig, *First World War*, p. 422. The lower estimate represents 20 per cent of the 300,000-strong cohort of 1900 added to the same percentage of the 70,000 convalescents returned to the army each month. The upper estimate also takes into consideration a further 197,200 men transferred from rear-echelon and home units who may or may not have used the transports. For desertion from transports carrying fresh troops, see Deist, 'Military Collapse', 201 and Rupprecht von Bayern, *Kriegstagebuch*, III, pp. 29–30.

[123] BA-MA Freiburg, PH 7/ 2: Report of W. Giffenig (former *Chef des Stabes des stellvertretenden Generalkommandos VII. AK*), written in 1922 and then, after the original was destroyed with the *Heeresarchiv* in April 1945, again in 1952 at the request of the *Bundesarchiv*.

Such behaviour was relatively restrained compared to incidents which took place in other military districts. In one case, 500 troops under the jurisdiction of the Eleventh Military District had to be disarmed before departure to the front and escorted to the station. When their weapons were returned, they opened fire on the platform. Fifty deserted from the station and a further twenty-five disappeared during the journey. Similarly, a relief column in the Eighth Military District was able to delay its departure by one day in mid-August by mutinying and threatening to shoot *Landsturm* troops who attempted to interfere.[124] During such altercations, officers were not only verbally abused but in some cases assaulted and injured: as an order issued in late July by the Prussian War Ministry complained, 'in many cases, it has come to open resistance and violent attacks on superiors'.[125]

In his memoirs, Ludendorff asserted that soldiers of the 1919 class conscripted into the army at the end of the war had been subject to 'secret agitation' at home, thus implying that these men, not loyal veterans, were responsible for the indiscipline.[126] Although no direct evidence regarding the ringleaders of the troop transport rioting exists, such a scenario appears highly unlikely. An examination of reports collected in August 1918 from units in the First Bavarian Military District clearly demonstrates that in the summer of 1918, inexperienced recruits were far better disposed towards service on the Western Front than veterans who had already fought there. Among the twenty-four training units which submitted information on soldiers' morale, ten reported negative findings but no less than fourteen stated that morale was satisfactory or good. In contrast, four of the regions' five hospitals expressed concerns about patients' morale and the fifth remarked only that in its wards the atmosphere was 'not bad'.[127] Moreover, a number of training units specifically noted that while young, untried troops were usually receptive to propaganda, older veterans were openly demoralised and presented their inexperienced comrades with a poor example to follow. As the *Vertrauensmann* of *Landsturm-Infanterie-Ersatz-Bataillon I* found, '[the] old, in part

124 These examples are taken from *Why Germany Capitulated*, pp. 54–5.

125 HStA Stuttgart, M 38/ 17 Bü 5, Blatt 53: Order of *Kriegsministerium* of 22 July 1918, reissued by *württ. 26. Infanterie-Division* entitled 'Disziplinlosigkeiten bei Ersatztransporten', dated 20 Aug. 1918. Cf. ibid., Bü 8, Blatt 34 for the original order.

126 Ludendorff, *War Memories*, II, p. 586.

127 HStA Munich/IV, Stellv. Gen.-Kdo I b.AK, 1980: Monatsberichte der Vertrauensleute, Aug. 1918.

already front-experienced men, have a disquieting effect on younger elements eager for action'.[128]

It is thus highly probable that disgruntled veterans, not allegedly Bolshevik recruits, were primarily responsible for the disorder on the railways. The contrast between their overt insubordination on the lines of communication and the passivity and obedience they displayed when actually in the battle zone can only be ascribed to the very different conditions present in each of these areas. Soldiers travelling to the front by rail were still safe, fresh and found themselves in what Ziemann has referred to as a weak link in the disciplinary and surveillance organisation of the German army.[129] The length of the trains, which often carried more than 1,000 soldiers, made them difficult to police and the escorts provided were usually inadequate. Often, men were accompanied by officers whom they did not know and for whom they had little respect. While the trains were in Germany, desertion remained far easier than it was in the battle zone, where controls were tighter and the land and language foreign. Moreover, mutiny and desertion on the transports were less risky than at the front, because until the regulations changed at the end of the war, troops on them were not considered *mobil* (i.e. not yet on active service), with the result that the authorities were unable to use their harshest punishments as deterrents.[130] In contrast, once in the area of operations disobedience ceased because men were closely supervised by officers, NCOs and Military Police, liable to face heavy penalties for insubordination, directly threatened by enemy action and were usually too tired, apathetic and isolated to mutiny or protest.

Thus, neither a 'covert strike' nor massive overt disobedience or revolution took place at the front in late 1918. Until the October Peace Note, discipline, exhaustion and apathy combined to ensure that the German army maintained its cohesion. 'Shirking', in its broadest sense, certainly did increase, but not so much through defiance as fatigue.

128 Ibid., report from the *Ersatz-Batl. Landsturm-Inf. I.*, 26 Aug. 1918. Cf. also those from *Ersatz-Batl. Landwehr Inf. Rgt Nr. 12*, 27 Aug. 1918, *2 Ersatz-Abt. Bayr. 1. Feldart-Regt*, 28 Aug. 1918 and *k.9. Feldart.-Regiment*, 27 Aug. 1918 and HStA Dresden, 11348 Stellv. Gen.-Kdo XII AK KA(P) 12888, Bl. 34: Report by *Leutnant* Oehme of the *II. Ersatz-Bataillon, Reserve-Infanterie-Regiment 102*, 13 June 1918.

129 Ziemann, 'Verweigerungsformen', p. 119.

130 For punishments see Jahr, *Gewöhnliche Soldaten*, p. 162. For an explanation of why transport trains were particularly attractive as places in which to protest and mutiny see HStA Stuttgart, M38/ 17 Bü 5, Blatt 53: Order of *Kriegsministerium* of 22 July 1918, reissued by *württ. 26. Infanterie-Division* entitled 'Disziplinlosigkeiten bei Ersatztransporten', dated 20 Aug. 1918 and Altrichter, *Seelischen Kräfte*, pp. 120–3.

Desertion and absence without leave also became more common, as men took advantage of the disorder caused by the retreat to abscond. Yet, as the figures for 'missing and prisoners' prove, until the very end of the war the number of soldiers committing these crimes at the front remained modest. Only on the lines of communication did overt anti-war protest and mass desertion take place during the summer of 1918, primarily because conditions there were very different from those in the battle zone. The soldiers who absconded from the transports perhaps numbered nearly 200,000 men in total and represented a very serious loss for an army fighting against a vastly superior enemy. Yet they alone were not decisive in the German army's defeat on the Western Front. Rather, in order to understand the military collapse at the front in the summer and autumn of 1918, it is necessary to investigate further the manifestations of decreased combat efficiency displayed by those soldiers actually manning the line. In particular, the mass surrenders which were such a feature of the final Allied advance require closer inspection.

Surrender at the front: an 'ordered surrender'?

Exhaustion and disillusionment did not result in the disintegration of the German army by a process of protest and revolt but rather caused its demise by sponsoring a gradual decline in its combat efficiency. Already at the beginning of the Allied counteroffensive in mid-July, apathy and indifference characterised the mood of the German army and, as the example of the *241. Division* shows, had an important effect on units' ability to resist attack. As has been argued, until October disobedience and desertion remained at a relatively low level. Indeed, judging from British intelligence reports, the number of mutinies taking place in combat units may actually have declined from a high point in mid-summer 1918. The beginning of the Allied counteroffensive not only increased the level of fatigue on the German side of the lines, making protest against the war impossible, but it also made it unnecessary. Rather than attempting to alleviate or escape the strain of war by active disobedience, many combat troops saw their salvation in passively awaiting an enemy advance and then giving themselves up without resistance. Soldiers surrendering to the British, who had numbered 142,217 men in the four years of war before the Amiens Offensive, totalled 186,053 men in the final three months of fighting before the armistice (see Figure 5); 385,000 German soldiers surrendered to the Allies along the entire Western Front between 18 July and 11 November, of whom the majority were irreplaceable combat veterans, not new recruits, poorly trained rear-line troops or imperfectly healed

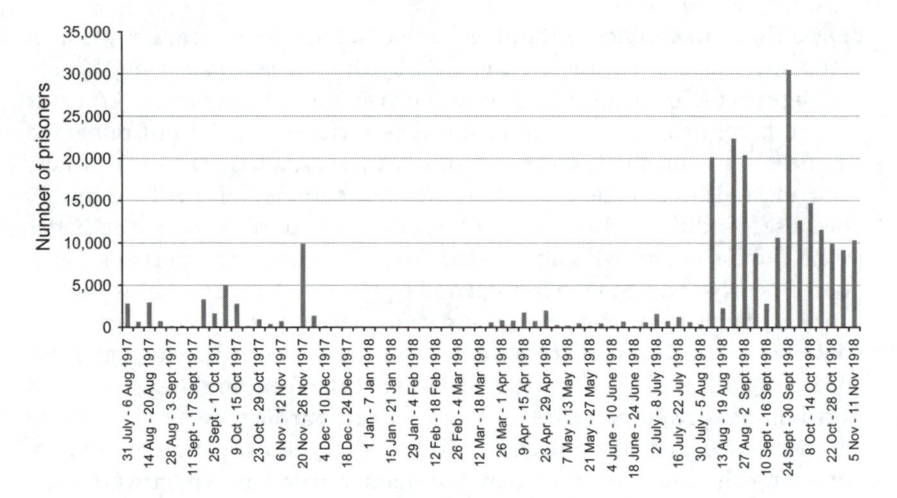

Figure 5. *German prisoners captured weekly in the British sector of the Western Front, 31 July 1917–11 November 1918*
Source: *Military Effort*, p. 632

wounded deserting on the railways.[131] Niall Ferguson is surely correct to argue that 'surrender was the key to the outcome of the First World War'.[132]

The nearly 400,000 men who surrendered represented only the most obvious and permanent expression of poor combat motivation. In the front line, 'shirking' could take the form of group action, as whole units simply retreated in the face of the oncoming enemy, without making serious attempts at battle. Ludendorff himself noted on 24 October 1918, 'according to the existing reports there is no doubt that numerous divisions no longer stood firm'.[133] Lower-ranking officers also blamed the loss of spirit among their troops for the constant retreat rather than superior Allied resources or tactics: as the staff officer Helmuth Fuchs noted in early October, 'the Englishman is also exhausted. He is still advancing only there where he finds no resistance. These places are unfortunately common as the skeletons of the divisions no longer fill out the front and the exhausted men frequently no longer hold.'[134] *Leutnant* Ahrend, whose field artillery battery was overrun by British infantry at

[131] Altrichter, *Seelischen Kräfte*, p. 157.
[132] Ferguson, 'Prisoner Taking and Prisoner Killing', 155 and Ferguson, *Pity*, pp. 367–8.
[133] HStA Dresden, *Militärbevollmächtigter* Nr. 4216, Bl. 114–15: Report of the Saxon *Militärbevollmächtigter* to the War Minister of a speech given by *General* Ludendorff, 24 Oct. 1918.
[134] BA-MA Freiburg, MSg 1/ 2968: H. Fuchs, diary, 10. Oct. 1918.

the end of the war, reached a similar conclusion, complaining to his parents, 'our "heroic" infantry no longer hold. Unfortunately! For the Englishman is cowardly. He only attacks when he finds no resistance.'[135]

Often, however, Allied tactics made rearward movement impossible. Improvements in British assault techniques were, as Paddy Griffith and Gary Sheffield have shown, undoubtedly partially responsible for the advances and large prisoner hauls made at the end of the war.[136] Allied attacks in the final phase of the conflict tended to combine an overwhelming artillery barrage with a quick infantry advance, which left German troops sheltering in deep dugouts little opportunity to reach the surface to repel them. *Generalleutnant* Fortmüller of the *241. Division* observed that, 'in a major enemy attack with a dense swath of fire, mass deployment of storm infantry with tanks and smoke screening, our own forward infantry mostly almost totally becomes the booty of the enemy, if, as it were, with one jump the enemy can penetrate our forward infantry'.[137] Sometimes, a curtain of fire placed directly behind the German lines made escape to the rear impossible, which often left soldiers with little choice other than to fight against overwhelming odds or surrender.[138] Once the initial penetration had succeeded, the subsequent advance was also conducive to prisoner taking because it often trapped Germans behind Allied lines. Fritz Schmidt, serving as a field telephone operator in *Grenadier-Regiment Nr. 6*, had exactly this experience when his section was buried by a shell during the American attack on the St Mihiel Salient on 12 September. When he and his comrades dug themselves out, they found themselves surrounded by French and American reserve and artillery troops.[139]

Nonetheless, the main reason for the quick advance and large number of captures made by the Allies at the end of the war was the psychological incapacity of troops in the Kaiser's army to resist the superior forces arrayed against them. By early October, British intelligence was reporting cases of severe panic, in which German troops had simply fled before attacking tanks and infantry.[140] Ahrend himself had the unpleasant experience of being abandoned by his men when he had wanted to stand

[135] BA-MA Freiburg, MSg 2/ 1291: E. Ahrend, 'Die letzte Schlacht', letter to parents, p. 13, 6 Nov. 1918.

[136] See Griffith, *Battle Tactics*, pp. 93–100 and Sheffield, *Forgotten Victory*, pp. 198–220.

[137] HStA Dresden, *Militärbevollmächtigter* Nr. 4216, Bl. 72: Report of *Generalleutnant* Fortmüller, 7 Oct. 1918.

[138] Altrichter, *Seelischen Kräfte*, p. 156.

[139] DTA, 259: F. Schmidt, 'Erinnerungen aus meinem Leben', memoir written *c.* 1920, pp. 76–8.

[140] TNA, WO 157/ 199: Summary of Information, No. 289 (Fourth Army), 3 Oct. 1918, p. 7. Cf. Rupprecht von Bayern, *Kriegstagebuch*, II, pp. 441–2 (entry for 5 Sept. 1918).

Plate 19. Prisoners (2): captured German soldiers, 28 September 1918. Compare the relieved expressions of many of these men with the glumness of British troops captured earlier in the year. Official British photograph.

firm against an overwhelming British attack.[141] Refusal to fight was by no means always spontaneous: already by the end of August, letters indicating intentions to desert to the enemy had multiplied to 'a frightening level', according to the censor of the *5. Armee*.[142] Around the same time, rumours were circulating that large numbers of men had deserted to the enemy and men on leave were openly boasting of their intention to do so. As one letter from an outraged member of the public recounted, one such soldier had stated that, 'as soon as it began again, he and his friends would desert to the enemy; then everything would be over and they would then at least get something to eat, for the French had, as they had experienced, food in abundance'.[143] By early September, troops

[141] BA-MA Freiburg, MSg 2/ 1291: E. Ahrend, 'Die letzte Schlacht', letter to parents, p. 6, 6 Nov. 1918.

[142] BA-MA Freiburg, W-10/ 50794: Postüberwachung der *5. Armee*, 31 Aug. 1918, pp. 77–8.

[143] HStA Dresden, 11352 Stellv. Gen.-Kdo XIX AK KA(P) 24170, Bl. 145: Letter of R. Peyke to *Kriegsminister*, 23 Aug. 1918.

about to be sent to the front were actively seeking information on the safest method by which to surrender. An ex-prisoner of war sent to give a lecture to a battalion in Baden on the hardships of French captivity was pleased at the interest his talk had excited but concerned that 'the inquiries and formulation of the questions of quite a number of comrades after the talk could scarcely leave any doubt that these men sought to find out how one could best manage inconspicuously and safely to be taken prisoner'.[144] Even British intelligence was unconvinced that improved tactics were the main cause of German surrenders. A report of 23 September expressed scepticism at German prisoners' claims that they had been surprised by Allied infantry, noting that 'although orders have been to "stand to" during the hours of dawn, most men were captured either half asleep or down in dugouts. With both NCO's [*sic*] and men, our artillery barrage is quite sufficient excuse for not manning rifles or machine guns.'[145] In some instances, large numbers of troops surrendered to trivial Allied forces: for example, eighty armed men of the *237. Division* surrendered to four French soldiers in August 1918. In September 1918, Brigadier-General E.A. Wood of the 55th Brigade, 18th Division was able to force more than twenty German soldiers to surrender to him, simply by throwing chalk and old boots at them.[146]

Despite the apathy and exhaustion among German other ranks and the improved Allied tactics, surrender nonetheless remained a highly risky course of action on the Western Front. Front-line soldiers knew that men who attempted to give themselves up to the enemy were by no means always welcomed. Schmidt recorded that when his unit had discovered that it was surrounded at St Mihiel, near panic broke out among his comrades. A decision was deferred for twenty-four hours, during which time the soldiers hid in their dugout, but eventually 'the agonising uncertainty' became too much to bear and the section's *Feldwebel* suggested that they surrender. All of the men knew the danger involved in attracting the French and American troops surrounding them and none wished to be the one to wave a dirty handkerchief bound to a stick, so that ultimately the matter had to be settled by drawing straws. The French troops who came in response clearly matched the Germans'

144 GLA Karlsruhe, 456 F 8 /106, Bl. 444: 'Stimmung der Truppe', 11 Sept. 1918.

145 TNA, WO 157/ 198: Summary of Information, No. 279 (Fourth Army), 23 Sept. 1918, p. 5. Cf. the behaviour of troops in the *21. Division* and the German 75th MG Marksman Detachment cited in TNA, WO 157/ 199: Summary of Information, No. 289 (Fourth Army), 3 Oct. 1918, p. 7.

146 See, respectively, United States War Office, *Histories*, p. 730 and P. Simkins, 'The War Experience of a Typical Kitchener Division. The 18th Division, 1914–1918', in H. Cecil and P.H. Liddle (eds.), *Facing Armageddon. The First World War Experienced* (London: Leo Cooper, 1996), p. 304.

apprehension with distrust of their own, for they advanced in combat formation and halted 50 metres away, well out of grenade range, while an officer and two men went forward and disarmed the prisoners. Schmidt and his comrades were fortunate: although passing Americans insulted them and pricked them with bayonets, the French soldiers who had captured them treated them kindly. Schmidt was surprised and grateful to be given white bread, a tin of sardines and a mug of wine by one of his captors. His memoir, written two years after the event, emphasises that 'the French front soldier was also a comrade to his enemies'.[147]

The French soldiers who handled Schmidt and his comrades well were surely more sensible than the Americans who threatened them and poked them with bayonets. As Ferguson has observed, 'no matter how hopeless their situation, German soldiers still had to feel they could risk surrendering before the war could end. And that meant that Allied soldiers had to be ready to take prisoners, rather than kill surrenderers.'[148] Ferguson suggests that the major propaganda campaign conducted by the Allies at the end of the war played an important part in encouraging German soldiers that surrender was a safe course of action.[149] Millions of leaflets extolling the virtues of captivity were dropped over German lines. Some stated baldly, 'the English do not kill prisoners', while others extolled the good rations and excellent treatment given to those taken captive.[150] Certainly, it appears that at the very least such propaganda proved highly demoralising, even for soldiers who remained sceptical of its honesty, as a passage from *Leutnant* Müller's diary shows:

> Here one is forever finding leaflets dropped by Tommy. Forged letters from German prisoners of war, who all write that it's very good there; much to eat, music, gymnastics festival etc. also among them are postcards with illustrations of well-clothed people, who are meant to portray prisoners. One album on German prisoner camps in England that one is always finding has illustrated on its title page a strapping rifleman, a real, fat Mecklenburger, who is emptying his mess tin. – And that while we here often have to starve.[151]

The Americans, in particular, favoured this type of propaganda, dropping more than 1 million copies of a 'prisoner leaflet', which contained an excerpt from the AEF's orders on prisoner treatment and appended a list

[147] DTA, 259: F. Schmidt, 'Erinnerungen aus meinem Leben', memoir written *c.* 1920, p. 79.
[148] Ferguson, 'Prisoner Taking and Prisoner Killing', 160.
[149] Ibid., 162–3.
[150] G.G. Bruntz, *Allied Propaganda and the Collapse of the German Empire in 1918* (Stanford University Press, 1938), p. 55.
[151] Staatsbib. Berlin, Ms. Germ. fol. 1651: C.F. Müller, diary, 30 Jan. 1918.

of rations issued to both American soldiers and those who surrendered to them.[152]

Although Ferguson is certainly correct to argue that 'such [propaganda] tactics ... surely did more to hasten the war's end than orders to "take no prisoners"', propaganda alone does not explain why Germans became more willing to surrender. Hungry farmers' sons or disaffected former industrial workers might well have believed what they read in Allied propaganda leaflets but it is clear that despite the millions of leaflets dropped over their lines, many soldiers retained a latent fear of captivity. One man, for example, whose letter was picked up by the German censor in October, acknowledged that the mood in the infantry was 'totally devastating' but explained that rather than surrender, they 'immediately go back, for all are frightened of being caught by the Americans, [in whose hands] prisoners do very badly and are mostly beaten to death or shot'.[153] Despite the German army's heavy losses, NCOs and officers were still present at the front and could themselves take direct action or otherwise report desertions to the enemy, for which punishment was extremely strict. By mid-1918, the penalty for this offence was death on return to Germany, loss of citizenship and the confiscation of property and belongings.[154]

Two possible explanations for why NCOs and officers did not stop surrenders taking place suggest themselves. The first is that after its heavy losses in the spring offensive, the German army's junior leadership was no longer capable of enforcing obedience from its men. Between March and July 1918, the German officer corps lost 5,602 of its members killed and significant numbers wounded and missing.[155] These losses in themselves do not appear to have fatally eroded its numerical strength, for, at least in the Bavarian army, statistics survive indicating that although there was a shortage of officers in the infantry in August 1918, the situation was less serious than it had been one year previously.[156] However, the heavy casualties did prompt the Chief of the General Staff to order regiments to set aside a cadre of junior leaders

152 Bruntz, *Allied Propaganda*, p. 111. For an example of a similar French leaflet see ibid., p. 108.

153 BA-MA Freiburg, W-10/ 50794: Postüberwachung der *5. Armee*, 17 Oct. 1918, pp. 114–15.

154 See the order issued by *Chef des Gen.Stabes des Feldheeres*, 25 June 1918, reproduced in Ulrich and Ziemann (eds.), *Frontalltag*, pp. 177–8.

155 *Sanitätsbericht III*, p. 132*.

156 Teicht, 'Offiziersausbildung', p. 122. In August 1917, the number of *Leutnants* serving with the Bavarian infantry was 904 instead of an authorised strength of 1,032. One year later their numbers had risen to 943 while the authorised strength remained unchanged.

before entering battle, in order to aid recovery in the event of heavy losses.[157] While a sensible decision in the longer term, this reduced the number of officers and NCOs at the front just at the time at which they were most urgently needed there. Still worse, those officers who were sent to replace the losses of the German offensives were not able to command the same respect possessed by their predecessors. Many, such as those transferred to the already mentioned *241. Division* in August, were *Landwehr* officers who had little experience of the western *Materialschlacht* at its worst and no wish to gain any. Many were fearful and resentful at being sent to active units: *Leutnant* Hans Muhsal, serving in the Vosges well away from the main action, recorded that the demand for volunteers to lead such units came as 'cold water on every joy' for himself and his fellow officers in *Landwehr-Infanterie-Regiment Nr. 119*.[158] The remaining replacement officers were young, inadequately trained *Kriegsoffiziere*, incapable of commanding the battle-hardened and war-weary veterans placed under them. Many, according to Altrichter, 'did not always understand or dare to take vigorous action with sufficient severity' and a variety of orders from the summer and autumn of 1918 testify to the frustration divisional COs felt at their new junior officers' failure to control their charges.[159] The men too were fully aware of the inadequacy of their leadership: prisoners of *19. Division* claimed that discipline had deteriorated because 'the NCO's [*sic*] who were being promoted were too much in sympathy with the men to have much authority, and the officers themselves were young, untrained and no longer respected as in the past'.[160] By the end of the year, the German high command had recognised this problem and was making desperate attempts to solve it. In October, Ludendorff even suggested that one-armed and other seriously disabled officers should be returned to the front, in the hope that their example would inspire the men to further feats of endurance.[161]

157 See BA-MA Freiburg, PH 3/ 455: Order from *Chef des Generalstabes des Feldheeres* entitled 'Angriffserfahrungen', 17 Apr. 1918 (p. 21 in folder) and also TNA, WO 157/ 197: Annexe to Fourth Army Summary, 13 Aug. 1918. This latter report cites captured documents showing that on 1 July 1918 *Infanterie-Regiment Nr. 15* detailed six officers and ninety-four NCOs as its leadership reserve.

158 BA-MA Freiburg, MSg 1/ 3109: H. Muhsal, diary, 4 June 1918.

159 Altrichter, *Seelischen Kräfte*, p. 152. For criticism of officers' grasp of authority, see the order issued by the CO of *41. Division* mentioned in United States War Office, *Histories*, p. 450 and also those of the *38.* and *10. Divisionen* and the *2. Garde-Reserve-Division* reproduced in *Why Germany Capitulated*, pp. 52–3.

160 TNA, WO 157/ 198: Summary of Information, No. 268 (Fourth Army), 12 Sept. 1918, p. 7.

161 HStA Dresden, *Militärbevollmächtigter* Nr. 4216, Bl. 115: Report of a speech by Ludendorff to the representatives of the *Militärbevollmächtigen*, 24 Oct. 1918.

The failure of junior officers to gain their men's respect may thus have resulted in the latter simply ignoring orders to fight and, instead, surrendering. Certainly, by October, some officers had lost control of their soldiers and doubted whether they could lead them in battle: one battalion commander in *24. Division*, for example, expressly stated to a superior that his men would not fire if attacked.[162] Particularly among poorer quality formations, the shock of enemy assault could lead to spontaneous disobedience and command collapse. One officer recounted how even shooting down ten of his subordinates had failed to stop them fleeing in panic. Another, serving with *Infanterie-Regiment Nr. 145*, himself took to his heels when his company, in disarray from a French surprise attack, ignored his orders to shoot and began to surrender to the troops overrunning them.[163] In other cases, desertion on the part of officers actually rendered disobedience superfluous: one entry in British intelligence files reports that three officers had abandoned their sleeping men and fled rearwards during an attack.[164] 'Shirking' also increased among the officer class. According to the Field Police Commissioner in charge of the Military Police post at Strassburg, 'the discontentedness of our soldiers is frequently traced back to the fact that many officers give a deficient example in exerting their full character. In the rear and administrative formations are said to be far too many officers; at the front, in contrast, too few.'[165]

Despite its plausibility, however, compelling evidence exists to reject the notion that command disintegration was the primary cause of the mass surrendering at the end of the war. As has already been observed, even in the second half of 1918 evidence of mutinies in combat units is scant. Hermann Cron concluded from his examination of the *Reichsarchiv*'s letter collection that inter-rank relations at the front remained good and British intelligence also believed that, despite heavy casualties and

[162] See the reported statement of a battalion commander in the *24. Division* in HStA Munich/IV, Gen.-Kdo I b.AK Bund 52 Akt 12: Report from *Generalkommando bayr. I AK* to *Armee-Oberkommando 18*, 29 Oct. 1918.

[163] See P. Gibbs, *Open Warfare. The Way to Victory* (London: William Heinemann, 1919), p. 377 and BA-MA Freiburg, W-10/ 50677: Letter of *Leutnant* Metzler, *6 Komp., I.R. 145*, probably Oct. 1918 (p. 1517 in file). Units rated third and fourth class by Allied intelligence generally surrendered with fewer officers than better formations, possibly indicating that they were more likely to experience command disintegration. See the table in A.A. Montgomery-Massingberd, *The Story of the Fourth Army in the Battles of the Hundred Days August 8th to November 11th 1918* (London: Hodder and Stoughton, 1920), p. 277.

[164] TNA, WO 157/ 199: Summary of Information, No. 289 (Fourth Army), 3 Oct. 1918, p. 5.

[165] HStA Stuttgart, M 30/ 1 Bü 49: Gerüchte und Stimmung. Wöchentliche Mitteilung No. 54, 8, from *Feldpolizeikommissar* Brand to *Abteilung IIIb, Oberkommando der Heeresgruppe Herzog Albrecht*, 19 Oct. 1918.

extreme stress, German officers had not lost control of their men at the end of the war. As one intelligence summary of late September noted, prisoners continued to acknowledge that their leaders could still make soldiers resist: 'the officers' word "MUST" is still the driving force'.[166] Moreover, extant prisoner statistics do not support the notion of large-scale mutinies or a widespread command deficit during the final Allied offensive. Among the 186,053 German soldiers captured by the British army between 6 August 1918 and the armistice on 11 November 1918 were 4,728 officers, meaning that officers and other ranks were surrendering in the ratio of one to thirty-eight. Unfortunately, no figures for the actual ratio of men to officers in late 1918 survive but, according to the German army's official medical history, the formal establishment (*Sollstärke*) of the Field Army in July 1918 was 135,619 combat officers and 5,115,849 men, which significantly translates as one officer to every thirty-eight other ranks. Had men been mutinying or officers deserting, the proportion of officers captured by the British should have been lower. The fact that the share of officers in the Field Army and their representation among prisoners was identical suggests a possibility hitherto neglected by historians: that in fact many front officers were leading their men into surrender.[167]

Narrative evidence also bears out this conclusion. By October 1918, Crown Prince Rupprecht was complaining that large units and officers had repeatedly surrendered themselves voluntarily.[168] The war correspondent Philip Gibbs saw what appeared to be a whole battalion march behind their officers into captivity after defending against an Australian attack.[169] Many commissioned leaders clearly viewed further bloodshed as pointless by the end of the war: one came over to the Allied lines in his smart 'peace clothes' while another admitted to Gibbs that he had 'advised his men to surrender ... if hard pressed'.[170] Unlike NCOs, who, as the example of Schmidt's *Feldwebel* demonstrates, were often reluctant to accept the full responsibility and undergo the risks of negotiating surrenders themselves, paternalistic officers sometimes went to extraordinary

[166] TNA, WO 157/ 198: Summary of Information, No. 279 (Fourth Army), 23 Sept. 1918, p. 5.

[167] See *Military Effort*, p. 632 and *Sanitätsbericht III*, p. 4*. The exact ratios between officers and other ranks in the Field Army and among prisoners were 1 to 37.72 and 1 to 38.35. The ratio of officers to men among prisoners captured between 6 August and 11 November was also marginally higher than the average for the entire war, in which 1 officer was captured to every 41.58 men. As the vast majority of medical and veterinary officers would have been well behind the lines and thus unable to surrender, I have excluded them from these calculations.

[168] Rupprecht von Bayern, *Kriegstagebuch*, III, p. 28 (letter to father dated 14 Oct. 1918).

[169] Gibbs, *Open Warfare*, pp. 384–5.

[170] Ibid., pp. 479 and 432.

Plate 20. Prisoners (3): captured German officers, 10 August 1918. The participation of demoralised and exhausted officers was an essential precondition for the mass surrenders at the war's end. Official Canadian photograph.

lengths to ensure their men's safety. One platoon commander, for example, actually went across no-man's-land to surrender and then requested permission to return to his position in order to fetch his men, who also wished to give themselves up.[171] The important role played by officers in the actual process of surrender does not, of course, exclude the possibility that their men were also able to pressure, or at least encourage, their leaders to take a particular course of action. In mid-October, Field Police were receiving reports that officers and men in war-weary Austrian units serving on the Western Front had agreed 'that they would allow themselves to be taken prisoner as soon as they come to the front' and it is not out of the question that similar arrangements were made between German

171 TNA, WO 157/ 199: Summary of Information, No. 287 (Fourth Army), 1 Oct. 1918, p. 7. This was not an isolated incident. For another, similar example, see Gibbs, *Open Warfare*, pp. 524–5.

soldiers and their leaders.[172] However, officers were crucial in making surrender a viable option for front soldiers as they vastly reduced the risks involved in the process. The presence of an officer bestowed some security on the men accompanying him, as his rank was likely to be respected by the enemy. Secondly, and still more importantly, officers had the authority to organise group surrenders, which made prisoner killing almost impossible; a rogue Allied soldier with a grudge might shoot or bayonet a lone prisoner but could not realistically murder an entire platoon or company. Far more than the promises of Allied propaganda, it was the presence of officers organising group capitulations which made surrender attractive to German soldiers in 1918.

A good example demonstrating the process of surrender – and officers' particular importance in it – at the end of the war is to be found in the memoir of Captain G.B. McKean of the 14/Canadian Infantry. At the beginning of September, McKean was ordered to take part in an offensive which was designed first to capture the line of strong fortifications known as the Wotan Switch and then advance to the Canal Du Nord. His battalion was designated as part of the second wave of attack, to be launched from the German support line. Due to an error, the attack began before McKean and his men were present. When they arrived at the front line, they found that the rest of the battalion had run into its own bombardment and was scattered. Nonetheless, having discovered a company commander with twenty men, McKean planned to attack his unit's objective, a village directly in front of them. An unlucky shell killed many of the men McKean had managed to gather and injured his fellow officer. McKean, himself wounded in the leg, detailed some soldiers to dress the wounded and with the remaining eight men moved towards the village. The subsequent events show the varying ways in which German troops acted according to the behaviour of their enemy and whether officers were present. McKean's first encounter with Germans was the discovery of a dugout situated in front of the village:

> I shouted down, and there was instantly a chorus of 'Kamerads' from the depths of it. I trifled with my German:
>
> 'Kommen Sie up hier or we'll shoot you verdamtt quick.'
>
> 'Ya! ya!' came back a chorus of agreement ...
>
> In a few seconds a German appeared and scrambled up the dug-out steps, trying his best to get a footing on the broken woodwork, and at the same time to keep his hands above his head in the approved style of the 'Kamerading' German. There was the bang of a rifle at my elbow and the Hun toppled backwards, and a chorus

[172] HStA Stuttgart, M 30/ 1 Bü 49: Report by *Feldpolizeibeamter* Hummel on morale in Austrian units on the Western Front, 18 Oct. 1918.

of shouts, shrieks and moans came from the assembled Huns below. I turned and saw a scout standing with a smoking rifle in his hand and a broad, expansive, satisfied smile on his face.

'Now you've done it,' I exclaimed angrily; 'we'll never get those Huns out of that dug-out in a blue moon now.'

Leaving the prisoner killer and another man with orders to persuade the remaining Germans out and not to use 'such harsh methods', McKean pushed on, cleared one more dugout himself and then left four men to take prisoner the Germans in three further shelters while he and two soldiers advanced on the village. In it were 'scores of scared-looking Huns', many of whom had probably straggled back after the first attack on the Switch. Certainly, from McKean's account, it appears that they were completely unorganised and did not have any officers with them. Faced with hordes of enemy soldiers, McKean decided to bluff and waved his arms and shouted, pretending that his battalion was behind him. He then charged the largest German soldier within his reach, who 'promptly turned, dropped his rifle, and ran for his life'. McKean continues:

This was the deciding act, the cue to the rest of the Huns. Their rifles clattered noisily as they threw them as far from them as they could, then scrambled out of the houses and 'footed' it for all they were worth! I was soon in the midst of a mob of fleeing Huns.

Catching the German whom he had originally charged, McKean threatened him with a revolver and then 'gave him a parting kick, and sent him scurrying back in the direction of our lines'. What then happened was an interesting demonstration of crowd psychology in action:

Seeing the tall one . . . running wildly back towards our lines, the majority of [the Germans] promptly turned round and followed him . . . At least fifty Huns went past us. Looking around I could see, at a distance, scores more of them making frantic efforts to get away.

McKean and his men now advanced, blocked off the panicking Germans' escape routes and directing them back towards British lines, after which, he estimated, there were at least 200 Germans fleeing behind them and a mob running in front of them. Following this mob, McKean turned a bend and came face to face with a German Captain standing at the entrance to a dugout. Significantly, far from trying to organise resistance this officer not only cooperated with McKean's demands but was actually proactive in helping him:

He smiled genially and pointed down the dug-out entrance. I looked down. It was too dark down there to see anything, but I heard the murmur of many excited voices. I motioned to the captain to bring them up. He assented with a smile, and very soon afterwards the Huns started trooping out. As each one came out I pointed up the road and gave him a good healthy kick, which none of them waited to have repeated. I had expected ten or twelve Huns to come up, but the number almost reached forty before the captain made a sign that they were all gone. He pointed to another dug-out a few yards further on.

'All right,' I said, 'shoot 'em up.'

He called down the dug-out, and very soon more Huns appeared. They all received the same impartial treatment . . .

Included amongst the prisoners were two officers who, in the excitement and exuberance of the moment, received the same undignified treatment. This dug-out yielded thirty more prisoners. The captain then indicated a third dug-out, smiling broadly all the time . . . He proceeded to persuade the occupants of the third dug-out to come out, and over forty of them filed past us . . . Altogether we collected well over one hundred prisoners from those three large dug-outs.[173]

McKean's experience raises a number of interesting points. Firstly, it is clear that deep dugouts played an important role in the German surrender; McKean himself described them as 'Fritz's undoing – he had stayed in them until invited by our men to come out and surrender'.[174] The dugouts offered German soldiers safety during the Allied bombardment and then made it impossible for them to resist when the enemy arrived. However, deep shelters had been used successfully at the Somme in 1916 and despite the considerable advances made by the Allies in tactics by 1918, it seems that the main reason shelters became traps was that the combat troops simply did not want to fight and stayed in them. Secondly, the account supports Ferguson's theory that prisoner killing was counterproductive: McKean's (largely) non-violent behaviour and corresponding success at capturing Germans contrasts sharply with the difficulties which his subordinate caused at the beginning of the attack by shooting a surrendering man. Thirdly, the behaviour of the stragglers shows both the effects of lack of formal leadership and the human need in times of stress for guidance: the tall German whom McKean singled out became the example to be copied by his compatriots. If the surrenders in the village demonstrate the horrific effects of what a leadership vacuum could do to a unit, then the second set of surrenders involving the Captain shows that by this time the junior leadership of the German army was also unwilling to continue fighting. By 1918, Captains were commanding battalions in the Germany army, so it seems unlikely that the officer encountered by McKean was lacking in military experience or

173 G.B. McKean, *Scouting Thrills* (London: Humphrey Milford and Oxford University Press, 1919), pp. 216–32. See also the similar account and excellent analysis of a mass German surrender in Ferguson, 'Prisoner Taking and Prisoner Killing', 160–2.

174 McKean, *Scouting Thrills*, p. 219.

training. Moreover, unlike the troops encountered in the village, the soldiers under the Captain's command were organised, with two further officers among them: as McKean was alone it does not seem unreasonable to suggest that the Germans and particularly the Captain he captured could have put up more resistance. Yet far from fighting, the Captain actively assisted in the surrender, pointing out the position of his dugouts and ordering his men to come to the surface and surrender.

Surrendering thus became more attractive to German soldiers in the late summer and autumn of 1918 due to a variety of factors. Intense exhaustion and depression combined to erode the army's combat motivation and make its troops apathetic. Surrender became easier due to the Allied advance: rather than having to brave the dangers of no-man's-land, would-be prisoners could simply wait for their trenches to be occupied by the enemy's assault troops. Barrages put down directly behind the lines and surprise attacks by overwhelmingly superior forces also combined to increase the number of men surrendering to Allied armies. The propaganda campaign certainly contributed to making surrender appear safer than it had been over the previous four years. In the last resort, however, it was the officers, whose presence and whose ability to organise group surrenders made that mode of exit from the war unprecedentedly safe, who made captivity a viable option for the majority of German soldiers. Thus, far from being left, in Ziemann's words, as an 'officer corps without troops' at the end of the war, many officers were intimately involved with and implicated in the disintegration of the German Field Army during the second half of 1918.[175] Rather than being a process based on protest and disobedience, the disintegration was characterised by apathy, indifference and fatalism among all ranks. Neither 'covert strike' nor overt mutiny marked the bankruptcy of the German war effort at the front; rather, the form disintegration took was foremost that of an ordered surrender.

The exhaustion and disillusionment caused by the failure of the German spring and early summer offensives, the increasingly apparent Allied material superiority and the unending operational demands made on combat troops resulted less in an attitude of anger and bitterness than in a rise in apathy and indifference. Disaffected national minorities, who had little interest in a German victory, become increasingly non-compliant to military demands from early in 1918. Among the German rank and file, despair took root once the prospects for their own side became ever more bleak after the failure of the first attacks to win decisive victory. Already by early summer, minor cases of disobedience

175 Ziemann, 'Enttäuschte Erwartungen', p. 165.

caused by intense exhaustion and disillusionment began to manifest themselves in front-line units. Officers, whose quality and numbers had declined due to their disproportionate losses in German attacks early in the year, shared in the general depression once the Allied counteroffensive began. The German army's ability to ward off the growing threat from the Entente decreased as combat motivation among fighting troops deteriorated. The Peace Note of 3 October set the seal on defeat, signalling the war's imminent end to the army's broken soldiers and giving rise to increased disobedience in its rear, thus catalysing the process of disintegration.

Contrary to the current historiographical consensus, disintegration at the front was not the result of widespread insubordination and indiscipline. Until the disorder sparked by the October Peace Note, mutinies at the front appear to have peaked in mid-summer 1918. Nor was there a 'covert strike' aimed at ending the war at the front. Desertion and long-term 'shirking' remained at numerically low levels until the last weeks of hostilities. Temporary 'shirking' should not be regarded as either an uncoordinated or a coordinated movement demanding peace but rather an expression of the intense fatigue felt by troops in autumn 1918. It was a manifestation of their need for rest and respite from the overwhelming demands of battle. Self-preservation, not political aims, occupied German soldiers in the front zone during late 1918; only behind the lines, in the troop transports, where men were fresher and discipline less tight, was anti-war protest visible and desertion high. Apathy and indifference in the trenches did not engender protest or revolt but rather inaction, a fatalistic attitude towards the war and a corresponding decline in combat motivation.

The decline in combat motivation provides the key to understanding how the German army broke down in 1918. Rather than resulting from active confrontation, like that which threatened the French and in more extreme form actually tore apart the Russian army in 1917, the German army's disintegration was first and foremost the product of apathetic indifference. As a comparison of German figures for missing and prisoners and Allied prisoner statistics reveals, surrenders, not desertions, were the major source of manpower loss apart from sickness and battle casualties in late 1918. Rather than confront their own military hierarchy covertly or overtly in order to escape the hardships of war, exhausted German soldiers simply waited for the advancing Allies to roll over them. Crucially, this was made possible by the complicity of front officers, whose quality and enthusiasm had declined over the course of the year so that by the autumn of 1918 their disillusionment and exhaustion equalled that of their men. By refusing to fight further for a lost cause, officers made mass surrenders possible, providing security for their men and organising entire groups to go into captivity. Neither an open revolution nor a 'covert strike' marked the demise of the German army in 1918. Rather, the fabric of the army and its position at the front crumbled due to exhaustion, apathy and mass surrender *led* by junior officers. Advocates of the 'Stab in the Back' theory after the war were correct to argue that, unlike on the home front, revolution never overtook the Kaiser's army. Its soldiers did indeed follow their orders to the end. Crucially, however, these orders were not to fight on; as the Allied superiority became clear and the Kaiser's cause increasingly hopeless, German soldiers followed their officers into captivity in a process which fatally weakened their army's front, destabilised its rear and ultimately hastened the end of the war.

Conclusion

This book set out to answer three questions: why did soldiers and armies in the First World War fight for such a long time? How were they able to cope psychologically with conditions at the front? And, finally, why did they eventually stop fighting? In order to answer these questions, it was necessary first to examine the conditions in which men operated, the fears they confronted and the resilience they demonstrated. The fighting on the Western Front between 1914 and 1918 subjected men to unprecedented levels of stress. This was not because it was bloodier than other wars, or more uncomfortable or more physically demanding. Rather, the intense strain experienced by soldiers at the front came about due to the extremely disempowering style of fighting there. Overwhelming artillery fire and the spatial restrictions of the trenches hindered men's 'fight or flight' instincts, leading to an intense sense of loss of control, which in turn generated emotionally wearing feelings of fear, anger and depression. Permanent and temporary exits were available from the trenches; soldiers no longer willing or able to withstand the pressures of combat could report sick, desert or, if with like-minded comrades, mutiny or 'strike'. Others found refuge from the front in psychiatric disorders, self-inflicted wounds or suicide. Curiously, however, given the extreme demands of front service and the long duration of the war, surprisingly few soldiers took advantage of these exits. Contrary to the impression given by some historiography, resilience not collapse was the norm among men on the Western Front.

At the root of this robustness lay a combination of societal influences, military factors and human psychological defence mechanisms. Societal factors are important in explaining why men fought for so long. Combat motivation was based on fear and distrust of the enemy. Germans rushed to obey mobilisation orders or volunteer when war began in August 1914 because they believed that their country was under threat of invasion. The extent of volunteering in Britain also leaves no room for doubt about its inhabitants' readiness to fight in 1914. Like the Germans, Britons enlisted because they feared the consequences of an enemy victory on their country, homes and, above all, loved ones. Despite the disenchantment with their governments and anger against civilians which grew among combatants on both sides, this motivation never left the majority. Patriotic and idealistic language may have receded gradually during the conflict (although it certainly never disappeared altogether, particularly among officers), but however much soldiers wished for peace, fear of the consequences of defeat for themselves and their families left them no option other than to fight on.

Three other factors supported this continued combat readiness. Firstly, on entering their national armies, soldiers were inculcated with obedience and encouraged to develop new military loyalties towards their leaders, units and comrades. The majority, motivated to defend their home communities, accepted the army as a 'legitimate authority' for the war's duration and were correspondingly receptive to this socialisation. Those few reluctant to serve were carried along by peer pressure and fear of punishment. Secondly, active service, contrary to the beliefs of some historians, did not lead to pacifism or liking for the enemy. Respect was certainly felt on both sides for martial prowess but the experience of being shot at did nothing to convince a soldier that he had little to fear from an enemy invasion. Prisoner killing and rumours of battlefield atrocities both strengthened men's identification with their comrades and countrymen, and encouraged distrust or even inflamed hatred against the enemy. Finally, the innate tendency of men to interpret information in accordance with pre-existing beliefs also strengthened combat motivation. This was probably particularly strong in the trenches, where the unattractiveness of all alternatives meant that soldiers had every reason to embrace justifications for continuing the fighting. Propaganda naturally reinforced these views, yet its effectiveness was undoubtedly enhanced by the fact that its listeners were themselves eager to see meaning in the war.

The key to surviving death and disempowerment at the front psychologically and physically lay in assessing risk optimally. Soldiers new to the line who ignored immediate threats out of bravado or ignorance often wantonly sacrificed their lives. Veterans who had been at the front too long either became numbed to risk, apathetic and were also liable to be killed unnecessarily or alternatively developed such intense feelings of fear that they suffered mental breakdown or deliberately sought death as a release. On both sides of the line, men thus survived mentally the terrifying conditions of the Western Front by failing to view them objectively. In the face of danger and discomfort, they consistently refused to accept that they as individuals could be killed. Statistical fallacies and misguided assumptions were used to 'prove' the correctness of this conclusion. The universal tendency to ignore cumulative risk and focus only on the short-term placed the chances of survival in an artificially positive light. Personal control was also overestimated, with the result that many soldiers asserted confidently that they could dodge shellfire and avoid danger. For most, religion or superstition lent sense and meaning to the chaotic environment and offered an opportunity of imposing order on it. The human capacity for hope, optimism and, not least, self-deception made the war subjectively less threatening and lent men peculiar powers of resilience.

While men may have been remarkably resilient, they still required leadership in order to make them militarily effective. Historians examining battlefield dynamics have underplayed the central role of junior officers in determining men's actions. In the chaos of the battlefield, these figures provided certainty and order. Behind the lines, they were supposed to act paternalistically, gaining men's trust and deference by ensuring that they were well looked after and rested. Most evidence indicates that British officers executed these duties better than their German counterparts; during 1916–18, a well-attested 'officer hate' (*Offiziershaß*) spread throughout the Kaiser's army. Partly this was caused by the corps' exaggerated concern for its aristocratic leadership principle, which, by placing unnecessary restrictions on recruitment, limited the number of officers at the front and distanced the corps from its subordinates. The young officers appointed during the war were overburdened with responsibility and thus had less time to care for each man's welfare than did commissioned leaders in the British army. Worse still, food shortages undermined inter-rank relations by making once established officers' privileges no longer acceptable to the rank and file. Theoretically, the 'officer hate' should have drastically undermined the combat efficiency of the German army. That this did not happen was largely because it was directed primarily against middle-ranking staff officers and rear-line unit commanders, not the junior combat officers who led men at the front. The inter-rank *Frontgemeinschaft* survived, a fact which in the medium term provided the army with the means to keep fighting but which contributed to its rapid collapse in 1918.

Ultimately, Hindenburg was incorrect in his belief that the nation which possessed the better nerves would win the war. Contrary to the claims of most historians, there was in fact little difference between the coping strategies, motivation and resilience of men in the German and British armies. Rather, it was the pressure exerted on those men by the enemy which proved decisive. Due to their material inferiority, the Germans remained permanently at a disadvantage in this respect; only superior operational doctrine and tactical advantage allowed them to stave off a defeat which became inevitable as soon as the Battle of the Marne had been lost in 1914. When they once more briefly achieved a material superiority in the west during the spring of 1918, their attack on the British was marked less by confidence than by desperation. Lacking transport, equipped inadequately and manned by hungry, war-weary soldiers, the German army had neither the material nor the psychological strength to smash the Allies. Well-fed and supplied British soldiers, reminded of their cause by the sight of refugees fleeing and towns devastated, maintained their cohesion in the face of the severe but temporary pressure and withstood the German attack.

The collapse of the German army in the second half of 1918 thus came about not because soldiers were politically radicalised or disobedient but primarily because they were too physically and mentally exhausted to continue fighting. Already by April 1918, the failure to defeat the British army had caused depression among many other ranks; the highly successful Allied attacks in July and August also convinced the majority of junior officers that the war was irretrievably lost. The exhaustion and dejection in the Germany army combined to create apathy, not anger. Indiscipline at the front was made impossible by the fatigue felt by the majority of combat soldiers and unnecessary due to the fact that officers, no less affected than their men, began to seek ways out of the conflagration. The conflict ended not by mass desertion or mutiny but principally by an ordered surrender, in which officers led their weary men into Allied captivity. Human resilience, not military discipline, had finally reached its limit.

Appendix 1

Walter Ludwig's study of Württemberg soldiers' coping strategies

Walter Ludwig's investigation of soldiers' coping strategies is probably the most sophisticated piece of psychological research to be undertaken on either side during the First World War. Ludwig served as an infantry officer on the Western Front, fought against British and French troops in the Vosges, the Argonne, the Somme and at Ypres and was wounded three times. He conducted his study, however, during two brief periods out of the line, while acting as a teaching officer at an officer training course and a teacher at a school for wounded. In total, 200 pupils were asked to write an essay entitled, 'Beobachtung aus dem Feld, an was der Soldat im Augenblick der höchsten Gefahr denkt, um die Furcht vor dem Tod zu überwinden' ('Observations from the field regarding what the soldier thinks in the moment of greatest danger in order to overcome the fear of death'). After the war, Ludwig analysed the essays by picking out the themes which he identified as most common and important and rating them for frequency. Personal statements on soldiers' own thoughts in danger were separated from general observations of how men acted or thought in danger. His results are reproduced in Table 4.

The results of Ludwig's study are not necessarily an entirely accurate reflection of German soldiers' coping strategies during the First World War. The presence of large numbers of officer cadets in the sample (the exact figure is not stated) indicates that the results were perhaps skewed by social or educational bias. Troops from regions outside Württemberg may have reported their experiences differently from Ludwig's soldiers. The lack of information about the ranks, religion and lengths of service of subjects and the limited data provided about their age also hinders any judgement of the sample's representativeness. Nonetheless, the size of the sample, the fact that all of the essay authors had participated in combat and the limited effect of social or cultural factors on coping

Table 4. *Results of Ludwig's study into Württemberg soldiers' coping strategies*

Coping strategies	Mentions (I)	Mentions (general)	Total	Position
Religious feelings	43	47	90	1
Memories of home	36	29	65	2
Social emotions	24	30	54	3
Fatalism	17	27	44	4
Consideration of the degree of possible unpleasantness	19	17	36	5
Indifference	15	18	33	6
Humour	10	20	30	7=
General hope	12	18	30	7=
Feelings of duty and honour	10	19	29	9
Feeling of activity and passivity	14	12	26	10
Combat emotions	7	14	21	11
Anaesthetising aids	8	12	20	12
Driving away of fear	10	8	18	13
Belief in invincibility	10	7	17	14
Recalling past life	9	7	16	15=
Discipline	3	13	16	15=
Fearlessness	10	5	15	17
Patriotism	2	9	11	18
Curiosity	4	6	10	19

Source: Translated and reproduced from Ludwig, 'Psychologie der Furcht', p. 172.

strategies (see chapter 3) suggests that despite possible biases, the study provides a good insight into how men coped with the danger, disempowerment and death of the trench fighting on the Western Front.[1]

[1] For background information on Ludwig and his study, see 'Psychologie der Furcht', pp. 128–30.

Appendix 2

Psychiatric casualties in the German and British armies

Any estimation of the psychiatric casualties suffered by the German and British armies during the First World War is fraught with difficulty due to contemporaries' categorisation and treatment of patients. Particularly in Britain, although also elsewhere, the dominant view within the medical profession before 1914 was that most mental disease had organic origins. Psychiatric illness was believed to be hereditary and caused by minute lesions in the brain. No intermediate state between sanity and insanity was recognised by English law.[1] When men began to suffer mental collapse in the trenches, doctors were thus poorly equipped to recognise and treat the psychological root of their problems. In 1914, the somatic symptoms displayed by many men were confusing and invited misdiagnosis. Some diseases resembling organic ailments continued to baffle doctors throughout the war. Functional cardiac disorders such as 'Disordered Action of the Heart' and 'Valvular Disease of the Heart' particularly concerned British medical authorities.[2] The German army was inflicted by a rash of digestive nervous disorders at Verdun in 1916.[3] On both sides in the last years of the war psychiatric patients were often misdiagnosed as gas casualties: after examining men allegedly suffering from mustard gas poisoning in 1918, Lord Moran argued that in most, 'the organic lesions were negligible or absent, it was the mind that had suffered hurt'.[4] The result of this confusion was that, as one psychiatrist observed, 'the true proportion which neurosis bore to the total

[1] Shephard, *War of Nerves*, p. 6 and T. Bogacz, 'War Neurosis and Cultural Change in England, 1914–1922. The Work of the War Office Committee of Enquiry into "Shell-Shock"', *Journal of Contemporary History* 24, 2 (April 1989), 229–30.

[2] See Medical Research Committee (ed.), *Report upon Soldiers Returned as Cases of 'Disordered Action of the Heart' (D.A.H.) or 'Valvular Disease of the Heart' (V.D.H.)* (London: HMSO, 1917).

[3] *Sanitätsbericht II*, p. 655.

[4] Moran, 'Wear and Tear', 1099–1100. Cf. J.S.Y. Rogers and A.B. Soltau in *RWOCIS*, pp. 63 and 74 respectively. Also Gaupp, 'Schreckneurosen', p. 71.

medical casualties of the War was vastly underestimated in official statistics'.[5]

Clouding the issue further was armies' tendency to consider psychiatric disorder as a disciplinary, rather than medical, issue. As the psychiatrist Robert Ahrenfeldt later observed, 'it appears to have been largely a matter of chance, and of individual outlook, whether a soldier suffering from a psychoneurotic breakdown was considered to be ill from "shell-shock", or to be a "malingerer" or deserter'.[6] Generally, however, the chances of the latter seem to have been highest at the beginning of the war in the British army. The former Medical Officer William Tyrrell asserted that 'the old Regular Army had a much fiercer way of looking upon anything approaching cowardice' than the New Army and many other contemporaries agreed.[7] Even as late as 1916, however, some men suffering from battle stress were executed for cowardice.[8] Although the German army shot fewer men than its British opponent, it nonetheless imprisoned rather than treated many of the so-called 'psychopaths' who committed military crimes.[9] The result is that some of the men who might under more enlightened regimes have been classified as psychiatric casualties instead appear in the disciplinary statistics of each army.

Despite these problems, official statistics nonetheless remain the best guide to the psychiatric casualties suffered by armies in the First World War. The official medical history of the German army shows that it treated 613,047 such cases between August 1914 and July 1918, or 4.58 per cent of the men who passed through the army during the war.[10] Figures for the British army are fragmentary. Statistics published in 1923 for 'Shell-shock, Wounded' indicate that 28,533 men fell into this category between September 1914 and December 1917.[11] More complete information was released in the 1931 official medical history. This contained statistics for 'nervous disorders' during the first year and a half of war and information on 'functional diseases of the nervous system' within

[5] E. Mapother in United Services Section with Section of Psychiatry, 'Discussion on Functional Nervous Disease', 859. Occasionally, however, ignorance and confusion could work the other way: J.W. Stock recorded a case in the autumn of 1915, in which a paralytic comrade was mistakenly diagnosed as a 'shellshock' casualty and evacuated to England. See IWM, 84/1/1: J.W. Stock, journal, autumn 1915.

[6] R.H. Ahrenfeldt, *Psychiatry in the British Army in the Second World War* (London: Routledge and Kegan Paul, 1958), p. 7.

[7] *RWOCIS*, p. 35. Cf. Shephard, *War of Nerves*, pp. 23–7.

[8] Corns and Hughes-Wilson, *Blindfold*, pp. 212–14.

[9] K. Bonhoeffer, 'Psychopathologische Erfahrungen und Lehren des Weltkriegs', *Münchener Medizinische Wochenschrift* 81, 31 (3 August 1934), 1213.

[10] *Sanitätsbericht III*, pp. 12, 145 and 42*–3*.

[11] *J&R*, p. 4.

Table 5. *Estimated psychiatric casualties and their percentage of German and British battle losses (physically wounded and mentally injured), 1914–18*

Casualties / period	1914	1915	1916	1917	1918
German 'Krankheiten des Nervengebiets' (KdN) (western Field Army)	14,184	53,801	63,461	57,099	39,004
British 'nervous disorders' (1916–18 adjusted)	1,906	20,327	50,849	37,476	33,346
Total British psychiatric casualties (1916–18 adjusted)	3,938	43,098	95,751	87,546	94,978
Percentage of 'KdN' among German battle casualties	3.67	9.88	8.46	9.29	5.60
Percentage of 'nervous' among British battle casualties	3.27	8.42	13.37	8.98	8.28
Percentage of psychiatric among British battle casualties	6.54	16.31	22.52	18.73	20.45

Sources: Sanitätsbericht III, pp. 42*–3* and 82*–5* and *Medical Services*, pp. 115, 123, 137, 277 and 298–9. 1914 refers only to the months August to December. The German 1918 figures refer only to the period January to July.

a sample of 1,043,653 casualties from 1916–20. Figures for 'mental diseases', 'debility' and 'functional diseases of the heart' were also included as separate categories. Table 5 displays (1) the only German psychiatric casualty figures available, (2) British statistics for 'nervous disorders' and 'functional diseases of the nervous system' adjusted up from the sample to give estimates for the total incidence of these cases in 1916–18 and (3) these British figures added to the other categories of psychiatric casualty recorded in the 1931 volume. It also shows the proportion of these casualties among the armies' total battle losses. Extrapolations from the data in the 1931 volume indicate that 143,903 British soldiers were treated for 'functional diseases of the nervous system (including neurasthenia and shell-shock)' during the war. If figures for 'mental diseases', 'debility' and 'functional diseases of the heart', all of which appear as separate categories, are included, then the figure for psychiatric diseases rises to 325,312, representing 5.70 per cent of all Britons mobilised.[12]

[12] See *Medical Services*, particularly pp. 298–9; extrapolations are possible because the 1916–20 sample comprised 18.5 per cent of all sick and wounded during this period. 5,704,416 men served in the wartime British army. See Beckett, 'Nation in Arms', p. 8.

Appendix 3

Military ranks and status in the German and British armies

German soldiers were distinguished not only by rank but also according to their place in their army's mustering organisation. In peacetime, conscripts underwent two years of training (three in the cavalry and horse artillery) in *Aktive* units after which they passed into the reserve where they were categorised by age: *Reservist* (aged 23–7), *Landwehrmann* (Class I aged 28–32 and Class II aged 33–8) and *Landsturmmann* (Class II aged 39–45; Class I comprised men of 17–39 who had not yet served). Men under 33 who were not trained before 1914 but recruited during the war were known as *Ersatzreservisten*. *Kriegsfreiwillige* were wartime volunteers and *Einjährig-Freiwillige* were soldiers with the educational and social qualifications necessary to be commissioned as reserve officers and who, before the war, undertook one year of military training which they paid for themselves. Officers were divided into active, *Reserve* and *Landwehr*. Those who had retired were categorised as *außer Dienst* (out of service) or *zur Disposition* (at disposal). Members of both groups rejoined the army at the outbreak of war.[1]

British troops were additionally categorised according to the type of service for which they had contracted. Regular soldiers were pre-war professionals. NCOs could serve for up to twenty-one years, but most of the rank and file spent seven years in the army, before being transferred to the 'Regular Reserve' for five years and, in some cases, the 'National Reserve' thereafter. Special Reservists were civilians with six months' peacetime training, intended in an emergency to replace Regular Army losses. Territorials were members of Britain's auxiliary military units, which had originally been intended for home defence. In peacetime, these civilians had agreed to serve for four years, committing themselves to participation in a statutory number of drills and an annual fifteen-day

[1] See W. Schmidt-Richberg, 'Die Regierungszeit Wilhelms II', in Militärgeschichtliches Forschungsamt (ed.), *Handbuch zur deutschen Militärgeschichte 1648–1939. Von der Entlassung Bismarcks bis zum Ende des Ersten Weltkrieges (1890–1918)* (10 vols., Frankfurt am Main: Bernard & Graefe, 1968), V, pp. 50–1 and General Staff, *German Army Handbook April 1918*, p. 25.

Table 6. *German military ranks (in descending order)*

Officers (with Patent)	*Generalfeldmarschall*
	Generaloberst
	General der Infanterie / Kavallerie / Artillerie
	Generalleutnant
	Generalmajor
	Oberst
	Oberstleutnant
	Major
	Hauptmann / Rittmeister†
	Oberleutnant
	Leutnant
Intermediate ranks	*Feldwebelleutnant* (officer without *Patent*)
	Offizierstellvertreter
	Fähnrich (active officer aspirant)
Other ranks	*Feldwebel / Wachtmeister**
	*Vizefeldwebel / Vizewachtmeister**
	Sergeant
	Unteroffizier
	*Obergefreiter***
	Gefreiter
	Gemeiner (*Musketier / Grenadier / Kanonier etc.*)

Note

† cavalry and train

* cavalry, field artillery and train

** artillery only

Sources: General Staff, *German Army Handbook April 1918*, pp. 21–3 and D.B. Nash, *Imperial German Army Handbook 1914–1918* (London: Ian Allan, 1980), pp. 140–1.

Table 7. *British military ranks (in descending order)*

Officers (with commission)	Field Marshal
	General
	Lieutenant General
	Major General
	Brigadier-General
	Colonel
	Lieutenant-Colonel
	Major
	Captain
	Lieutenant
	Second Lieutenant
Other ranks	First Class Staff Sergeant-Major/ Warrant Officer 1st Class (from 1915)
	Warrant Officer 2nd Class (from 1915)
	Quartermaster-Sergeant
	Company, Battery or Squadron Sergeant-Major
	Sergeant
	Corporal
	Bombardier*
	Lance Corporal / Acting Bombardier*
	Private / Gunner / Sapper etc.

Note
* artillery only

Sources: S. Bull, *Brassey's History of Uniforms. World War One British Army* (London: Brassey's, 1998), pp. 43–6, War Office (ed.), *Soldiers' Small Book* (London: HMSO, 1911), p. 16 and General Staff, *Field Service Pocket Book. 1914*, p. 179.

camp. Finally, there were wartime volunteers, 'Derby men' and (from 1916) conscripts who enlisted for the duration of the war and could be posted to Regular, Territorial or New Army 'Service' units.[2]

[2] See French, *Military Identities*, pp. 20–1, Samuels, *Command or Control?*, p. 119, Beckett, 'Territorial Force', p. 128 and Simkins, *Kitchener's Army*, p. 39.

Glossary of German terms

(For German ranks, see Appendix 3.)

GERMAN	ENGLISH
Armee	Army
Armee-Abteilung	Army detachment
Armeekorps	Army corps
Bataillon	Battalion
Batterie	Artillery battery
bayerisch	Bavarian (adjective)
Einjährig-Freiwillige	'One-year volunteers' wishing to become reserve officers (see also Appendix 3)
Eisenbahnreisende	Railway Police
Etappe-Munitions-Kolonne	Rear-zone ammunition column
Fahnenflucht	Desertion
Feldartillerie	Field artillery
Feldunterarzt	Junior Army Doctor
Frontgemeinschaft	Front-line community of comradeship
Fußartillerie	Heavy artillery
Garde-Regiment	Guards regiment
Gymnasium (pl. *Gymnasien*)	Elite secondary school. *Realgymnasien* and *Oberrealschulen* were similar but less prestigious institutions
Heeresgruppe	Army group
Heimatschuß	A non-life-threatening wound serious enough to require evacuation home. Also known as a *Tangoschuß*
Jäger-Bataillon	Light infantry battalion
Junker	East Prussian nobleman
Kadettenanstalt	Army school for future officers
Kaiserreich	Germany during the period 1871–1918

Kaiserschlacht	The German offensive of spring and summer 1918
Kriegsoffiziere	Wartime-appointed officers
kriegsverwendbar	'Fit for combat service'
Landsturm-Infanterie-Regiment	Infantry regiment composed of oldest group of reservists (see also Appendix 3)
Landwehr-Infanterie-Regiment	Infantry regiment predominantly composed of middle band of reservists (see also Appendix 3)
Marine-Division	Naval division
Materialschlacht	'Battle of material'. Used to refer to the artillery-intensive offensives which took place from 1916
Militär-Polizeistelle	Military Police post
Oberheeresleitung	High command of the German army
Offizierswahl	'Officer election', in which active or reserve officers voted on whether to accept a cadet into their ranks
Regiment	Regiment
Reichsarchiv	German central archive (1919–45) which contained the Prussian army's records. Destroyed by an air-raid in April 1945
Reichstag	German Parliament
Reserve-Infanterie-Regiment	Infantry regiment composed mainly of youngest reservists (see also Appendix 3)
sächsisch	Saxon (adjective)
Spartakus	Left-wing revolutionary group involved in the 1919 insurrections
Standesbewußtsein	The aristocratic caste ethos and identity cultivated by the German officer corps
Stollen	Large dugouts
Sturm-Bataillon	Assault battalion (elite troops)
unerlaubte Entfernung	Absence without leave
Unteroffizier	Both a German non-commissioned rank and a generic term for NCOs
Vaterländischer Unterricht	Patriotic Instruction – a propaganda programme introduced in 1917
Vertrauensmann (pl. *Vertrauensleute*)	Man tasked with reporting on morale in his military unit
württembergisch	Württemberg (adjective)

Bibliography

MANUSCRIPT AND ARCHIVAL SOURCES

All German combatants' surnames cited in the bibliography and in the main text (including those taken from official reports and unpublished compilations) are pseudonyms except for those held in the author's private collection and in the Staats- und Universitätsbibliothek, Handschriftabteilung, Hamburg. This is due to German archive regulations regarding privacy.

BAYERISCHES HAUPTSTAATSARCHIV MÜNCHEN, ABTEILUNG IV: KRIEGSARCHIV (HSTA MUNICH/IV)

Official documentation	Gen.-Kdo I. AK 52
Official documentation	Gen.-Kdo I. AK 104
Training of officer cadets (Bavarian War Ministry)	MKr 1857–8
Documentation of the Bavarian War Ministry	MKr 1980
Training of officer cadets (Bavarian War Ministry)	MKr 4751
Documentation of the Bavarian War Ministry	MKr 11254
Documentation regarding mishandling of men	Stellv. Gen.-Kdo I. AK 591
Monatsberichte der Vertrauensleute, Aug. 1918	Stellv. Gen.-Kdo I. AK 1980

BIBLIOTHEK FÜR ZEITGESCHICHTE, STUTTGART (BZ)

Papers of A. Bauer

BUNDESARCHIV-MILITÄRARCHIV FREIBURG (BA-MA FREIBURG)

Auszüge aus Kriegsbriefen Untererthaler Soldaten, 1914–1917, gesammelt von Heinrich Ullrich	MSg 2/ 4563
Papers of anonymous volunteer	MSg 2/ 65

Papers of E. Ahrend	MSg 2/ 1291
Papers of K. Alefeld	MSg 1/ 909
Papers of E. Berner	MSg 1/ 1941
Papers of W. Dietl	MSg 2/ 5290
Papers of K.J. Fierz	MSg 1/ 3060
Papers of H. Fuchs	MSg 1/ 2965–8 and 2970
Papers of H. Genscher	MSg 2/ 2735
Papers of Gothe [no initial]	MSg 2/ 628
Papers of R. Güldenberg	MSg 1/ 121
Papers of K. Kießler	MSg 2/ 5460
Papers of G. Klein	MSg 2/ 3788
Papers of J. Kohler	MSg 2/ 5458
Papers of E.W. Küpper	MSg 2/ 5254
Papers of W. Lüthje	MSg 2/ 2797
Papers of A. Meier	MSg 2/ 5799
Papers of F. and K. Meier	MSg 2/ 5800
Papers of L. Moeller	MSg 2/ 428
Papers of H. Muhsal	MSg 1/ 3109
Papers of F.O. Nawrath	MSg 1/ 1383
Papers of H. von Obergassel	MSg 1/ 805
Papers of Oertel [no initial]	MSg 1/ 690
Papers of K. Reiter	MSg 1/ 161
Papers of G. Schaub	MSg 2/ 2961
Papers of S. Scheer	MSg 2/ 4470
Papers of P. Seese	MSg 2/ 1247
Papers of R. Vettermann	MSg 2/ 2901
Papers of E. Vogt	MSg 1/ 3183
Papers of E. Vollmar	MSg 1/ 843
Papers of A. Volquartz	MSg 1/ 571
Papers of F. Wedlich	MSg 2/ 4667
Papers of G. Kroschel	PH 10 II/ 501
Denkschrift über die von der deutschen Untersuchungsbehörde seit Ende des Jahres 1917 neu festgestellten Völkerrechtsverletzungen englischer Truppen	PH 2/ 26
Order addressed to officers and men, 13 Nov. 1918	PH 3/ 18
Herstellung einer neuen Ausbildungsvorschrift für die Infanterie-Befehl und Besprechungen der Arbeiter. November 1916	PH 3/ 28
Ausbildung von Offizieren und Mannschaften des östlichen Kriegsschauplatzes in der westlichen Kriegsführung (November 1917)	PH 3/ 33

Mitteilungen 1–107. Tägliche Lageberichte von den Kriegsschauplätzen Jul. 1914–Sept. 1918	PH 3/ 53
Politisch Propaganda bei den Truppenteil des Feldheeres. Verordung des Generalquartiermeisters vom 25/7/1917	PH 3/ 62
Form der Propaganda und Soldatensprache. Feldpressestelle, Mai 1916–Mai 1918	PH 3/ 93
Copy of Order Ia No. 9670, OHL of 4 Aug. 1918	PH 3/ 293
Berichte, Mitteilungen Vervielfältigen Druck	PH 3/ 409
Denkschrift der Obersten Heeresleitung über die deutsche Volks- und Wehrkraft	PH 3/ 446
Die 'Große Schlacht in Frankreich' ('Offensive Michael') vom 21. März–5. April 1918) und daraus gewonnene Erfahrungen	PH 3/ 455
AOK 2 NO Eingangene Meldungen vom 1. Januar 1916 bis 30. Juni 1916	PH 3/ 546
Divisionen Engländer. Chef.d.Gen.St d.F.H. Abt. IIIb	PH 3/ 553
Vernehmungsprotokolle und beschlagnahmte Dokument franz. und engl. Kriegsgefangener sowie deren Auswertung im Gefangenlager Cambrai. Aug.–Okt. 1916	PH 3/ 556
Aufklärungsmeldungen sowie Zeitungsauswerten des Nachrichtenoffiziers beim AOK 4 (Juni 1915)	PH 3/ 573
Aussagen deutscher Gefangene an den Nachrichtenoffizier beim AOK 4 Okt. 1914–Sept. 1915	PH 3/ 582
Vernehmungsprotokolle französischer & englischer Kriegsgefangener im Bereich des AOK 4, Bd. 3 Aug.–Sept. [1917]	PH 3/ 585
NO 4 Gefangenen-Aussagen. 1.6–31.7.1918	PH 3/ 589
NO 4 Gefangenen-Aussagen. 1.8–31.10.1918	PH 3/ 590
OHK 6, Die September Offensive [1915]	PH 5 II/ 64
Leitsätze für den Vaterländischen Unterricht der Armee-Abteilung A	PH 5 IV/ 2
Wander-Theater. Armee-Abteilung A	PH 5 IV/ 42

Unterrichtung der höheren Kommandobehörden über den Zustand der im Kampfe stehende Truppen und die Verhältnisse auf dem Kampffeld	PH 6 V/ 6
Neu aufgestellter Bericht des Oberst a.D. Walter Giffenig auf die vom Reichsarchiv im Jahre 1922 für das Weltkriegswerk gestellten Fragen betr. Entstehung und Vorbereitung der Revolution von 1918/19	PH 7/ 2
Handakten Prof. Dr Stursberg über fachärtliche Tätigkeit beim stellv. VIII AK	PH 7/ 6
Geheimer Nachrichtendienst u. Spionageabwehr des Heeres von Generalmajor a.D. Gempp	RW 5/v. 41 and v. 43
Auszüge aus Feldpostbriefen von Januar 1914–November 1918. Enthält u.a.: Frankreich	W-10/ 50677
Anonymous Reichsarchiv study on training	W-10/ 50755
Postüberwachung der 5. Armee. Erfaßungen der letzten Kriegsjahre	W-10/ 50794
Ueberblick über Organisation und Regelung des Mannschaftsersatzes für das deutsche Heer während des Weltkrieges. I. Von der Mobilmachung bis zum Herbst 1916	W-10/ 50900
Denkenschrift über die Ersatzstellung für das Deutsche Heer von Mitte September bis Ende 1914	W-10/ 50902
Entwicklung der Stimmung im Heere 1916/17 im Winter 1916/17. Forschungsarbeit von Obkircher (1936)	W-10/ 51507
Reichsarchiv historical work	W-10/ 51921

DEUTSCHES TAGEBUCHARCHIV, EMMENDINGEN (DTA)

Letter extracts collected by A. Schulz	91
Papers of A. Geyer	262,1
Papers of G. Gruber	138a–c
Papers of E. Huthmacher	930
Papers of P. Keppeler	758
Papers of G. Kirchner	9/II
Papers of K. Kramer	506
Papers of F. Schmidt	259
Papers of H. Weber (within larger recipient's collection)	865
Papers of L. Wernicke	1040, II

GENERALLANDESARCHIV KARLSRUHE (GLA KARLSRUHE)

Armee-Abteilung B. Armee-Oberkommando. Feldjustiz Beamter. Bestimmungsakten betr. Misshandlung Untergebener	456 F 3 /88
Miscellaneous documention	456 F 8 /106
Tätigskeitbericht der Militärpolizeistelle Karlsruhe (Oktober 1917–März 1918)	456 F 8 /231
Eisenbahnüberwachungsreisen	456 F 8 /260
Miscellaneous documentation	456 F 8 /331

HAUPTSTAATSARCHIV STUTTGART (HSTA STUTTGART)

Kriegsministerium: Justiz-Abteilung	M 1/ 7/ 304
Stimmungsberichte und Meldungen der Geheimen Feldpolizeistellen	M 30/ 1/ 49
Heeresgruppe Herzog Albrecht documents	M 30/ 1/ 73
Heeresgruppe Herzog Albrecht documents	M 30/ 1/ 336–7
Heeresgruppe Herzog Albrecht documents	M 30/ 2
26. Infanterie-Division documents	M 38/ 17
27. Infanterie-Division documents	M 39/ 15
Stellvertrendes General-Kommando XIII AK Denkschriftsammlung	M 77/ 2/ 4
Kriegsstammrolle der 8. Kompanie, Inf. Regt. Nr. 121	M 461/ 25

DEPARTMENT OF DOCUMENTS, IMPERIAL WAR MUSEUM, LONDON (IWM)

Papers of anonymous soldier	Misc 99 Item 1515
Papers of W.H.J.St L. Atkinson	02/16/1
Papers of G.R. Barlow	86/40/1
Papers of E.H. Bennett	79/35/1
Papers of O.H. Best	87/56/1
Papers of F.H. Bracey	94/46/1
Papers of V.S. Braund	83/6/1
Papers of P.A. Brown	91/3/1
Papers of G. Calverley	02/30/1
Papers of E.F. Chapman	92/3/1
Papers of A. Cornfoot	97/37/1
Papers of P.G. Copson	86/30/1
Papers of A.H. Crerar	P 323
Papers of T.H. Cubbon	78/4/1
Papers of R. Cude	Con Shelf
Papers of B.O. Dewes	84/22/1
Papers of J.H. Dible	Con Shelf

Papers of H.M. Dillon	82/25/1
Papers of G. Donaldson	69/25/1
Papers of R. Downing	88/7/1
Papers of W. Edgington	88/52/1
Papers of J.P. Fowler	82/3/1
Papers of P. Fraser	85/32/1
Papers of S.T. Fuller	86/32/1
Papers of A.H. Habgood	P 115 & Con Shelf
Papers of R.P. Hamilton	87/8/1
Papers of M. Hardie (Third Army censorship reports)	84/46/1
Papers of R.P. Harker	Con Shelf
Papers of R.J. Hartley	86/30/1
Papers of J.T. Keeping	90/37/1
Papers of S.A. Knight	96/29/1
Papers of G.A. Loyd	98/2/1
Papers of E.A. Luther	P 262
Papers of J. McIlwain	96/29/1
Papers of P.D. Mundy	80/43/1
Papers of B.C. Myatt	97/4/1
Papers of R.H. Owen	90/37/1
Papers of F.E. Packe	Con Shelf
Papers of H. Panton	P 262
Papers of C.J. Paterson	79/51/1
Papers of C.P. Quayle	92/19/1
Papers of C.S. Rawlins	76/121/1 & Con Shelf
Papers of A. Reeve	90/20/1
Papers of A.J. Rixon	99/13/1
Papers of A.H. Roberts	97/37/1
Papers of W.A. Rogers	87/62/1
Papers of D.L. Rowlands	93/20/1
Papers of W.B. St Leger	P 239
Papers of C.R. Smith	99/56/1
Papers of S.H. Steven	96/29/1
Papers of J.W. Stock	84/1/1
Papers of W.H. Tait	PP/MCR/161
Papers of C.M. Tames	85/1/1
Papers of O.P. Taylor	92/3/1
Papers of W. Tyrrell (Southborough Commission)	68/84/1–38 (29)
Papers of A.R. Williams	82/26/1
Papers of N.L. Woodroffe	95/31/1
Papers of A.E. Wrench	85/51/1
Papers of H.W. Yoxall	P 317 Con Shelf
German Methods of Trench Warfare (First Army, 1916)	K.85/ 3374

LANDESKIRCHLICHES ARCHIV NÜRNBERG (LA NUREMBERG)

Divisional chaplains' reports	3209

THE NATIONAL ARCHIVES, KEW (FORMERLY PUBLIC RECORD OFFICE) (TNA)

Cambrai Inquiry. Memorandum by General Smuts	CAB 24/ 37
Report upon Soldiers returned as Cases of 'Disordered Action of the Heart' (Medical Research Committee)	CSC 5/ 93
Rationing: Food Queues: notes and memoranda on their prevention, 1917–1918	MAF 60/ 243
Secretary of State for War: Organised gatherings	WO 32/ 5455
Discipline incidents connected with indiscipline of 11 Border Regiment	WO 32/ 17700
Enquiry into 'Discontent among Battalion owing to Col. Harvey's unsympathetic consideration for officers & men under his command.' (1/4 Norfolks)	WO 32/ 18563
Intelligence Series. Belgium. 1914	WO 33/ 613
War Diary. Director General Medical Services, British Armies in France	WO 95/ 45
War Diary. Assistant Director of Medical Services, 1st Division	WO 95/ 1242
War Diary. Assistant Director of Medical Services, 2nd Division	WO 95/ 1320
War Diary of 2/York and Lancs	WO 95/ 1610
War Diary of 3/Monmouthshires	WO 95/ 2274
War Diary of 20/Middlesex	WO 95/ 2615
War Diary of 1/4 Battalion East Yorks	WO 95/ 2834
War Diary of 6/Durham Light Infantry	WO 95/ 3840
Memorandum on the question of an extension of the British Front, 15 December 1917	WO 106/ 1517
Translation of German manual 'War organisation in the event of mobilization'	WO 106/ 1529
Inquiry into the surrender of the 1st Gordon Highlanders	WO 141/ 37–8
Intelligence reports and prisoner interrogations (GHQ)	WO 157/ 1–26
Intelligence reports and prisoner interrogations (4th Army)	WO 157/ 188–99
Intelligence Section. GHQ. Daily War Diary	WO 158/ 5
Cambrai Enquiry File No. 1	WO 158/ 53
Lord Haig's Diary. Volume XXXI	WO 256/ 28 and 33

Official documentation relating to F.R. Hill	WO 339/ 12350
Official documentation relating to G. Whitbread	WO 339/ 111286
Official documentation relating to R. Railton	WO 339/ 115371
Short Service Attestation Form for Private Henry Fairhurst, 14/York and Lancs	WO 363/ FO 22

PRIVATE COLLECTION (AUTHOR)

Papers of H. Anthes
Papers of K. Beier
Papers of W. Enders
Papers of K. Fritsche
Papers of H. Hausbalk
Papers of A.H. Just
Papers of R. Kühne
Papers of G. Schneider
Papers of O. Steinhilber

PRIVATE COLLECTION (COSTELLOE)

Papers of J.P. MacKay

SÄCHSISCHES HAUPTSTAATSARCHIV DRESDEN (HSTA DRESDEN)

Aufklärung im Heer, Band II	11348 Stellv. Gen.-Kdo XII AK KA(P) 12779
Berichte der Vertrauensoffiziere 1918, Band 12	11348 Stellv. Gen.-Kdo XII AK KA(P) 12888
Kriegsakten betr. Eisenbahnüberwachungsreisen	11352 Stellv. Gen.-Kdo XIX AK KA(P) 24135
Kriegsakten betr. Eisenbahnüberwachungsreisen	11352 Stellv. Gen.-Kdo XIX AK KA(P) 24139–40
Geheime Angelegenheiten betr.	11352 Stellv. Gen.-Kdo XIX AK KA(P) 24158–9
Kriegsakten betr. Truppenbelehrung	11352 Stellv. Gen.-Kdo XIX AK KA(P) 24170
Fahnenflüchtige betr. Bd. 1	11352 Stellv. Gen.-Kdo XIX AK KA(P) 24179
Letters to Ersatz-Bataillon Fussartillerie 12	11363 Ersatz-Bataillon Fussartillerie 12, 34288
Mitteilungen vom Militärbevollmächtigten vom 1.10.–31.12.16	Militärbevollmächtigter 4201
Mitteilungen pp. vom Militärbevollmächtigten vom 1.1.–31.3.18 – kurze Zusammenstellung über die britische Armee	Militärbevollmächtigter 4210

Mitteilungen pp. vom Militärbevollmächtigten	Militärbevollmächtigter 4216
Mitteilungen pp. vom Militärbevollmächtigten	Militärbevollmächtigter 4221

STAATSBIBLIOTHEK ZU BERLIN, PREUSSISCHER KULTURBESITZ, HANDSCHRIFTABTEILUNG, BERLIN (STAATSBIB. BERLIN)

Papers of F. Brussig	Ms. Boruss. fol. 1084
Papers of C.F. Müller	Ms. Germ. fol. 1651

STAATS- UND UNIVERSITÄTSBIBLIOTHEK, HANDSCHRIFTABTEILUNG, HAMBURG (STAATSBIB. HAMBURG)

Papers of R. Dehmel (including letter of H. Carossa)	6179

WELLCOME LIBRARY FOR THE HISTORY AND UNDERSTANDING OF MEDICINE, LONDON (WLHM)

Papers of C. Chamberlain	RAMC 699 Box 136
Papers of H.J.S. Shields	RAMC 383 Box 41
Major General Sir Maurice Holt. Field message book containing orders, notes etc., as ADMS, 2nd Division, in France and Flanders. Sept.–Oct. 1914	RAMC 380/1/10 Box 40
Major General Sir Maurice Holt. Confidential instructions re clearing a battlefield. 1914	RAMC 380/2/4 Box 40
Extracts regarding 'shell shock' / shirking in 11/Border Regiment, 1/5 Warwickshires and among officers	RAMC 446/18 Box 66
War Diary of 1/2 North Midland Field Ambulance RAMC, 138th Infantry Brigade, 46th Division. From 2 Aug. 1914 to 16 April 1915	RAMC 1402 Box 300

PRINTED PRIMARY SOURCES

'A.F.B.D.', 'Some Military Causes of the German Collapse', *United Service Magazine* 60 (October 1919 to March 1920), 286–93.

Aldren Turner, W., 'Remarks on Cases of Nervous and Mental Shock Observed in the Base Hospitals in France', *British Medical Journal* (15 May 1915), 833–5.

Altrichter, F., *Die seelischen Kräfte des Deutschen Heeres im Frieden und im Weltkriege* (Berlin: E.S. Mittler & Sohn, 1933).
Altrock, C. von (ed.), *Vom Sterben des deutschen Offizierkorps* (Berlin: E.S. Mittler & Sohn, 1922).
Anon., 'Notes on the Man Power and Fighting Strength of Germany: 1st August–1st November, 1914', *Journal of the Royal United Services Institution* 66, 461 (February 1921), 148–51.
Anon., 'Note on the French Effort during the War', *Journal of the Royal United Services Institution* 67, 465 (February 1922), 149–54.
Army Chaplain, *Can England's Church Win England's Manhood? A Study in Camp, Field and Hospital of the Spiritual Condition of English Soldiers* (London: Macmillan & Co., 1917).
Aschaffenburg, G., 'Die konstitutionellen Psychopathen', in K. Bonhoeffer (ed.), *Geistes- und Nervenkrankheiten.* Part 1 (Leipzig: Johann Ambrosius Barth, 1922), pp. 123–53.
Ashley, R.S., *War-Diary of Private R.S. (Jack) Ashley 2472 7th London Regiment 1914–1918* (London: Philippa Stone, 1982).
Bächtold, H., *Deutscher Soldatenbrauch und Soldatenglaube* (Strassburg: Karl J. Trübner, 1917).
Bairnsfather, B., *More Fragments from France.* Vol. II (8 vols., London: *The Bystander*, 1916).
Berliner Tageblatt und Handels-Zeitung (August 1914).
Bierwagen, M., *Zwischen Somme und Pripjet. Geschichte des Res. Infanterie-Regiments Nr. 271 im Weltkriege 1914 bis 1918* (Oldenburg: Gerhard Stalling, 1927).
Bird, C., 'From Home to the Charge. A Psychological Study of the Soldier', *American Journal of Psychology* 28, 3 (July 1917), 315–48.
Blake, R. (ed.), *The Private Papers of Douglas Haig 1914–1919. Being Selections from the Private Diary and Correspondence of Field-Marshal the Earl Haig of Bemersyde, K.T., G.C.B., O.M., etc.* (London: Eyre and Spottiswoode, 1952).
Bonhoeffer, K., 'Über die Bedeutung der Kriegserfahrungen für die allgemeine Psychopathologie und Ätiologie der Geisteskrankheiten', in K. Bonhoeffer (ed.), *Geistes- und Nervenkrankheiten.* Part I (Leipzig: Johann Ambrosius Barth, 1922), pp. 3–44.
———, 'Psychopathologische Erfahrungen und Lehren des Weltkriegs', *Münchener Medizinische Wochenschrift* 81, 31 (3 August 1934), 1212–15.
Boraston, J.H. (ed.), *Sir Douglas Haig's Despatches (December 1915–April 1919)* (London: J.M. Dent & Sons, 1919, 1979)
Brophy, J. and Partridge, E., *The Long Trail. Soldiers' Songs and Slang 1914–18*, revised edn (London: Sphere Books, 1965, 1969).
Brown, W., *Psychology and Psychotherapy* (London: Edward Arnold, 1921).
Bruntz, G.G., *Allied Propaganda and the Collapse of the German Empire in 1918* (Stanford University Press, 1938).
Burton-Fanning, F.W., 'Neurasthenia in Soldiers of the Home Forces', *The Lancet* (16 June 1917), 907–11.

Cairns, D.S. (ed.), *The Army and Religion. An Enquiry and its Bearing upon the Religious Life of the Nation* (London: Macmillan & Co., 1919).

Cambell, H., 'The Biological Aspects of Warfare. I', *The Lancet* (15 September 1917), 433–5.

———, 'The Biological Aspects of Warfare. II', *The Lancet* (29 September 1917), 505–8.

Camena d'Almeida, P., *L'armée allemande avant et pendant la guerre de 1914–1918* (Nancy: Berger-Levrault, 1919).

Carrington, C.E., 'Kitchener's Army. The Somme and After', *Journal of the Royal United Services Institute for Defence Studies* 123, 1 (March 1978), 15–20.

Chambers, W.D., 'Mental Wards with the British Expeditionary Force. A Review of Ten Months' Experience', *Journal of Mental Science* 65, 270 (July 1919), 152–80.

Chapman, G., *A Passionate Prodigality* (Leatherhead: Ashford, Buchan & Enright, 1933, 1993).

Core, D.E., 'The "Instinct-Distortion", or "War Neurosis"', *The Lancet* (10 August 1918), 168–72.

['A Correspondent'], 'Medical Aspects of Severe Trauma in War', *British Medical Journal* (12 December 1914), 1038–9.

Crick, P.C.T., 'The Soldier's Religion', in F.B. MacNutt (ed.), *The Church in the Furnace. Essays by Seventeen Temporary Church of England Chaplains on Active Service in France and Flanders* (London: Macmillan & Co., 1917), pp. 349–74.

Crile, G.W., *A Mechanistic View of War and Peace* (London: T. Werner Laurie, 1915).

Croft, W.D., 'The Application of Recent Developments in Mechanics and other Scientific Knowledge to Preparation and Training for Future War on Land', *Journal of the Royal United Services Institution* 65, 459 (August 1920), 443–76.

Cron, H., *Imperial German Army 1914–18. Organisation, Structure, Orders of Battle* (Solihull: Helion and Company, 1937, 2002).

Delbrück, H., *Über den kriegerischen Charakter des deutschen Volkes. Rede am 11. September 1914* (Berlin: Carl Heymann, 1914).

Dillon, F., 'Neuroses among Combatant Troops in the Great War', *British Medical Journal* (8 July 1939), 63–6.

Eder, M.D., *War-Shock. The Psycho-Neuroses in War. Psychology and Treatment* (London: William Heinemann, 1917).

[Editorial], 'The War and Nervous Breakdown', *The Lancet* (23 January 1915), 189–90.

[Editorial], 'Soldiers' Dreams', *The Lancet* (23 January 1915), 210.

[Editorial], 'The Medical Examination of Recruits', *The Lancet* (13 May 1916), 1006.

Edmonds, J.E., *History of the Great War based on Official Documents. Military Operations. France and Belgium, 1914. Antwerp, La Bassée, Armientières, Messines, and Ypres. October–November 1914* (London: Macmillan & Co., 1925).

———, *History of the Great War based on Official Documents. Military Operations. France and Belgium, 1914. Mons, the Retreat to the Seine, the Marne and the Aisne. August–October 1914* (London: Macmillan & Co., 1926).

———, *History of the Great War based on Official Documents. Military Operations. France and Belgium, 1915. Battles of Aubers Ridge, Festubert, and Loos* (London: Macmillan & Co., 1928).

———, *History of the Great War based on Official Documents. Military Operations. France and Belgium, 1918. The German March Offensive and its Preliminaries* (London: Macmillan & Co., 1935).

———, *History of the Great War based on Official Documents. Military Operations. France and Belgium, 1918. March–April: Continuation of the German Offensives* (London: Macmillan & Co., 1937).

Einem, K. von, *Ein Armeeführer erlebt den Weltkrieg. Persönliche Aufzeichnungen des Generalobersten v. Einem*, ed. J. Alter (Leipzig: v. Hase / Koehler, 1938).

Elliot, T.R., 'Transient Paraplegia from Shell Explosions', *British Medical Journal* (12 December 1914), 1005–6.

Elliot Smith, G., 'Shock and the Soldier', *The Lancet* (22 April 1916), 853–7.

Erzberger, M., *Die Mobilmachung* (Stuttgart: Deutsche Verlags-Anstalt, 1914).

Everth, E., *Tat-Flugschriften 10. Von der Seele des Soldaten im Felde. Bemerkungen eines Kriegsteilnehmers* (Jena: Eugen Diederich, 1915).

Feiling, A., 'Loss of Personality from "Shell Shock"', *The Lancet* (10 July 1915), 63–6.

Fraser, D. (ed.), *In Good Company. The First World War Letters and Diaries of the Hon. William Fraser, Gordon Highlanders* (Salisbury: Michael Russell, 1990).

Friedländer, Prof., Dr, 'Grundlinien der psychischen Behandlung. Eine Kritik der psychotherapeutischen Methoden', *Zeitschrift für die gesamte Neurologie und Psychiatrie* 42 (1918), 99–139.

Frost, E.P., 'Dreams', *Psychological Bulletin* 13, 1 (15 January 1916), 12–14.

Fuller, J.F.C., *Training Soldiers for War* (London: Hugh Rees, 1914).

———, *The Army in My Time* (London: Rich & Cowan, 1935).

Gaupp, R., 'Schreckneurosen' und Neurasthenie', in K. Bonhoeffer (ed.), *Geistes- und Nervenkrankheiten.* Part I (Leipzig: Johann Ambrosius Barth, 1922), pp. 68–101.

General Staff, *Field Service Pocket Book. 1914* (London: HMSO, 1914).

———, *German Army Handbook April 1918*, ed. D. Nash (London and New York: Arms and Armour Press and Hippocrene Books, 1977).

The German Army from Within by a British Officer who has Served in it (London: Hodder & Stoughton, 1914).

Gibbs, P., *Open Warfare. The Way to Victory* (London: William Heinemann, 1919).

———, *Realities of War* (London: William Heinemann, 1920).

———, *The War Dispatches* (Isle of Man: Anthony Gibbs and Phillips, 1964).

Gilchrist, H.L., *A Comparative Study of World War Casualties from Gas and other Weapons* (Washington, DC: United States Government Printing Office, 1928).

Göhre, P., *Tat-Flugschriften 22. Front und Heimat. Religiöses, Politisches, Sexuelles aus dem Schützengraben* (Jena: Eugen Diederich, 1917).

Gothein, G., *Warum verloren wir den Krieg?* (Stuttgart: Deutsche Verlags-Anstalt, 1919).

Graves, R., *Goodbye to All That,* revised edn (London: Penguin, 1929, 1960).

Hall, S.G., *Morale. The Supreme Standard of Life and Conduct* (New York: D. Appleton, 1920).

Harbutt Dawson, W., *The German Danger and the Working Man* (London: The Central Committee for National Patriotic Organisations, n.d.).

Heeresgruppe Herzog Albrecht, *Deutscher Staat und Kultur. Auf Grund an der Kaiser-Wilhelms-Universität in Straßburg bei Hochschullehrgängen der Heeresgruppe gehaltener Vorträge* (Strasburg: Karl J. Trübner, 1918).

Heeres-Sanitätsinspektion des Reichskriegsministeriums (ed.), *Sanitätsbericht über das Deutsche Heer (Deutsches Feld- und Besatzungsheer) im Weltkriege 1914/1918 (Deutscher Kriegssanitätsbericht 1914/18).* Vol. III: *Die Krankenbewegung bei dem deutschen Feld- und Besatzungsheer im Weltkriege 1914/1918* (3 vols., Berlin: E.S. Mittler & Sohn, 1934).

——— (ed.), *Sanitätsbericht über das Deutsche Heer (Deutsches Feld- und Besatzungsheer) im Weltkriege 1914/1918 (Deutscher Kriegssanitätsbericht 1914/18).* Vol. II: *Der Sanitätsdienst im Gefechts- und Schlachtenverlauf im Weltkriege 1914/1918* (3 vols., Berlin: E.S. Mittler & Sohn, 1938).

Herwig, B., 'Psychotechnische Methoden im Verkehrswesen', in E. Abderhalden (ed.), *Handbuch der biologischen Arbeitsmethoden.* Part VI: *Methoden der experimentellen Psychologie.* Part C/I (Berlin: Urban & Schwarzenberg, 1928), pp. 689–812.

Hirschfeld, M., *Deutsche Kriegsschriften.* Part *20*: *Kriegspsychologisches* (Bonn: A. Marcus & E. Webers Verlag, 1916).

———, *Sittengeschichte des Ersten Weltkrieges*, revised edn (Hanau am Main: Karl Schustek, 1929, *c.* 1965).

Hobohm, M., *Soziale Heeresmißstände als Teilursache des deutschen Zusammenbruches von 1918. Die Ursachen des Deutschen Zusammenbruches im Jahre 1918.* Part *2*: *Der innere Zusammenbruch.* Vol. XI.1 (12 vols., Berlin: Deutsche Verlagsgesellschaft für Politik und Geschichte, 1929).

Hocking, W.E., *Morale and its Enemies* (New Haven: Yale University Press, 1918).

Hofmann, H., 'Die deutsche Nervenkraft im Stellungskrieg', in F. Seeßelberg (ed.), *Der Stellungskrieg 1914–18* (Berlin: E.S. Mittler & Sohn, 1926).

Holmes, E., *The Nemesis of Docility. A Study of German Character* (London: Constable and Company, 1916).

Holtz, G. vom, *Das Württembergische Reserve-Inf.-Regiment Nr. 121 im Weltkrieg 1914–1918* (Stuttgart: Chr. Belsersche Verlagsbuchhandlung, 1922).

Home, A., *The Diary of a World War I Cavalry Officer* (Tunbridge Wells: Costello, 1985).

Hottenroth, J.E. (ed.), *Sachsen in großer Zeit in Wort und Bild. Gemeinverständliche sächsische Kriegsgeschichte und vaterländisches Gedenkswerk des Weltkrieges.* Vol. III (3 vols., Leipzig: Verlag der Literaturwerke 'Minerva' R. Max Lippold, 1923).

Housman, L. (ed.), *War Letters of Fallen Englishmen* (Philadelphia: Pine Street Books, 1930, 2002).

Huber, M. (ed.), *La population de la France pendant la Guerre* (Paris and New Haven: Les Presses Universitaires de France and Yale University Press, 1932).

Jany, C., *Geschichte der Preußischen Armee vom 15. Jahrhundert bis 1914*. Vol. IV: *Die Königlich Preußische Armee und das Deutsche Heer 1807 bis 1914* (5 vols., Osnabruck: Biblio, 1933, 1967).

Johann, E. (ed.), *Innenansicht eines Krieges. Bilder, Briefe, Dokumente 1914–1918* (Frankfurt am Main: Heinrich Scheffer, 1968).

Johnson, W. and Rows, R.G., 'Neurasthenia and War Neuroses', in W.G. MacPherson, W.P. Herringham, T.R. Elliott and A. Balfour (eds.), *History of the Great War based on Official Documents*. Vol. II: *Medical Services. Diseases of the War* (London: HMSO, 1923), pp. 1–67.

Jungblut, [no initial], 'Die Tätigkeit der deutschen Ärzte im Weltkriege', *Deutsches Ärzteblatt* 65, 15 (13 April 1935), 368–72.

Kantorowicz, H., *Der Offiziershaß im deutschen Heer* (Freiburg im Breisgau: J. Bielefelds Verlag, 1919).

King, E.J., *The History of the 7th Battalion Middlesex Regiment* (London: Harrison & Sons, 1927).

Klemm, O., 'Eignungsprüfungen an meßtechnischem Personal', in E. Abderhalden (ed.), *Handbuch der biologischen Arbeitsmethoden*. Part VI: *Methoden der experimentellen Psychologie*. Part C/I (Berlin: Urban & Schwarzenberg, 1928), pp. 565–619.

Klemperer, V., *Curriculum Vitae. Erinnerungen 1881–1918*. Vol. II, ed. W. Nowojski (2 vols., Berlin: Aufbau Taschenbuch Verlag, 1996).

Kriegsminsterium, *Felddienst-Ordnung (F.O.)* (Berlin: Ernst Siegfried Mittler und Sohn, 1908).

Krüger-Franke, Dr, 'Ueber truppenärztliche Erfahrungen in der Schlacht', *Berliner Klinische Wochenschrift* 1 (4 January 1915), 7–9.

Laffin, J. (ed.), *Letters from the Front 1914–1918* (London: J.M. Dent & Sons, 1973).

Laudenheimer, Dr, 'Die Anamnese der sogenannten Kriegspsychoneurosen', *Münchener Medizinische Wochenschrift* 62, 38. *Feldärztliche Beilage* 38 (21 September 1915), 1302–4.

Lemmermann, H. (ed.), *Kriegserziehung im Kaiserreich. Studien zur politischen Funktion von Schule und Schulmusik 1890–1918*. Vol. II: *Dokumentation* (Lilienthal: Eres Edition, 1984).

Lewin, K., 'Kriegslandschaft', *Zeitschrift für angewandte Psychologie* 12, 5 & 6 (1917), 440–7.

Lipscomb, F.M., 'Contribution to Discussion on Anxiety Neurosis in the Army', *Journal of the Royal Army Medical Corps* 68, 1 (January 1937), 32–8.

Loewenfeld, L., 'Die Suggestion in ihrer Bedeutung für den Weltkrieg', *Grenzfragen des Nerven- und Seelenlebens. Einzeldarstellungen für Gebildete aller Stände*. Vol. XVI (Part 101–6) (Munich: J.F. Bergmann, 1923), 5–77.

Ludendorff, E., *My War Memories. 1914–1918*, 2nd edn (2 vols., London: Hutchinson & Co., 1923).

Ludwig, W., 'Beiträge zur Psychologie der Furcht im Kriege', in W. Stern and O. Lipmann (eds.), *Beihefte zur Zeitschrift für angewandte Psychologie. 21. Beiträge zur Psychologie des Krieges* (Leipzig: Johann Ambrosius Barth, 1920), pp. 125–72.

MacCurdy, J.T., *War Neuroses* (Cambridge University Press, 1918).

McKean, G.B., *Scouting Thrills* (London: Humphrey Milford and Oxford University Press, 1919).

McTaggart, M.F., 'Danger Values', *Journal of the Royal United Services Institution* 66, 462 (May 1921), 284–92.

Mapother, E., 'War Neurosis', *Journal of the Royal Army Medical Corps* 68, 1 (January 1937), 38–48.

Marcks, E., *Politische Flugschriften. Der Deutsche Krieg.* Part 19: *Wo Stehen Wir? Die politischen, sittlichen und kulturellen Zusammenhänge unseres Krieges* (Stuttgart: Deutsche Verlagsanstalt, 1914).

Medical Research Committee (ed.), *Report upon Soldiers Returned as Cases of 'Disordered Action of the Heart' (D.A.H.) or 'Valvular Disease of the Heart' (V.D.H.)* (London: HMSO, 1917).

Mitchell, T.J. and Smith, G.M. (eds.), *History of the Great War based on Official Documents. Medical Services. Casualties and Medical Statistics of the Great War* (London: Imperial War Museum, 1931, 1997).

Moll, A., 'Ueber psycho-pathologische Erfahrungen vom westlichen Kriegsschauplatz', *Berliner Klinische Wochenschrift* 4 (25 January 1915), 95–6.

Montgomery-Massingberd, A.A., *The Story of the Fourth Army in the Battles of the Hundred Days August 8th to November 11th 1918* (London: Hodder and Stoughton, 1920).

Moran, Lord [Wilson, C.], *The Anatomy of Courage* (London: Constable, 1945, 1966).

———, 'Wear and Tear', *The Lancet* (17 June 1950), 1099–1101.

Mott, F.W., 'Two Addresses on War Psycho-Neurosis. (II.) The Psychology of Soldiers' Dreams', *The Lancet* (2 February 1918), 169–72.

Moynihan, M. (ed.), *Greater Love. Letters Home 1914–1918* (London: W.H. Allen, 1980).

Muirhead, I.B., 'Shock and the Soldier', *The Lancet* (13 May 1916), 1021.

Müller, H., 'Der Ersatz des Heeres', *Münchener Medizinische Wochenschrift* 81, 31 (3 August 1934), 1160–2.

Münzer, A., 'Die Psyche des Verwundeten', *Berliner Klinische Wochenschrift* 10 (8 March 1915), 234–5.

Myers, C.S., *Shell Shock in France 1914–18. Based on a War Diary* (Cambridge University Press, 1940).

Napier Pearn, O.P., 'Psychoses in the Expeditionary Forces', *Journal of Mental Science* 65, 269 (April 1919), 101–8.

Neumann, K.E., 'Psychologische Beobachtungen im Felde', *Neurologisches Centralblatt* 33, 23 (1 December 1914), 1243–5.

Neymann, C.A., 'Some Experiences in the German Red Cross', *Mental Hygiene* 1, 3 (July 1917), 392–6.

Nonne, M., 'Therapeutische Erfahrungen an den Kriegsneurosen in den Jahren 1914–1918', in K. Bonhoeffer (ed.), *Geistes- und Nervenkrankheiten*. Part 1 (Leipzig: Johann Ambrosius Barth, 1922), pp. 102–21.

Palmer, R., '*What a Lovely War*'. *British Soldiers' Songs from the Boer War to the Present Day* (London: Michael Joseph, 1990).

Pfeilschifter, G., 'Seelsorge und religiöses Leben im deutschen Heere', in G. Pfeilschifter (ed.), *Deutsche Kultur, Katholizismus und Weltkrieg. Eine Abwehr des Buches La guerre allemande et la catholicisme* (Freiburg im Breisgau: Herdersche Verlagshandlung, 1916), pp. 235–68.

Plaut, P., 'Psychographie des Kriegers', in W. Stern and O. Lipmann (eds.), *Beihefte zur Zeitschrift für angewandte Psychologie. 21. Beiträge zur Psychologie des Krieges* (Leipzig: Johann Ambrosius Barth, 1920), pp. 1–123.

———, 'Prinzipien und Methoden der Kriegspsychologie', in E. Abderhalden (ed.), *Handbuch der biologischen Arbeitsmethoden*. Part VI: *Methoden der experimentellen Psychologie*. Part C/I (Berlin: Urban & Schwarzenberg, 1928), pp. 621–87.

Procter, T.H., 'The Motives of the Soldier', *International Journal of Ethics* 31, 1 (October 1920), 26–50.

Pulkowski, von [no initial], *Handbuch für Unteroffiziere, Obergefreite und Gefreite der Fußartillerie*. Vol. I (Berlin: R. Eisenschmidt, 1914).

Raimes, A.L., *The Fifth Battalion, the Durham Light Infantry 1914–1918* (n.p.: Committee of Past and Present Officers of the Battalion, 1931).

Rehm, O., 'Hysterie und Nervenschock. (Untersuchungen über Blutdruck, Puls und psychische Arbeitsleistung)', *Zeitschrift für die gesamte Neurologie und Psychiatrie* 42 (1918), 89–98.

Reichsarchiv, *Der Weltkrieg 1914 bis 1918*. Vol. V: *Der Herbst-Feldzug 1914. Im Westen bis zum Stellungskrieg. Im Osten bis zum Rückzug* (14 vols., Berlin: E.S. Mittler & Sohn, 1929).

———, *Der Weltkrieg 1914 bis 1918*. Vol. XIV: *Die Kriegsführung an der Westfront im Jahre 1918* (14 vols., Berlin: E.S. Mittler & Sohn, 1944).

Richardson, L.F., *Mathematical Psychology of War* (Oxford: W.M. Hunt, 1919).

Rivers, W.H.R., 'An Address on the Repression of War Experience', *The Lancet* (2 February 1918), 173–7.

Roberts, F.J. (ed.), *The Wipers Times. A Complete Facsimile of the Famous World War One Trench Newspaper, Incorporating the 'New Church' Times, The Kemmel Times, The Somme Times, The B.E.F. Times, and the 'Better Times'*, Introduction, Notes and Glossary by P. Beaver (London: Papermac, 1973).

Rohde, M., 'Neurologische Betrachtungen eines Truppenarztes im Felde', *Zeitschrift für die gesamte Neurologie und Psychiatrie* 29, 5 (19 October 1915), 379–415.

Roth, K., *Das K.B. Reserve-Infanterie-Regiment Nr. 23* (Munich: Max Schick, 1927).

Rüdt von Collenberg, L. *Die deutsche Armee von 1871 bis 1914* (Berlin: Ernst Siegfried Mittler und Sohn, 1922).

Rupprecht von Bayern, Kronprinz, *In Treue fest. Mein Kriegstagebuch* (3 vols., Munich: Deutscher National Verlag A.-G., 1929).

Salmon, T.W., 'The Care and Treatment of Mental Diseases and War Neuroses ("Shell Shock") in the British Army', *Mental Hygiene* 1, 4 (October 1917), 509–47.

Schaible, C., *Standes- und Berufspflichten des deutschen Offiziers. Für angehende und jüngere Offiziere des stehenden Heeres und des Beurlaubtenstandes* (Berlin: R. Eisenschmidt, 1917).

Schauwecker, F., *Im Todesrachen. Die deutsche Seele im Weltkriege* (Halle: Heinrich Diekmann, 1921).

Schiche, E., 'Ueber Todesahnungen im Felde und ihre Wirkung', in W. Stern and O. Lipmann (eds.), *Beihefte zur Zeitschrift für angewandte Psychologie. 21. Beiträge zur Psychologie des Krieges* (Leipzig: Johann Ambrosius Barth, 1920), pp. 173–8.

Schmahl, [no initial], 'Die Gewehre der europäischen Mächte', *Illustrierte Geschichte des Weltkrieges 1914/15.* Allgemeine Kriegszeitung 30 (n.d.), 99–100.

———, 'Infanteriegeschosse', *Illustrierte Geschichte des Weltkrieges 1914/15. Allgemeine Kriegszeitung* 36 (n.d.), 215–16.

Scholz, L., *Seelenleben des Soldaten an der Front. Hinterlassene Aufzeichnungen des im Kriege gefallenen Nervenarztes* (Tübingen: J.C.B. Mohr, 1920).

Schuhmacher, W., *Leben und Seele unseres Soldatenlieds im Weltkrieg* (Frankfurt am Main: Moritz Diesterweg, 1928).

Schulenburg, Graf von der (ed.), *Das Infanterie-Regiment Keith (1. Oberschlesisches) Nr. 22 im Kriege 1914–1918* (Berlin: Mars-Verlag Carl Siwinna, n.d.).

Schultz, J.H., 'Einige Bemerkungen über Feindschaftsgefühle im Kriege', *Neurologisches Centralblatt* 34, 11 (1 June 1915), 373–8.

Schultze-Großborstel, E., *Deutsche Kriegsschriften.* Part *16*: *Die Mobilmachung der Seelen* (Bonn: A. Marcus & E. Webers Verlag, 1915).

Selle, H. von and Gründel, W. (eds.), *Das 6. Westpreußische Infanterie-Regiment Nr. 149 im Weltkriege* (Berlin: Tradition Wilhelm Kolk, 1929).

Singer, K., 'Wesen und Bedeutung der Kriegspsychosen', *Berliner Klinische Wochenschrift* 8 (22 February 1915), 177–80.

Skaife, E.O., *R.W.F. A Short History of the Royal Welch Fusiliers* (London: Gale & Polden, n.d.).

Sombart, W., *Händler und Helden. Patriotische Besinnungen* (Munich: Dunker und Humblot, 1915).

'Some Mascots and Trifles that have Saved Lives', *The War Illustrated. A Picture-Record of Events by Land, Sea and Air* 2, 28 (27 February 1915), 47.

Sommer, R., *Krieg und Seelenleben. Akademische Festrede zur Feier des Jahresfestes der Großherzoglich Hessischen Ludwigs-Universität am 1. Juli 1915* (Giessen: Hof- und Universitäts-Druckerei Otto Kindt, 1915).

Southard, E.E., *Shell-Shock and other Neuropsychiatric Problems Presented in Five Hundred and Eighty-Nine Case Histories from the War Literature, 1914–1918* (New York: Arno Press, 1919, 1973).

Stanford Read, C., *Military Psychiatry in Peace and War* (London: H.K. Lewis, 1920).

Steiner, [no initial], 'Neurologie und Psychiatrie im Kriegslazarett', *Zeitschrift für die gesamte Neurologie und Psychiatrie* 30, 2/3 (27 November 1915), 305–18.

Stirling Taylor, G.R., *The Psychology of the Great War* (London: Martin Secker, 1915).

Thaer, A. von, *Generalstabsdienst an der Front und in der O.H.L. Aus Briefen und Tagebuchaufzeichnungen 1915–1919*, ed. S.A. Kaehler (Göttingen: Vandenhoeck & Rupprecht, 1958).

Ulrich, B. and Ziemann, B. (eds.), *Frontalltag im Ersten Weltkrieg. Wahn und Wirklichkeit* (Frankfurt am Main: Fischer Taschenbuch, 1994).

United Services Section with Section of Psychiatry, 'Discussion on Functional Nervous Disease in the Fighting Services', *Proceedings of the Royal Society of Medicine* 29 (1935–6), 855–68.

United States War Office, *Histories of Two Hundred and Fifty-One Divisions of the German Army which Participated in the War* (London: London Stamp Exchange, 1920, 1989).

Volkmann, E.-O., *Soziale Heeresmißstände als Mitursache des deutschen Zusammenbruches von 1918. Die Ursachen des Deutschen Zusammenbruches im Jahre 1918.* Part 2: *Der innere Zusammenbruch.* Vol. XI.2 (12 vols., Berlin: Deutsche Verlagsgesellschaft für Politik und Geschichte, 1929).

War Office (ed.), *Soldiers' Small Book* (London: HMSO, 1911).

——— (ed.), *The General Annual Report on the British Army for the year ending 30th September, 1913, with which is incorporated the Annual Report on Recruiting, prepared by command of the Army Council. Presented to both Houses of Parliament by Command of His Majesty [Cd. 7252.]* (London: HMSO, 1914), pp. 1–139.

——— (ed.), *Statistics of the Military Effort of the British Empire during the Great War. 1914–1920* (London: HMSO, 1922).

——— (ed.), *Report of the War Committee of Enquiry into 'Shell-Shock'* (London: HMSO, 1922).

A War Record of the 21st London Regiment (First Surrey Rifles), 1914–1919 (London: no publisher, 1928).

Weiler, K., *Arbeit und Gesundheit. Sozialmedizinische Schriftenreihe aus dem Gebiete des Reichsministeriums*. Part 22: *Nervöse und seelische Störungen bei Teilnehmern am Weltkriege, ihre ärztliche und rechtliche Beurteilung*. Part I: *Nervöse und seelische Störungen psychogener und funktioneller Art* (Leipzig: Georg Thieme, 1933).

Weygandt, W., 'Kriegspsychiatrische Begutachtungen', *Münchener Medizinische Wochenschrift* 62, 37. *Feldärztliche Beilage* 37 (14 September 1915), 1257–9.

White, O.W., 'Battle Supply', *Journal of the Royal United Services Institution* 67, 465 (February 1922), 93–105.

Why Germany Capitulated on November 11, 1918. A Brief Study Based on Documents in the Possession of the French General Staff (London: Hodder and Stoughton, 1919).

Wintterlin, G., *Kriegsgemäße Ausbildung der Kompagnie. Eine Anleitung für Kompagnie- und Zugführer* (Berlin: Ernst Siegfried Mittler & Sohn, 1917).

Wirth, J., 'Kampfstofferkrankungen im Weltkrieg', *Der Deutsche Militärarzt* 1, 4 (July 1936), 155–9.

Witkop, P. (ed.), *Kriegsbriefe gefallener Studenten* (Munich: Albert Langen / Georg Müller, 1933).

Wittermann, E., 'Kriegspsychiatrische Erfahrungen aus der Front', *Münchener Medizinische Wochenschrift* 62, 34. *Feldärztliche Beilage* 34 (24 August 1915), 1164–6.

Wolfsohn, J.M., 'The Predisposing Factors of War Psycho-Neuroses', *The Lancet* (2 February 1918), 177–80.

Wright, W.K., 'Psychology and the War', *Psychological Bulletin* 13, 12 (15 December 1916), 462–6.

Wurmb, E. von, *'Zum Offizier befördert!' Kameradschaftlicher Ratgeber für junge Offiziere und den Offiziersersatz der Linie und des Beurlaubtenstandes* (Berlin: R. Eisenschmidt, 1917).

Wyrall, E., *The Die-Hards in the Great War. A History of the Duke of Cambridge's own (Middlesex Regiment), 1914–1919, Compiled from the Records of the Line, Special Reserve, Service, and Territorial Battalions* (2 vols., London: Harrison & Sons, n.d.).

PRINTED SECONDARY WORKS

Afflerbach, H., '"Bis zum letzten Mann und letzten Groschen?" Die Wehrpflicht im Deutschen Reich und ihre Auswirkungen auf das militärische Führungsdenken im Ersten Weltkrieg', in R.G. Foerster (ed.), *Die Wehrpflicht. Entstehung, Erscheinungsformen und politisch-militärische Wirkung* (Munich: R. Oldenbourg, 1994), pp. 71–90.

Agrell, J., 'Stress. Military Implications – Psychological Aspects', in L. Levi (ed.), *Emotional Stress. Physiological and Psychological Reactions. Medical, Industrial and Military Implications. Proceedings of an International Symposium arranged by the Swedish Delegation for Applied Medical Defense Research* (Basel: S. Karger, 1967), pp. 214–19.

Ahrenfeldt, R.H., *Psychiatry in the British Army in the Second World War* (London: Routledge and Kegan Paul, 1958).

Armor, D.A. and Taylor, S.E., 'When Predictions Fail. The Dilemma of Unrealistic Optimism', in T. Gilovich, D. Griffin and D. Kahneman (eds.), *Heuristics and Biases* (Cambridge University Press, 2002), pp. 334–47.

Ashworth, T., *Trench Warfare 1914–1918. The Live and Let Live System* (London: Macmillan, 1980, 2000).

Audoin-Rouzeau, S., *Men at War, 1914–1918. National Sentiment and Trench Journalism in France during the First World War* (Oxford: Berg, 1992).

——— and Becker, A., *1914–1918. Understanding the Great War* (London: Profile Books, 2002).

Bailey, J., 'British Artillery in the Great War', in P. Griffith (ed.), *British Fighting Methods in the Great War* (London: Frank Cass, 1996), pp. 23–49.

Barham, P., *Forgotten Lunatics of the Great War* (New Haven: Yale University Press, 2004).

Bartov, O., *Hitler's Army. Soldiers, Nazis and War in the Third Reich* (Oxford University Press, 1992).

Baynes, J., *Morale. A Study of Men and Courage. The Second Scottish Rifles at the Battle of Neuve Chapelle 1915* (London: Leo Cooper, 1967, 1987).

Becker, A., *War and Faith. The Religious Imagination in France 1914–1930* (Oxford: Berg, 1998).

Becker, E., *The Denial of Death* (London: Free Press, 1973, 1997).

Becker, F., *Bilder von Krieg und Nation. Die Einigungskriege in der bürgerlichen Öffentlichkeit Deutschlands 1864–1913* (Munich: R. Oldenbourg, 2001).

Beckett, I., 'The Nation in Arms', in I.F.W. Beckett and K. Simpson (eds.), *A Nation in Arms. A Social Study of the British Army in the First World War* (Manchester University Press, 1985), pp. 1–35.

———, 'The Territorial Force', in I.F.W. Beckett and K. Simpson (eds.), *A Nation in Arms. A Social Study of the British Army in the First World War* (Manchester University Press, 1985), pp. 127–63.

Bendele, U., *Krieg, Kopf und Körper. Lernen für das Leben – Erziehung zum Tod* (Frankfurt am Main: Ullstein, 1984).

Bernstein, P.L., *Against the Gods. The Remarkable Story of Risk* (Chichester: John Wiley & Sons, 1996).

Bessel, R., *Germany after the First World War* (Oxford: Clarendon Press, 1993).

———, 'Die Heimkehr der Soldaten. Das Bild der Frontsoldaten in der Offentlichkeit der Weimarer Republik', in G. Hirschfeld, G. Krumeich and I. Renz (eds.), *Keiner fühlt sich hier mehr als Mensch ... Erlebnis und Wirkung des Ersten Weltkriegs* (Essen: Klartext, 1993), pp. 221–39.

———, 'Mobilizing German Society for War', in R. Chickering and S. Förster (eds.), *Great War, Total War. Combat and Mobilization on the Western Front, 1914–1918* (Cambridge: German Historical Institute and Cambridge University Press, 2000), pp. 437–52.

Bidwell, S., *Modern Warfare. A Study of Men, Weapons and Theories* (London: Allen Lane, 1973).

Binger, L., '"Ein tiefer Sinn im kindschen Spiel". Sozialisation für den Krieg', in Berliner Geschichtswerkstatt (ed.), *August 1914. Ein Volk zieht in den Krieg* (Berlin: Dirk Nishen, 1989), pp. 38–48.

Bogacz, T., '"A Tyranny of Words". Language, Poetry, and Antimodernism in England in the First World War', *Journal of Modern History* 58, 3 (September 1986), 643–68.

———, 'War Neurosis and Cultural Change in England, 1914–1922. The Work of the War Office Committee of Enquiry into "Shell-Shock"', *Journal of Contemporary History* 24, 2 (April 1989), 227–56.

Bond, B., *The Unquiet Western Front. Britain's Role in Literature and History* (Cambridge University Press, 2002).

Bourke, J., *Dismembering the Male. Men's Bodies, Britain and the Great War* (London: Reaktion Books, 1996).

———, *An Intimate History of Killing. Face-to-Face Killing in Twentieth-Century Warfare* (London: Granta Books, 1999).

———, 'The Emotions in War. Fear and the British and American Military, 1914–45', *Historical Research* 74, 185 (August 2001), 314–30.

Bourne, J., 'The British Working Man in Arms', in H. Cecil and P.H. Liddle (eds.), *Facing Armageddon. The First World War Experienced* (London: Leo Cooper, 1996), pp. 336–52.

———, 'A Personal Reflection on the Two World Wars', in P. Liddle, J. Bourne and I. Whitehead (eds.), *The Great War 1914–45. Lightning Strikes Twice* (London: HarperCollins, 2000).

Bowman, T., *The Irish Regiments in the Great War. Discipline and Morale* (Manchester University Press, 2003).

Brocks, C. and Ziemann, B., '"Vom Soldatenleben hätte ich gerade genug." Der Erste Weltkrieg in der Feldpost von Soldaten', in R. Rother (ed.), *Die letzten Tage der Menschheit. Bilder des Ersten Weltkrieges* (Berlin: Deutsches Historisches Museum, 1994), pp. 109–20.

Brown, C.G., *The Death of Christian Britain. Understanding Secularisation 1800–2000* (London: Routledge, 2001).

Brown, I.M., *British Logistics on the Western Front, 1914–1919* (London: Praeger, 1998).

Bryant, R.A. and Harvey, A.G., *Acute Stress Disorder. A Handbook of Theory, Assessment and Treatment* (Washington, DC: American Psychological Association, 2000).

Bull, S., *Brassey's History of Uniforms. World War One British Army* (London: Brassey's, 1998).

Buschmann, N., 'Der verschwiegene Krieg. Kommunikation zwischen Front und Heimat', in G. Hirschfeld, G. Krumeich, D. Langewiesche and H.-P. Ullmann (eds.), *Kriegserfahrungen. Studien zur Sozial- und Mentalitätsgeschichte des Ersten Weltkriegs* (Tübingen: Klartext, 1997), pp. 215–26.

Christadler, M., *Kriegserziehung im Jugendbuch. Literarische Mobilmachung in Deutschland und Frankreich vor 1914* (Frankfurt am Main: Haag und Herchen, 1978).

Clayton, A., *Paths of Glory. The French Army 1914–18* (London: Cassell, 2003).

Clemente, S.E., *For King and Kaiser! The Making of the Prussian Army Officer, 1860–1914* (London: Greenwood, 1992).

Corns, C. and Hughes-Wilson, J., *Blindfold and Alone. British Military Executions in the Great War* (London: Cassell, 2001, 2002).

Corrigan, G., *Mud, Blood and Poppycock. Britain and the First World War* (London: Cassell, 2003).

Cox, J., *The English Churches in a Secular Society. Lambeth, 1870–1930* (Oxford University Press, 1982).

Creveld, M. van, *Supplying War. Logistics from Wallenstein to Patton*, 2nd edn (Cambridge University Press, 1977, 2004).

———, *Fighting Power. German and US Army Performance, 1939–45* (London: Arms and Armour, 1983).

Damasio, A.R., *Descartes' Error. Emotion, Reason and the Human Brain* (London: Picador, 1995).

Deist, W., 'Zur Geschichte des preussischen Offizierkorps 1888–1918', in H.H. Hofmann (ed.), *Das deutsche Offizierkorps 1860–1960* (Boppard am Rhein: Harald Boldt, 1980), pp. 39–57.

———, 'Der militärische Zusammenbruch des Kaiserreichs. Zur Realität der "Dolchstoßlegende"', in U. Büttner (ed.), *Das Unrechtsregime. Internationale Forschung über den Nationalsozialismus*. Vol. I: *Ideologie-Herrschaftssystem-Wirkung in Europa* (Hamburg: Christians, 1986), pp. 101–29.

———, 'Verdeckter Militärstreik im Kriegsjahr 1918?', in W. Wette (ed.), *Der Krieg des kleinen Mannes. Eine Militärgeschichte von unten* (Munich: Piper, 1992, 1995), pp. 146–67.

———, 'The Military Collapse of the German Empire. The Reality Behind the Stab-in-the-Back Myth', *War in History* 3, 2 (April 1996), 186–207.

———, 'The German Army, the Authoritarian Nation-State and Total War', in J. Horne (ed.), *State, Society and Mobilization in Europe during the First World War* (Cambridge University Press, 1997), pp. 160–72.

Demeter, K., *The German Officer-Corps in Society and State 1650–1945* (London: Weidenfeld and Nicolson, 1962, 1965).

Dewey, P.E., 'Military Recruiting and the British Labour Force during the First World War', *Historical Journal* 27, 1 (March 1984), 199–223.

Douglas, R., 'Voluntary Enlistment in the First World War and the Work of the Parliamentary Recruiting Committee', *Journal of Modern History* 42, 4 (December 1970), 564–85.

Driskell, J.E. and Salas, E., 'Overcoming the Effects of Stress on Military Performance. Human Factors, Training, and Selection Strategies', in R. Gal and A.D. Mangesdorff (eds.), *Handbook of Military Psychology* (Chichester: John Wiley & Sons, 1991), pp. 183–93.

Dülffer, J., 'Einleitung. Dispositionen zum Krieg im wilhelminischen Deutschland', in J. Dülffer and K. Holl (eds.), *Bereit zum Krieg. Kriegsmentalität im wilhelminischen Deutschland 1890–1914. Beiträge zur historischen Friedensforschung* (Göttingen: Vandenhoeck und Ruprecht, 1986), pp. 9–19.

———, 'Kriegserwartung und Kriegsbild in Deutschland vor 1914', in W. Michalka (ed.), *Der Erste Weltkrieg. Wirkung, Wahrnehmung, Analyse* (Munich: Piper, 1992), pp. 778–98.

Dupuy, T.N., *A Genius for War. The German Army and General Staff, 1807–1945* (London: MacDonald and Jane's, 1977).

Eckart, W.U. and Gradmann, C., 'Medizin im Ersten Weltkrieg', in R. Spilker and B. Ulrich (eds.), *Der Tod als Maschinist. Der industrialisierte Krieg 1914–1918. Eine Ausstellung des Museums Industriekultur Osnabrück im Rahmen des Jubiläums '350 Jahre Westfälischer Friede' 17. Mai – 23. August 1998. Katalog* (Bramsche: Rasch, 1998), pp. 203—15.

Eksteins, M., *Rites of Spring. The Great War and the Birth of the Modern Age* (London: Bantam Press, 1989).

Elias, N., *Studien über die Deutschen. Machtkämpfe und Habitusentwicklung im 19. und 20. Jahrhundert* (Frankfurt am Main: Suhrkamp, 1989).

Ellis, J., *Eye-Deep in Hell* (London: Penguin, 1976, 2000).

——— and Cox, M., *The World War I Databook. The Essential Facts and Figures for all the Combatants* (London: Aurum Press, 1993).

Englander, D., 'Discipline and Morale in the British Army, 1917–1918', in J. Horne (ed.), *State, Society and Mobilization in Europe during the First World War* (Cambridge University Press, 1997), pp. 125–43.

——— and Osborne, J., 'Jack, Tommy and Henry Dubb. The Armed Forces and the Working Class', *Historical Journal* 21, 3 (1978), 593–621.

English, A.D., 'Leadership and Operational Stress in the Canadian Forces', *Canadian Military Journal* (Autumn 2000), 33–8.

Feldman, G.D., *Army, Industry, and Labor in Germany 1914–1918* (Princeton University Press, 1966).

Ferguson, N., *The Pity of War* (London: Allen Lane. The Penguin Press, 1998).

———, 'Prisoner Taking and Prisoner Killing in the Age of Total War. Towards a Political Economy of Military Defeat', *War in History* 11, 2 (April 2004), 148–92.

Fiedler, G., *Jugend im Krieg. Bürgerliche Jugendbewegung, Erster Weltkrieg und sozialer Wandel 1914–1923* (Cologne: Verlag Wissenschaft und Politik, 1989).

Fischer, J., 'Das württembergische Offizierkorps 1866–1918', in H.H. Hofmann (ed.), *Das deutsche Offizierkorps 1860–1960* (Boppard am Rhein: Harald Boldt, 1980), pp. 99–138.

Flack, W.F., Jr, Litz, B.T. and Keane, T.M., 'Cognitive-Behavioural Treatment of War-Zone-Related Posttraumatic Stress Disorder. A Flexible, Hierarchical Approach', in V.M. Follette, J.I. Ruzele and F.R. Abeeg (eds.), *Cognitive-Behavioural Therapies for Trauma* (New York: Guilford, 1998), pp. 77–99.

Foley, R.T., *German Strategy and the Path to Verdun. Erich von Falkenhayn and the Development of Attrition, 1870–1916* (Cambridge University Press, 2005).

Fong, G., 'The Movement of German Divisions to the Western Front, Winter 1917–1918', *War in History* 7, 2 (April 2000), 225–35.

Förster, J., 'Ludendorff and Hitler in Perspective. The Battle for the German Soldier's Mind, 1917–1944', *War in History* 10, 3 (July 2003), 321–34.

French, D., 'The Meaning of Attrition, 1914–1916', *English Historical Review* 103, 407 (April 1988), 385–405.

———, *Military Identities. The Regimental System, the British Army, and the British People, c. 1870–2000* (Oxford University Press, 2005).

Frevert, U., *A Nation in Barracks. Modern Germany, Military Conscription and Civil Society* (Oxford: Berg, 2004).

Fritsche, G.-W., 'Bedingungen des individuellen Kriegserlebnisses', in P. Knoch (ed.), *Kriegsalltag. Die Rekonstruktion des Kriegsalltags als Aufgabe der historischen Forschung und der Friedenserziehung* (Stuttgart: J.B. Metzlersche Verlagsbuchhandlung, 1989), pp. 114–52.

Fuller, J.G., *Troop Morale and Popular Culture in the British and Dominion Armies 1914–1918* (Oxford: Clarendon Press, 1990).

Funck, M., 'In den Tod gehen. Bilder des Sterbens im 19. und 20. Jahrhundert', in U. Breymayer, B. Ulrich and K. Wieland (eds.), *Willensmenschen. Über deutsche Offiziere* (Frankfurt am Main: Fischer Taschenbuch, 1999), pp. 227–36.

Fussell, P., *The Great War and Modern Memory* (Oxford University Press, 1975).

Gabriel, R.A., 'Introduction', in R.A. Gabriel (ed.), *Military Psychology. A Comparative Perspective* (London: Greenwood Press, 1986), pp. 1–6.

Gestrich, A., '"Leicht trennt sich nur die Jugend vom Leben" – Jugendliche im Ersten Weltkrieg', in R. Spilker and B. Ulrich (eds.), *Der Tod als Maschinist. Der industrialisierte Krieg 1914–1918. Eine Ausstellung des Museums Industriekultur Osnabrück im Rahmen des Jubiläums, 350 Jahre Westfälischer Friede, 17. Mai–23. August 1998. Katalog* (Bramsche: Rasch, 1998), pp. 32–45.

Gilbert, A.D., *Religion and Society in Industrial England. Church, Chapel and Social Change, 1740–1914* (London: Longman Group, 1976).

Gill, D. and Dallas, G., 'Mutiny at Etaples Base in 1917', *Past and Present* 69 (November 1975), 88–112.

———, *The Unknown Army* (London: Verso, 1985).

Gray, J.A., *The Psychology of Fear and Stress* (Cambridge University Press, 1971, 1987).

Gregory, A., 'British "War Enthusiasm" in 1914. A Reassessment', in G. Braybon (ed.), *Evidence, History and the Great War. Historians and the Impact of 1914–18* (New York: Berghahn Books, 2003), pp. 67–85.

Grieves, K., *The Politics of Manpower, 1914–18* (Manchester University Press, 1988).

Griffith, P., *Battle Tactics on the Western Front. The British Army's Art of Attack, 1916–18* (New Haven: Yale University Press, 1994).

———, 'The Extent of Tactical Reform in the British Army', in P. Griffith (ed.), *British Fighting Methods in the Great War* (London: Frank Cass, 1996), pp. 1–22.

Gudmundsson, B.I., *Stormtroop Tactics. Innovation in the German Army, 1914–1918* (London: Praeger, 1989, 1995).

Guth, E.P., *Der Loyalitätskonflikt des deutschen Offizierkorps in der Revolution 1918–20* (Frankfurt am Main: Peter Lang, 1983).

Habeck, M.R., 'Technology in the First World War. The View from Below', in J. Winter, G. Parker and M.R. Habeck (eds.), *The Great War and the Twentieth Century* (New Haven: Yale University Press, 2000), pp. 99–131.

Hall, R.C., '"The Enemy is Behind Us": The Morale Crisis in the Bulgarian Army during the Summer of 1918', *War in History* 11, 2 (April 2004), 209–19.

Hamilton, R.F. and Herwig, H.H., *Decisions for War, 1914–1917* (Cambridge University Press, 2004).

Harris, J.P. and Barr, N., *Amiens to the Armistice. The BEF in the Hundred Days' Campaign, 8 August–11 November 1918* (London: Brassey's, 1998).

Hartcup, G., *The War of Invention. Scientific Developments, 1914–18* (London: Brassey's Defence Publishers, 1988).

Hawley, A., 'People not Personnel. The Human Dimension of Fighting Power', in H. Strachan (ed.), *The British Army, Manpower and Society into the Twenty-First Century* (London: Frank Cass, 2000), pp. 213–26.

Herwig, H.H., *The First World War. Germany and Austria-Hungary 1914–1918* (London: Arnold, 1997).

Hettling, M. and Jeismann, M., 'Der Weltkrieg als Epos. Philipp Witkops "Kriegsbriefe gefallener Studenten"', in G. Hirschfeld, G. Krumeich and I. Renz (eds.), *Keiner fühlt sich hier mehr als Mensch . . . Erlebnis und Wirkung des Ersten Weltkriegs* (Essen: Klartext, 1993), pp. 175–98.

Hirschfeld, G., 'Die Somme-Schlacht von 1916', in G. Hirschfeld, G. Krumeich and I. Renz (eds.), *Die Deutschen an der Somme 1914–1918* (Essen: Klartext, 2006), pp. 79–161.

Holmes, R., *Tommy. The British Soldier on the Western Front 1914–1918* (London: HarperCollins, 2004).

Horne, A., *The Price of Glory. Verdun 1916* (London: Macmillan, 1962).

Horne, J. and Kramer, A., *German Atrocities, 1914. A History of Denial* (New Haven: Yale University Press, 2001).

Horowitz, M.J. and Wilner, N., 'Field Studies on the Impact of Life Events', in M.J. Horowitz (ed.), *Stress Response Syndromes* (Northvale, NJ: Jason Aronson, 1997), pp. 43–68.

Howard, M., 'Men against Fire. Expectations of War in 1914', in S.E. Miller, S.M. Lynn-Jones and S. Van Evera (eds.), *Military Strategy and the Origins of the First World War* (Princeton University Press, 1991), pp. 3–19.

Hughes, C., 'The New Armies', in I.F.W. Beckett and K. Simpson (eds.), *A Nation in Arms. A Social Study of the British Army in the First World War* (Manchester University Press, 1985), pp. 99–125.

Hüppauf, B., '"Der Tod ist verschlungen in den Sieg". Todesbilder aus dem Ersten Weltkrieg und Nachkriegszeit', in B. Hüppauf (ed.), *Ansichten vom Krieg. Vergleichende Studien zum Ersten Weltkrieg in Literatur und Gesellschaft* (Königsten: Forum Academicum, 1984), pp. 55–91.

———, 'Schlachtenmythen und die Konstruktion des "Neuen Menschen"', in G. Hirschfeld, G. Krumeich and I. Renz (eds.), *Keiner fühlt sich hier mehr als Mensch . . . Erlebnis und Wirkung des Ersten Weltkriegs* (Essen: Klartext, 1993), pp. 43–84.

Ingenlath, M., *Mentale Aufrüstung. Militarisierungstendenzen in Frankreich und Deutschland vor dem Ersten Weltkrieg* (Frankfurt: Campus, 1998).

Jackman, S.D., 'Shoulder to Shoulder. Close Control and "Old Prussian Drill" in German Offensive Infantry Tactics, 1871–1914', *Journal of Military History* 68, 1 (January 2004), 73–104.

Jaeger, H., 'Der Unternehmer als Vater und Patriarch', in W. Faulstich and G.E. Grimm (eds.), *Sturz der Götter? Vaterbilder im 20. Jahrhundert* (Frankfurt am Main: Suhrkamp, 1989), pp. 98–120.

Jahr, C., *Gewöhnliche Soldaten. Desertion und Deserteure im deutschen und britischen Heer 1914–1918* (Göttingen: Vandenhoeck & Ruprecht, 1998).

Janowitz, M. and Shils, E.A., 'Cohesion and Disintegration in the Wehrmacht in World War II', in M. Janowitz (ed.), *Military Conflict. Essays in the Institutional Analysis of War and Peace* (Los Angeles: Sage Publications, 1975), pp. 177–220.

Jarausch, K.H., 'German Students in the First World War', *Central European History* 17, 4 (December 1984), 310–29.

John, H., *Das Reserveoffizierkorps im Deutschen Kaiserreich 1890–1914. Ein sozialgeschichtlicher Beitrag zur Untersuchung der gesellschaftlichen Militarisierung im Wilhelminischen Deutschland* (Frankfurt am Main: Campus, 1981).

Jones, E. and Wessely, S., 'Psychiatric Battle Casualties. An Intra- and Interwar Comparison', *British Journal of Psychiatry* 178, 3 (March 2001), 242–7.

———, Hodgins Vermaas, R., McCartney, H., Beech, C., Palmer, I., Hyams, K. and Wessely, S., 'Flashbacks and Post-Traumatic Stress Disorder. The Genesis of a 20th-Century Diagnosis', *British Journal of Psychiatry* 182, 2 (February 2003), 158–63.

——— and Wessely, S., 'War Syndromes. The Impact of Culture on Medically Unexplained Symptoms', *Medical History* 49, 1 (January 2005), 55–78.

Joseph, S., 'Attributional Processes, Coping and Post-traumatic Stress Disorders', in W. Yule (ed.), *Post-traumatic Stress Disorders. Concepts and Therapy* (Chichester: John Wiley & Sons, 1999, 2000), pp. 51–70.

Katz, D. and Kahn, R.L., *The Social Psychology of Organizations*, 2nd edn (Chichester: John Wiley & Sons, 1978).

Keegan, J., *The Face of Battle. A Study of Agincourt, Waterloo and the Somme* (Harmondsworth: Penguin, 1976, 1983).

———, *The First World War* (London: Pimlico, 1999).

Keene, J.D., 'Intelligence and Morale in the Army of a Democracy. The Genesis of Military Psychology during the First World War', *Military Psychology* 6, 4 (1994), 235–53.

Kelman, H.C. and Hamilton, V.L., *Crimes of Obedience. Toward a Social Psychology of Authority and Responsibility* (New Haven: Yale University Press, 1989).

Kitchen, M., *The German Officer Corps 1890–1914* (Oxford: Clarendon Press, 1968).

———, *The German Offensives of 1918* (Stroud: Tempus, 2001).

Kluge, U., *Soldatenräte und Revolution. Studien zur Militärpolitik in Deutschland 1918/19* (Göttingen: Vandenhoeck & Ruprecht, 1975).

Knoch, P. (ed.), *Menschen im Krieg 1914–1918. Bilder- und Lesebuch zur Ausstellung in Ludwigsburg (Dezember 1987 bis Februar 1988)* (Ludwigsburg: Pädagogische Hochschule Ludwigsburg, 1987).

———, 'Kriegsalltag', in P. Knoch (ed.), *Kriegsalltag. Die Rekonstruktion des Kriegsalltags als Aufgabe der historischen Forschung und der Friedenserziehung* (Stuttgart: J.B. Metzlersche Versbuchhandlung, 1989), pp. 222–51.

———, 'Erleben und Nacherleben. Das Kriegserlebnis im Augenzeugenbericht und im Geschichtsunterricht', in G. Hirschfeld, G. Krumeich and I. Renz (eds.), *Keiner fühlt sich hier mehr als Mensch ... Erlebnis und Wirkung des Ersten Weltkriegs* (Essen: Klartext, 1993), pp. 199–219.

Komo, G., *'Für Volk und Vaterland'. Die Militärpsychiatrie in den Weltkriegen* (Münster: Lit, 1992).

Kramer, A., 'Wackes at War. Alsace-Lorraine and the Failure of German National Mobilization, 1914–1918', in J. Horne (ed.), *State, Society and Mobilization in Europe during the First World War* (Cambridge University Press, 1997), pp. 105–21.

Kraul, M., *Das deutsche Gymnasium 1780–1980* (Frankfurt am Main: Suhrkamp, 1984).

Kruse, W., 'Die Kriegsbegeisterung im Deutschen Reich zu Beginn des Ersten Weltkrieges', in M. van der Linden and G. Mergner (eds.),

Kriegsbegeisterung und mentale Kriegsvorbereitung. Interdisziplinäre Studien (Berlin: Duncker und Humblot, 1991), pp. 73–87.

———, *Krieg und nationale Integration. Eine Neuinterpretation des sozialdemokratischen Burgfriedensschlusses 1914/15* (Essen: Klartext, 1993).

———, 'Krieg und Klassenheer. Zur Revolutionierung der deutschen Armee im Ersten Weltkrieg', *Geschichte und Gesellschaft. Zeitschrift für Historische Sozialwissenschaft* 22, 4 (1996), 530–61.

———, 'Krieg und nationale Identität. Die Ideologisierung des Krieges', in W. Kruse (ed.), *Eine Welt von Feinden. Der Große Krieg 1914–1918* (Frankfurt am Main: Fischer Taschenbuch, 1997), pp. 167–76.

Kulka, R.A., Schlenger, W.E., Fairbank, J.A., Hough, R.L., Jordan, B.K., Marmar, L.R. and Weiss, D.S., *Trauma and the Vietnam War Generation. Report of Findings from the National Vietnam Veterans Readjustment Study* (New York: Brunner / Mazel, 1990).

Labott, S.M. and Martin, R.B., 'The Stress-moderating Effects of Weeping and Humour', *Journal of Human Stress* 13, 4 (winter 1987), 159–64.

Labuc, S., 'Cultural and Societal Factors in Military Organizations', in R. Gal and A.D. Mangesdorff (eds.), *Handbook of Military Psychology* (Chichester: John Wiley & Sons, 1991), pp. 471–89.

Latzel, K., *Vom Sterben im Krieg. Wandlungen in der Einstellung zum Soldatentod vom Siebenjährigen Krieg bis zum II. Weltkrieg* (Warendorf: Fahlbusch & Co., 1988).

———, 'Die mißlungene Flucht vor dem Tod. Töten und Sterben vor und nach 1918', in J. Duppler and G.P. Groß (eds.), *Kriegsende 1918. Ereignis, Wirkung, Nachwirkung. Beiträge zur Militärgeschichte. Herausgegeben vom Militärgeschichtlichen Forschungsamt.* Vol. LIII (Munich: R. Oldenbourg, 1999), pp. 183–99.

Lee, J., 'Some Lessons of the Somme. The British Infantry in 1917', in British Commission for Military History (ed.), *'Look to Your Front'. Studies in the First World War* (Staplehurst: Spellmount, 1999), pp. 79–88.

Leed, E.J., *No Man's Land. Combat and Identity in World War I* (Cambridge University Press, 1979, 1981).

Leese, P., *Shell Shock. Traumatic Neurosis and the British Soldiers of the First World War* (Basingstoke: Palgrave Macmillan, 2002).

Lerner, P., *Hysterical Men. War, Psychiatry, and the Politics of Trauma in Germany, 1890–1930* (Ithaca: Cornell University Press, 2003).

Liddle, P., *Testimony of War 1914–1918* (Salisbury: Michael Russell, 1979).

———, *The Soldier's War 1914–18* (London: Blandford Press, 1988).

———, 'British Loyalties. The Evidence of an Archive', in H. Cecil and P.H. Liddle (eds.), *Facing Armageddon. The First World War Experienced* (London: Leo Cooper, 1996), pp. 523–38.

Linden, M. van der and Mergner, G., 'Kriegsbegeisterung und mentale Kriegsvorbereitung', in M. van der Linden and G. Mergner (eds.), *Kriegsbegeisterung und mentale Kriegsvorbereitung. Interdisziplinäre Studien* (Berlin: Duncker und Humblot, 1991), pp. 9–23.

Linnenkohl, H., *Vom Einzelschuß zur Feuerwalze. Der Wettlauf zwischen Technik und Taktik im Ersten Weltkrieg* (Koblenz: Bernard & Graefe, 1990).

Linse, U., 'Das Wahre Zeugnis. Eine psychohistorische Deutung des Ersten Weltkriegs', in K. Vondung (ed.), *Kriegserlebnis. Der Erste Weltkrieg in der literarischen Gestaltung und symbolischen Deutung der Nationen* (Göttingen: Vandenhoeck & Ruprecht, 1980), pp. 90–114.

———, '"Saatfrüchte sollen nicht vermahlen werden!" Zur Resymbolisierung des Soldatentods', in K. Vondung (ed.), *Kriegserlebnis. Der Erste Weltkrieg in der literarischen Gestaltung und symbolischen Deutung der Nationen* (Göttingen: Vandenhoeck & Ruprecht, 1980), pp. 262–74.

Lipp, A., *Meinungslenkung im Krieg. Kriegserfahrungen deutscher Soldaten und ihre Deutung 1914–1918* (Göttingen: Vandenhoeck & Ruprecht, 2003).

Liulevicius, V.G., *War Land on the Eastern Front. Culture, National Identity, and German Occupation in World War I* (Cambridge University Press, 2000).

———, 'Ostpreußen', in G. Hirschfeld, G. Krumeich and I. Renz (eds.), *Enzyklopädie Erster Weltkrieg* (Paderborn: Ferdinand Schöningh, 2004), pp. 764–6.

Ljunberg, L., 'Stress. Military Implications – Medical Aspects', in L. Levi (ed.), *Emotional Stress. Physiological and Psychological Reactions. Medical, Industrial and Military Implications. Proceedings of an International Symposium Arranged by the Swedish Delegation for Applied Medical Defense Research* (Basel: S. Karger, 1967), pp. 220–4.

Loewenberg, P., 'Germany, The Home Front (1). The Physical and Psychological Consequence of Home Front Hardship', in H. Cecil and P.H. Liddle (eds.), *Facing Armageddon. The First World War Experienced* (London: Leo Cooper, 1996), pp. 554–62.

Lupfer, T.T., *The Dynamics of Doctrine. The Changes in German Tactical Doctrine during the First World War* (Fort Leavenworth, KS: Combat Studies Institute, 1981).

McCartney, H.B., *Citizen Soldiers. The Liverpool Territorials in the First World War* (Cambridge University Press, 2005).

MacCrae, R.R. and John, O.P., 'An Introduction to the Five-Factor Model and its Applications', *Journal of Personality* 60, 2 (June 1992), 175–215.

McGinnies, E., 'Emotionality and Perceptual Defence', in R.D. Gross (ed.), *Key Studies in Psychology* (London: Hodder & Stoughton, 1990), pp. 10–20.

MacKenzie, S.P., 'Morale and the Cause. The Campaign to Shape the Outlook of Soldiers in the British Expeditionary Force, 1914–1918', *Canadian Journal of History* 25, 2 (August 1990), 215–32.

McKibbin, R., *The Ideologies of Class. Social Relations in Britain 1880–1950* (Oxford: Clarendon Press, 1990, 1994).

McLeod, H. *Secularisation in Western Europe, 1848–1914* (London: Macmillan, 2000).

McNally, R.J. and Shin, L.M., 'Association of Intelligence with Severity of Posttraumatic Stress Disorder Symptoms in Vietnam Combat Veterans', *American Journal of Psychology* 152 (1995), 936–8.

———, Bryant, R.A. and Ehlers, A., 'Does Early Psychological Intervention Promote Recovery from Posttraumatic Stress?', *Psychological Science in the Public Interest* 4, 2 (November 2003), 45–79.

Malinowski, S., *Vom König zum Führer. Sozialer Niedergang und politische Radikalisierung im deutschen Adel zwischen Kaiserreich und NS-Staat* (Berlin: Akademie, 2003).

Manning, F.J., 'Morale, Cohesion, and Esprit de Corps', in R. Gal and A.D. Mangesdorff (eds.), *Handbook of Military Psychology* (Chichester: John Wiley & Sons, 1991), pp. 453–70.

Marlowe, D., 'The Human Dimension of Battle and Combat Breakdown', in R.A. Gabriel (ed.), *Military Psychology. A Comparative Perspective* (London: Greenwood Press, 1986), pp. 7–24.

Marquis, A.G., 'Words as Weapons. Propaganda in Britain and Germany during the First World War', *Journal of Contemporary History* 13, 3 (July 1978), 467–98.

Marshall, S.L.A., *Men Against Fire. The Problem of Battle Command* (Norman: University of Oklahoma Press, 1947, 2000).

Middlebrook, M., *The Kaiser's Battle, 21 March 1918. The First Day of the German Spring Offensive* (London: Allen Lane. The Penguin Press, 1978).

Milgram, S., 'Behavioural Study of Obedience', in R.D. Gross (ed.), *Key Studies in Psychology* (London: Hodder & Stoughton, 1990), pp. 116–29.

Miller, D.T. and Taylor, B.R., 'Counterfactual Thought, Regret, and Superstition. How to Avoid Kicking Yourself', in T. Gilovich, D. Griffin and D. Kahneman (eds.), *Heuristics and Biases* (Cambridge University Press, 2002), pp. 367–78.

Mitchinson, K.W., *Gentlemen and Officers. The Impact and Experience of War on a Territorial Regiment 1914–1918* (London: Imperial War Museum, 1995).

Mommsen, W.J., *Der autoritäre Nationalstaat. Verfassung, Gesellschaft und Kultur im deutschen Kaiserreich* (Frankfurt am Main: Fischer Taschenbuch, 1990).

———, 'Der Erste Weltkrieg und die Krise Europas', in G. Hirschfeld, G. Krumeich and I. Renz (eds.), *Keiner fühlt sich hier mehr als Mensch … Erlebnis und Wirkung des Ersten Weltkriegs* (Essen: Klartext, 1993), pp. 25–41.

Moncure, J., *Forging the King's Sword. Military Education between Tradition and Modernization. The Case of the Royal Prussian Cadet Corps, 1871–1918* (New York: P. Lang, 1993).

Mosse, G.L., *Fallen Soldiers. Reshaping the Memory of the World Wars* (Oxford University Press, 1990).

Nash, D.B., *Imperial German Army Handbook 1914–1918* (London: Ian Allan, 1980).

Nipperdey, T., *Deutsche Geschichte 1866–1918*. Vol. I: *Arbeitswelt und Bürgergeist* (2 vols., Munich: C.H. Beck, 1990).

———, *Deutsche Geschichte 1866–1918*. Vol. II: *Machtstaat vor der Demokratie* (2 vols., Munich: C.H. Beck, 1992).

Nonn, C., 'Oh What a Lovely War? German Common People and the First World War', *German History* 18, 1 (January 2000), 97–111.

Offer, A., *The First World War. An Agrarian Interpretation* (Oxford: Clarendon Press, 1989).

Ostertag, H., *Bildung, Ausbildung und Erziehung des Offizierkorps im deutschen Kaiserreich 1871–1918. Eliteideal, Anspruch und Wirklichkeit* (Frankfurt am Main: Peter Lang, 1990).

Overmans, R., 'Kriegsverluste', in G. Hirschfeld, G. Krumeich and I. Renz (eds.), *Enzyklopädie Erster Weltkrieg* (Paderborn: Ferdinand Schöningh, 2004), pp. 663–6.

Palazzo, A., *Seeking Victory on the Western Front. The British Army and Chemical Warfare in World War I* (Lincoln: University of Nebraska, 2000).

Palmer, I.P., 'Lest we Forget, Again', *British Journal of Psychiatry* 179, 2 (August 2001), 179.

Parker, P. *The Old Lie. The Great War and the Public-School Ethos* (London: Constable, 1987).

Peaty, J., 'Capital Courts-Martial during the Great War', in British Commission for Military History (ed.), *'Look to Your Front'. Studies in the First World War* (Staplehurst: Spellmount, 1999), pp. 89–104.

Pedroncini, G., *Les mutineries de 1917* (Paris: Presses Universitaires de France, 1967).

Peterson, C., Maier, S.F. and Seligman, M.E.P., *Learned Helplessness. A Theory for the Age of Personal Control* (Oxford University Press, 1993).

Pitman, R.K., Orr, S.P., Lowenhagen, M.J., Macklin, M.L. and Altman, B., 'Pre-Vietnam Contents of Posttraumatic Stress Disorder Veterans' Service Medical and Personal Records', *Comparative Psychology* 32 (1991), 416–22.

Prior, R. and Wilson, T., *Command on the Western Front. The Military Career of Sir Henry Rawlinson, 1914–18* (Oxford: Blackwell, 1992).

———, *Passchendaele. The Untold Story* (New Haven: Yale University Press, 1996).

———, *The Somme* (New Haven: Yale University Press, 2005).

Rachman, S.J., *Fear and Courage* (New York: W.H. Freeman and Company, 1978, 1990).

Rahne, H., *Militärische Mobilmachungsplanung und -technik in Preußen und im Deutschen Reich von Mitte des 19. Jahrhunderts bis zum Zweiten Weltkrieg* (Berlin: Militärverlag der deutschen Demokratischen Republik, 1983).

Reimann, A., 'Die heile Welt im Stahlgewitter. Deutsche und englische Feldpost aus dem Ersten Weltkrieg', in G. Hirschfeld, G. Krumeich, D. Langewiesche and H.-P. Ullmann (eds.), *Kriegserfahrungen. Studien zur Sozial- und Mentalitätsgeschichte des Ersten Weltkriegs* (Tübingen: Klartext, 1997), pp. 131–45.

———, *Der große Krieg der Sprachen. Untersuchungen zur historischen Semantik in Deutschland und England zur Zeit des Ersten Weltkriegs* (Essen: Klartext, 2000).

Ritter, G.A. and Tenfelde, K., *Arbeiter im Deutschen Kaiserreich 1871 bis 1914* (Bonn: J.H.W. Dietz Nachf., 1992).

Robbins, K., 'The British Experience of Conscientious Objection', in H. Cecil and P.H. Liddle (eds.), *Facing Armageddon. The First World War Experienced* (London: Leo Cooper, 1996), pp. 691–706.

Rohkrämer, T., 'Der Gesinnungsmilitarismus der "kleinen Leute" im Deutschen Kaiserreich', in W. Wette (ed.), *Der Krieg des kleinen Mannes. Eine Militärgeschichte von unten* (Munich: Piper, 1992), pp. 95–109.

———, 'August 1914 – Kriegsmentalität und ihre Voraussetzungen', in W. Michalka (ed.), *Der Erste Weltkrieg. Wirkung, Wahrnehmung, Analyse* (Munich: Piper, 1992), pp. 759–77.

Rojahn, J., 'Arbeiterbewegung und Kriegsbegeisterung. Die deutsche Sozialdemokratie 1870–1914', in M. van der Linden and G. Mergner (eds.), *Kriegsbegeisterung und mentale Kriegsvorbereitung. Interdisziplinäre Studien* (Berlin: Duncker und Humblot, 1991), pp. 57–71.

Rose, A.M., 'The Social Psychology of Desertion from Combat', in P. Karsten (ed.), *Motivating Soldiers. Morale or Mutiny* (New York: Garland Publishing, 1998), pp. 250–65.

Rose, E., 'The Anatomy of Mutiny', in P. Karsten (ed.), *Motivating Soldiers. Morale or Mutiny* (New York: Garland Publishing, 1998), pp. 169–82.

Ross, L. and Anderson, C.A., 'Shortcomings in the Attribution Process. On the Origins and Maintenance of Erroneous Social Assessments', in D. Kahneman, P. Slovic and A. Tversky (eds.), *Judgment under Uncertainty. Heuristics and Biases* (Cambridge University Press, 1982), pp. 129–52.

Roth, K.H., 'Die Modernisierung der Folter in den beiden Weltkriegen. Der Konflikt der Psychotherapeuten und Schulpsychiater um die deutschen "Kriegsneurotiker" 1915–1945', 1999. *Zeitschrift für Sozialgeschichte des 20. und 21. Jahrhunderts* 2, 3 (1987), 8–75.

Rothwell, V.H., *British War Aims and Peace Diplomacy 1914–1918* (Oxford: Clarendon Press, 1971).

Rumschöttel, H., 'Der bayerische Offizierkorps 1866–1918', in H.H. Hofmann (ed.), *Das deutsche Offizierkorps 1860–1960* (Boppard am Rhein: Harald Boldt, 1980), pp. 75–98.

Rürup, R., 'Der "Geist von *1914*" in Deutschland. Kriegsbegeisterung und Ideologisierung des Krieges im Ersten Weltkrieg', in B. Hüppauf (ed.), *Ansichten vom Krieg. Vergleichende Studien zum Ersten Weltkrieg in Literatur und Gesellschaft* (Königsten: Forum Academicum, 1984), pp. 1–30.

Samuels, M., *Command or Control? Command, Training and Tactics in the British and German Armies, 1888–1918* (London: Frank Cass, 1995).

Sanders, M.L. and Taylor, P.M., *British Propaganda during the First World War* (London: Macmillan, 1982).

Schmidt-Richberg, W., 'Die Regierungszeit Wilhelms II', in Militärgeschichtliches Forschungsamt (ed.), *Handbuch zur deutschen Militärgeschichte 1648–1939*. Vol. V: *Von der Entlassung Bismarcks bis zum Ende des Ersten Weltkrieges (1890–1918)* (10 vols., Frankfurt am Main: Bernard & Graefe, 1968), pp. 9–156.

Schubert-Weller, C., *'Kein schönrer Tod'. Die Militarisierung der männlichen Jugend und ihr Einsatz im Ersten Weltkrieg 1890–1918* (Weinheim: Juventa, 1998).

Schweitzer, R., *The Cross and the Trenches. Religious Faith and Doubt among British and American Great War Soldiers* (London: Praeger, 2003).

Scott, P.T., *'Dishonoured'. The 'Colonels' Surrender' at St Quentin, the Retreat from Mons, August 1914* (London: Tom Donovan, 1994).

See, K. von, *Die Ideen von 1789 und die Ideen von 1914. Völkisches Denken in Deutschland zwischen Französischer Revolution und Erstem Weltkrieg* (Frankfurt am Main: Athenaion, 1975).

Sheffield, G., 'British Military Police and their Battlefield Role, 1914–18', *Sandhurst Journal of Military Studies* 1 (1990), 33–46.

———, 'Officer–Man Relations, Discipline and Morale in the British Army of the Great War', in H. Cecil and P.H. Liddle (eds.), *Facing Armageddon. The First World War Experienced* (London: Leo Cooper, 1996), pp. 413–24.

———, *Leadership in the Trenches. Officer–Man Relations, Morale and Discipline in the British Army in the Era of the First World War* (Basingstoke: Macmillan, 2000).

———, *Forgotten Victory. The First World War. Myths and Realities* (London: Headline, 2001).

Shephard, B., *A War of Nerves. Soldiers and Psychiatrists 1914–1994* (London: Pimlico, 2002).

Showalter, D.E., 'Mass Warfare and the Impact of Technology', in R. Chickering and S. Förster (eds.), *Great War, Total War. Combat and Mobilization on the Western Front, 1914–1918* (Cambridge University Press, 2000).

Silva, P. de, 'Cultural Aspects of Post-traumatic Stress Disorder', in W. Yule (ed.), *Post-traumatic Stress Disorders. Concepts and Therapy* (Chichester: John Wiley & Sons, 1999, 2000), pp. 116–38.

Simkins, P., *Kitchener's Army. The Raising of the New Armies, 1914–16* (Manchester University Press, 1988).

———, 'Everyman at War. Recent Interpretations of the Front Line Experience', in B. Bond (ed.), *The First World War and British Military History* (Oxford: Clarendon Press, 1991), pp. 289–313.

———, 'The War Experience of a Typical Kitchener Division. The 18th Division, 1914–1918', in H. Cecil and P.H. Liddle (eds.), *Facing Armageddon. The First World War Experienced* (London: Leo Cooper, 1996), pp. 297–313.

———, 'Co-Stars or Supporting Cast? British Divisions in the "Hundred Days", 1918', in P. Griffith (ed.), *British Fighting Methods in the Great War* (London: Frank Cass, 1996), pp. 50–69.

———, 'Somme Reprise. Reflections on the Fighting for Albert and Bapaume, August 1918', in British Commission for Military History (ed.), *'Look to Your Front'. Studies in the First World War* (Staplehurst: Spellmount, 1999), pp. 147–62.

Simpson, A., *Hot Blood and Cold Steel. Life and Death in the Trenches of the First World War* (Staplehurst: Spellmount, 1993, 2000).

Simpson, K., 'The Officers', in I.F.W. Beckett and K. Simpson (eds.), *A Nation in Arms. A Social Study of the British Army in the First World War* (Manchester University Press, 1985), pp. 63–97.

———, 'The British Soldier on the Western Front', in P.H. Liddle (ed.), *Home Fires and Foreign Fields. British Social and Military Experience in the First World War* (London: Brassey's Defence Publishers, 1985), pp. 135–58.

Slovic, P., Fischoff, B. and Lichtenstein, S., 'Facts versus Fears. Understanding Perceived Risk', in D. Kahneman, P. Slovic and A. Tversky (eds.),

Judgment under Uncertainty. Heuristics and Biases (Cambridge University Press, 1982), pp. 464–89.

Smith, L.V., *Between Mutiny and Obedience. The Case of the French Fifth Infantry Division during World War I* (Princeton University Press, 1994).

Snape, M., *God and the British Soldier. Religion and the British Army in the First and Second World Wars* (London: Routledge, 2005).

Spiers, E.M., *The Army and Society 1815–1914* (London: Longman, 1980).

———, 'The Regular Army in 1914', in I.F.W. Beckett and K. Simpson (eds.), *A Nation in Arms. A Social Study of the British Army in the First World War* (Manchester University Press, 1985), pp. 37–61.

———, 'The Scottish Soldier at War', in H. Cecil and P.H. Liddle (eds.), *Facing Armageddon. The First World War Experienced* (London: Leo Cooper, 1996), pp. 314–35.

Stibbe, M., *German Anglophobia and the Great War, 1914–1918* (Cambridge University Press, 2001).

Stone, N., *The Eastern Front 1914–1917* (Abingdon: Purnell Book Services, 1975, 1976).

Stouffer, S.A., Suchman, E.A., DeVinney, L.C., Star, S.A. and Williams, Jr, R.M. *The American Soldier. Adjustment during Army Life.* Vol. I (2 vols., New York: John Wiley & Sons, 1949, 1965).

———, Lumsdaine, A.A., Lumsdaine, M.H., Williams Jr, R.M., Smith, M.B., Janis, I.L., Star, S.A. and Cottrell, Jr, L.S., *The American Soldier. Combat and its Aftermath.* Vol. II (2 vols., New York: John Wiley & Sons, 1949, 1965).

Strachan, H., 'The Morale of the German Army, 1917–18', in H. Cecil and P.H. Liddle (eds.), *Facing Armageddon. The First World War Experienced* (London: Leo Cooper, 1996), pp. 383–98.

———, 'The Soldier's Experience in Two World Wars. Some Historiographical Comparisons', in P. Addison and A. Calder (eds.), *Time to Kill. The Soldier's Experience of War in the West 1939–1945* (London: Pimlico, 1997), pp. 369–78.

———, 'The Battle of the Somme and British Strategy', *Journal of Strategic Studies* 21, 1 (March 1998), 79–95.

———, *The First World War.* Vol. I: *To Arms* (3 vols., Oxford University Press, 2001).

———, 'Ausbildung, Kampfgeist und die zwei Weltkriege', in B. Thoß and H.-E. Volkmann (eds.), *Erster Weltkrieg Zweiter Weltkrieg. Ein Vergleich* (Paderborn: Ferdinand Schöningh, 2002), pp. 265–86.

———, *The First World War. A New Illustrated History* (London: Simon and Schuster, 2003).

Sutherland, S., *Irrationality. The Enemy Within* (London: Penguin Books, 1994).

Tate, T., *Modernism, History and the First World War* (Manchester University Press, 1998).

Taylor, A.J.P., *The First World War. An Illustrated History* (London: Penguin, 1963, 1966).

Taylor, S.E. and Brown, J.D., 'Illusion and Well-Being. A Social Psychological Perspective on Mental Health', *Psychological Bulletin* 103, 2 (1988), 193–210.

Terraine, J., *White Heat. The New Warfare 1914–18* (London: Sidgwick and Jackson, 1982).

Thomson, M., 'Status, Manpower and Mental Fitness. Mental Deficiency in the First World War', in R. Cooter, M. Harrison and S. Sturdy (eds.), *War, Medicine and Modernity* (Stroud: Sutton Publishing, 1998, 1999).

Travers, T., *How the War Was Won. Command and Technology in the British Army on the Western Front, 1917–1918* (London: Routledge, 1992).

Trice, A.D., 'Ratings of Humor Following Experience with Unsolvable Tasks', *Psychological Reports* 51, 2 (December 1982), 1148.

Tversky, A. and Kahneman, D., 'Judgment under Uncertainty. Heuristics and Biases', in D. Kahneman, P. Slovic and A. Tversky (eds.), *Judgment under Uncertainty. Heuristics and Biases* (Cambridge University Press, 1982), pp. 3–20.

———, 'Judgments of and by Representativeness', in D. Kahneman, P. Slovic and A. Tversky (eds.), *Judgment under Uncertainty. Heuristics and Biases* (Cambridge University Press, 1982), pp. 84–98.

———, 'Causal Schemas in Judgements under Uncertainty', in D. Kahneman, P. Slovic and A. Tversky (eds.), *Judgment under Uncertainty. Heuristics and Biases* (Cambridge University Press, 1982), pp. 117–28.

Ulrich, B., 'Kriegsfreiwillige. Motivationen – Erfahrungen – Wirkungen', in Berliner Geschichtswerkstatt (ed.), *August 1914. Ein Volk zieht in den Krieg* (Berlin: Dirk Nishen, 1989), pp. 232–41.

———, 'Feldpostbriefe im Ersten Weltkrieg – Bedeutung und Zensur', in P. Knoch (ed,), *Kriegsalltag. Die Rekonstruktion des Kriegsalltags als Aufgabe der historischen Forschung und der Friedenserziehung* (Stuttgart: J.B. Metzlersche Verlagsbuchhandlung, 1989), pp. 40–83.

———, '"Eine wahre Pest in der öffentlichen Meinung". Zur Rolle von Feldpostbriefen während des Ersten Weltkrieges und der Nachkriegszeit', in G. Niedhart and D. Riesenberger (eds.), *Lernen aus dem Krieg? Deutsche Nachkriegszeiten 1918 und 1945. Beiträge zur historischen Friedensforschung* (Munich: C.H. Beck, 1992), pp. 319–30.

———, 'Die Desillusionierung der Kriegsfreiwilligen von 1914', in W. Wette (ed.), *Der Krieg des kleinen Mannes. Eine Militärgeschichte von unten* (Munich: Piper, 1992), pp. 110–26.

———, '"... als wenn nichts geschehen wäre". Anmerkungen zur Behandlung der Kriegsopfer während des Weltkriegs', in G. Hirschfeld, G. Krumeich and I. Renz (eds.), *Keiner fühlt sich hier mehr als Mensch ... Erlebnis und Wirkung des Ersten Weltkriegs* (Essen: Klartext, 1993), pp. 115–29.

———, 'Kampfmotivationen und Mobilisierungsstrategien. Das Beispiel Erster Weltkrieg', in H. von Stietencron and J. Rüpke (eds.), *Töten im Krieg* (Freiburg: Karl Alber, 1995), pp. 399–419.

———, *Die Augenzeugen. Deutsche Feldpostbriefe in Kriegs- und Nachkriegszeit 1914–1933* (Essen: Klartext, 1997).

Unruh, K., *Langemarck. Legende und Wirklichkeit* (Koblenz: Bernard & Graefe, 1986).

Verhey, J., *The Spirit of 1914. Militarism, Myth and Mobilization in Germany* (Cambridge University Press, 2000).

Vondung, K., 'Deutsche Apokalypse 1914', in K. Vondung (ed.), *Das wilhelminische Bildungsbürgertum. Zur Sozialgeschichte seiner Ideen* (Göttingen: Vandenhoeck & Ruprecht, 1976), pp. 153–71.

Wagenaar, W.A., *Paradoxes of Gambling Behaviour* (London: Lawrence Erlbaum Associates, 1988).

Watson, A., '"For Kaiser and Reich". The Identity and Fate of the German Volunteers, 1914–1918', *War in History* 12, 1 (January 2005), 44–74.

Watson, J.S.K., *Fighting Different Wars. Experience, Memory, and the First World War in Britain* (Cambridge University Press, 2004).

Watson, P., *War on the Mind. The Military Uses and Abuses of Psychology* (London: Hutchinson, 1978).

Wehler, H.-U., *Deutsche Gesellschaftsgeschichte*. Vol. III: *Von der 'Deutschen Doppelrevolution' bis zum Beginn des Ersten Weltkrieges. 1849–1914* (4 vols., Munich: C.H. Beck, 1995).

Wesbrook, S.D., 'The Potential for Military Disintegration', in S.C. Sarkesian (ed.), *Combat Effectiveness. Cohesion, Stress and the Volunteer Military* (London: Sage Publications, 1980), pp. 244–78.

Whalen, R.W., *Bitter Wounds. German Victims of the Great War, 1914–1939* (Ithaca: Cornell University Press, 1984).

Wildman, A.K., *The End of the Russian Imperial Army. The Old Army and the Soldiers' Revolt (March–April 1917)*. Vol. I (2 vols., Princeton University Press, 1980).

———, *The End of the Russian Imperial Army. The Road to Soviet Power and Peace*. Vol. II (2 vols., Princeton University Press, 1987).

Wilkinson, P., 'English Youth Movements, 1908–30', *Journal of Contemporary History* 14, 2 (April 1969), 3–23.

Williams, M.J., 'Thirty Per Cent. A Study in Casualty Statistics', *Journal of the Royal United Services Institution* 109, 633 (February 1964), 51–5.

———, 'The Treatment of the German Losses on the Somme in the British Official History. "Military Operations France and Belgium, 1916" Volume II', *Journal of the Royal United Services Institution* 111, 641 (February 1966), 69–74.

Williams, R., 'Personality and Post-traumatic Stress Disorder', in W. Yule (ed.), *Post-traumatic Stress Disorders. Concepts and Therapy* (Chichester: John Wiley & Sons, 1999, 2000), pp. 92–115.

Winter, D., *Death's Men. Soldiers of the Great War* (London: Allen Lane, 1978, 1979).

Winter, J., 'Britain's "Lost Generation" of the First World War', *Population Studies. A Journal of Demography* 31, 3 (November 1977), 449–66.

———, 'Army and Society. The Demographic Context', in I.F.W. Beckett and K. Simpson (eds.), *A Nation in Arms. A Social Study of the British Army in the First World War* (Manchester University Press, 1985), pp. 193–209.

———, *The Great War and the British People* (London: Macmillan, 1986).

———, *The Experience of World War I* (London: Greenwich Editions, 1988, 2000).

———, *Sites of Memory, Sites of Mourning. The Great War in European Cultural History* (Cambridge University Press, 1995).

Wohl, R., *The Generation of 1914* (Cambridge, MA: Harvard University Press, 1979).

Yule, W., Perrin, S. and Smith, P., 'Post-traumatic Stress Reactions in Children and Adolescents', in W. Yule (ed.), *Post-traumatic Stress Disorders. Concepts and Therapy* (Chichester: John Wiley & Sons, 1999, 2000), pp. 25–50.

———, Williams, R. and Joseph, S., 'Post-traumatic Stress Disorders in Adults', in W. Yule (ed.), *Post-traumatic Stress Disorders. Concepts and Therapy* (Chichester: John Wiley & Sons, 1999, 2000), pp. 1–24.

Ziemann, B., 'Verweigerungsformen von Frontsoldaten in der deutschen Armee 1914–1918', in A. Gestrich (ed.), *Gewalt im Krieg. Ausübung, Erfahrung und Verweigerung von Gewalt in Kriegen des 20. Jahrhunderts* (Münster: Lit, 1996), pp. 99–122.

———, 'Fahnenflucht im deutschen Heer 1914–1918', *Militärgeschichtliche Mitteilungen* 55 (1996), 93–130.

———, *Front und Heimat. Ländliche Kriegserfahrung im südlichen Bayern 1914–1923* (Essen: Klartext, 1997).

———, 'Enttäuschte Erwartung und kollektive Erschöpfung. Die deutschen Soldaten an der Westfront 1918 auf dem Weg zur Revolution', in J. Duppler and G.P. Groß (eds.), *Kriegsende 1918. Ereignis, Wirkung, Nachwirkung. Beiträge zur Militärgeschichte. Herausgegeben vom Militärgeschichtlichen Forschungsamt.* Vol. LIII (Munich: R. Oldenbourg, 1999), pp. 165–82.

Zillmann, D., Rockwell, S., Schweitzer, K. and Sundar, S.S., 'Does Humor Facilitate Coping with Physical Discomfort?', *Motivation and Emotion* 17, 1 (March 1993), 1–21.

Zuber, T., 'The Schlieffen Plan Reconsidered', *War in History* 6, 3 (July 1999), 262–305.

UNPUBLISHED THESES

Beach, J.M., 'British Intelligence and the German Army, 1914–1918' unpublished Ph.D. thesis, University College London (2005).

Klingenschmidt, R., 'Motive und Entwicklung der allgemein-schulischen Unteroffiziersausbildung in der königlich bayerischen Armee von 1866 bis 1914' unpublished Staats- und Sozialwissenschaft Diplomarbeit, Universität der Bundeswehr Munich (1997).

Rice, A.K., 'Morale and Defeatism in the Bavarian "Heer und Heimat" in the First World War (1916–18)' unpublished M.Phil. thesis, University of Oxford (2004).

Sieber, C., 'Das Soldatenlied im 1. WK – Analyse und didaktische Verwertbarkeit' unpublished Wissenschaftliche Hausarbeit, Pädagogische Hochschule Freiburg (1995).

Teicht, A., 'Die Offiziersausbildung in Bayern während des 1. Weltkriegs' unpublished Pädagogik Diplomarbeit, Hochschule der Bundeswehr Munich (1978).

Wilson, J.B., 'Morale and Discipline in the British Expeditionary Force, 1914–1918' unpublished MA thesis, University of New Brunswick (1978).

Index